MOTHERING CANADA
INTERDISCIPLINARY VOICES
LA MATERNITÉ AU CANADA
VOIX INTERDISCIPLINAIRES

MOTHERING CANADA
INTERDISCIPLINARY VOICES
LA MATERNITÉ AU CANADA
VOIX INTERDISCIPLINAIRES

EDITED BY
SHAWNA GEISSLER
LYNN LOUTZENHISER
JOCELYNE PRAUD
LEESA STREIFLER

DEMETER
DEMETER PRESS
TORONTO, CANADA

Demeter Press
c/o Motherhood Initiative for Research and Community Involvement (MIRCI)
140 Holland St. West, P.O. 13022
Bradford, ON, L3Z 2Y5
Telephone: 905.775.5215 Email: info@motherhoodinitiative.org

Demeter Press gratefully acknowledges the support of the Saskatchewan Arts Board and the University of Regina.

Demeter Press logo based on Skulptur "Demeter" by Maria-Luise Bodirsky
<www.keramik-atelier.bodirsky.edu>

Cover Art:
Leesa Streifler, untitled, 2010, ink and acrylic on acetate, 27.94 x 20.32 cm.
Cover Design/Interior Design: Luciana Ricciutelli
Printed and Bound in Canada

Library and Archives Canada Cataloguing in Publication

Mothering Canada: interdisciplinary voices = La maternité au Canada: voix interdisciplinaires / edited by Shawna Geissler ... [*et al.*].

Texts in English and French.
Includes bibliographical references.
ISBN 978-1-55014-504-5

1. Mothers--Canada. 2. Motherhood--Canada. 3. Mothers in art. 4. Mothers in literature. I. Geissler, Shawna, 1967- II. Title: Maternité au Canada.

HQ759.M68 2010 306.874'30971 C2010-901269-0E

Catalogage avant publication de Bibliothèque et Archives Canada

Mothering Canada: interdisciplinary voices = La maternité au Canada: voix interdisciplinaires / edited by Shawna Geissler ... [*et al.*].

Textes en anglais et en français.
Comprend des références bibliographiques.
ISBN 978-1-55014-504-5

1. Mères--Canada. 2. Maternité--Canada. 3. Mères dans l'art. 4. Mères dans la littérature. I. Geissler, Shawna, 1967- II. Titre: Maternité au Canada.

HQ759.M68 2010 306.874'30971 C2010-901269-0F

for our mothers and our children

Statement of Authorship:

Mothering Canada: Interdisciplinary Voices
La Maternité au Canada: Voix Interdisciplinaires
edited by
Shawna Geissler, Lynn Loutzenhiser, Jocelyne Praud and Leesa Streifler

The order of authorship is in alphabetical order to reflect the equal contributions by each editor.

CONTENTS

SUPPORTING

Acknowledgements

We would like to thank the University of Regina for the funding received from the SSHRC/President's Fund, the Humanities Research Institute, and the President's Office. We are grateful to the Saskatchewan Arts Board for its support. We are indebted to Andrea O'Reilly for giving us the opportunity to publish this anthology with Demeter Press and Renée Knapp for her support in making this text a reality. Special thanks to Luciana Ricciutelli for her inspired and dedicated work on the design of the book. We would also like to thank Angela Beck, who created the webpage for our call for papers, Danielle Goulden for compiling bibliographic materials on mothering research in Canada, Chrystene Ells, who helped co-ordinate the visual art contributions, and Angela Alquist, who maintained our correspondence with the contributors. We sincerely thank Helen Yum for her timely advice regarding the book publishing process. We are indebted to our contributors for their wisdom, experience, and talent. Finally, we are immensely grateful to our partners, Kelly Geissler, Eldon Soifer, Karl A. Henriques, and Kenneth Bell, for their support of our work.

This book is dedicated to our mothers: Helen Guenther, Nancy Underwood, Marcelle Praud, and Sheila Streifler, and to our children: Justin, Adam, Evan, Maya, Joshua, Justine, Franz, and Daniel.

Introduction

SHAWNA GEISSLER, LYNN LOUTZENHISER, JOCELYNE PRAUD AND LEESA STREIFLER

MOTHERING CANADA: Interdisciplinary Voices/La maternité au Canada: Voix interdisciplinaires is a feminist anthology of English and French scholarly and creative texts and visual art exploring myriad facets of mothering in Canada. This interdisciplinary and bilingual anthology, which is co-edited by four academics from different fields of study, namely, English Literature, Psychology, Political Science and Visual Art, illustrates Canadian mothering through its presentation of diverse academic methodologies (quantitative, qualitative, and critical) as well as literary and visual expressions of personal experience. From the overwhelming number of submissions we received for this anthology, we selected works to highlight diverse Canadian experiences of being a mother. These experiences include pregnancy, birthing, breastfeeding, multiple births, childhood illness, mothering late in life, public and institutional support, feminism, "supermoms," stay-at-home mothers, immigrant mothers, queer mothers and working/student mothers. Our contributors, whose biographies can be found within the text, include English and French academics, writers, and visual artists from across Canada, representing the many different voices of mothering.

In combination with the valuable research of the academic works in this anthology, we believe that the inclusion of non-academic pieces and visual art in the anthology contributes to the academic arena in several important ways. First, the diverse, yet common, Canadian mothering experiences, such as the physical and mental well-being of mothers, traditional aboriginal practices, the place of mothering in academia, birth and pregnancy experiences, and social pressures on women, are often not represented and thus are not being recognized as important issues for academic research. Second, these pieces value mothers and the mothering experience, giving voice to "Othered" mothers, who may be underrepresented or marginalized, such as adoptive, foster, single, surrogate, disabled, step, immigrant, or poor mothers, but need to be centrally located in our country's consciousness, socially and academically. Third, the visual art and the artists' statements and essays, and the poetry, fiction, and creative non-fiction works are generative rather than simply reflective of experience. These works place mothering experience and insight in the realm of feminist thought. Additionally, they are valuable in drawing attention to areas that require government and social changes, as well as scientific, medical, and other forms of academic research that will contribute to and benefit Canadian society. Mothering and its range of lived experiences must be legitimized as necessary, valuable, and of national importance, and must be part of twenty-first-century feminist discourse.

While arranging the anthology, we observed common threads binding groups of works together. In balancing the marginalized voices and the more mainstream perspectives, we discovered that although each piece is unique, together they approach similar issues from various perspectives, disciplines, and methodologies to create more complex, and perhaps, more accurate, representations of important mothering issues. We chose four themes to represent these works on mothering: Becoming, Connecting, Challenging, and Supporting.

It seems appropriate to begin an anthology on mothering with a section on "Becoming." And although this may, at first, seem a simple truth—a woman becomes a mother by having a baby—the realities are much more complex. For example, there are many ways that women can become mothers that do not require actually becoming pregnant. This first section explores real experiences of becoming mother from pregnancy and birth to the care of newborns. Collectively, these works question the very foundation of what it means to be a mother in Canada. A mother's worries about the future of her unborn child, a woman's pain in delivering a stillborn child, and the naturalness of birth and breastfeeding are intricately woven together through experiential narrative. In support of these stories, examinations of governmental involvement in mothering, the commercialization of breast milk, and the medicalization of labour and delivery comprise the remainder of this section.

The second section, "Connecting," explores powerful and complicated familial bonds. Poems, personal reflections, and literary criticism highlight the relationships between mothers and daughters, stages in a child's life, and child/parent role reversals in complex circumstances. As well, the relationship between motherhood and fatherhood as it has been portrayed in social science and personal narratives is analyzed, showing the disparate social realities of contemporary Canadian mothering and fathering. This section of the anthology re-evaluates the traditional and current roles of mothers and fathers, and the changing realities of Canadian families.

"Challenging," the third section, illuminates real-life scenarios of some of the difficulties facing mothers and families in Canada today. These works tell stories of mothers experiencing violence, discrimination, poverty, haunting pasts, physical and mental illness, and sexual abuse, as well as the difficulties and joys of caring for special needs children. Throughout this section, long-held perceptions of the "Canadian mother" are themselves challenged, and bureaucratic and social institutions are examined critically: Where is the support for these mothers and these families? What governmental, social, private sector, and academic changes can be affected? Where is further research needed to assist mothers and families facing real challenges in Canada today?

The final section of the anthology, "Supporting," draws on diverse quantitative and qualitative sources to discuss the importance of support to mothers, be they spiritual, cultural, institutional, financial, social, or personal. These works illuminate situations, such as the discrepancies between expectant parents' intentions to share child-rearing duties, and the rights of same-sex parents, facing twenty-first-century Canadian families. Incompatibilities between the ideal universal affordable and quality advocacy, social, and governmental organizations and the realities of actual mothering experiences in this country are highlighted in this section, proving the need for serious reform in public policies and social programming.

Mothering Canada: Interdisciplinary Voices/La maternité au Canada: Voix interdisciplinaires provides a set of academic and non-academic written and visual works that focus on, and celebrate, the variety and diversity (including bilingualism, aboriginal culture, queer and immigrant experiences) that is Canada. The anthology introduces areas of mothering that are under-represented in the current literature and practice, and suggests new areas of research. This volume acts as an effective and informative textbook for courses in several academic disciplines including Sociology, Social Work, Psychology, Women's and Gender Studies, Human Justice, Education, and Health Sciences. The text also provides a resource for students seeking careers in areas such as counseling, nursing, health care, midwifery, and women and children's advocacy, as well as being of interest to a larger audience—mothers. Finally, as mothers, we hope that this anthology works as an impetus for change, stimulating further interest on mothering in Canada, and validating the need for developing and widening consideration of mothering issues in government, business, education, and communities.

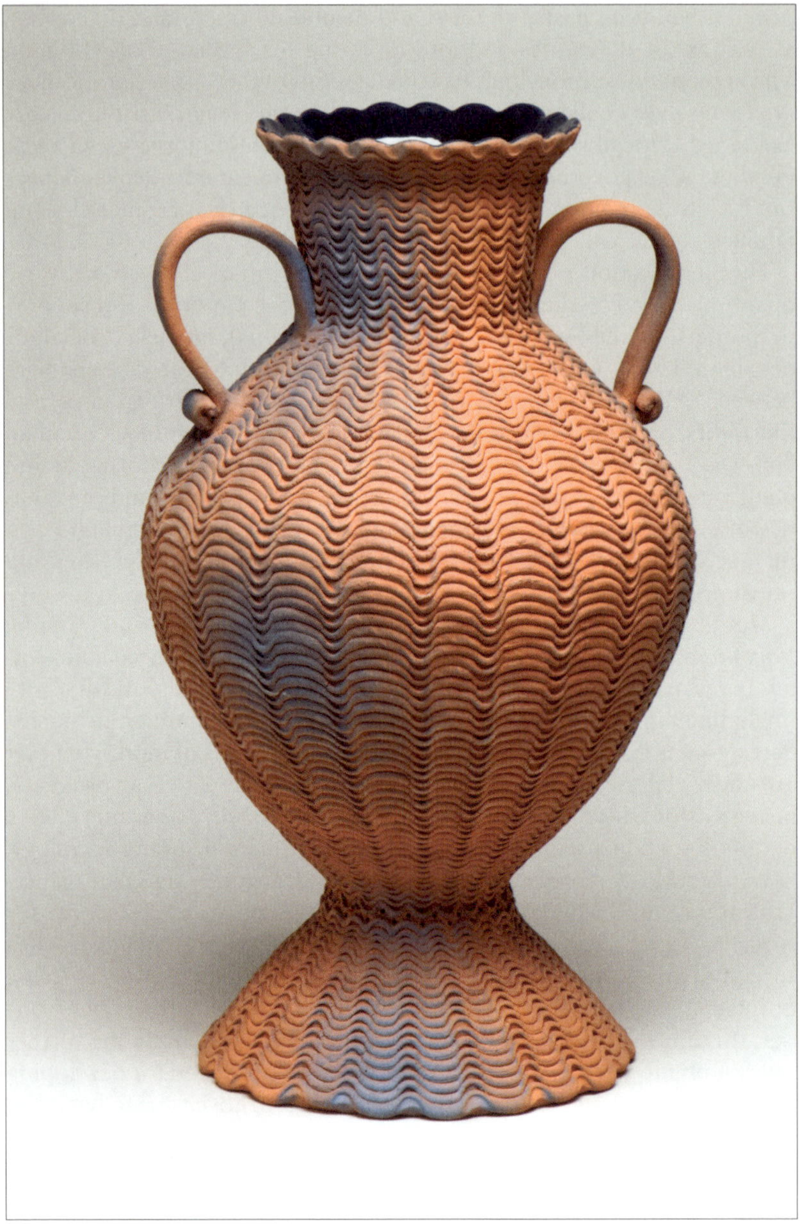

Cara Gay Driscoll, *Earthen Woman*, 2007, earthenware clay with terra sigillata, 39 x 23 cm.

Earthen Woman is a hand-coiled clay vessel that pays homage to mother earth. The vessel contains a spiritual message etched into its base: "blessed are you women of the earth, your memory etched, formed and fired into new life, reflecting the one who calls you by name" (inspired by M. Cessna).

BECOMING

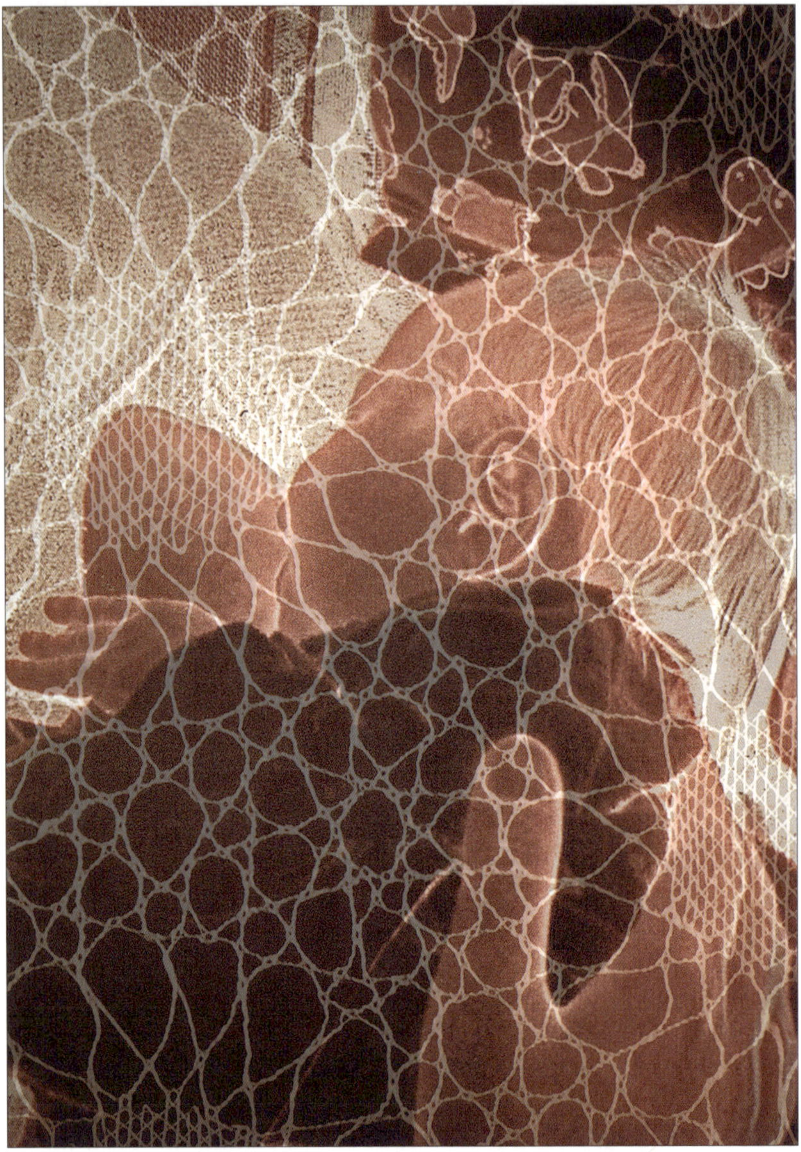

Gaëtanne Sylvester, *Sofia,* 2007, Digital print on photorag acid free paper with permanent acrylic inks. Printed at Centre Sagamie, Alma, Québec, 50.80 x 71.12 cm.

Sofia is a digital composition/collage of a photograph and images of lace. Lace presents us with a duality; it reveals while it conceals, it decorates while it restrains. Lace, familiar and accessible, becomes symbolic of the genome, fertility, sexuality, and the social reality of a mother today.

Mother's Wish

ROSA HONG CHEN

A place for you to wonder

A place that is not uncommon,
for you, my child,
another or any other.

It may be meagre and scant,
in no parallel to a sumptuous palace,
but a hub hatching your awed rarities.

A place that is nice and warm,
just for a sound sleep, my child,
and for a prolonged breath of fresh air.

It is a home-place, my child,
new, yet secured and freer,
merely for you to wonder.

A place that opens the door
to your virgin land, and
probes your curiosity to prosper.

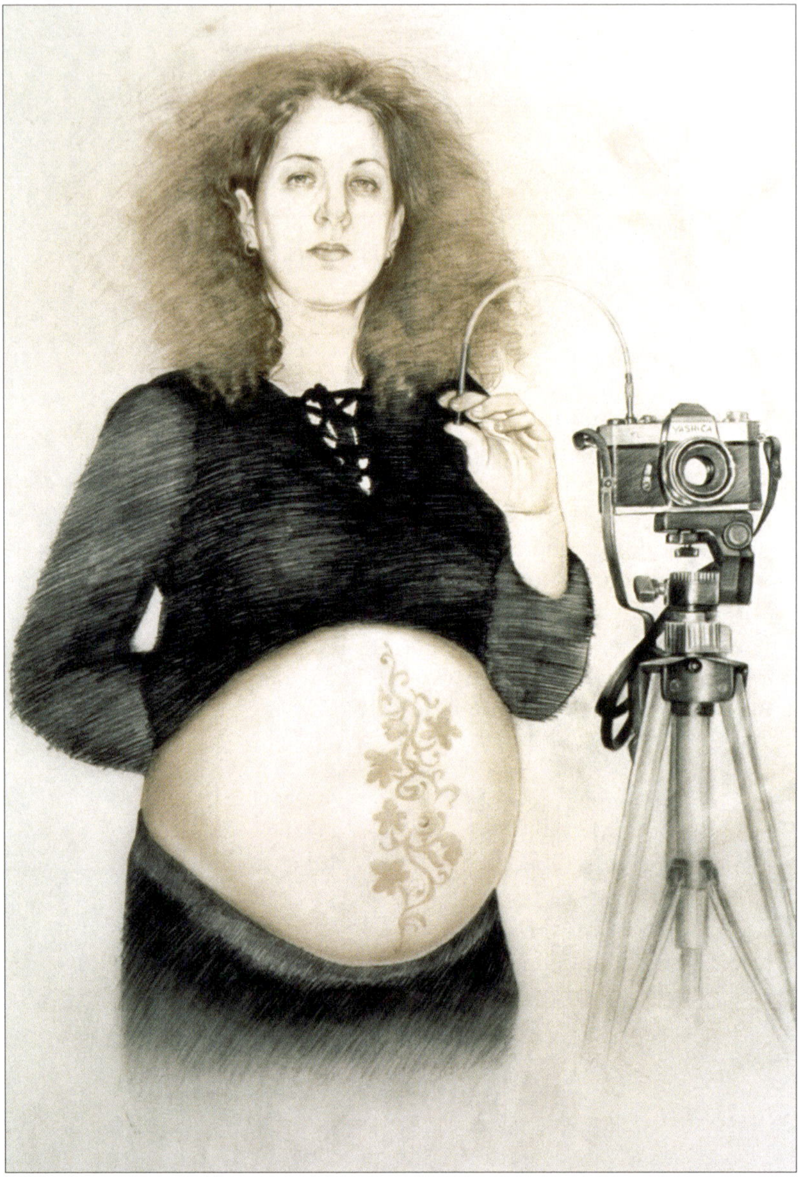

Jennifer Linton, *Linea Negra,* 2005, coloured pencil on mylar, 52.07 x 60.96 cm.

The "linea negra" is a pigmented line that can appear on the skin of the lower abdomen during pregnancy. I imagined mine fuelled with a natural, generative power and assuming the form of a twisting floral vine.

When a Pregnant Body Becomes Visible

ELENA NEITERMAN

THIS PAPER EXAMINES the discourse in which the body of a pregnant woman becomes visible through the public management of its weight and shape. Although women's weight management has been under social control for a long time, pregnant women have predominantly been exempt from this control for fear of potential danger to the fetus (Brooks-Gardner 194). Instead, the bodies of pregnant women have been controlled by medical specialists, who suggested the appropriate nutrition for, and defined the standard weight gain during pregnancy. Here, I identify a new direction: weight control in the realm of pregnancy where the pregnant body is seen as not only pregnant, but also as a feminine, sexualized body. By analyzing the content of popular websites for pregnant women, I show how the bodies of pregnant women are introduced to the readers of pregnancy press, and the context in which the pregnant body is discussed in terms of weight and shape.

A WOMAN'S BODY AND WEIGHT

There is significant scholarship devoted to the subject of women's body weight control (such as Bordo; Germov and Williams; McKinley). Empirical research shows that women are worried about their weight during their adolescent years (O'Dea and Abraham) and adulthood (Germov and Williams; Halliwell and Dittmar), and that they continuously work on the shape of their bodies.

Some researchers, such as Bordo, suggest that weight management is yet another form of social control over women's bodies. To follow the popular standards of beauty and slimness, women must constantly discipline and monitor their bodies, making them docile (Bartky 25-27, 37, 41). This bodywork is a never-ending process, unifying women of all ages, ethnicities, and social statuses (Bordo 176).

Recent studies involving postpartum women reveal that the after-pregnancy body is regarded as one needing repair and needing to "bounce back" in order to conform to regular and acceptable norms (Dworkin and Wachs 615; Upton and Han 684, 686-688). As Rebecca Upton, Sallie Han, Shari Dworkin and Faye Wachs show, the concept of the "right body" is so dominant that discourse is framed in terms of loss-of-body during pregnancy and return-of-the-body in the postpartum stage.

Although there is ample literature suggesting that women fight to "get their bodies back" after pregnancy, there are only a few studies looking at weight discourse during pregnancy. Some researchers indicate that women enjoy the time when their bodies are out of their control, exempting them from supervising their shapes and sizes (Baily 119-120; Warren and Brewis 223-224, 226; Wiles 34). Sarah Earle's study, in contrast, suggests that pregnant women are indeed concerned about their weight and shape (245). They signify their bodies as pregnant rather than fat by either verbally stating so or donning maternity clothes and looking forward to the postpartum period and "getting their bodies back."

The "body work" that engages women from early in their socialization is assumed to stop during pregnancy and start over during the postnatal period. This hiatus from "body work" may occur because the pregnant body is perceived as a maternal body, rather than a feminine, sexualized body. This paper shows that popular pregnancy magazines use weight discourse to add an additional dimension to the maternal image: the image of a feminine, sexualized body that must conform to the disciplining practices and regulations of femininity.

DATA AND METHOD

This paper uses the discursive approach to explore the construction of pregnancy as it is represented in popular websites available to North American women. I analyze text to identify the main discourses raised by popular media with regard to pregnant body forms. I refer to text as it is defined by Bernhard Radloff: "a structure composed of elements of signification by which the greater or the lesser unity of those elements makes itself manifest" (as cited in Makaryk 639). For this study, I have chosen to concentrate on the following Internet sources that are most commonly suggested by online search engines:

- The website of *Today's Parent*—a popular Canadian magazine. The articles in the website cover the period from 2002 to 2006. < www.todaysparent.com/pregnancybirth/index.jsp>.
- The website of *FitPregnancy*, an American magazine. It includes sixty-six articles in its "Health" section and seventy-seven publications in its "Food and Nutrition" section. <www.fitpregnancy.com>.
- The AmericanBaby.com website provides online information

for planning pregnancy, expectant mothers, and new parents. Forty-six articles from this website were analyzed. <www.americanbaby.com/common/magazine>.

- The Pregnancy website contains material identical to that published in the popular American magazine of the same name. < www.pregnancymagazine.com>.
- The Parents website carries articles published between 1998 and 2006 in the *Parents, Babytalk,* and *Parenting* magazines. *Parenting* <www.parenting.com>; *Parents* <www.parents.com/parents/category.jsp?catref=AB2>.

The websites are easy to navigate and fully accessible to the public. The only website that requires registration is the Pregnancy website, and there is no charge involved. The websites contain a wealth of potentially useful information for expectant mothers. The information includes topics such as labour and delivery, the postpartum period, and pregnancy itself. Analyzing the content of these texts, I looked at the discourse on the pregnant body: the body's image, weight, shape, and behaviour. I identified three avenues by which weight discourse is presented to expectant mothers: linking excessive weight during pregnancy to the discourse on obesity; examining weight gain as a factor that could lead to health problems in both mother and fetus; and discussing the emotional and psychological damage caused by being overweight during pregnancy.

THE DANGERS OF PREGNANCY: A LINK TO OBESITY

The discourse on obesity has recently become very popular in medical literature (such as Reynolds, Saito and Crimmins). However, while medicine is concerned with the biological factors leading to obesity and the implications of obesity on an individual's overall health, social theorists examine the social construction of fatness (Sobal and Mauer 108, 241-242). Some theorists critically address the development of the discourse on obesity and extra weight, a discourse that sees these phenomena as abnormal and pathological, requiring diagnosis and treatment (Monaghan 303-304, 309-311). Pregnant women often experience cravings and thus they are often seen as incapable of controlling their appetite. FitPregnancy magazine, in contrast, suggests that there is a thin line between excess weight gained during pregnancy and obesity:

> Close to 50 percent of first-time American moms begin pregnancy overweight, and 85 percent of them gain more than is recommended while pregnant. Experts now believe this cycle of weight gain is a major contributor to female obesity and the nation's obesity epidemics. (Vogel)

In the article "Does Size Matter?" the author, Amanda Vogel, does not identify the experts who are concerned with women's body weights, but readers are most likely to assume that the experts are doctors and dietitians. The article suggests that the extra weight gained during pregnancy introduces the "cycle of weight gain," something that every modern woman seeks to avoid. Thus, weight gain during pregnancy is not viewed as a temporary symptom of an uncontrollable pregnant body, which can be fixed in the postpartum period, but, rather, weight gain during pregnancy is considered to have long-term, wide-spread implications. Pregnancy weight gain is being considered a cause for female obesity in the United States of America.

The Parents website features an article on weight gain under the guise of pregnancy fitness. The author, Ellie Krieger, links obesity and pregnancy:

> Sharon Biddinger, 24, now pregnant with her second child, was almost 50 pounds heavier going into this pregnancy than she was the first time around.... You might think a diagnosis of obesity is reserved only for extreme cases. But according to the most recent National Health and Nutrition Examination Survey, 3 of 10 women are clinically obese... Sadly, the percentage of women entering pregnancy obese parallels the national statistic.

The article asks pregnant women to become aware of the problem of obesity. If a woman becomes pregnant, she is in danger of gaining extra weight. What used to be called "baby weight" becomes a link between the pregnant and obese body. Therefore, according to pregnancy media, food consumption and nutrition intake should be constantly monitored by expectant mothers.

In our society, obesity is not only a health issue, but a moral issue (Gard and Wright 3, 14-17; Jones). Instead of targeting social circumstances that lead people to gain extra weight, our society targets the individuals themselves, stigmatizing them as unworthy, immoral, unable to control "animal instincts," and in need of moral and physical repair (Gard and Wright 32, 181; Campos 218-219; 227-228). We routinely link obesity with various medical complications. Yet, as the following section suggests, health concerns become a central site for public attention to the body size of pregnant women.

THE DANGERS OF FATNESS: MEDICAL COMPLICATIONS

> In what might be a sign of the times, the American College of Obstetricians and Gynecologists (ACOG) has released its first committee opinion on obesity during pregnancy. The ACOG

> document, "Obesity in Pregnancy," explains the known risks that obesity poses to pregnant women and their babies. There are ... elevated risks to the babies of women who are obese, including stillbirth, prematurity, macrosomia (large for gestational age), neural tube defects, and higher rates of childhood obesity. (Parents)

As the quotation above suggests, extra weight gained during pregnancy not only puts a woman at risk of becoming obese after pregnancy, it can also create numerous complications during pregnancy, potentially endangering her and her unborn child. These complications include, but are not limited to, gestational diabetes, premature birth, and caesarean section procedures. Laura Riley, cited in the article "Plus-Size and Pregnant," says, "We are talking about a medical disorder [obesity] that has major implications for 1) your pregnancy, 2) your fetus, and 3) your life" (Krieger). The article lists medical complications resulting from obesity, citing even the practical difficulties inherent in caring for overweight bodies in hospital settings, stating that "it also is harder to transfer a heavy patient if she needs to be moved, a real problem in an emergency" (Krieger). Thus, extra weight endangers not only the health of the pregnant woman, but also that of her unborn child, rendering her unworthy of motherhood and not sufficiently competent to be a parent. By giving in to her "animal," bodily instincts, she not only sacrifices her own moral image, but also the body of an unborn child that she carries inside her. In this sense, she becomes an ultimate "villain," one that should be judged and condemned morally and publicly (Brooks-Gardner 193-194).

The rhetoric of obesity as a medical disorder, and the medical risks resulting from excess weight gain during pregnancy concern the pregnant body in its maternal image. It does not concern the pregnant body as a feminine, sexualized body. As Carol Brooks-Gardner points out, pregnant women are seen as potentially dangerous to their fetuses: their behaviour, mood, and nutrition can harm their unborn child (189-191). In a sense, the body of a pregnant woman is not perceived as an individual body, but as a carrier-body: the body of the woman becomes invisible as it is concealed by the growing body of an expectant mother. Yet, as I will demonstrate further, negative emotions associated with gaining extra weight are closely linked to the social norms of expectant mothers' pre-pregnancy body shape.

EXPERIENCING PREGNANT BODY

It seems that women who are larger-than-average size experience negative consequences even during their pregnancy. "Many plus-size women don't look pregnant until late in their pregnancies, which can be disappointing and frustrating," says the author of "Weigh to Go." According to this statement, the only excuse for a woman to have a growing abdomen is her pregnancy. The possibility of creating a false impression, of being considered fat and not pregnant, carries a negative social assessment of a woman: that she is unable to control her appetite and deviates from the acceptable beauty norms. Although the article implies that pregnancy provides an excuse for a woman to gain extra weight, it also suggests that the added pounds should be carefully calculated.

Even when a woman is identified as pregnant, however, the concern with her weight gain does not disappear from public interest. In "The Weighting Game," Christina Boyle introduces readers to the emotional saga of a pregnant woman struggling with others' reactions to her growing body:

> Near the end of my second trimester, people started asking me how much weight I'd gained so far. I never responded with a number, only a smart-ass comeback. I was thrilled, of course, that my baby was thriving inside my belly, but I also was terrified that I'd never fit into my favorite clothes again. One day, I was flagging a cab on the street when a woman came up and asked when my twins were due. "I'm just having one baby," I replied. "I'm large and in charge. Have a nice day!" I wanted to slap her. I wanted to cry.

A pregnant body is a public body. People feel at liberty to touch a pregnant body, to advise the mother on what to eat and drink, and what to not eat and drink, and to ask personal questions. When weight gain enters the terrain of pregnancy, people also feel free to comment directly on a woman's shape and size. Even though our society often perceives pregnant bodies as maternal bodies, the quotations above demonstrate that the habit of monitoring body shape, which most women have done since their early years of adolescence, does not magically disappear once a woman becomes pregnant. What does seem to disappear is pregnant women's ownership of their bodies: pregnant bodies become public bodies and, as such, they can be taught and advised by others.

ON VISIBILITY OF A PREGNANT BODY AND SOCIAL CONTROL

Previous research suggested that pregnancy was one of the periods in women's lives when they were not judged according to weight standards (Baily 119-120; Warren and Brewis 223-224, 226). However, my findings indicate that progressively more attention is being paid to weight gain on the part of expectant mothers. I suggest that this attention is the result of the transformation of pregnancy from an asexualized construction into a sexualized construction, a development that invites it to be measured according to standardized ideals of proper aesthetic femininity.

Sarah Earle notes that over the past ten years, a significant number of maternity stores and maternity fashion lines have cropped up in the United Kingdom (251). The abundance of maternity stores is also apparent in North America. In addition, large retail companies such as the Gap, Old Navy, and Sears are producing their own line of maternity clothes. Every popular pregnancy magazine, whether in print or online, lists websites that specialize in the consumer needs of pregnant women. Most websites directed at pregnant women also provide a consumer guide educating women about less-expensive clothes, locations to find apparel, and the most important things to buy during pregnancy. The Parents website informs women of the new industry of maternity photography and invites women to celebrate their growing bodies:

> In 1991, a very pregnant Demi Moore appeared nude on the cover of *Vanity Fair*. With that iconic cover, a sea change occurred in how pregnancy is portrayed in print. Pregnancy is no longer something to be hidden underneath a muumuu, but something to be celebrated in all its glory.

Magazines and websites feature glowing pregnant women and new mothers hugging their newborns. Although these happy women appear to be of different skin colour, they are all similar in one way: they all look young and slim. They show off their abdomens and model a variety of consumer goods for purchase.

The image of the pregnant body is not limited to the media directed at pregnant readers; it is also found in media directed at the public. The March 6, 2006 issue of *Star* magazine features a cover story article entitled "Hollywood's Baby Boom." Two pages of this popular magazine are dedicated to images of pregnant celebrities including Gwen Stefani, Gwyneth Paltrow, Angelina Jolie, and Rachel Weisz. In addition to the images, the magazine presents a physician's comments regarding the weight gain of each star: each woman's weight gain is examined, and suggestions are given whether each star should gain more weight or watch her diet. These bodies are not depicted as the productive, pregnant bodies of baby-carriers. Rather, these bodies are depicted as women: constructed as sexy, feminine, and attractive.

Over the past two decades, the pregnant body has become increasingly visible. It now appears on the television screen, in the media, and in the world of consumerism. The bodies of pregnant women have begun to receive attention as consumers, and as women's bodies in its aesthetical form. Pregnancy magazines feature articles on sexy, glowing, and desirable pregnant women. The magazine covers and illustrations offer images of pregnant models showing off their bellies. These slender pregnant bodies, I suggest, are the representation of a normative pregnant body, of what is constructed as appropriate during pregnancy.

When weight gain discourse appears in the context of pregnancy, it is sometimes couched in the rhetoric of fetus-endangerment. By not conforming to the norm, pregnant women are considered deviant in two respects: they lose social respect for being unable to control their flesh (as every overweight person does), and their social status suffers because they are endangering their unborn child (since weight gain potentially harms fetus development). How pregnant women respond to this discourse—whether they comply with it or resist it—is a topic for further investigation.

WORKS CITED

Bailey, Lucy. "Gender Shows: First-Time Mothers and Embodied Selves." *Gender and Society* 15 (2001): 110-29.

Bartky, Sandra Lee. "Foucault, Femininity and Modernization of Patriarchal Power." *Politics of Women Bodies: Sexuality, Appearance and Behaviour.* Ed. Rose Weitz. Oxford: Oxford University Press, 2003. 25-45.

Bordo, Susan. *Unbearable Weight: Feminism, Western Culture, and the Body*. Los Angeles: University of California Press, 1995.

Boyle, Christina. "The Weighting Game." 09 Dec 2008. <http: //www.parenting.com/article/Pregnancy/Health/pregnancy-weight>.

Brooks-Gardner, Carol. "Pregnant Women as Social Problem." *Social Problems: Constructionist Readings.* Ed. D. R. Loseke and J. Best. New York: Aldine De Gruyter, 2003. 188-95.

Campos, Paul. *The Obesity Myth: Why America's Obsession with Weight Is Hazardous to Your Health*. New York: Gotham, 2004.

Dworkin, Shari L. and Faye L. Wachs. "'Getting Your Body Back': Postindustrial Fit Motherhood in Shape Fit Pregnancy Magazine." *Gender and Society* 18.5 (2004): 610-24.

Earle, Sarah. "'Bumps and Boobs': Fatness and Women's Experiences of Pregnancy." *Women's Studies International Forum* 26.3 (2003): 245-52.

Gard, Michael and Jan Wright. *The Obesity Epidemic: Science, Morality, and Ideology.* London: Routledge, 2005.

Germov, John and Lauren Williams. "Dieting Women: Self-Surveillance and the Body Panopticon." *Weighty Issues: Fatness and Thinness as Social Problems*. Ed. J. Sobal and D. Maurer. New York: Aldine De Gruyter, 1999. 117-32.

Halliwell, Emma and Helga Dittmar. "Does Size Matter? The Impact of Model's Body Size on Women's Body-Focused Anxiety and Advertising Effectiveness." *Journal of Social and Clinical Psychology* 23.1 (2004): 104-22.

Jones, Curtis. "Social Problems and Social Recovery in Weight Loss Reality Television." *The Annual Sociology Mini Conference.* McMaster University, 2008.

Krieger, Ellie. "Plus-Size and Pregnant." March 2006. *American Baby Magazine.* 09 Nov 08. <http: //www.parents.com/pregnancy/my-body/fitness/plus-size-and-pregnant>.

Makaryk, Irene R., ed. *Encyclopedia of Contemporary Literary Theory.* Toronto: University of Toronto Press, 1993.

McKinley, Nita M. "Ideal Weight/Ideal Women: Society Constructs Female." *Weighty Issues: Fatness and Thinness as Social Problem.* Eds. J. Sobal and D. Maurer. New York: Aldine De Gruyter, 1999. 97-115.

Monaghan, Lee F. "Discussion Piece: A Critical Take on the Obesity Debate." *Social Theory and Health* 3.4 (2005): 302-14.

O'Dea, Jennifer A. and Suzanne Abraham. "Onset of Disordered Eating Attitudes and Behaviors in Early Adolescence: Interplay of Pubertal Status, Gender, Weight, and Age." *Adolescence* 34.136 (1999): 671-79.

Parents. "Pregnancy Weight Gain." Online: <http://www.parents.com /pregnancy/my-body/weight-gain/>. Accessed 15 July 2007.

Reynolds, Sandra L., Yasuhiko Saito, and Eileen M. Crimmins. "The Impact of Obesity on Active Life Expectancy in Older American Men and Women." *The Gerontologist* 45.4 (2005): 438-44.

Sobal, Jeffery and Donna Maurer, eds. *Weighty Issues: Fatness and Thinness as Social Problems.* New York: Aldine de Gruyter, 1999.

Upton, Rebecca L. and Sallie S. Han. "Maternity and Its Discontents: 'Getting the Body Back' after Pregnancy." *Journal of Contemporary Ethnography* 32.6 (2003): 670-92.

Vogel, Amanda. "Does Size Matter?" 09 Nov 2008. <www.fitpregnancy.com/fitness/711>.

Warren, Samantha and Joanna Brewis. "Matter over Mind? Examining the Experience of Pregnancy." *Sociology* 38.2 (2004): 219-36.

"Weigh to Go." *Pregnancy Magazine.* July 15, 2007. Online: <http://www.pregnancymagazine.com/site/index.php?option=com_content&task=view&id=23&Itemid=3>.

Wiles, Rosemary. "'I'm Not Fat, I'm Pregnant': The Impact of Pregnancy on Fat Women's Body Image." *Women and Health: Feminist Perspectives.* Ed. S. Wilkinson and C. Kitzinger. London: Taylor and Francis, 1994. 33-48.

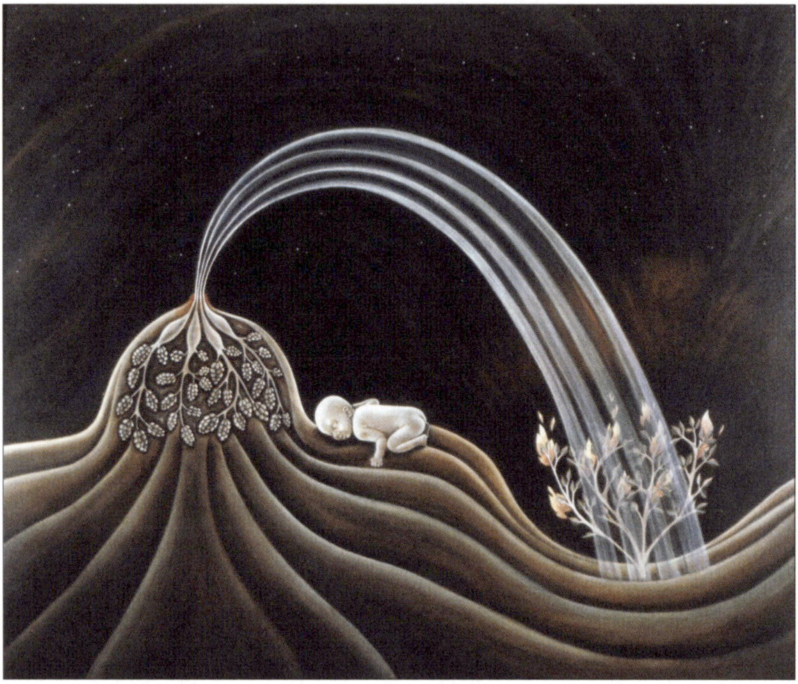

Marsha Kennedy, *Burning Bush*, 1988-89, gouache, varnish on rag board, 55.88 x 66.04 cm.

Burning Bush is from a series called *The Return* where the fertile human body is related to the earth. The interior lactating breast visually resembles the 'Burning Bush' of the Old Testament, which burnt without being consumed, symbolized for me a personal understanding of the unbroken passage of life. The birth of my son, Erin, was the inspiration for Burning Bush.

One Day at a Time

SHANNON WALL BIXBY

I'M IN LABOUR. The contractions overtake me, minute after minute, like giant waves crashing against the shore. "How much longer do you think I have?" I ask my midwife, expecting her to tell me I am only minutes away from meeting my first child.

"Oh, about an hour and a half, I'd guess," she answers, unaware of the blow she is delivering. I fall back on the hospital bed, deflated, exhausted, winded by her response. There is no way I will last that long, I think. Twenty minutes seems an eternity right now. I won't make it. There is no way I will make it.

And then I hear it. A little voice. A whisper. A feeling, really. I don't know where it is coming from, but it has my attention. I imagine it is Max, speaking to me from within the womb. His message surrounds me. He tells me to forget the "hour and a half," to turn off the calculator in my mind that is busy calculating how many more contractions I'll have to endure in the next 90 minutes.

"All you have to worry about right now," he tells me, "is *this* moment; *this* contraction. Forget the ones you've had. Forget the ones to come. Be present now. Your body knows the way." I listen. I breathe. I trust my body. The next wave comes in, crashes over me, and disappears. I can do this, I think. One contraction at a time. I can do this.

Hours later, I lie in bed with him on my chest. There are no words to describe his perfection. I can't stop staring at his tiny perfect lips, stroking his puffy perfect cheeks, and gawking at the incredible wonder of it all. He is only minutes old, and I am already drunk with love for this perfect little being.

But as I gaze into his brand new, sea-coloured eyes, I feel another wave wash over me: this time, one of panic. I don't know anything about babies, I think! My heart beats a little bit faster. Yes, my husband and I attended prenatal classes, but they didn't teach us how to keep this fragile, unpredictable little baby *alive* for the first few days of his life. And they didn't cover how to breastfeed him, or toilet train him, or teach him to read, or how to deal with him when he's a teenager. In a few hours, I think, they are going to release us from this hospital and leave us to *parent* this complicated little person for the rest of our lives! "Help! Help!" I want to scream out.

As I lie there sweating about all the stages of life Max is going to have to go through with an unprepared, most likely incompetent, mother, I hear the little voice once more. Again, it is just barely a whisper—and once again, it calms my heart.

"All you have to worry about right now," says the voice, "is how to look after a one-day-old baby. Forget the terrible twos. Forget the teenage years. Focus on today. You already know everything you need to know right now, in this moment. You can change a diaper. You are learning to breastfeed. You can comfort him and tell him you love him. Relax. That is enough."

I know this sounds a bit strange. I know unborn and newborn babies don't talk. But somehow, lying there in that hospital bed, I heard the messages I needed to hear, and I listened to them.

Max is now a vivacious, bright-eyed four-year-old. For the past four years, I've been taking it day-by-day. And, yes, there are still moments when I think about the future and feel panicked or ill equipped to face the challenges I will undoubtedly face by virtue of being his mother. But then, I look at him, and realize that I will deal with those challenges just as I have with the ones I've faced so far: one day at a time. Just how Max likes it.

Scars

JOY L. EIDSE

SCENE 6: THE BELLY

This scene is written like a collection of journal entries from two different journals. The actor should have two journals in front of her and pick up each separately to read from them. She is just skimming, flipping pages, and reading a little from each page. There is a recorded heartbeat that plays between each entry. As the scene progresses, the heartbeat speeds up.

Journal 1:

Derek fasts and prays one day each week that we would get pregnant. Lord, hear our prayer. Jesus, son of David, have mercy on us ... Everyone else is having children ... my friends can't seem to talk about anything else ... I get it. It's just hard ... going for testing ... sperm count normal ... ovulation normal ... taking temperature, checking mucus, position of cervix, ovulation test kits ... lots of sex, careful not to deplete the sperm, no hot tubs for you ... Twenty-four months of concentrated effort ... *(Flips ahead a ways in the journal)* ... Eight weeks pregnant. I can hardly believe it! I didn't think it would ever happen ... Dear baby, your daddy and I have been waiting for you for so long, we didn't know if you would ever come ... Today I've got a headache. I'm exhausted and nauseous and I'm so grateful because it means I'm going to have a baby! *(Flips ahead some more)* ... Ultra sound one ... inconclusive ... can't get a good picture of the head ... fetal assessment two ... Genetic testing ... a condition called anencephaly ... incompatible with life ... forebrain not developed ... not treatable ... 50 % chance of surviving birth ... maybe live for a few hours ... decide whether or not to carry to term ... it's a boy ... River Creedance Eidse. *(pause, then flip to another page)*

Son, you are my treasure, son, love beyond measure fills my heart for you ... My grief overwhelms me ... I celebrate you and I grieve the loss of hope ... the loss of dreams ...

Sound of a heartbeat.

Journal 2:

Tomorrow we will find out if this baby is healthy ... *(flip ahead)* He's perfect ... another boy and we've used up our one good boy's name ... it really is going to happen ... *(pause and read as if reading a quote from another book, in a slightly different voice)* "The woman's changing body is a marvellous thing to behold ... the best odds diet ... 6 helping of grain, 3 of yellow vegetables, 3 of green, 4 proteins, 3 fruit, 3 dairy, 1 cheat a month, like ice cream ..." *(own voice again)* Can this cheat be for next month? ... *(reading quote)* "No alcohol, no sugar, no honey, no fresh water fish..." *(back to own voice)* Dominic, Dominic, we need a little song for Dominic, Dominic, we need a love song for Dominic, Dominic, he's the sweetest boy I know ... Do I dare hope? ... Let's not have a baby shower until after he is born ...

Sound of a heartbeat.

Journal 1:

I want to cherish every moment I have with you and be the best parent I can be, even if it's only for a few more months ... Why carry to term? Aren't you just making it harder on yourself? ... Deformed, no human without a brain ... more love equals more pain ... maybe they made a mistake ... maybe everything will be fine ... *(sarcastic)* "Don't worry, you can always have another one." *(pause)* Bouncing baby boys never stop moving ... move slowly in the night and don't wake him up or he'll start kicking and you'll never get back to sleep ... starting to get excited; can't wait to see him ... starting to dread the end, but I so want to see him ... can hardly bend over ... peeing all the time ... short of breath ... no stretch marks yet ... oh, there they are.

Sound of a heartbeat.

Journal 2:

Just need to write this exam before he comes ... due date approaching ... guess I should get stuff together soon ...

Sound of a heartbeat.

Journal 1:

Notice from the Department of Health to the Winnipeg Centre Vineyard Funeral Home: Expected death of newborn, River Creedance Eidse, no special precautions necessary ... phone call from the Health Division, "We're concerned about your intentions to take your baby home, dead or alive ... unsanitary ... psychological trauma" ... ask Theresa to sing at funeral, ask Andy to read story ... ask Brian to pray ...

Sound of heartbeat.

Journal 2:
Birth plan ... go to hospital at five centimeters ... Derek cut the cord, bathe the baby ... prefer to be drug-free.
Heartbeat.

Journal 1:
Neonatal recessitation plan ... if not breathing, but has a pulse ... if struggling to breathe ... if not breathing and no pulse, give to mother without intervention ... decline fetal heart monitor during labour ... ways to initiate labour ... sex three times a day ... with this belly? ... enema? ... no thanks ... 10 mile walks, in 30 degree weather ... cod liver oil equals the burning ring of fire ... three hours of nipple stimulation equals two Harry Potter movies ... blue cohash, red raspberry leaf tea, homeopathy, acupuncture, sweeping the membranes, all to no avail ... stretch marks growing.
Heartbeat.

Journal 2:
Ways to stimulate labour ... a big meal, three weeks before due date ... Watch out, here he comes!

SCENE 8: THE PERINEUM

"How many stitches am I getting, doc?" "Enough." There is something to be said about either the strength or the sanity of a woman who can go through 28 hours of the worst pain she will ever know and then choose to do it again. River was induced. It did not end well. The labour was so complicated and traumatic that they gave me an amnesiac in my IV so I wouldn't remember the intensity. Maybe that's why I was willing to try again. We went in for induction 17 days after River's due date. They said he probably wouldn't initiate labour on his own because he didn't have a forebrain. I was given cervical gel. The contractions started out slowly and then began to pick up over the next few hours and then suddenly stopped. They gave me another dose of gel around 10: 00 p. m. This time the contractions started out strong and picked up in intensity 'til about 1:00 a. m. Then they plateaued. Plateau, such a calm and peaceful sounding word, makes it sound like you're getting a break ... After a couple of hours, the contractions starting piggybacking. This is apparently quite normal with the gel. One after another, without a break, no time to relax or breathe. This went on for hours. The nurse asked if I wanted Demerol. I said, "No, I'll wait and see how dilated I am. If I'm progressing well, I can keep this up for a bit longer." Finally, at 8: 00 a. m., the doctor came to check me. One centimetre. After 12 hours of labour, I was only one centimetre. *(angry)* I was one f'in' centimetre when I came in. What the f$and# is the point of this!? "We need to increase the intensity of your contractions." "Are you serious? " "I think it's time for an epidural," she said. I could definitely see her point and felt that since she was the doctor, she would know when it was time for an epidural. So who was I to disagree? This is the point when the birth plan went out the window, never to be referred to again. Heplock took three tries. It's really hard to sit still when there are constant bursts of excruciating pain, one after another wracking your body so intensely that you can hardly breathe. The needle in the spine had to be done twice as well. That doesn't seem like an area of the body that should be pierced more than once at a time. I don't know, maybe I'm just squeamish. Finally, blessed sleep for a few hours, but I could only lay on one side. River's feet were in my ribs and it hurt to be on that side. I awoke when my water broke. There was a lot of meconium. Not a good sign. I don't remember feeling him move at all after that. A while later, I don't know how long it was—the day and night seemed to all meld together. I was checked again and was at ten centimetres. I was given permission to start pushing. The medication was allowed to wear off so that I could feel the urge to push, and push with the contractions. I had in my mind how things would go at this point. I had attended the birth of my best friend's daughter. Once they told her she could push, the baby pretty much slid out within about half an hour. This seemed like a reasonable time frame to me.

Three hours later, it was clear that River was a face presentation. They said he was probably protecting the soft tissue on the top of his head, where there was no skull. They did an episiotomy ... unlike "plateau," the word "episiotomy" gives no illusion of calmness or peacefulness. It sounds like it is: a cut, a stinging slice. There was very little progression in the labour after the episiotomy. They brought me a mirror so I could see his face, his full lips were puckered up like he was giving us a kiss, but his face was dark and swollen. He did not move or respond to touch. I think I knew he was dead, but had not fully processed it at that point. They said that, if he survived the labour, he would be deaf, blind, and unconscious, but I guess they still expected him to react to touch. It wasn't until my second pregnancy that I found out that once a baby's head is out you only have minutes to get the rest of him out before his breathing would be compromised. The doctor reached in to see what the trouble was ... River's shoulder was stuck. She tried to free him. It was a deep pain, involving my bones. I screamed and screamed, and begged her to stop. She kept going, thinking that any second now he would be free. Finally ... finally, she stopped. I had to be moved down the hall to the operating room for more light and more room. I remember that move. My baby's tiny, deformed head between my legs, a sheet thrown over me, the bright lights ... still pushing ... the nurses' desk, the crying newborn in the room we were passing, visitors for the new baby cooing over his new life. A second obstetrician was called in, along with the anaesthesiologist, a bunch of nurses, my midwife, my friend, and my husband. They tried laughing gas—I screamed in pain and hyperventilated. They gave me more and more drugs ... I don't even know what all they gave me. The anaesthesiologist advised the doctor to wait at least ten minutes before trying again. They couldn't wait. I remember hearing my voice further and further away and then all went dark.

When I opened my eyes, I felt the heavy weight of my son lying on my belly. He was naked, except for the little hat our midwife had crocheted. I looked down and said, "Wake up little baby. Wake up." He did not wake up. They wrapped him up and I held him. He was a big boy. Perfect, to me, in every way. He weighed in at eight pounds, eight ounces, even without a fully developed head. He would for sure have been nine pounds, if all had been normal. The OB wrote "second degree tearing" on the report, from vagina through perineum, but the midwife said it was more like third degree, because I tore a little into the anus. Right through is fourth degree. Whatever the degree, the healing was slow and excruciating. But I embraced that pain; it was the only physical proof I had that I had had a son. That pain was a physical manifestation of the pain of my soul. I don't wonder why people who grieve used to tear at their hair and cut themselves. They just needed to feel something tangible that they could deal with, not the elusive internal pain that comes from a soul being shredded. It's so hard to find medication for that kind of pain.

SCENE 12: CONCLUSION

These are the scars of my body. They are mine, and I cherish the markers that prove that I lived, here, on this planet, for a time. I will not hide my scars. They speak of experience and of wisdom. They are beautiful to me, each with their story of pain, whether chosen or inflicted. I have no scars of war, of torture, or disease or poverty. I will not take scars to hide my scars or speak negatively about the beauty marks I bear. My scars have become part of me; they tell a story, a story worth sharing, a story that invites a story. This is my story.

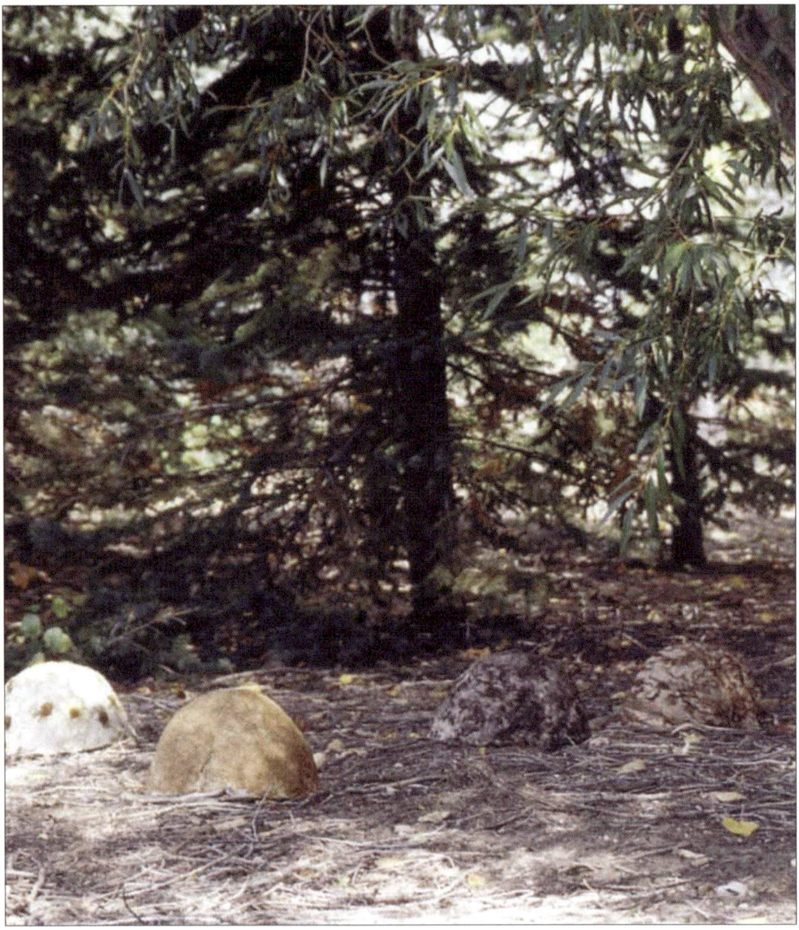

Judy Anderson, *Looking Beyond*, 2004, mixed media, handmade paper and natural items, 38.10 x 25.40 cm.

Looking Beyond, cast from my pregnant belly, represents a tiny version of the womb of Mother Earth. Through the use of handmade paper and natural items I reference Mother Earth, spirituality and the cyclical nature of life and death.

Severed (in Northern Alberta)

SUSAN PICARD

We are severed from the wildlife
that knows how long
a babe should suckle
instincts dulled
in the swelter of progress
that *borrows* my *most basic* biology
packages it without
my powerful alchemy
attachment bond
milk on the lips
now written into stories
as weakness.

Out of the food chain
you are strong
ripping roadways into well sites
creating all terrain access
disrupting
a suckling baby.
Mother bear lumbers
with lightning speed
roars
slashes the air
shakes her head
deadly protective
when you stumble into her home.

Do you wonder why
I am fierce
when they find her shaggy body
by the river

dead
two cubs clawing
shriveled nipples
their death sentence?

Damn your fear
discomfort at *my bare breast*
how many babies died
when your powdered capitalism
was diluted with
poverty
while you...
revved your engine?

A Fragile Moment

REINIE HEYDEMANN

"At least I heard him cry!"
she sobbed into my arms
holding tenderly
the suffering mother
who lost her little one
born prematurely from her womb
too fragile to live
beyond his first breath
and cry.

Words of pain and joy
mixed like a bitter medicine.

What anguish and despair.

Anger at the man who planted the seed
deserting the birthing mother
who asks the question "Why?"
and mourning two more losses
regretting previous abortions.

She voices her anger and rage
while tenderly holding
and smiling at her little one
wrapped in his diaper shroud.

No more life, no more dream.

Yet embracing a new kind of spirit
its preciousness in her arms
despite the fact that I must
take her son back to the morgue.

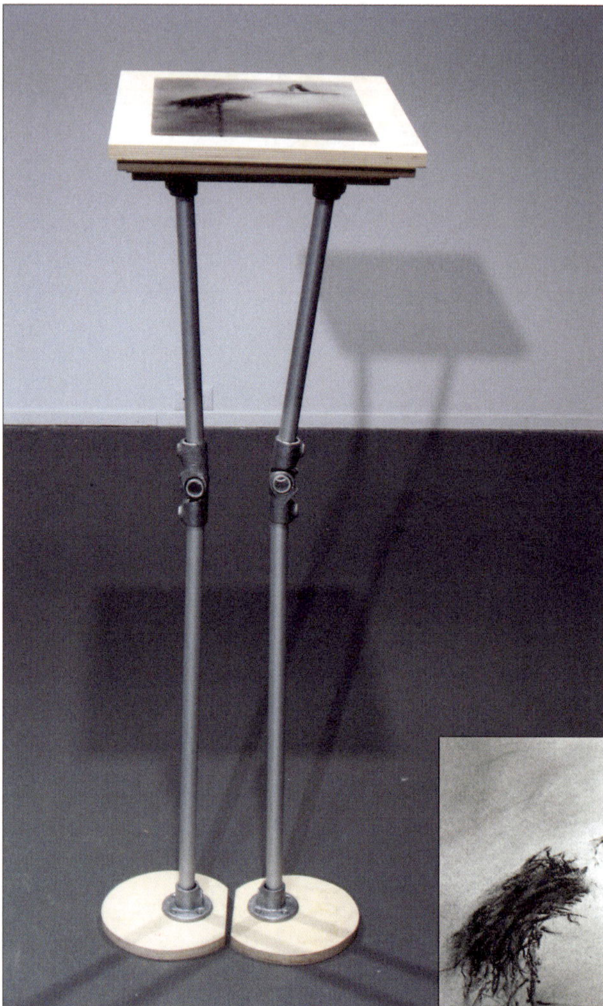

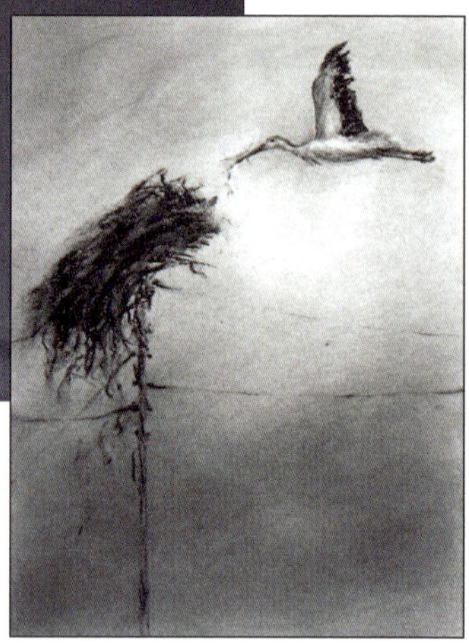

Wendy Peart, (from top to bottom) *Teeter* (from *The Stork Project*) and *Teeter* detail, 2006, aluminum, plywood, steel, and charcoal on paper, 127 x 38 x 47 cm.

The work, *Teeter* (from *The Stork Project*), considers the tenuous, vulnerable condition of the White Stork's nest, its place of home, nurturing and sanctuary. Preferring to perch atop human dwellings or industrial structures, the White Stork creates a romantic utopia in which to raise its young.

Tenuto

TRONI Y. GRANDE

Should I record
  what passed between us
    without a net
who would believe

How such a lithe ephemeral frame
  so strong a beating
    could bend   and supple
me contain in such fragility

How could this lilt
  this pressure
    so small a difference
    (who would believe)
    turn word to note
    confer on each
the slightest accent of grace

(Floating attention, you called it,
waiting for this moment
where other resonance
and slightest pressure
yield net effect)

In this hugely ordinary moment
  pause of men
      two women sign into the air
       draw generations deep
       the pain of birth and stalled delivery
labour failing / to progress

one mother pushes
  forces to a head
    where dents and bruises
      bear the cleft of union
one mother gestures wildly
    moves beyond words
      keening
grafts a mark on the heart of pain

Should I record
  how joined / how separate
    bereft
who would bear this   resonance

Où sont les sage-femmes?

Le choc culturel d'une femme immigrée en Ontario face aux pratiques de santé concernant la maternité

AURÉLIE LACASSAGNE

LES PRATIQUES DE santé, aussi variées soient-elles, font partie intégrante des pratiques culturelles d'un groupe. Au même titre que l'éducation—ses principes et son fonctionnement—la manière dont les professionnels de santé reçoivent les personnes, le degré de médicalisation, le degré de contrôle sur les corps et autres pratiques forment la culture d'un groupe. Par là même, la culture médicale s'avère être un marqueur identitaire assez puissant si l'on considère qu'elle touche à l'intimité de la personne. Si les pratiques de santé varient dans l'espace-temps et qu'elles construisent en partie une société, les immigrés, en arrivant dans un nouveau lieu, se trouvent donc confrontés à des pratiques sociales inconnues, qu'il va falloir appréhender, comprendre, et intégrer à ses schèmes de pensée. Maintenant le cas des femmes immigrées est encore plus illustratif des problèmes potentiels qui se posent face à ces pratiques différentes. Plusieurs raisons renforcent cet aspect problématique. Tout d'abord, les femmes immigrées sont souvent dans des situations de vulnérabilité plus grande liées à leur précarité sociale (niveau d'éducation plus faible, connaissance imparfaite voire ignorance complète de la langue d'accueil, pas d'emploi, pas d'accès à des réseaux sociaux, etc.), mais également à leur statut de femme (risque de violence accrue, risque d'exploitation sexuelle, etc.). Ensuite, comme je l'ai déjà remarqué, les pratiques de santé sont liées de façon inhérente à l'intimité et au corps. Or, pour les femmes, ces deux aspects revêtent une dimension plus particulière, plus profonde que pour les hommes. En outre, les professionnels de la santé, et en particulier les médecins—occupant le haut de la pyramide médicale—étant en majorité des hommes, les femmes immigrées doivent non seulement faire face au choc culturel de pratiques différentes, mais en plus, il faut les gérer avec une personne de l'autre sexe.

On imagine donc aisément la somme des complications à laquelle doivent faire face les femmes immigrées lors d'une maternité. La maternité est un moment de vie qui démultiplie les émotions, les sensations, les peurs, les interrogations. Lors d'une première maternité en particulier, la femme rentre dans une expérience de vie radicalement nouvelle. Le besoin de «se raccrocher» à des expériences connues, à des pratiques sociales intégrées socialement et psychologiquement, à des professionnels dont on connaît les principes et méthodes s'avère indispensable dans la mesure où cela permet de ne pas rajouter de stress inutile, d'anxiété déjà présente liée à l'état même de femme enceinte. L'art des sages-femmes renvoie à ces dimensions de gestion des appréhensions liées à la maternité.

BRÈVE HISTORIQUE DE LA PROFESSION DES SAGES-FEMMES ET DE LEUR PERCEPTION

Les sages-femmes ont existé depuis la nuit des temps et dans de nombreuses cultures (Coulon-Arpin). Elles représentent une des rares figures universelles. Bien sûr, cette figure a évolué au fil de l'histoire. En différents lieux, à différentes époques, les sages-femmes ont connu des statuts sociaux variés, tantôt extrêmement respectées, tantôt considérées comme sorcières et pourchassées. Leurs pratiques aussi varient (Jordan): pratique orientée plus vers l'aspect médical de la maternité, ou plus vers l'aspect humain. Le degré d'avancement biomédical a aussi des conséquences importantes, notamment la place des savoirs ancestraux, de la spiritualité par rapport aux avancées scientifiques dans les pays en voie de développement (voir par exemple: Sesia).

Le Canada, et dans une moindre mesure les États-Unis, se distinguent de la vaste majorité des pays du monde de par la place qu'occupe l'art des sages-femmes. En effet, dans ces deux pays, cette figure universelle avait quasiment été éliminée du paysage social et médical. Les médecins s'étaient arrogés leur savoir et eux seuls étaient en charge de la maternité. Il aura fallu un très long travail pour que les sages-femmes puissent réapparaître au grand jour et que leur art soit de nouveau reconnu. Mon objectif ici n'est pas d'en relater l'histoire, ce qui a été fait brillamment ailleurs. Mon expérience étant limitée à l'Ontario, c'est sur cette province que je focaliserai mon attention. Il aura fallu attendre 1991 pour qu'une loi provinciale (la Loi sur les sages-femmes) vienne réglementer leur pratique. D'après l'Association des sages-femmes de l'Ontario, on en dénombre 390 dans toute la province. Ce nombre progresse; mais il reste bien en dessous de ce qui existe dans d'autres pays. À titre de comparaison, on estime à 15 000 le nombre de sages-femmes pratiquant en France. En outre, il apparaît que les sages-femmes canadiennes doivent lutter pour faire leur place au sein du système de santé. D'ailleurs, leur statut social dans le système est très bas (selon leurs propres paroles) parce qu'elles sont des femmes, mais également parce que leur expertise de la maternité n'est pas reconnue comme telle (Benoit 311).

Mon hypothèse est donc la suivante: pour les femmes immigrées arrivant en Ontario dans une période de maternité, il existe un véritable choc culturel car elles ne retrouvent pas la figure connue et rassurante de la sage-femme. La pratique des sages-femmes ontariennes reste très restreinte comparée à d'autres cas. En effet, dès qu'une grossesse ou un accouchement se complique, c'est un médecin qui prend le relais; ces derniers ne travaillent pas vraiment en collaboration; la frontière entre ces deux professions s'avère très hermétique. À cela s'ajoute que le statut social des sages-femmes (le manque de reconnaissance sociale) de leur savoir-faire n'a rien de très rassurant pour une femme immigrée perdue.

Qu'en est-il de la recherche féministe sur la maternité? Comment s'assurer que la parole des mères ne soit pas simplement mobilisée dans le discours académique mais soit insérée dans un projet émancipateur? L'objet de ce texte consiste à relever l'importance de la narration et de la réflexivité dans la recherche sur la maternité au moyen d'un récit de vie autobiographique. La méthodologie du récit de vie est de plus en plus souvent usitée surtout dans les recherches féministes. Elle permet de laisser parler les femmes au lieu de parler en leur nom, mais également d'apporter« une dimension diachronique qui permet de saisir les logiques d'action dans leur développement biographique, et les configurations de rapports sociaux dans leur développement historique» (Bertaux 13). Le récit autobiographique par rapport au récit de vie classique offre plusieurs avantages: c'est un récit plus travaillé car il a fait l'objet d'une réflexion approfondie alors que le récit de vie est brut et lisse; il enlève également le filtre de l'interprétation posé par le chercheur; enfin, il permet une forme de cohérence entre le Moi privé et le Moi public en apportant une réflexivité. Sa validité est assurée par la proximité herméneutique qu'il offre. En tant que chercheure féministe, la narration permet d'introduire une distance réflexive par rapport à l'analyse; cela permet de se comprendre en tant que chercheure féministe.

PREMIÈRE MATERNITÉ À SAULT STE MARIE

«Je suis arrivée de France en septembre 2001 à Sault Ste Marie pour m'installer avec mon mari. En octobre, je suis tombée enceinte. J'étais sous statut de touriste et par conséquent, je n'avais pas de couverture santé. Je suis donc rentrée en décembre en France pour voir mon médecin de famille. J'ai fait ma première échographie là-bas. Moment merveilleux, tout allait bien, les indicateurs étaient au beau fixe: trois segments à chaque membres, épaisseur nucale dans les normes. J'ai même pu avoir des photos et une cassette vidéo. Mon médecin était cependant moins enthousiaste. Je venais de passer un an (de septembre 2000 à juin 2001) au Bélarus. Or, ce pays a été gravement touché par la catastrophe de Tchernobyl; les taux de radioactivité y sont très élevés et les conséquences sanitaires en pâtissent gravement.[1] Mon médecin, très consciencieux, a fait mesurer mon taux de radioactivité. Aucune surprise, le taux de radioactivité dans mon corps avait augmenté, malgré les précautions prises. Cependant, mon médecin savait qu'une fois rentrée en France, la radioactivité devrait naturellement baisser. Mon médecin décide donc de m'envoyer au département de génétique d'un grand hôpital pour évaluer ce risque. Le diagnostic ne se fait pas attendre: je suis considérée comme une patiente à haut risque. Cela signifie surtout que ma grossesse est considérée comme à haut risque. Concrètement, en France, d'après les pratiques en vigueur, les médecins m'expliquent que les tests sanguins seront plus nombreux et également que je devrais passer une échographie chaque mois pour suivre le développement du fœtus. Le risque ne pèse pas sur moi mais sur la santé du bébé que je porte.

Je reviens au Canada un peu secouée: comment assurer le suivi médical? Heureusement, j'obtiens un contrat de travail ce qui me permet d'être couverte par le RAMO (Régime d'assurance-maladie de l'Ontario). Mais là, je découvre que le parcours du combattant ne fait que commencer: il faut trouver un médecin. Inutile d'essayer de trouver un médecin de famille, des dizaines de milliers de personnes sont sur liste d'attente. Je découvre la pauvreté extraordinaire du système de santé ontarien en région (dans le Nord comme on dit ici). Je me tourne vers mes étudiantes, la plupart sont toutes déjà mères, et compatissent à mon sort. Une d'entre elles contacte son gynécologue-obstétricien qui accepte de suivre ma grossesse. Je lui dis que, malgré les risques liés à ma grossesse, une sage-femme serait mieux car je me sentirais plus en confiance. Dans ma culture, ce sont elles qui ont le savoir-faire et qui s'occupent de la grossesse. Elle m'explique que les sages-femmes ici n'occupent pas une telle position: 'd'ailleurs il n'y a qu'un seul cabinet de sages-femmes et puis il faudra que tu accouches chez toi.' Deuxième choc, cette fois plus violent: je n'avais jamais imaginé qu'il puisse exister une société où les sages-femmes n'auraient pas le droit de cité. Et puis accoucher à domicile, quelle drôle d'idée ! Je n'en avais jamais entendu parler sauf à travers les récits de ma grand-mère qui, dans notre petit village, faisait office d'infirmière et de sage-femme, et qui accouchait les femmes chez elles dans les années 50 et 60. Je n'imaginais même pas que cela puisse encore arriver.[2] Je réplique à mon étudiante que ce n'est pas possible. Elle me dit que les sages-femmes n'ont pas le droit de rentrée à l'hôpital. Je n'en crois mes oreilles et m'en vais demander à d'autres étudiantes leurs avis. Elles sont toutes unanimes, elles me disent toutes la même chose: 'si tu vas avec une sage-femme, tu dois accoucher à la maison et elles ne pourront pas venir avec toi à l'hôpital.'

Prise de panique, le temps avançant, je ne vérifie pas les informations et me rends à ce premier rendez-vous avec le gynécologue-obstétricien (appelons-le Dr. X) qui a bien voulu me recevoir. La rencontre ne se passe pas très bien. Une multitude de chocs culturels m'arrivent en pleine face: Dr. X voit trois patientes en même temps dans trois pièces différentes; il me fait attendre très longtemps pour finalement ne même pas m'examiner, ne même pas m'écouter, l'entretien dure quelques minutes à peine. Je n'ai pas le temps de lui expliquer mon cas. Je ressors du cabinet médical tétanisée: que va-t-il arriver à mon enfant? Au deuxième rendez-vous, j'attaque tout de suite sur le Bélarus, lui expliquant ce que m'avaient dit les médecins en France. Dr. X me regarde interloqué, un peu comme si j'étais une folle furieuse, et me répond: 'je ne vois pas le rapport entre le Bélarus et la santé du bébé. Vous ne courrez aucun risque. Et je ne vous ferai certainement pas passer des échographies tous les mois. Ici au Canada, c'est une par grossesse, mais vous, bien sûr en France, c'est différent, vous êtes un pays socialiste, vous payez beaucoup d'impôts, alors vous pouvez vous amuser à ce genre de choses!' Le lien de confiance n'avait pas eu le temps de naître, il ne pouvait plus naître.

Je décide donc de téléphoner à une sage-femme de Sault-Sainte-Marie. Je lui explique la situation. J'étais persuadée qu'une sage-femme comprendrait et m'aiderait et puis je n'ai pas l'impression de lui demander la lune: je reste avec Dr. X pour pouvoir accoucher à l'hôpital, mais j'aimerais vous rencontrer pour assurer un vrai suivi de ma grossesse. Refus catégorique: il ne peut y avoir de doublon, ou vous êtes suivie par une sage-femme ou vous êtes suivie par un gynécologue-obstétricien. Nouveau choc, je me sens désemparée.

Arrive le temps de faire l'échographie du deuxième trimestre, la seule que l'on fait au Canada (quand la grossesse n'est pas considérée à risque). J'arrive à l'hôpital avec mon mari, le rapport et les photos de ma première échographie. Là, c'est la rencontre du troisième type. Tout d'abord les deux techniciennes (ce ne sont pas des docteurs ou des sages-femmes qui font les échographies: quelle bizarrerie!) refusent que mon mari soit présent. Ensuite elles tournent consciemment leur écran pour que je ne puisse rien voir (en France, j'avais un écran pour moi toute seule); elles regardent les photos comme si cela venait de la planète Mars (leur appareil date des années 80 et ne fait pas de photos); et rigolent au vue du rapport écrit en français. Ensuite silence complet pendant tout l'examen. À la fin, j'ose demander le verdict (j'utilise ce mot volontairement). La réponse se veut nonchalante: 'on transmet les infos à Dr. X qui vous dira ce qu'il juge utile.'

Au rendez-vous suivant avec Dr. X, je n'obtiens guère plus de renseignements. Je demande à ce qu'au moins j'aie des tests sanguins, refus. Un seul pendant toute la grossesse. Le seul suivi médical consistera donc aux tests d'urine mensuels; une seule échographie; une seule prise de sang. En tout et pour tout, j'ai dû voir Dr. X une vingtaine de minutes. Jamais aucune question concernant mon moral, comment j'envisageais ma grossesse, comment je voulais accoucher. Rien, le néant: suivi psychologique zéro, aspect personnel nul, suivi médical très médiocre. Et bien sûr, tout cela se passe à Sault Ste Marie, soit à quelques 5 000 kilomètres de ma famille, de mes amies. Je suis seule, au moment où j'aurais le plus besoin de soutien. Je commence pour la première fois à comprendre les traumatismes que peuvent engendrer le statut de femme immigrée. De nombreux éléments différentient la culture française de la façon dont les gens vivent à Sault Ste Marie.

Mais l'expérience la plus traumatique fut bel et bien ma première maternité et son déroulement. Sûrement parce que la maternité est la chose la plus intime qu'une femme soit amenée à vivre. Sûrement parce que la maternité a ce caractère d'ambivalence d'être tout à la fois le révélateur d'une grande force tout en étant un moment de vulnérabilité extrême. Je me consolais en me disant que, contrairement à beaucoup d'autres femmes immigrées en Ontario, je pouvais au moins communiquer en anglais. Même si j'avais préféré pouvoir utiliser ma langue maternelle, le français, il y a des moments, notamment durant l'accouchement, où on oublie toutes les langues sauf sa langue maternelle; il y a des sentiments intimes si profonds qu'on ne peut les exprimer que dans sa langue maternelle; et puis, j'avais les moyens financiers de rentrer en France si vraiment je le voulais, tout du moins jusqu'au septième mois de la grossesse. Par rapport à beaucoup d'autres femmes immigrées, mon isolement n'était donc pas aussi grand. Je n'avais pas à me soucier de questions matérielles. L'accouchement se déroula aussi mal que la grossesse. Le fœtus était en détresse respiratoire et mal positionné, il fallait aller vite pour me faire une péridurale dans l'imminence d'une possible césarienne. Mais il n'y a qu'un seul anesthésiste en service à Sault Ste Marie et on attend un grave accidenté de la route. Finalement, la décision est prise d'envoyer l'hélicoptère sur Sudbury pour que l'anesthésiste puisse s'occuper de moi, de longues minutes d'angoisse, encore. Au dernier moment, Dr. Y (Dr. X n'était pas de service) arrive et décide d'essayer les forceps (sans me demander mon avis, sans faire d'épisiotomie, les spécialistes apprécieront...). Le bébé sort, c'est une fille, on me l'emmène toute de suite. De longues minutes d'angoisse, encore. Elle va bien. Nous sortirons le lendemain de l'hôpital, sans que personne ne m'ait lavée, sans que personne ne m'ait examinée, sans que personne ne m'ait donnée de conseils sur l'allaitement. Ce grand moment de joie que la maternité doit être, fut le moment le plus terrifiant, angoissant et solitaire de ma vie.»

DEUXIÈME MATERNITÉ À SUDBURY

«Octobre 2005, je découvre que j'attends un deuxième enfant: moment de joie mêlé d'appréhension. Tous les souvenirs de ma première maternité que j'avais su si bien enfouir comme l'humain est seul capable de le faire des expériences traumatiques, remontent à la surface. Néanmoins, la situation est différente, j'habite maintenant à Sudbury, une plus grande ville. Une chose est sûre dans ma tête: je serai suivie par une sage-femme, même si je dois accoucher à domicile. Je prends contact avec la pratique à côté de chez moi. Que de bonnes surprises ! Tout d'abord, on me rassure en me disant que si je veux accoucher à l'hôpital, il n'y a aucun problème, qu'ici on respecte la volonté des futures mères. Deux des trois sages-femmes sont aussi francophones, facilitant ainsi l'expression de mes sentiments. Et puis surtout, on m'écoute, on prend le temps, on comprend mes angoisses et on essaye de les atténuer. Les sages-femmes ont fait un travail psychologique fantastique en m'apprenant à gérer le traumatisme de ma première maternité. Elles sont également très ouvertes quand je leur raconte comment cela se passe en France. Elles se montrent très ouvertes aux différences culturelles et les prennent en compte du mieux possible. Car même si j'avais à faire à des sages-femmes, comme dans mon pays d'origine, cette pratique n'est pas monolithique.[3]

Là aussi donc il y a eu un choc culturel dans la mesure où j'ai découvert une autre approche de l'art des sages-femmes. Une approche fondée sur la dimension humaine, une approche souvent féministe, une approche psychologique. À aucun moment, on ne considère la grossesse comme une pathologie. La relation qui s'installe entre la sage-femme et la future mère est faite de confiance, de proximité, d'intimité, d'écoute, d'ouverture. Chacune s'est enrichie du regard de l'autre. Les différences culturelles n'ont pas été un mur qui a brisé la communication et qui a pénalisé la maternité; au contraire, elles ont été un facteur d'épanouissement pour toutes. J'ai accouché à l'hôpital. Tout s'est formidablement bien passé: une deuxième petite fille est née qui tout de suite fut posée sur mon ventre et est allée crapahuter pour prendre sa première tétée. Les sages-femmes ont été présentes également par la suite pour m'aider pendant l'allaitement, toujours disponibles au moindre coup de fil. Aujourd'hui je suis convaincue que nulle part ailleurs je n'aurais eu une telle expérience. J'avais enfin découvert les joies de devenir mère.»

CONCLUSION

Chaque maternité est une expérience unique. Elle peut s'avérer un moment rempli de joie et de bonheur ou se révéler un traumatisme. La situation des femmes immigrées relève d'une catégorie particulière. De part leur statut, des difficultés spécifiques peuvent surgir pendant une maternité: problèmes de communication liés à la langue, problèmes médicaux particuliers, problèmes liés à la situation socio-économique. Ce que j'ai voulu montrer au travers du récit de vie présenté, c'est que, plus généralement, des problèmes d'ordre culturel liés aux pratiques de santé peuvent se poser. La part des femmes dans les mouvements migratoires, et notamment de femmes éduquées et formées, augmente (Kofman). Si le gouvernement de l'Ontario souhaite poursuivre une politique d'immigration active—nécessaire à l'activité économique de la province—il devient urgent de mettre en place des politiques publiques qui facilitent non seulement la venue de ces femmes, mais également leur intégration à la société d'accueil. Une augmentation drastique du nombre de sages-femmes, un accroissement de leur financement, des campagnes publiques de promotion de cette profession ainsi que des mesures coercitives pour les hôpitaux qui ne seraient pas« ouverts » aux sages-femmes représentent quelques éléments d'une véritable politique publique en faveur des sages-femmes. C'est un besoin urgent pour les femmes immigrées venant sous d'autres statuts (regroupement familial et asile) étant donné que ces femmes se trouvent souvent dans une situation de vulnérabilité, qui s'accroît durant la maternité. De façon générale, toute la population ontarienne y gagnerait dans la mesure où il semble qu'il existe une corrélation entre l'institutionnalisation et la formation hautement qualifiée de sages-femmes et le taux de mortalité à la naissance (Benoit 315).

[1]Des études indépendantes montrent que le nombre de problèmes de santé liés à la contamination radioactive chez les enfants—allant de l'asthme chronique à la leucémie en passant par les malformations cardiaques et physiques—ont augmenté de façon exponentielle (OECDNEA; Lazjuk *et al.*).

[2]Un rapport du Haut Comité de la Santé Publique de 1994 estimait à 0,5 % soit 3 800 le nombre d'accouchements à domicile en France (Munier).

[3]Elle varie suivant les traditions nationales. En France, les sages-femmes ont une approche très médicale de leur pratique. Cela s'explique par des facteurs historiques et éducatifs. Historiquement, les sages-femmes ont d'abord été assimilées aux chirurgiens. Les statuts et règlements corporatifs concernant les chirurgiens adoptés en 1730 s'appliquaient aux sages-femmes. Par conséquent, leur enseignement s'est orienté vers une perspective très médicale. Au vingtième siècle, comme ailleurs, il y aura une différenciation croissante entre la profession de sage-femme et celle de chirurgien. Néanmoins, la France ne perdra jamais ce caractère, qui s'est même renforcé au cours des dernières années. En effet, depuis 2002, les étudiantes sages-femmes suivent la première année des cours de médecine et elles doivent valider l'examen classant de fin de première année du premier cycle des études médicales, avant d'entamer leurs études de sages-femmes. Le champ des actes médicaux est aussi assez large: elles sont en charge des échographies et surtout en cas de pathologie, elles exercent avec les obstétriciens. Elles ne doivent pas abandonner le suivie de la future mère au profit de ces derniers.

OUVRAGES CITÉS

Benoit, Cecilia.« Paradigm Conflict in the Sociology of Service Professions: Midwifery as a Case Study. » *Canadian Journal of Sociology* 19.3 (1994): 303-329.

Bertaux, Daniel. *L'enquête et ses méthodes. Le récit de vie.* Paris: Armand Colin, 2006.

Coulon-Arpin, Madeleine. *La maternité et les sages-femmes, de la préhistoire au XXème siècle.* Paris: Éditions Roger Dacosta, 1981.

Jordan, Brigitte. *Birth in Four Cultures: A Cross-Cultural Investigation of Chidbirth in Yucatan, Holland, Sweden and the United States.* Prospect Heights, IL: Waveland Press, 1993.

Kofman, Eleonore.«Female 'Birds of Passage' a Decade Later: Gender and Immigration in the European Union. » *International Migration Review* 33.2 (1999): 269-299.

Lazjuk, G. I. *et al.*«Frequency Changes of Inherited Anomalies in the Republic of Belarus After the Chernobyl Accident.» *Radiation Protection Dosimetry* 62.1/2 (1995): 71-74.

Munier, Mathilde. *Accompagnement global avec accouchement à domicile en France de 1997 à 2001.* Mémoire de fin d'études pour le diplôme d'État de sage-femme, Université Paris V, 2005.

Organization for Economic Co-operation and Development Nuclear Energy Agency (OECDNEA).« Chernobyl Ten Years on, Radiological and Health Impact. An Assessment by the Nuclear Energy Agency Committee on Radiation Protection and Public Health. » 1995. 1er septembre 2007. <http: //www.nea.fr/html/rp/chernobyl/chernobyl-1995.pdf>.

Sesia, Paola. «'Women Come Here on Their Own When They Need to': Prenatal Care, Authoritative Knowledge, and Maternal Health in Oaxaca.» *Medical Anthropology Quaterly* 10.2 (1996): 121-140.

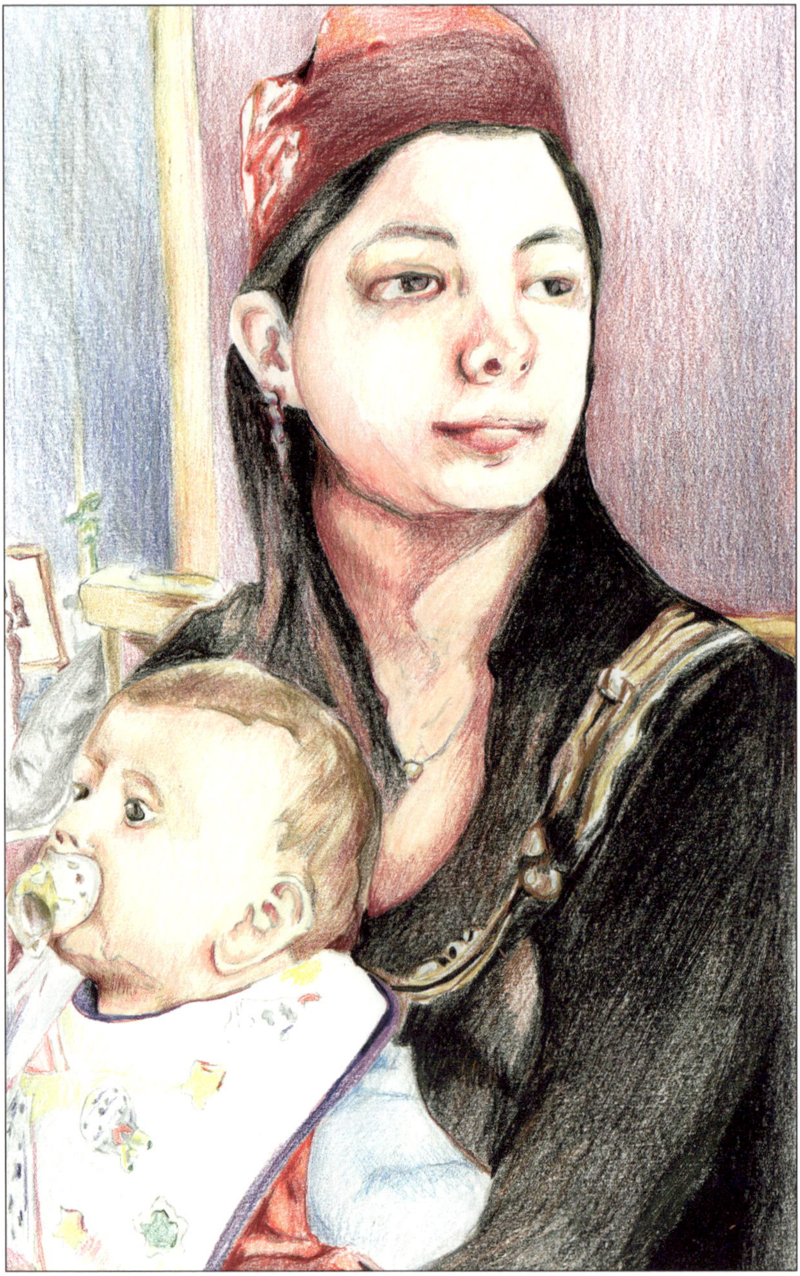

Michelle Glennie, *Mélanie and Zaak*, 2007, coloured pencil on bristol board, 25.40 x 38.10 cm.

In *Mélanie and Zaak*, I want to express the binding nature of a mother's oath. The drawing renews the iconic representations of the seated Madonna and Child. I swapped angels and gold for contemporary elements: Zaak's bib symbolizes constant care; his pacifier breaks away from ideologies placed on motherhood.

Une nouvelle avenue d'intervention développée au Québec pour soutenir les mères déprimées dans le contexte de l'allaitement maternel

MARIE LACOMBE, MARIE HATEM, LINDA BELL
ET EDWARD Z. TRONICK

L'ARRIVÉE D'UN ENFANT dans une famille est généralement perçue comme un évènement heureux. Pourtant, d'après les écrits consultés 8 à 15% des mères souffrent de dépression postnatale suite à la naissance d'un enfant (Perfetti, Clark et Fillmore 56-63). Souvent, ces mères souffrent en silence du fait de la représentation sociale du bonheur associée à la maternité et au rôle de mère. Elles sont moins nombreuses à poursuivre leur allaitement (Field, Hernandez-Reif et Feijo 539-545; Galler *et al.* 80-87). D'ailleurs, les différentes instances concernées par la qualité de l'allaitement maternel telles que l'Organisation mondiale de la santé, l'American Academy of Pediatrics, la Société canadienne de pédiatrie, l'Ordre des Infirmières et Infirmiers du Québec et Santé Canada recommandent l'allaitement maternel exclusif jusqu'à six mois de vie comme mode d'alimentation privilégié pour tous les nouveau-nés. Dans le présent article, il sera question d'une intervention développée au Québec pour aider les intervenantes en milieu clinique à apporter un soutien aux femmes qui allaitent. Pour y arriver, il sera fait mention de la dépression postnatale et de l'établissement de la relation mère-enfant dans le contexte de l'allaitement maternel.

LA DÉPRESSION POSTNATALE, SES SYMPTÔMES, SA PRÉVALENCE, SES FACTEURS PRÉDICTIFS ET SON DÉPISTAGE

La dépression postnatale réfère à un épisode de dépression majeure temporaire associé à la naissance d'un enfant. Cette dépression postnatale survient chez la mère au cours des quatre semaines suivant l'accouchement (DSM-IV). Cependant, les chercheurs font consensus pour signifier par dépression postnatale, la dépression qui s'installe dans les trois mois suivant la naissance de l'enfant (Wisner, Parry et Piontek 194-199).

Les symptômes de la dépression postnatale peuvent s'étendre sur une période variant de quelques semaines et persister au-delà de la première année de vie de l'enfant (Wisner, Parry et Piontek 194-199). Au plan clinique, la dépression postnatale se manifeste par l'humeur dépressive ou par la perte d'intérêt ou de plaisir dans la plupart des activités, perturbant le fonctionnement quotidien de la mère depuis au moins deux semaines. La présence de quatre ou plus des symptômes suivants sont requis pour établir le diagnostic: la perte ou le gain de poids, l'insomnie ou l'hypersomnie, l'agitation ou le ralentissement psychomoteur, la perte d'énergie ou la fatigue, la labilité émotionnelle, le sentiment de culpabilité, l'anxiété sévère, les attaques de panique, la difficulté à penser et à se concentrer, les pensées récurrentes de suicide ou de mort avec ou sans un plan prédéterminé, les hallucinations auditives, les idées délirantes ainsi que les comportements désorganisés en regard des soins à donner à l'enfant (Americain Psychiatric Association).

Il est possible de supposer que la dépression postnatale affecte plus de 12 000 femmes chaque année au Québec et 55 000 femmes au Canada. Le taux de prévalence de la dépression postnatale peut s'élever jusqu'à 26% chez les mères adolescentes et de 22 à 34% chez les mères à faible revenu.

Selon Uriel Halbreich, les facteurs prédictifs de la dépression postnatale peuvent être classifiés comme suit (1-7): 1) l'histoire personnelle; 2) l'histoire familiale; 3) les facteurs socio-économiques; 4) les relations familiales perturbées; 5) le réseau de soutien social; 6)les facteurs liés à la grossesse, à l'accouchement ou à la période postnatale; 7) les facteurs liés à l'enfant; et 8) les différents autres facteurs (hormonaux, biologiques).

Or, le dépistage systématique s'avère primordial pour intervenir précocement afin de favoriser la poursuite de l'allaitement maternel et ce, pour le bien-être de la mère, de l'enfant et de la famille. Ceci requiert une évaluation précoce des symptômes de la dépression postnatale. Par exemple, les intervenantes peuvent utiliser un instrument tel que l'échelle d'Edinburgh qui est traduit dans plus de 20 langues et facile à auto-administrer à la période pré et postnatale pour le dépistage des symptômes de dépression (Cox 185-189).

LA DÉPRESSION POSTNATALE ET L'ALLAITEMENT MATERNEL

La dépression postnatale peut-être un obstacle à l'initiation et à la poursuite de l'allaitement. Au niveau national, selon l'Enquête sur la santé dans les collectivités canadiennes menée en 2003, 85% des mères ont déclaré avoir essayé d'allaiter comparativement à 76% chez les mères québécoises (Santé Canada). En dépit de l'importance de l'allaitement maternel comme principal mode d'alimentation de l'enfant jusqu'à six mois, moins de 50% des femmes québécoises et canadiennes allaitent leur enfant jusqu'à six mois. Seulement 17% des mères canadiennes allaitent exclusivement jusqu'à six mois et moins de 3% au Québec (Institut de la Statistique du Québec; Millar et Maclean 25-33). Il est tout à fait plausible de croire qu'un des facteurs de sevrage chez certaines mères était la dépression postnatale. Chez les mères qui allaitent, les résultats de l'étude rapportent une relation inverse entre les symptômes de dépression et l'allaitement à six semaines de vie, même après avoir contrôlé l'histoire de dépression antérieure, les évènements de vie stressants et la médication en cours (Hatton 444-449). De plus, d'autres résultats d'études démontrent que ces mères allaitent moins longtemps (Dubois *et al.*; Galler *et al.* 80-87a).

Une des raisons rapportées fréquemment chez les mères déprimées qui cessent leur allaitement est la perception de l'insuffisance de lait (Schwartz *et al.* 439-444). Il est fort possible que la dépression postnatale puisse interférer avec la production de lait. Certains auteurs rapportent que le stade de la lactogenèse est retardé chez les mères qui présentent un taux élevé de cortisol (Grajeda et Perez-Escamilla 3055-3060). Par ailleurs, Katheryn Dewey rapporte que la présence d'évènements stressants dans la vie a un effet négatif sur le processus de lactation rendant difficile l'initiation de l'allaitement (3012S-3015S).

LES EFFETS DE LA DÉPRESSION POSTNATALE SUR LA RELATION MÈRE-ENFANT

La dépression postnatale affecte le comportement de la mère de même que celui de l'enfant ainsi que la qualité des interactions mère-enfant (Cohn *et al.* 31-45; Field *et al.* 7-14). D'ailleurs, la dépression postnatale est bien reconnue comme étant une condition de santé pouvant compromettre le développement cognitif et émotionnel de l'enfant (Kendall-Tackett; Tronick *et al.* 406-423).

Des résultats d'observation des enfants de trois à six mois en interaction avec leur mère déprimée indiquent que ces enfants présentent davantage d'asymétrie frontale droite (Field *et al.* 216-229). Cependant, les enfants allaités par une mère déprimée ne présentent aucune activité cérébrale asymétrique et ils parviennent à vivre une relation plus positive avec leur mère (Jones, McFall et Diego 103-124). D'ailleurs, les mères déprimées sont moins positives en ce qui a trait à l'humeur, aux expressions faciales, aux vocalisations, au ton de la voix ainsi qu'aux comportements ludiques (Field 25-29).

Quoique la qualité des échanges entre la mère et son enfant semble être affectée par la présence de dépression chez la mère, certains facteurs peuvent nuancer cet effet. Certaines mères sont probablement capables de s'auto-motiver à interagir positivement avec l'enfant, guidées par des valeurs profondes ou des connaissances sur l'importance des interactions positives pour le développement de l'enfant ou par un désir profond de se connecter positivement avec leur enfant.

LES EFFETS DE LA DÉPRESSION POSTNATALE DANS LE CONTEXTE DE L'ALLAITEMENT MATERNEL

Certains auteurs suggèrent que l'allaitement contribue à favoriser une humeur positive chez la mère (Hatton 444-449). Aussi, Mezzacappa et Katlin rapportent que l'allaitement maternel pourrait jouer un rôle protecteur contre l'humeur négative chez les mères (187-193). Les mères allaitantes rapportent un niveau de stress plus bas et la tétée au sein amène des sentiments plus positifs chez cette dernière. Enfin, Deborah McCarter-Spaulding et June Horowitz rapportent que les mères plus âgées, vivant avec un partenaire et détenant un revenu élevé sont plus enclines à allaiter même si elles sont déprimées (10-17).

LA RELATION MÈRE-ENFANT DANS LE CONTEXTE DE L'ALLAITEMENT MATERNEL

L'établissement de la relation parent(s)-enfant est d'une importance majeure pour le développement de l'enfant tout comme pour le développement de l'identité du parent. De prime abord, l'allaitement a l'avantage de favoriser des échanges affectifs entre la mère et l'enfant. Chaque tétée est en effet l'occasion de multiples échanges visuels et verbaux ainsi que de plusieurs minutes de contact peau à peau (Beaudry, Chiasson et Lauzière).

Actuellement, les intervenantes apportant le soutien aux mères sont formées davantage pour résoudre les problèmes techniques de l'allaitement et axent particulièrement leurs interventions sur cet aspect (Shaw-Flach 432-435). Alors, les intervenantes pourraient élargir leurs interventions à l'aspect relationnel vécu par la dyade mère-enfant en plaçant le focus sur les interactions mère-enfant. Lors des rencontres prénatales, les intervenantes devraient donner l'information sur les bienfaits d'une bonne relation affective pour le développement physique et affectif de l'enfant et de l'identité maternelle dans le contexte de l'allaitement (Bell *et al.* 2004). Dès que la mère accouche, il est recommandé d'utiliser le développement de la qualité des interactions mère-enfant pour favoriser la poursuite de l'allaitement. Pour ce faire, les auteures ont eu recours au modèle de Linda Bell *et al.* pour le développement d'un outil afin d'évaluer la qualité des interactions mères-enfant.

LE MODÈLE DE BELL ET SES COLLÈGUES

Une série d'études réalisée au Québec par Bell et ses collègues a permis de développer le modèle de la relation parent(s)-enfant à partir des représentations parentales. Globalement, ces différentes études ont permis d'identifier les cinq composantes de cette relation qui se définissent comme

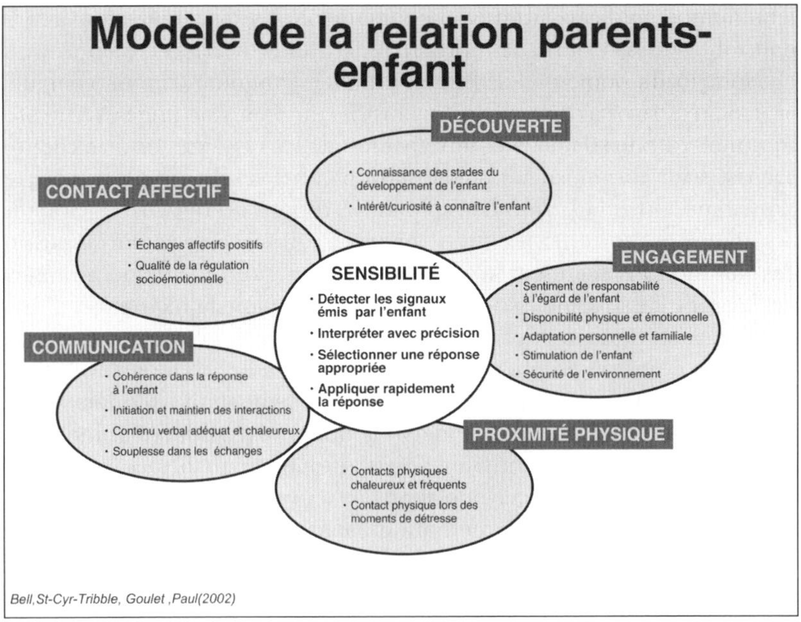

suit (voir Figure 1, ci-dessus): 1) la découverte de l'enfant: c'est le processus par lequel les parents font la connaissance de leur enfant afin de mieux comprendre l'expression de ses besoins; 2) le contact physique entre le parent et son enfant fait appel aux comportements adoptés par le parent et l'enfant pour interagir; 3) le développement de la relation affective qui se caractérise par la disposition affective des parents à l'égard de leur enfant et de leur nouveau rôle; celui-ci se manifeste dans l'expression de plaisir, de sentiment de compétence à s'occuper de l'enfant et de contrôle sur leur expérience; 4) l'initiation des interactions par les parents avec leur enfant qui correspond à l'habileté et à la motivation des parents à initier, à maintenir et à terminer ces interactions en tenant compte des capacités interactives de ce dernier; et 5) l'investissement du rôle parental réfère à la capacité du parent à assumer de nouvelles responsabilités et à s'engager réellement envers l'enfant. Les parents se sentent responsables de la sécurité, de la croissance et du développement de leur enfant. Au cœur de ces cinq composantes se trouve la sensibilité maternelle. D'après Carl Lacharité, celle-ci s'exprime en quatre phases: 1) la détection des signaux émis par l'enfant; 2) la signification juste et appropriée des signaux; 3) la sélection d'une réponse juste et appropriée aux signaux; et 4) l'application rapide de la réponse sélectionnée.

LE DÉVELOPPEMENT ET L'UTILISATION DE L'OUTIL

Le but de l'observation à domicile était de documenter le rôle des interactions mère-enfant dans la poursuite de l'allaitement maternel à partir de l'observation des interactions d'une dyade mère-enfant au Québec. Deux séances d'allaitement d'une durée de 30 minutes ont été enregistrées sur bande vidéo. La consigne donnée à la mère était de se comporter naturellement et librement avec leur enfant. La chercheuse prenait soin de noter toute information contextuelle ne pouvant être captée sur bande vidéo. L'objectif poursuivi pour cet outil est de donner des ateliers pour initier les intervenantes à l'observation et l'évaluation des interactions mère-enfant dans le contexte de l'allaitement maternel à partir du modèle. Nous suggérons un temps de formation d'une durée de sept heures et un suivi six mois après l'expérimentation sur le terrain. Dans un premier temps, le modèle de Bell et de ses collègues est expliqué pour bien comprendre les fondements du modèle. Pour la deuxième étape, une durée de trois heures est allouée: d'une part, pour initier les intervenantes à l'observation de la qualité de la relation mère-enfant selon le critère de sensibilité maternelle à l'intérieur des cinq composantes à partir de bande vidéo, d'exercices et d'échanges et, d'autre part, pour initier les intervenantes à des interventions de soutien à l'allaitement maternel par l'établissement de la relation mère-enfant. Cet outil peut-être utilisé par toute intervenante qui côtoie les mères plus particulièrement les infirmières. Afin de mieux comprendre l'observation des interactions mère-enfant d'après une composante de ce modèle, une illustration clinique est présentée comme exemple à partir d'une bande vidéo.

ILLUSTRATION CLINIQUE

Mélanie, une jeune québécoise de 26 ans, vient de donner naissance à son premier enfant. Sa grossesse s'est bien déroulée. Elle vit avec le père de son enfant depuis trois ans. Le père travaille à temps complet. Elle détient un baccalauréat en communication et a travaillé jusqu'à 37 semaines de grossesse. Mélanie souffre d'une allergie sévère. À la naissance, le médecin lui a conseillé de nourrir son bébé au sein, sous prétexte que l'allaitement pourrait réduire le risque d'allergie. Amy, le nouveau-né, a une chance sur trois d'être affectée par les allergies. Le père désirait que Mélanie allaite son bébé tout en lui laissant le choix de prendre sa décision. Au départ, la mère n'était pas certaine d'allaiter, actuellement Amy a 15 jours, voici les propos de sa mère: «Je n'étais pas sûre d'allaiter, aussitôt que j'ai accouché, elle a pris le sein. J'aime ça allaiter, c'est drôle de voir le petit bébé qui se colle après toi, qui se nourrit ». Lors de notre rencontre avec l'intervenante, la mère est fière de sa fille et dit bien s'adapter à son nouveau rôle de mère. Elle raconte qu'elle a un bon réseau de soutien et que sa relation conjugale avec son conjoint est très satisfaisante.

Les observations de l'intervenante

Voici l'ensemble des observations de l'intervenante lors de l'évaluation des interactions mère-enfant lors d'une session d'allaitement: 1) la mère tente d'initier des interactions lorsque le bébé a faim; 2) la mère a de la difficulté à décoder les signaux lorsque le bébé a faim ou l'inverse; 3) la mère dit que le bébé dort lorsqu'il est éveillé; 4) la mère est plus ou moins habile dans ses gestes avec le bébé (positionnement pour le rot ou la mise au sein, elle ne se préoccupe pas de la position du bébé); 5) la mère le stimule souvent pour qu'il boive; 6) la mère observe plus ou moins les réactions de l'enfant; et 7) la mère cherche à comprendre ce qui se passe lorsque le bébé tète plus ou moins bien.

La formulation de l'hypothèse de travail

Suite à ces observations, l'intervenante formule une hypothèse de travail sur la relation mère-enfant pour soutenir l'allaitement maternel qui se décrit comme suit: le fait que le bébé de Mélanie n'a pas suffisamment faim lorsqu'elle le met au sein augmente chez elle le besoin de le stimuler exagérément lors des sessions d'allaitement. De ce fait, une tendance se dessine vers une prolongation des séances d'allaitement. Ainsi, la mère risque de se décourager et de croire que son bébé boit mal, d'avoir des problèmes avec ses seins et de sevrer l'enfant. Quelques axes d'intervention sont suggérées afin d'aider les intervenantes à initier leur rôle dans l'observation et l'évaluation de la qualité des interactions mère-enfant dans les contextes de l'allaitement. En premier lieu l'intervenante cherche: 1) à augmenter la connaissance des parents quant aux caractéristiques individuelles de l'enfant; 2) à informer la mère sur les caractéristiques particulières de l'enfant au niveau de son alimentation, des poussées de croissance, du cycle de sommeil et d'éveil, de fatigue, de malaise et de bien-être de l'enfant; 3) à valoriser, renforcer et développer les habiletés de la mère à détecter des signaux de faim et de satiété émis par l'enfant; 4) à augmenter les habiletés à interpréter correctement les signaux de l'enfant; et 5) à encourager la mère à observer son enfant et lui demander d'interpréter les signaux de l'enfant.

Aussi, l'intervenante se concentre sur l'observation de l'interaction mère-enfant en relevant les signaux émis par l'enfant, en les partageant avec la mère et en l'informant sur leur signification ainsi qu'en encourageant la mère à les interpréter. De même, l'intervenante donne des pistes concrètes à la mère lors de l'alimentation au sein: 1) encourager la mère à patienter si l'enfant ne démontre pas suffisamment des signes de faim; 2) attirer l'attention de la mère sur les réactions de l'enfant; 3) demander à la mère de chuchoter quelques mots à l'oreille pour augmenter son réflexe de succion; et 4) proposer à la mère de parler à la place de l'enfant.

À la lumière de la prévalence du phénomène de sevrage chez les mères qui allaitent, il nous apparaît donc important d'observer et d'évaluer la relation mère-enfant lors du contexte de l'allaitement pour soutenir les mères qui allaitent. Ces interventions permettent d'augmenter la sensibilité de la mère à décoder, interpréter et ajuster une réponse appropriée lors du contexte de l'allaitement maternel. Bref, pour ce faire, il faut d'abord que les intervenantes soient bien formées à l'observation et à l'évaluation de la relation parent(s)-enfant selon l'outil développé à partir du modèle de Bell, ainsi qu'à l'intervention précoce auprès des mères.

CONCLUSION

La dépression postnatale est une condition médicale qui peut avoir un impact négatif sur la poursuite de l'allaitement maternel. Or, la qualité des interactions vécues par la mère et l'enfant peuvent faire une différence sur l'initiation et la poursuite de l'allaitement. Le modèle de Bell et de ses collaboratrices développé au Québec permet de guider le jugement clinique de l'intervenante en regard de la qualité des interactions parent(s)-enfant observées. Elle peut ainsi orienter des interventions de soutien à l'établissement de cette relation pour la poursuite de l'allaitement jusqu'à six mois de vie de l'enfant. Au plan clinique, il importe que les intervenantes soient habilitées à observer la qualité des interactions mère-enfant. L'intervention précoce dans le contexte de l'allaitement maternel est un moment privilégié pour observer un répertoire varié d'interactions afin d'être à l'affût de toute difficulté d'interaction susceptible d'affecter la dyade mère-enfant et mener au sevrage de l'enfant. Ces interventions permettent d'augmenter la sensibilité de la mère à décoder, interpréter et ajuster une réponse appropriée lors du contexte de l'allaitement maternel. Le soutien donné par l'intervenante est une activité de promotion de la santé pour assurer un développement cognitif et socio-émotionnel chez l'enfant et aider le parent à développer sa propre identité comme parent à l'adaptation au nouveau rôle parental.

OUVRAGES CITÉS

American Academy of Pediatrics. «Breastfeeding and the Use of Human Milk». *Pediatrics* 115.2 (2005): 496-506.

American Psychiatric Association. *Diagnostic and Statistical Manual of Mental Disorders IV*. Washington, DC: 2000.

Beaudry, Micheline, Sylvie Chiasson et Julie Lauzière. *Biologie de l'allaitement: le sein, le lait, le geste*. Québec: Presses de l'Université du Québec, 2006.

Bell, Linda. *Perceptions parentales de l'établissement de la relation avec leur enfant à la période périnatale et selon une perspective familiale.* Thèse de doctorat inédite. Université de Sherbrooke, Sherbrooke, 2002.

Bell, Linda *et al. Établissement de la relation parent(s)-enfant.* Université de Sherbrooke, Sherbrooke, 2002.

Bell, Linda *et al.* «Parent-Child Relationship in the Perinatal Period: Evaluation and Intervention». *Perspectives infirmières* 1.6 (2004): 32-36.

Cohn, Jeffery F. *et al.* «Face-to-Face Interactions of Depressed Mothers et their Infants». *New Directions Child Development* 34 (1986): 31-45.

Cox, John L. «Validation of the Edinburgh Postnatal Depression Scale (EPDS) in Non-Postnatal Women». *Journal of Affectives Disorders* 39.3 (1996): 185-189.

Dewey, Katheryn G. «Maternal and Foetal Stress are Associated with Impaired Lactogenesis in Humans». *Journal of Nutrition* 131.11 (2001): 3012S-3015S.

Dubois, Lise. «Étude longitudinale du développement des enfants du Québec». Institut de la Statistique du Québec: Québec, 2000.

Field, Tiffany. «Early Interactions between Infants and their Postpartum Depressed Mothers». *Infant Behavior and Development* 25.1 (2002): 25-29.

Field, Tiffany. «Prenatal Depression Effects on the Foetus and the Newborn». *Infant Behavior Development* 27 (2004): 216-229.

Field, Tiffany *et al.* «Behavior State Matching and Synchrony in Mother-Infant Interactions of Nondepressed versus Depressed Dyads». *Developmental Psychology* 26.1 (1990): 7-14.

Field, Tiffany, Maria Hernandez-Rief et Larissa Feijo. «Breastfeeeding in Depressed Mother-Infant Dyads». *Early Child Development and Care* 172 (2002): 539-545.

Galler, Jania R. «Maternal Moods Predict Breastfeeding in Barbados». *Journal of Developmental and Behavioral Pediatrics* 20.2 (1999): 80-87.

Grajeda, Ruben et Rafael Perez-Escamilla. «Stress during Labor and Delivery is Associated with Delayed Onset of Lactation among Urban Guatemalan Women». *Journal of Nutrition 132* (2002): 3055-3060.

Halbreich, Uriel. «Postpartum Disorders: Multiple Interacting Underlying Mechanisms and Risk Factors». *Journal of Affective Disorders* 88.1 (2005): 1-7.

Hatton, Daniel C. «Symptoms of Postpartum Depression and Breastfeeding». *Journal of Human Lactation* 21.4 (2005): 444-449.

Institut de la Statistique du Québec. *L'allaitement maternel au Québec: coup d'œil sur les pratiques provinciales et régionales.* Montréal: Direction Santé Québec, 2006.

Jones, Nancy A., Barbara A.McFall et Miguel A Diego. «Patterns of Brain

Electrical Activity in Infants of Depressed Mothers Who Breastfeed and Bottle Feed: The Mediating Role of Infant Temperament». *Biological Psychology* 67 (2004): 103-124.

Kendall-Tackett, Kathleen A. *Depression in New Mothers*. Binghamton, New York: Haworth, 2005.

Lacharité, Carl. *Formation: évaluer et soutenir les compétences parentales dans les familles avec de jeunes enfants: le rôle de l'attachement et de la sensibilité parentale*. Montréal: Formation Porte-Voix, 2003.

McCarter-Spaulding, Deborah et June A. Horowitz. «How Does Postpartum Depression Affect Breastfeeding?». *The American Journal of Maternal Child Nursing* 32.1 (2007): 10-17.

Mezzacappa, Elizabeth S. et Edward S. Katlin. «Breastfeeding is Associated with Reduced Perceived Stress and Negative Mood in Mothers». *Health Psychology* 21.2 (2002): 187-193.

Millar, Wayne J. et Heather Maclean. «L'allaitement maternel». *Statistique Canada. Rapport* sur la santé 16.2 (2005): 25-33.

Orde des infirmiers et des infirmières du Québec (OIIQ). *Prise de position sur l'allaitement maternel,* 1999.

Organisation mondiale de la santé (OMS). *The Optimal Duration of Exclusive Breastfeeding. Report of an Expert Consultation.* Geneva, 2001.

Perfetti, Jennifer, Roseanne Clark and Capri M. Fillmore. «Postpartum Depression: Identification, Screening, Treatment». *Wisconsin Medical Journal* 103.6 (2004): 56-63.

Santé Canada. Breastfeeding in Canada: A Review and Update. Ottawa: 1999.

Santé Canada. *Enquête sur la santé dans les collectivités canadiennes. Fichier santé*. Canada: 2003.

Santé Canada. *Durée de l'allaitement maternel exclusif: recommandations*. Ottawa: 2004.

Schwartz, Kendra *et al.* «Factors Associated with Weaning in the First 3 Months Postpartum». *Journal of Family Practice* 51.5 (2002): 439-444.

Shaw-Flach, Adelle. «Management of Common Breastfeeding Problems». *Community Practitioner* 75.11 (2002): 432-435.

Société canadienne de pédiatrie. «Les pédiatres conseillent de privilégier l'allaitement exclusif pendant 6 mois». *Paediatrics and Child Health* 10.3 (2005): 148.

Tronick, Edward Z. *et al.* «Postpartum Exuberance: Not All Women in a Highly Positive Emotional State in the Postpartum Period are Denying Depression and Distress». *Infant Mental Health Journal* 18.4 (1997): 406-423.

Wisner, Katherine L. *et al.* «Clinical Practice. Postpartum Depression». *New England Journal of Medicine* 347.3 (2002): 194-199.

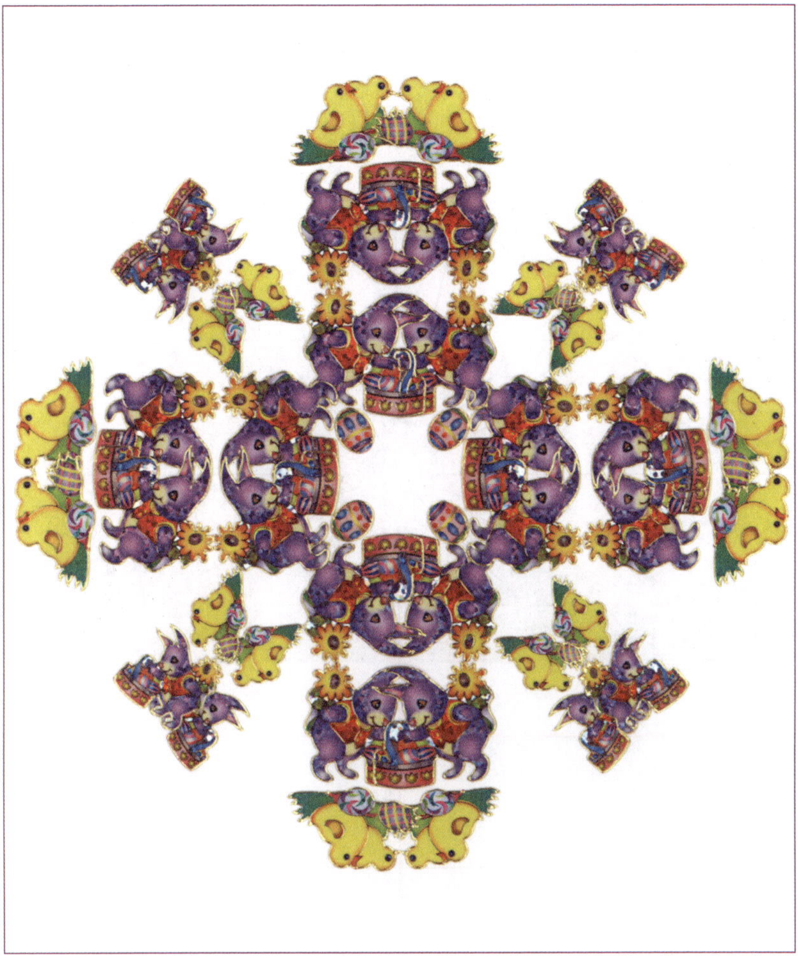

Corrina Beesley-Hammond, *Bunny Crossing*, 2006, stickers on paper, 27.94 x 27.94 cm.

The images and ideas represented in *Bunny Crossing* are about nesting, nurturing and family traditions. They are inspired by the daily rituals of South Indian Tamil homemakers. Tamil homemakers draw a Kollum at their home entrance each morning and re-draw it in the evening.

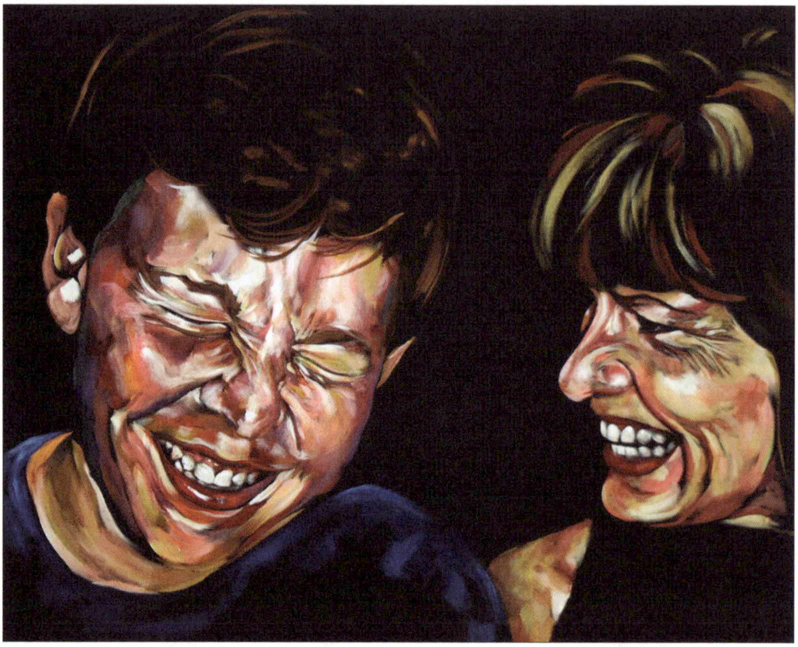

Belinda Kriek, *October 2006*, 2006, acrylic on canvas, 96.52 x 121.92 cm.

October 2006 reflects a mother's gaze, confirming the spiritual connection between me and my son in a hilarious moment of mutual happiness precipitated by a maternal bond. My son's perpetual, infectious disposition bridges the generation gap and permeates everyone he meets, including the viewer to whom he is unaware.

CONNECTING

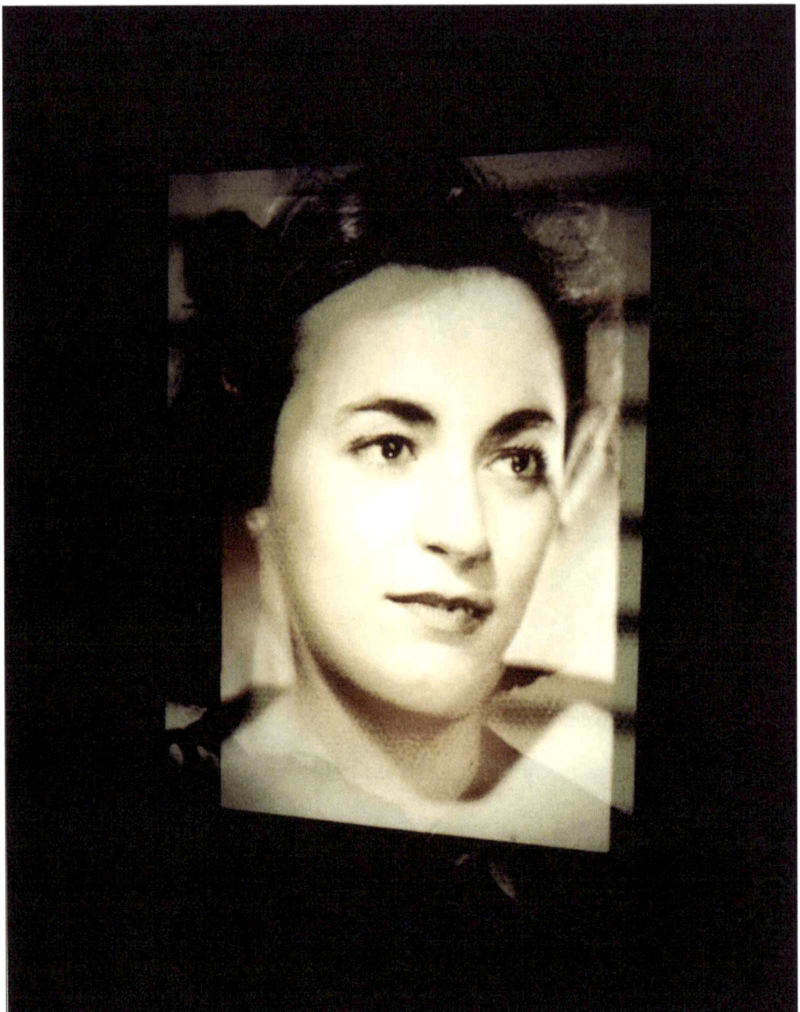

Sorel Cohen, *The Faces of Fate*, 1994, chromogenic print from slide projection, 101.60 x 76.20 cm and 182.88 x 121.92 cm.

This superimposed portrait of myself and my mother is one element in a larger series of photographs entitled, *Damaged Lives,* in which I use the text of a letter to Edgar Degas from his aunt Laura Belelli to examine states of intimacy and adversity that occur within families.

A Poem to My Mother

Aboriginal Day 2007

DONNA LESTER-SMITH

My grief since you have recently gone
is like an eaglet in first flight.

Afraid and awkward,
slowly, it transforms into the smoothness and poise
for which it was born.

In it rests the power to endure,
the courage to guide,
the clarity of vision to succeed.

Beside the one I love, to the rhythm of his breath,
silent and timid, a tear traces my cheek in the darkness,
absorbed between skin and cotton,
effortlessly,

the way the wings of a dragonfly inhale
the touches of spring rain.

More intrepidly, my grief appears in sunlight,
its tears spider-weaving through
lashes to the song of my sobs as I drive alone in my car,
right knee reflexing that common, inherent muscle-dance
as my toes rest on the edge of the brake petal at a stoplight.

My grief since you have gone appears when I least expect it.

Like when driving home from Richmond's Aboriginal celebration,
having met new friends and realizing our bonds of Métis bloodline —
theirs in you, the ancestor I reach for,

your gift of life in me, your only child.

And when meeting a friend from a lifetime ago,
a time when Richmond was first my home. And now,
after years in that other place of joy and struggle,

I've come home —

Bringing with me your spirit to rest,
my grief learning to gracefully soar.

A Question of Authorship

ELIZABETH BLANCHARD

"WRITE ABOUT ME," my son says loudly, his feet flat against the wall, his head dropped over the side of the couch, his mouth open, the ends of his blond hair touching the carpet, generating static that causes air-thin strands to rise slightly into an ion-charged halo.

"You never write about me," he repeats, his feet tapping the wall to an incessant rhythm, the same beat that twitches through his thin 12-year-old body when misbehaving on the school bus, riding the grocery cart in the parking lot, or lying in wait for his sister to come out of the bathroom before bedtime.

I write stories. I write stories in the basement of my home where he and I are now. I write stories, short not long, rarely fact, mostly fiction, only because fiction is safer, or it feels safer at least. I've written short stories inspired by my daughter's love of hockey, my father's life as a watchmaker, my mother's illness, my mother's death, always their identities veiled in unfamiliar names and couched in foreign circumstances.

"But you never write about me." He's now standing over my shoulder, grinning at my computer screen, pointing at a curse word that one of my characters blurted out for the sake of authenticity.

I have tried writing about him, started many times to take that huge feeling inside of me that is him in an attempt to give it a shape and form on the page. I've tried to write about his broad orthodontic grin and his rogue hair that makes him look like he's been up to something, or planning it at least, and the way he looks you straight in the eye when talking to you, or shakes your hand like he's already a man at 76 pounds, never failing to elicit a surprised smile from an unsuspecting recipient.

I have tried to manufacture a story about him, mask him in some promethean hero, dangerously quick-witted with that all-is-forgiven smile of his, but always the storyline falters. It is as though the fiction falls short, is unable to eclipse him, like pasting shreds of construction paper on the sun.

He came to me, or rather was handed to me, at 5: 35 a.m., twelve years ago in a staunchly lit hall of an obstetrics unit. His 17-year-old biological mother in the birthing room had fallen quiet. He too, I remember, was quiet as the nurse put him in my arms. Swaddled in a hospital blanket, he shivered and I felt awkward and lacking in my mock turtleneck sweater and slacks. His eyes tried to focus on my face and I fell in love, not a soft roll down a grassy hill, but a heart-thumping drop off the face of a cliff into an endless space of shifting winds. It is in this space my words not so much fail, but are swept away like confetti in a storm.

I told him early on that he grew in another lady's belly, only because trust cannot exist without truth. This is what I had read, over and over again, late at night in my bed, in the glow of a table lamp. I also told him that God's bean shooter had temporarily malfunctioned, and that as soon as the kernel of himself had landed in someone else's belly, heaven's GPS lit up in throbbing reds and yellows and he was quickly redirected back to our family. I told him this with a smile one Sunday morning as he crawled over our down comforter between my husband and I, his shoulders rolling like an imaginary lion on the African savanna, his milk teeth bared in a fierce roar. He laughed and asked me to tell the bean shooter story again, his small, smooth forehead pressed hard against mine. Belonging has a language of its own.

His younger sister took the conventional route; he knows this. Three months after I brought him home, I got pregnant.

"How come?" he asked me once as I stood at the kitchen sink peeling onions, folding back only the unnecessary layers of skin.

"Because when you came, your love healed whatever was broken," I told him patting the buckle of my leather belt, "Here, inside of me." He glanced sideways at his little sister sitting on the floor in the center of the kitchen, her dimpled arms flailing recycled yogurt containers at the refrigerator door.

"Daddy and I waited twelve long years for you, and as soon as you arrived, bam!" I slapped my hand against my thigh, "Your sister came along. My guess is that she was probably waiting for you too."

He eyed her suspiciously, as if seriously doubting he had or would ever have anything to do with this thumb-sucking sibling. Already he had forgotten the time I came home from work one day to find my elderly babysitter crying on the couch, rocking both babies in her arms. Always on the look-out for something to gnaw on, my daughter had crawled behind the couch having spotted a fistful of her brother's much coveted Cheerios, and was turning a noiseless shade of purple by the time the babysitter found her balled up on the living room floor. Relayed to me after the fact in halting sobs, the babysitter recounted how my son, who had inadvertently waddled upon the scene, bent over his sister, stuck his two-year-old index in her mouth, removed the impeding objects, identified them, then put them in *his* mouth and masticated loudly with his freshly cut canines.

My babysitter quit shortly thereafter.

Now, years later, my pre-teen daughter stomps her foot and tells me how her brother is completely ruining her life.

How fine is the spider silk that binds us together.

In Grade 2, he told me that flags live, but only in the wind.

In Grade 5, he convinced his schoolmates that I had bought him on eBay, then asked me to go along with it, just for a week or so.

"You mean she's not your real mom?"

"I wouldn't say that to her face if I were you."

In Grade 7, when I first took him out for a drive in our brand new Honda Civic with standard transmission, he commented on how my driving skills reflected my personality, his words delivered staccato style as his head bounced off the head rest every time I shifted gears. It is this ability of his to see me from a distance that is unsettling, as though having not inherited the emotional grime of my own biology, his view of me is unclouded, unapologetically dust free, somewhat akin to looking at a rock formation with no notion of its geological history to account for its striations or excuse its jaggedness.

I know what he wants. He wants me to write stories about him as a Jedi, a pre-Vader Anikin, before the lava-flow burn, adroitly maneuvering a light saber shoulder to shoulder with Obi Wan, or as a champion Quiddich seeker of Potter fame, lightening-swift in his broomstick pursuit of the Golden Snitch. "But these stories have all been done," I tell him. "Your story must be an original," I insist, knowing full well how feeble my argument sounds.

And so I sit here in my basement after he has gone to prepare for bed, startled by the sound of my daughter's screech as she comes out of the bathroom, my son's laughter followed by the pounding of angry feet down a darkened hall. Perhaps my inability lies in the fact that his story is not mine to fashion. I, having ultimately very little control over his narrative (or my daughter's for that matter), have become in some ways more of a reader than a writer, and as such, am carried away into that endless pace of shifting winds, gathering my breath in wait for the next chapter to unfold.

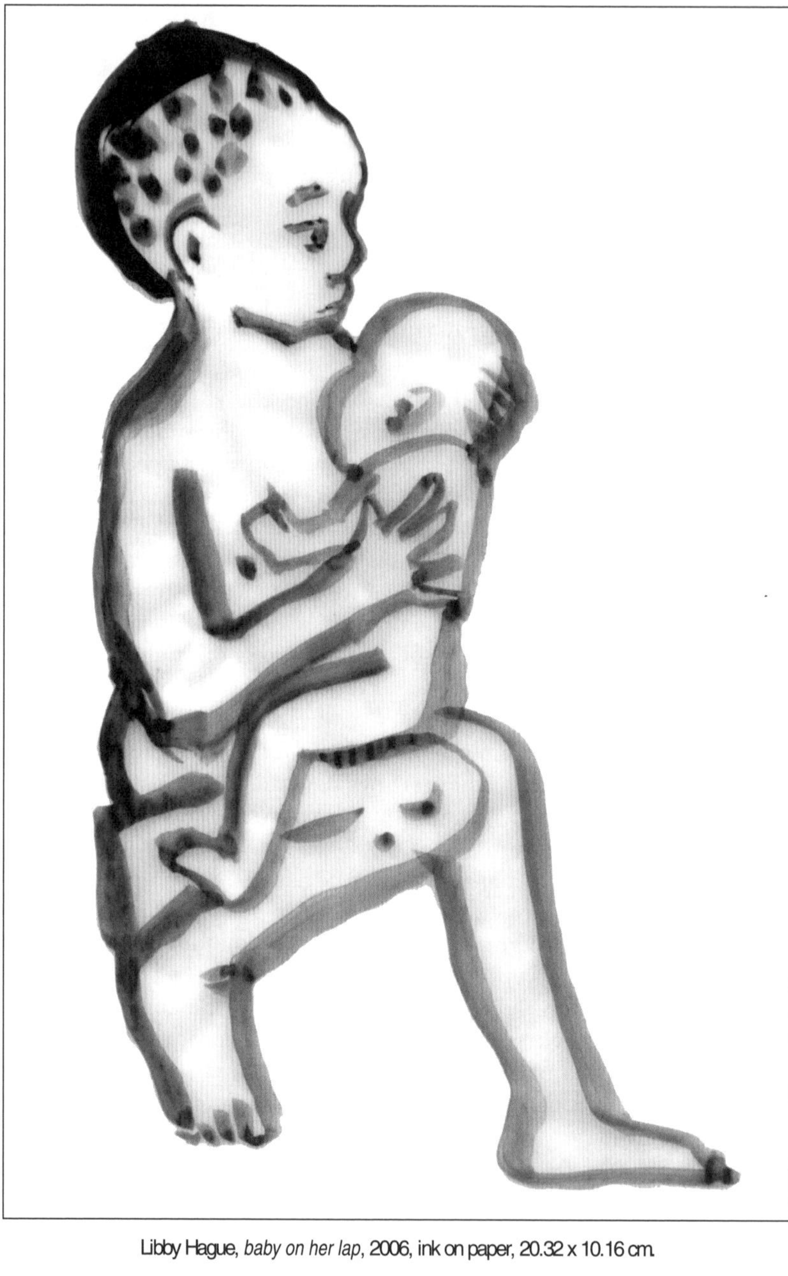

Libby Hague, *baby on her lap*, 2006, ink on paper, 20.32 x 10.16 cm.

This ink drawing is part of a more complicated narrative, *Martian Odyssey*, which examines human interdependencies, including mothering in the broad sense of caring for a dependent. As sometimes happens when war or disease erases a middle generation, children raise each other or grandmothers raise their daughters' children.

Papyrus

ELIZABETH F. HILL

The infant's life
Is a blank roll of papyrus,
Polished and smooth,
And, one hopes,
Constructed of sheets sufficiently strong
To withstand
The pressure of the pen.
As the scroll unfurls,
The child
Must choose with care
The scribes
Who will etch in the entries
So as to minimize tears
And prevent too many blots
On the record.

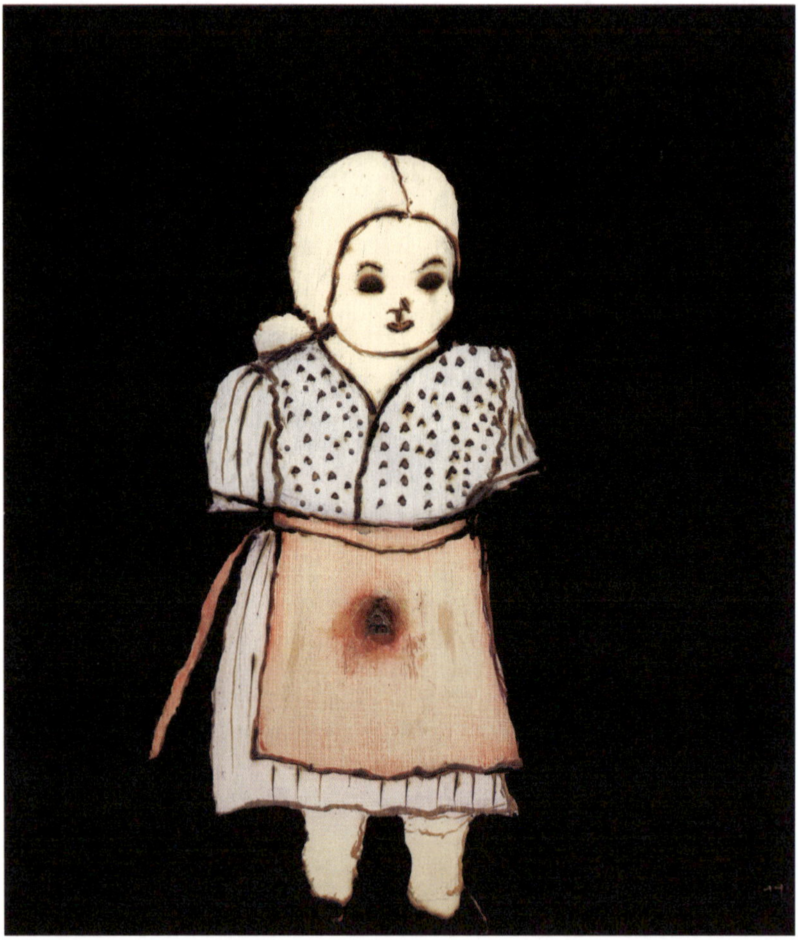

Jewell Goodwyn, *Heimlich*, 1995, acrylic, miniature metal house, wood, 25.40 x 22.86 cm.

Heimlich references the womb, the place that each one of us has lived, once upon a time and in the beginning. Heimlich refers to the realm of intimacy and comfort, as well as the uncanny. *Heimlich* is part of a series titled *Still Lives*, inspired by images of nineteenth-century dolls.

Contextualisation de la relation mère-fille dans *L'Ingratitude* de Ying Chen

NICOLE CÔTÉ

> In her introduction to *Supposing the Subject*, Joan Copjec warns against the shortsightedness of seeing history as antithetical to the purviews of psychoanalysis. She points out that history conceived linearly is truly ahistorical, while the psychoanalytical perspective teaches us to be attentive to the disjunctive and retroactive hauntedness of history.... Hauntedness alerts us to context, and it is from this attention to context that we might be able to begin to re-envision a politics attuned to the reality of grief in all its material and immaterial evidence. (Cheng 28-29)

YING CHEN, NÉE en 1961 à Shanghai, venue vivre à Montréal parce que l'Université McGill lui offrait une bourse pour poursuivre sa maîtrise, est peut-être l'auteure migrante la plus connue du Québec. Autrefois traductrice, Ying Chen traduit désormais sa culture, mais aussi la nouvelle vision du monde qui naît d'un changement de continent, et écrit en français, langue qu'elle avait choisi d'étudier.

Singulièrement, Chen déteste être associée à l'écriture migrante. Ses oeuvres de fiction, selon elle, visent l'universel de la condition humaine, bien qu'elle décrive dans ses premiers ouvrages les particularités de la vie en Chine. Peut-être afin de se débarrasser pour de bon des étiquettes, Chen montre au fil de son oeuvre de fiction un désir de plus en plus pressant de se délester des contingences les plus élémentaires de la vie humaine: l'âge, l'appartenance ethnique, l'époque, la vie sur terre. C'est dire que ses oeuvres s'attachent aux universaux de la condition humaine tout en étant ancrées (du moins les premières) dans les particularités socio-culturelles et géographiques d'un pays, d'une époque. Son roman *L'Ingratitude* (1995), dont je traiterai, a remporté, en France et au Québec, plusieurs prix,[1] autant en raison de son écriture puissante et dépouillée que du sujet tabou dont il traite: le «dressage» des filles par leur mère et l'une de ses conséquences les plus immédiates, la tentative de suicide de la fille.

En choisissant d'écrire *L'Ingratitude* d'abord en français et de publier ce roman au Québec, Ying Chen traduit l'expérience d'une relation mère-fille chinoise dans une autre langue. Si elle traduit un contexte, une langue, c'est que cette expérience a valeur exemplaire, comme toute littérature: ancrée dans un contexte particulier, elle n'en a pas moins valeur universelle, sinon, pourquoi son oeuvre s'attire-t-elle des prix sur deux continents ? Paradoxalement donc, l'institution de la maternité telle que *L'Ingratitude* la présente dans ses retranchements les plus dangereux peut faire réfléchir les Québécois «de souche». *L'Ingratitude* me semble une oeuvre de fiction d'autant plus intéressante qu'elle se situe dans un contexte chinois car, malgré sa contemporanéité, le récit met en scène un féminin des plus dévalués dans un pays lointain, ce qui permet de creuser en toute sécurité les racines idéologiques de l'institution de la maternité au Québec ainsi que ses conséquences sur les relations mères-filles et sur la famille. En effet, bien que le roman se situe en Chine, les conditions d'élevage des filles comportent certains invariants dus à la condition traditionnellement inférieure des femmes dans presque toutes les sociétés.[2] Ainsi, un texte littéraire comme *L'Ingratitude* pose des questions d'une grande pertinence quant à cette même institution de la maternité dans un pays comme le Canada, dans une province comme le Québec, où les femmes assument toujours l'essentiel de la tâche d'élever les enfants, en particulier les filles, malgré que, comme les Chinoises, elles travaillent à l'extérieur. Comme Montesquieu qui, avec ses *Lettres persanes*, oblige les Français à réfléchir sur les travers de leurs coutumes et intitutions politiques sous couvert d'une critique des Persans, Ying Chen, avec *L'Ingratitude*, présente au visage des Québécois un miroir pas si déformé de l'institution de la maternité dans le contexte d'une société patriarcale. Je ne nierai pas que la condition des femmes au Québec et au Canada a beaucoup évolué, mais la maternité, dernier bastion des idées reçues, peut être dangereuse en raison de l'idéalisme que son institution sécrète et à la barre duquel les mères doivent se mesurer.

Par ailleurs, le Canada étant multi-ethnique et ayant adopté une politique de multiculturalisme, c'est-à-dire de respect et de mise en valeur des différentes traditions culturelles et religieuses, les immigrants au Québec comme ailleurs au Canada ont le droit de poursuivre en privé des pratiques qui avaient cours dans leur pays, souvent même lorsqu'elles ne sont pas considérées comme respectant les droits de la personne, à moins que l'affaire ne soit amenée au public, devant un tribunal. La question de l'«accommodement raisonnable» au Québec vise justement à combler le fossé qui existe entre le respect des droits humains dans une démocratie libérale comme le Québec, le Canada et les coutumes d'une société plus traditionnelle, souvent sanctionnées par des textes religieux ou philosphiques anciens, qui risquent toujours d'éroder les droits et libertés des femmes.

Parce que la fiction a toujours une fonction exemplaire, qui permet de réfléchir sur un problème sans se sentir directement engagé—contrairement à la lecture d'un essai, par exemple—et parce que la relation mère-fille décrite ici n'est pas officiellement québécoise, les lectrices du roman de Chen peuvent réfléchir en toute impunité à une situation d'autant plus douloureuse qu'elle est doublement taboue: il y est question de maltraitance, et les racines de cette maltraitance peuvent être retracées dans la maltraitance de tout un peuple pour sa moitié féminine.

RÉSUMÉ DE L'INTRIGUE DE *L'INGRATITUDE*

Je résume brièvement l'intrigue de cette oeuvre bien connue mais avant, deux mots sur l'aspect formel qui fait, en partie du moins, l'originalité du roman: la voix de la narratrice-focalisatrice est narrée dès le début du roman depuis l'outre-tombe. Yan-Zi, jeune femme de 25 ans, projette de se suicider autant pour échapper à l'étouffante emprise maternelle que pour ravir à sa mère le seul plaisir qu'il lui reste: celui d'être mère, parce qu'être mère est une fonction dont on lui permet de s'acquitter et qui la définit presque exclusivement. Par un ironique tour du destin, Yan-Zi est frappée à mort par un camion lorsque son fiancé la poursuit pour l'empêcher de commettre l'irréparable. Il s'agit donc d'une mort dont le statut même pose problème: le geste suicidaire voulu par Yan-Zi aurait par la même occasion été un matricide, comme le suggère Lori Saint-Martin, puisqu'en s'anéantissant, Yan-Zi signerait par la même occasion la mort symbolique de sa mère, dont l'individualité se résorbe dans la fonction sociale du maternage. Mais Yan-Zi perd le contrôle de la situation et le suicide-matricide prévu pourrait n'être perçu par la première intéressée que comme un vulgaire accident. Dès lors, la mère innommée pourrait se décharger de la culpabilité que le suicide d'un enfant apporte toujours. Le récit ne semble pas résoudre l'ambivalence suicide-accident: ainsi, dès le début de son récit, Yan-Zi affirme: «ma mort est une honte démesurée, car je m'y suis condamnée moi-même, j'en ai exécuté la peine moi-même. Ils m'en veulent de ce que je ne les aime pas assez, que je m'enfuie de leur royaume» (7). Mais plus loin, elle discute l'interprétation que donne sa mère de sa mort: l'hypothèse du suicide est placidement évacuée par la mère, qui semble croire que sa réputation est sauve puisque sa fille est morte écrasée par un camion—un accident qui reproduit celui, non-mortel, du père. Yan Zi, passée dans le royaume des morts, mais déçue de ce que le seigneur Nilou—dont on lui avait dit qu'il accueillait les jeunes filles décédées dans son royaume—n'existe pas, se sent seule et réalise qu'elle aimait vraiment sa mère. Yan-Zi, s'éloignant irrémédiablement du royaume des vivants, entend «une dernière voix humaine, le cri d'un nourisson peut-être: maman!» (133).

CONTEXTUALISAITON DE L'ŒUVRE ET DE SES PERSONNAGES

J'ai voulu étudier cette dure oeuvre de Ying Chen en comtextualisant le rôle, institutionnalisé, de la mère. Comme le mentionne Lucie Lequin, la narratrice-focalisatrice Yan-Zi «ne fait que s'attaquer à sa mère sans voir en cette dernière aussi une victime d'une société opprimante, victime bien semblable à elle-même» (Lequin «À la croisée des chemins», 115). J'avancerais que la structure narrative de *L'Ingratitude* accorde à la mère une place encore bien ténue et qu'elle reflète les limites de la réception présupposée en ce qui concerne les relations mères-filles. La mère innommée de Yan-Zi demeure une mère patriarcale avec laquelle peu de lectrices s'identifieraient, contrairement, par exemple, à la grand-mère de *La mémoire de l'eau*, de la même auteure. Le portrait de la mère, si juste soit-il, n'est selon moi pas accompagné d'un contexte qui soit rédempteur pour cette dernière. Toutefois le texte contient en germe son contexte, et c'est ce dernier sur lequel j'aimerais m'attarder, c'est-à -dire sur l'institution de la maternité et ses conséquences pour la relation mère-fille telles qu'elles sont présentées dans *L'Ingratitude*. Si cette contextualisation, qui permet selon moi de mieux comprendre la violence de la mère à l'endroit d'une fille qu'elle aime, m'apparaît pertinente, c'est qu'elle met en lumière un phénomène qui n'est pas restreint à la famille chinoise traditionnelle, mais se retrouve, à différents degrés, également dans les familles québécoises, puisque la condition féminine crée une telle constellation familiale. Néanmoins, examiner de près le contexte idéologique qui a permis une telle constellation, c'est déjà accepter de corriger les sources sociologiques du problème, et cesser d'accuser soit la mère ou la fille.

Dans un ouvrage récent qui trace la condition des Chinoises depuis la tradition confucéenne jusqu'à la fin du vingtième siècle en passant par les années maoïstes, Ravni Thakur affirme que traditionnellement, les Chinoises «n'exercent de pouvoir réel que contre leur sexe, assurant ainsi la légitimité des structures de pouvoir masculines, ou l'acceptation des formes doxiques d'identification» (38).[3] Il semble qu'en Chine, une réflexion sur la situation des femmes et sur la nécessité d'une réforme n'ait duré que les premières décennies du vingtième siècle.

Dès le début des années 20, le Parti communiste chinois adoptait une position conservatrice quant à la condition des femmes pour des raisons intéressées: «Nos slogans actuels, affirme alors Gai Chang concernant la situation des femmes, ne sont plus 'un mariage libre' et 'l'égalité entre hommes et femmes'; ils sont plutôt 'sauvez les enfants et établissez une abondante et florissante famille de manière à ce que chaque foyer prospère'» (Johnson citée par Thakur 46).[4] Néanmoins, dans la Chine devenue république populaire (octobre 1949), «[a]ucune des activités ménagères entreprises par les femmes n'était quantifiée ou considérée comme productive; on disait aux femmes qu'elles contribuaient à l'édification de la société en gardant le moral de leurs maris au travail et en maintenant l'harmonie familiale. Pour les femmes au travail, le fardeau était double» (Thakur 50). Thakur affirme d'ailleurs que le parti tentait rarement de résoudre les contradictions inhérentes aux positions des femmes, bien que «la création rapide d'institutions socialistes, l'objectif de se rapprocher tout aussi rapidement du niveau de vie de l'Occident, soulevait la question du conflit entre l'égalité des femmes et la mise en oeuvre du rêve socialiste» (51). Jusqu'au début des années 60, années pendant lesquelles on peut imaginer que Yan-Zi a grandi—on notait beaucoup de confusion quant au rôle de la femme dans cette république communiste prônant l'égalité des sexes, puisqu'on assignait tacitement le foyer comme la place de la femme. Seulement durant la Révolution culturelle (1966-1976) cette remise en question des valeurs confucéennes comme garantes des relations entre les sexes a-t-elle pu renaître grâce à l'épouse de Mao, Jian Qing. Toutefois, à la mort de Mao, qui entraîna la chute de la Bande des Quatre, les politiques concernant le rôle de la femme changèrent de nouveau, et la féminité et la maternité furent de nouveau encouragées. Thakur affirme qu'il existe aujourd'hui «une différence remarquable entre l'idéologie très publicisée de l'égalité et la pratique de la subordination des femmes» (53). Thakur en concluait à la fin des années 90 qu'en dépit des grandes avancées économiques accomplies par la Chine, la rigide division sexuelle des tâches sur laquelle les relations entre les sexes s'appuient se maintient obstinément. Cela montre qu'une seule avancée des conditions économiques ne suffit pas, un travail idéologique concommittant devant avoir lieu. D'ailleurs, conclut Thakur, la naturalisation du rôle des femmes comme garante de l'éducation des enfants et du bien-être émotif de la famille a poussé les femmes modernes, qui travaillent à l'extérieur, vers un épuisant double fardeau plutôt que vers une redéfinition des rôles des sexes sociaux.

Après avoir discuté de la redéfinition flouée des rôles sexuels en Chine communiste, j'aimerais élargir ma contextualisation en discutant de la relation mère-fille sous l'angle de la socialisation de la fille, du point de vue de Françoise Couchard, anthropologue et psychanalyste, d'autant plus que nombre de points que soulève Couchard dans son ouvrage *Emprise et violence maternelle*[5] sont exemplifiés dans *L'Ingratitude*. Ainsi Couchard affirme que dans la plupart des sociétés, l'emprise de la mère sur la fille se situe entre autres dans l'imposition de modèles dès le berceau, passés d'une génération à l'autre. Cette emprise comprend «le modelage de l'image corporelle ... selon des canons de beauté et de séduction mis au service des hommes, mais définis par les mères» (3). Si cette emprise est si puissante, c'est que, selon Couchard, elle est autant constituée d'une «séduction tendre qui vient combler le narcissisme de l'enfant que de son versant sombre, qui peut même aller jusqu'à l'anéantir dans ses désirs et son individualité» (3). Couchard précise bien que le désir de maltraiter l'enfant ne correspond pas à une sorte de méchanceté naturelle, mais «a sa source dans une blessure narcissique, une humiliation permanente faite à la femme, dans son rapport avec l'homme: il serait trop dangereux de s'attaquer directement à ce dernier, le ressentiment et la vengeance sont donc dirigés vers l'enfant» (35). [6]

Particulièrement pertinent à l'étude de *L'Ingratitude* est le «terrorisme de la souffrance»,

> [c]'est-à-dire le spectacle du malheur que ... la mère impose à sa fille. C'est en effet sur [la fille] que reposera massivement le poids de l'aliénation et de l'affliction maternelle.... Les souvenirs d'un malheur imposé par la mère susciteront, quand ils seront matière à remémoration, une grande ambivalence. Un sentiment de sollicitude, de pitié et de culpabilité mêlées étreindra certaines à l'évocation de ce qu'a subi ou accepté cette mère. (126)

Ce sacrifice sera parfois présenté en spectacle à la fille, ce qui la convainc qu'elle «a contracté à l'endroit de la génitrice une dette sans fin et impossible à rembourser» (131). Couchard explique d'ailleurs que les mères «acceptent mal de voir leurs filles échapper à ce qu'elles ont dû affronter» parce que la répétition de leur rôle par leur fille leur permet une certaine emprise sur elle (133).

Par ailleurs, un facteur aggravant, selon Couchard, est que la majorité des mères, «intériorisant un surmoi personnel et social, s'obligeront à désinvestir leur libido amoureuse pour en reporter uniquement la charge sur la progéniture.... Le sentiment maternel exacerbé par l'ordre social enveloppe alors mère et enfants dans une 'peau commune' dont les autres, le père au premier chef, se trouvent exclus» (133). Pour cette raison, la mère, selon Couchard, s'avère incapable de percevoir «une différenciation entre cette fille qui la redouble et elle-même» (149) et se voit tout aussi incapable de la soutenir si elle la perçoit. Ce problème de frontières personnelles est présenté comme étant particulièrement dévastateur dans *L'Ingratitude* puisque la mère ne reconnaît pas de différence à sa fille, désirant garder sa fille dans le même, l'ipséité, «une illusion qui berce toute mère» (157), dont je tirerai des exemples dans mon analyse de *L'Ingratitude*. Selon Couchard, «[l]a mère violente n'abandonne jamais cette illusion qui opère alors un brouillage des limites entre imaginaire et réalité» (157).

Paradoxalement, comme Couchard l'explique, bien que la mère maltraitante veuille la plupart du temps amener sa fille à l'intérieur de ses frontières, lui refusant son altérité, dans les cas où elle lui reconnaît une différence avec elle-même, la mère violente projette sur sa fille ses propres traits de personnalité considérés comme mauvais, ou ceux de ses propres parents qu'elle a incorporés. Couchard apparente ce mécanisme à celui du bouc émissaire, figure que la mère maltraitante a dû assumer dans son enfance, «parce que ses parents ne l'avaient pas reconnue comme une individualité indépendante» (156). Toutefois, précisément parce que les frontières mère-fille sont particulièrement brouillées dans ce cas, cette mère meurtrière «est aussi meurtrière pour elle-même, se maltraitant et se punissant à travers ce double que représentait sa fille» (156).

Si j'ai cité si extensivement Thakur et Couchard, c'est que le contexte socio-culturel et politique de la mère dans *L'Ingratitude* ne me semble pas assez développé pour que la lectrice puisse comprendre la part quasi-inéluctable du rôle de la mère, qui n'est qu'un engrenage dans une société misogyne. C'est une généalogie féminine occultée qui me semble ici être une des parts d'ombre de *L'Ingratitude*, son aspect conservateur, malgré la poignante vérité de la description du rapport mère-fille: la mère est d'une cruauté implacable; mais somme toute, la contextualisation minimale de la formation de son caractère contribue à déplacer les allégeances du lecteur et de la lectrice du côté de la fille, comme c'est traditionnellement le cas.

AMBIVALENCE DANS LA RELATION MÈRE-FILLE

La grande popularité de ce roman[7] réside en partie dans la charge implacable, d'une ironie brûlante, de Yan-Zi contre sa mère. On a vu avec Thakur et Couchard comment la relation mère-fille est toujours piégée dans une société misogyne et à quel point les frontières entre mère et fille sont poreuses. Sylvie Bernier a noté ce leitmotif dans *L'Ingratitude*: «Ce poids de l'hérédité qui ancre le personnage et se traduit par une sorte de résistance cherche dans la mort à échapper à une relation spéculaire avec une mère toute-puissante et chez qui l'identification atteint les limites de l'obsession» (119).

Cependant Yan-Zi en tant que narratrice est d'autant plus attachante qu'elle ne perd pas de vue, malgré la sécheresse du portrait de sa mère, les instants de grâce et la luminosité qui traversent parfois son être autrement engoncé: «Son corps entier rayonnait.... Je n'en croyais pas mes yeux. Cette mère tant rêvée était là, enfin, cette femme éblouissante et divine»(33). La dénonciation de la mère y est donc ambivalente, laissant surgir en filigrane, parmi la cruauté des propos, un amour désespéré de la fille pour la mère, comme le passage suivant—abondamment cité par la critique pour sa représentation des enjeux du roman—le montre bien:

> Je brûlais d'envie de voir maman souffrir à la vue de mon cadavre. Souffrir jusqu'à vomir son sang. Une douleur inconsolable. La vie coulerait entre ses doigts et sa descendance lui échapperait. Mon

> corps commençant à pourrir par ses journées chaudes, ses gènes cesseraient de circuler dans mes veines, se perdraient au fond de la terre uniforme. Elle n'aurait plus d'enfant. Sa fille unique s'envolerait loin d'elle ainsi qu'un coup de vent mortel croise un arbre en le secouant, mais sans s'arrêter ... impitoyable. (16)

Yan-Zi signifie en mandarin *hirondelle*, un oiseau traditionnellement associé en Chine à l'harmonie familiale. Considérant que la mère inommée a élevé des oiseaux en cage avant la naissance de sa fille et après sa mort, le nom même de la fille semble pénétré d'ironie: selon l'interprétation insconsciente de la mère, cet oiseau symbole de l'harmonie familiale ne peut réussir sa mission qu'emprisonné, c'est-à-dire privé de son agentivité. En ce sens, l'oiseau *yan-zi* ne peut mener à bien sa tâche d'harmonisation des relations familiales qu'en sacrifiant son individualité: le symbole englobe donc mère et fille, interpellées par la société chinoise à renoncer à leur agentivité pour le bien de la famille. On voit que la systématicité de l'effacement des frontières mère-fille rejoint même la symbolique du nom —et de l'absence de nom—dans le cas de la mère. La conséquence de cette éradication de la subjectivité féminine est, nous l'avons vu, la violence des femmes sur leur progéniture féminine. Les critiques n'ont en outre pas manqué de noter le passage où Yan-Zi remarque que sa mère avait été battue «pour qu'elle apprenne à se soumettre et aussi à s'imposer dès le moment venu» (92), passage remarquable de concision où la structure de l'oppression est mise à nu: l'humiliée ne manquera pas d'humilier à son tour. Yan-Zi glisse ici et là des commentaires en apparence anodins, mais qui, accumulés, permettent à la lectrice attentive d'entrevoir le contexte socio-politique qui a pu créer une telle constellation psychique mère-fille.

La tragédie de Yan-Zi est qu'il lui faut, comme les héroines du vingt-et-unième siècle, opérer une désidentification du sort de sa mère et des autres femmes, ce qui ne lui laisse aucun modèle, une situation dont plusieurs théoriciennes féministes ont démontré qu'elle était dangereuse pour l'intégrité psychique de la fille. Dans ce cas, le désir de Yan-Zi de négocier sa place comme sujet à l'intérieur d'une relation se complique malheureusement du fait de l'absence de modèles féminins dans son entourage immédiat. Yan-Zi, dans un contexte où le rôle des femmes se réduit à être objet (fiancée, épouse) ou obstacle (mère), choisit de sortir de l'intrigue. «Les mères», dit Lori Saint-Martin, «sont les grandes responsables du conditionnement social. D'où le violent rejet de la mère» (Saint-Martin, *Le nom de la mère* 25). Ainsi, traditionnellement, toute fille qui possède un solide instinct de survie renie le lien avec la mère en faveur de celui avec le père. Toutefois, le père de Yan-Zi n'est d'aucun secours. Ainsi, il est fait allusion au désinvestissement émotif du père dans la scène où mère et fille partent bredouilles au marché après que la mère a frappé une dernière fois à la porte du bureau du père, espérant que le père les y accompagnera contre toute attente.

IMMANENCE DU CORPS DE LA MÈRE

La réduction de la mère par la fille reflète celle que la mère effectue sur la fille en lui refusant une différenciation rédemptrice --rappelons que la société, au départ, n'alloue pas cette différenciation à la mère, qui n'est plus que «fonction»: la mère est réduite à un corps dés-érotisé, mais surtout dépourvu d'agentivité, et donc d'avenir. Yan-Zi ne s'y trompe pas, elle que l'immanence du corps de la mère écoeure: «J'étais donc sortie de là! De ce ventre mou, sale, et gonflé de gras. J'aurais préféré naître d'une pierre ou d'une plante sans nom» (19), dit-elle. La comparaison n'est pas anodine ici, puisque la narratrice choisit le plus ancien, le plus chosifié des trois règnes, le minéral, puis suggère comme alternative le règne végétal—aucun des deux règnes ne se caractérisant par la conscience ou même la liberté de mouvement. D'ailleurs, la mère, comme la plante dont voudrait être sortie la narratrice, est sans nom. Ce passage traite donc en partie du désir de Yan-Zi d'échapper à la condition féminine, associée à l'immanence du corps et à des fonctions d'abord sexuelles, puis maternelles, sans possibilité de subjectivité, et donc d'agentivité. Cette ambivalence face à la mère, d'ailleurs, se retrouve dans la comparaison de l'odeur de la mère à celle de la rivière, également innommée, qui traverse la ville. À un moment, l'odeur riche de sa peau est associée au segment «maman sentait la rivière de notre ville» (34); plus loin dans le récit, l'odeur de la mère est associée à la puanteur de cette même rivière.

On sait d'ailleurs que la figure de la mère dans la littérature—de même dans la littérature québécoise jusque dans les années 80—est presque toujours déterminée par son corps. Cette objectification de la femme est liée au refus de reconnaissance de la mère, qui, selon Anne-Marie Vilaine, «se traduit par l'occultation ou la dévaluation de tout ce qui est lié à l'économie féminine et de tout ce qui est en rapport analogique avec le féminin/maternel» (Vilaine citée par Saint-Martin, *Le nom de la mère* 208).

Le rôle de la mère en devient d'autant plus uniforme: sans emploi, emmurée dans la maison, mariée par ses parents à un homme qu'elle n'aime pas et qui le lui rend bien, la mère est ainsi encouragée à se concentrer entièrement sur l'obsession, traditionnelle pour son sexe, d'assurer un bon avenir à sa fille. Il me semble que ce que l'oeuvre ne montre pas ici suffisamment, du moins pas clairement comme *La mémoire de l'eau* le fait, c'est que la mère est la dépositaire des frustrations de toute la lignée de femmes qu'elle perpétue en acceptant le rôle imparti par une société profondément misogyne. Mais comme on ne peut parler du corps de la mère sans aborder sa relation à celui de la fille, «celui de Yan-Zi semble encore rattaché au ventre de sa mère, menacé à tout moment de refoulement vers les entrailles maternelles», dit Sylvie Bernier (127).

VOIX NARRATOLOGIQUE SPECTRALE: LE RETOUR DU REFOULÉ

Malgré ces extraits où l'évidence du contexte répressif dans lequel évolue la mère est illustrée par la fille, l'oeuvre reste en grande partie monologique. Tout se passe ici comme si, puisqu'on a affaire à une société chinoise restée très traditionnelle, la narration adoptait une structure qui reflétait l'oppression de la mère, bouc émissaire d'un système patriarcal.[8] Car c'est la voix de la fille qui domine le récit. En effet, ces passages où la narratrice laisse entrevoir le meilleur et le pire de sa mère par sa propre pensée médiatisée sont presque toujours contrôlés par la narratrice; en d'autres mots, la mère n'atteint que rarement elle-même au statut de narratrice. Les rares passages où Yan-Zi laisse sa mère s'exprimer par la voie de dialogues sont concentrés dans le chapitre 22, où elle apprend à sa mère qu'elle vient de se donner au fiancé de sa collègue de bureau pour se dévaluer à ses yeux, puisque sa mère représente les valeurs sociales traditionnelles. Ces dialogues très durs ont néanmoins pour effet notable d'instaurer une possibilité de résolution du conflit générationel. On se demande alors pourquoi ces dialogues ne sont pas plus fréquents dans le récit puisque, comme Marianne Hirsch le dit elle-même, «parler pour la mère, c'est à la fois donner voix à son discours et le taire. C'est la marginaliser» (16).[9] Marianne Hirsch a d'ailleurs montré qu'au sein des littératures occidentales, la prise de parole de la mère dans les ouvrages de fiction commence dans les années 80, ce qui indique que certaines formes narratologiques sont clairement associées à l'état d'une société et à ses valeurs.[10]

On a vu que le système interpelle la mère à laisser son rôle social absorber sa singularité. Cet effacement de sa singularité, ce spectre de sa singularité niée qui est résistance à son oblation, à son effacement, hante la fille. Yan-Zi, en se suicidant, désire mettre fin à la mère, non pas en tant qu'individu, car elle existe si peu, mais à cette «a-mère» (Nicole Brossard), à cette institution maternelle hégémonique qui hante la mère, à cette Harmonie-Yan-Zi dont la condition de survie est paradoxalement la mort symbolique, l'adbication de son individualité, son absorption dans le «moi-peau» de la mère (comme le diraient Didier Anzieu et Françoise Couchard), qui lui-même se définit par sa réduction à l'institution maternelle incarnée dans un corps. Car la mère appelle également sa fille vers un destin de femme et de mère dépouillée de son individualité. Anne Cheng affirme d'ailleurs au sujet de l'interpellation: «Critics have pointed out all too often the coercions effected by interpellation, how terrible it is to be placed» (75). Dans cette optique, le brûlant désir qu'éprouve Yan-Zi d'être orpheline n'est que l'envers de celui de s'enlever la vie, car ces deux désirs traduisent celui d'éviter de se soustraire au regard constrictif de l'autre. D'un point de vue symbolique, c'est donc sa mort, accidentelle ou non, qui rend à Yan-Zi sa voix, sa subjectivité.

Mais puisque par ailleurs c'est le spectre de Yan-Zi qui tient lieu de voix narrative, on pourrait interpréter cette spectralité, dont Jacques Derrida affirme qu'elle est incorporation paradoxale (n'étant ni corps ni âme) comme le retour du refoulé—le minoritaire tel qu'il est incarné par la sujectivité résistante de la fille, cette résistance lui étant passée inconsciemment par la mère—l'hégémonique (incarné par la mère réduite à sa fonction de représentation de la reproduction de valeurs sexistes) organise la répression, et ainsi, la confirmation d'une spectralité (Derrida 37). En effet, la mère peut être interprétée comme l'incarnation de l'hégémonie—bien que paradoxalement, d'un point de vue individuel, elle soit «vidée»—parce qu'en elle s'incarne la fonction de mère, avec tout ce qu'elle charrie de *doxa*. La mère est quasi dépourvue d'individualité car elle ne connaît d'elle-même que ce qui est approuvé par le social, combattant tout ce qui y est étranger. Je cite ce passage révélateur en ce qu'il illustre le rejet symbolique de toute altérité de la part de la mère, qui recherche un univers clos, itératif, pour sa famille:

> Depuis qu'on commençait à parler de l'ouverture à l'étranger, maman essayait de ramener la nouvelle situation à la hauteur de sa nouvelle croyance: par bonheur, son pays et son peuple différaient beaucoup des autres; n'empêche que, afin d'affronter les influences nouvelles et de rester plus que jamais nous-mêmes, il était nécessaire de nous fortifier le cerveau et d'améliorer notre système immunitaire.... Chaque nuit, en allant aux toilettes, maman faisait donc un petit détour pour vérifier si la porte de l'appartement était bien verrouillée. Et, sous la pression de ses doigts, la serrure poussait un hurlement qui faisait sursauter toute la famille. (27)

Notons ici que le «hurlement» signale une violence faite aux êtres en repoussant ce qui pourrait surgir d'eux. On voit qu'il s'agit d'une métaphore assez limpide du désir de la mère de refermer la famille sur elle-même, symbolisée ici par la maison cadenassée pour la nuit. L'allusion à l'amélioration du système immunitaire, chargé de repousser l'intrus, est une autre métaphore qui dessert le même but. Mais ce désir d'ipséité qui obsède la mère se retourne également contre la famille, puisque c'est non seulement ce qui provient de l'extérieur de la famille qui est banni de son cercle, mais aussi la différence qui provient de sa fille, de l'intérieur. Et comme, pour Yan-Zi, le refus de n'être qu'une copie de sa mère ne trouve son expression que dans la mort, il laisse prévoir son spectre.

DEUIL ET MÉLANCOLIE

Depuis Freud, on sait que l'incorporation est une réponse à la réalité d'une perte et son déni (Butler 383), le deuil de l'autre, pour qui l'on ressent une grande ambivalence, n'étant pour ainsi dire pas digéré. On voit dès lors qu'autant la mère que Yan-Zi se trouvent dans une position mélancolique: la mère, qui a incorporé des parents maltraitants pour qui elle ne peut que ressentir une grande ambivalence; Yan-Zi, qui a si bien incorporé sa mère qu'elle connaît mal les frontières de sa propre identité. Cependant, toutes les actions entreprises avant la mort accidentelle de Yan-Zi la dirigent vers ce deuil de sa mère, dont la séparation est achevée au plus grand des prix. «Trahir les siens, succomber à la tentation de l'ailleurs paraît le passage obligé vers la liberté, la seule voie possible à une véritable individualité...», dit Sylvie Bernier, des oeuvres de Ying Chen. Si, «Yan-Zi assiste sereinement à l'incinération de son propre corps» (Bernier 127), c'est qu'elle a enfin accompli son deuil, qu'elle avait déjà entamé avec sa lettre d'adieu.

Par contre la mère reste dans son incorporation non digérée, puisqu'elle avoue à sa fille la préférer morte. La scène du buffet offert lors des obsèques de Yan-Zi montre en effet que la mère ne fera pas le deuil de sa fille, pas plus qu'elle n'a fait le deuil de parents parce qu'ils n'ont pas su l'accueillir dans le monde.[11] Au buffet funéraire les gens se gavent, y compris la mère, pour ne pas ressentir cette absence, qui ne pourrait être comblée que par des mots remplaçant la nourriture.

Ce repas des obsèques a donc la même valeur symbolique que la scène où est décrite la mère qui oblige Yan-Zi à souper tous les soirs avec elle, précisément parce qu'elle n'a pas de paroles «nourrissantes» à donner[12]:

> Pas question non plus de m'absenter de la maison à l'heure du repas: maman attachait une grande importance à la cérémonie de la table, à ce que les membres de la famille, chacun assis à sa place, mangent ensemble en écoutant les quelques remarques semblables à des reproches qu'elle faisait sur eux. (58)

Dans la famille de Yan-Zi, les repas ne sont pas un moment de partage affectif: ils *remplacent* l'affection. De la même manière, la valeur symbolique traditionnelle du buffet des obsèques est niée, puisque le buffet est présenté comme une scène de cannibalisme du fait que la viande y est abondante, alors que la chair y est traditionnellement interdite, par «respect pour le seigneur Nilou et les êtres qui l'ont rejoint dans son royaume, y compris les cochons et les poissons» (62). Yan-Zi, glissant en une phrase du littéral au figuratif, montre comment sa mère, l'associant au boeuf, en fait une victime émissaire du système social:

> Je sens même une odeur de boeuf juste au moment où l'on pousse mon corps dans le feu. C'est un véritable boeuf, vous savez, dit maman, en s'adressant à tout le monde. Je comprends qu'elle désigne par là non pas la viande qu'on est en train de déchirer à la table, ni mon signe astrologique, mais bien moi avec mon caractère de boeuf. J'ai soudain la stupide impression d'être mangée par les invités de maman. Maintenant, je crois connaître mieux la véritable raison pour laquelle on vient célébrer ma mort. On adore la chair. (63)

On assiste donc de la part de la mère à une incorporation de la défunte Yan-Zi.[13] Nicholas Abraham et Marie Torok notent que ce qui importe est moins le «cannibalisme» de l'incorporation que la destruction du langage figuratif (10), comme l'exemple qui précède le montre clairement. La mère[14] montre par son itinéraire circulaire—de l'élevage des hirondelles en cage, dont je rappelle qu'on les nomme *yan-zi* en mandarin, au nom de sa fille, à l'élevage de nouveaux oiseaux en cage une fois sa fille morte—son incapacité à rester dans la métaphorisation. Cette symbolisation attesterait de sa capacité à donner sens à la vie de sa fille par le biais du langage, outil symbolique par excellence, et lui permettrait par ailleurs de la laisser partir, le langage nouant des liens affectifs qui remplacent la proximité des corps.[15] Qu'à cela ne tienne, Yan-Zi renaîtra, comme le laisse entendre le cri du nourisson qui clôt le récit.

CONCLUSION

Sylvie Bernier interprète «ce lieu incertain entre la vie et la mort» d'où Yan-Zi relate son récit comme un «lieu de passage … ou, transposé dans le registre de l'exil, un voyage du pays natal à la terre d'accueil» (18). En présentant cette mort au sens littéral à ses lecteurs québécois, Chen ne leur fait-elle pas un clin d'œil, les invitant à prendre le relai de cette mère incapable de symboliser pour donner un sens à la vie de celle qui lui tient à coeur? De là le récit, raconté au sens littéral par une morte depuis l'au-delà. En fait, le récit est celui d'une femme revenue de la mort puisqu'il fait l'économie de la mère et de sa nourriture. Les mots du récit ont heureusement remplacé la nourriture, et la mort est devenue renaissance en terre d'accueil. En outre, ce récit chinois est singulièrement narré en français, depuis le Québec.

[1]La jaquette de la page couverture dit: «Finaliste au prix Femina, *L'Ingratitude* a reçu le prix Québec-Paris, le grand prix des lectrices de Elle-Québec, et le prix des libraires du Québec».
[2]Ces invariants sont la raison pour laquelle je ne crains pas de citer des

auteures comme Couchard, anthropologue et psychanalyste française, Cheng, auteure américaine d'origine chinoise, et plusieurs autres. Ce sont des invariants dus, bien sûr, à la condition inférieure des femmes dans une majorité de pays, condition d'ordre sociologique, mais qui sont naturalisées.

[3]Ma traduction.

[4]Ma traduction.

[5]Couchard définit ainsi la notion d'emprise: «la notion d'emprise renvoie dans son acceptation commune à l'idée de domination, de mainmise sur l'autre; elle sous-entend une hiérarchie: celle d'un fort sur un faible. Le sens originel du mot est juridique, l'emprise désignant d'abord la mainmise administrative sur une propriété privée; le terme enfin est lié à l'idée d'empreinte ou de trace visible» (3).

[6]Couchard ajoute que de nombreuses cultures imposent un double assujettissement à la mère, celui de procréer le plus possible et de procréer des mâles. Yan-Zi est née trop récemment à Shanghai pour appartenir à une famille nombreuse, et rien n'indique que sa mère est malheureuse de ne pas avoir accouché d'un garçon.

[7]Qui s'apparente, selon moi, davantage au récit, avec son univers centré sur un seul personnage—autour duquel gravitent quelques proches, à la conscience desquels le lecteur n'a pas accès—avec des coordonnées spatio-temporelles réduites ou floues.

[8]Les romans québécois, jusqu'à l'arrivée de *Bonheur d'occasion*, de Gabrielle Roy (1945), ne donnent jamais la parole à la mère. C'est une muette, une automate, dont l'individualité est absorbée par la tâche.

[9]Ma traduction de «[t]o speak for the mother is at once to give voice to her discourse and to silence and marginalize her» (Hirsch 16).

[10]On peut se demander ce qui se serait passé si le récit avait opté pour une polyvocalité qui aurait donné une voix à la mère. Mon hypothèse est que cette possibilité n'a pas été considérée pour des raisons de cohérence formelle. La narratrice, pour se venger du contrôle qu'exerce sa mère sur sa vie, choisit de prendre l'entier contrôle de son récit.

[11]Yan-Zi fait allusion (dans un passage cité plus haut) au fait que sa mère a été battue par ses parents «pour qu'elle apprenne à se soumettre et aussi à s'imposer dès le moment venu» (92). Abraham et Torok précisent au sujet du développement émotif des enfants: «The transition from breast-filled mouth to word-filled mouth is achieved through experiences of 'empty mouth'. Learning to fill the void of the mouth with words constitutes an early paradigm of introjection. Clearly this cannot occur without the constant presence of a mother who herself possesses language. Her constancy (...) is the necessary guarantee of the meaning of words. First the empty mouth, then the absence of objects become words, and finally experiences with words themselves are converted into other words. Thus the original oral void will have found a remedy for all its wants through

their conversion in linguistic intercourse with the speaking community. To introject a wish, a grief, or a situation is to dispose of it through language in a communion of empty mouths. Thus food absorption, in the literal sense, becomes introjection in the figurative sense. To achieve this transition, presence of the object must be superseded by auto-apprehension of its absence. Language, which makes up for that absence by representing presence, can be understood only within a 'community of empty mouths'» (5).

[12]En fait, la crise qui sort Yan-Zi de son foyer commence le soir où Yan-Zi rencontre par hasard Bi au restaurant Bonheur, et qu'il l'invite à y souper. La mère, avec raison, voit cette entrave au rituel de leur repas comme le début de la fin de son emprise.

[13]Incorporation qui refuse d'autant plus le deuil que la mère lui parle une fois les invités partis comme si rien ne s'était passé, comme si Yan-Zi n'était pas morte, mais toujours à s'obstiner avec elle.

[14]Selon Bernier, cette mère est «vampirique», précisément parce qu'elle a été vampirisée, comme beaucoup de mères chinoises, par le système de valeurs chinois.

[15]Sylvie Bernier, dans son très bel article sur l'oeuvre de Ying Chen, ne s'y est pas trompée lorsqu'elle a affirmé: «Un portrait de la Chine se lit dans cette mère cannibale qui cherche à ravaler en son ventre sa progéniture» (120).

OUVRAGES CITÉS

Abraham, Nicholas, et Torok, Maria. « Introjection-Incorporation. Mourning or Melancholia». *Psychoanalysis in France*. Sous la dir. S. Lebovici and D. Widlöcher. New York: International University Press, 1980: 3-16.

Anzieu, Didier. *Le moi-peau*. Paris: Dunod, 1995.

Bernier, Sylvie. «S'exiler de soi: Ying Chen». *Francofilia: Studie e Ricerche Sulle Letterature di Lingua Francese*. 1999, no 37: 115-131.

Butler, Judith. «Imitation and Gender Insubordination». *Inside/Out: Lesbian/Gay Theories*. Sous la dir. Diana Fuss. New York: Routledge, 1991: 371-387.

Chen, Ying. *La mémoire de l'eau*. Montréal: Leméac, 1993.

Chen, Ying. *L'Ingratitude*. Montréal: Leméac/Actes Sud, 1995.

Cheng, Anne Alin. *The Melancholy of Race*. New York: Oxford University Press, 2000.

Couchard, Françoise. *Emprise et violence maternelle. Étude d'anthropologie psychanalytique*. Paris: Dunod, 1991.

Derrida, Jacques. *Specters of Marx. The State of the Debt, the Work of Mourning, and the New International.* New York: Routledge, 1994 (traduit par Peggy Kamuf).

Hirsch, Marianne. *The Mother-Daughter Plot. Narrative, Psychoanalysis, Feminism.* Bloomington and Indiannapolis: Indiana University Press, 1989.

Lequin, Lucie. «À la croisée des chemins». *Trajectoires au féminin dans la littérature québécoise 1960-1990.* Sous la dir. de Lucie Joubert. Québec: Nota bene, 2000. 107-118.

Saint-Martin, Lori. *Le nom de la mère: mères, filles et écriture dans la littérature québécoise au féminin.* Québec: Nota bene, 1999.

Thakur, Ravni. *Rewriting Gender. Reading Contemporary Chinese Women.* London: Zed Books, 1997.

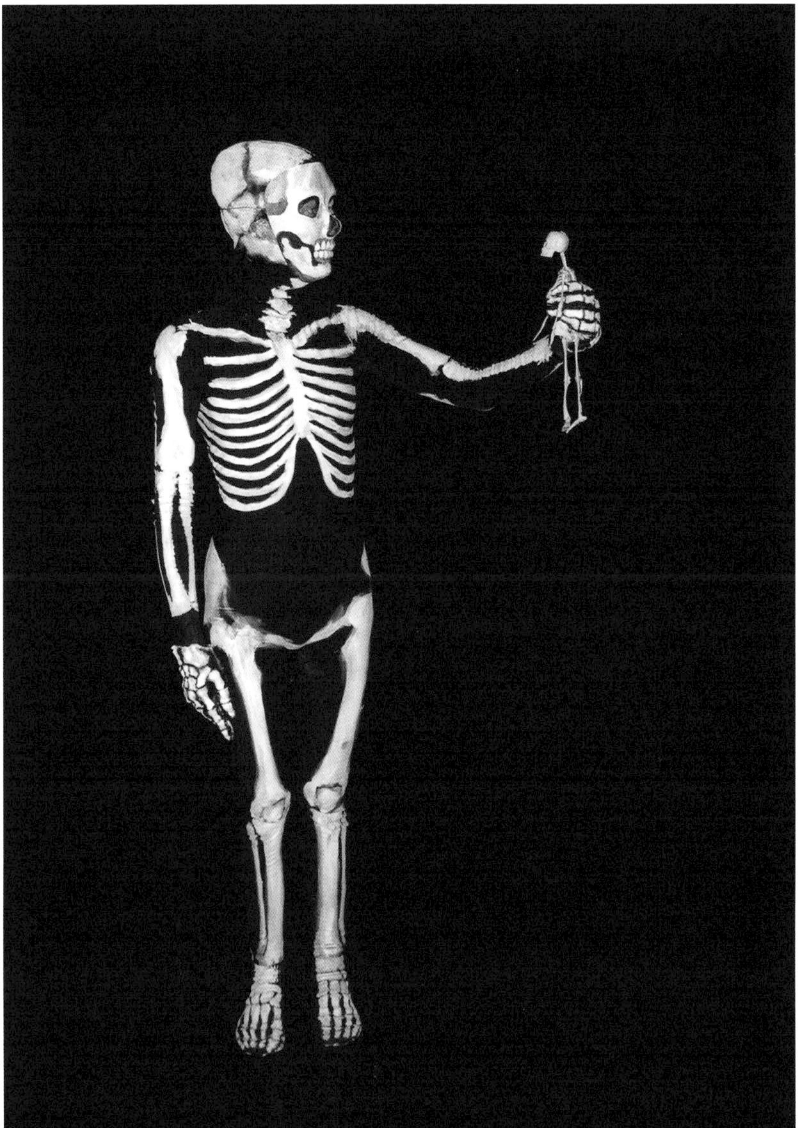

The Skeleton Crew (Seema Goel, Steve Kirkland, Robin Poitras), *a fellow of infinite jest*, 2003, photograph, of variable size.

a fellow of infinite jest comes from a collaborative photographic project by the Skeleton Crew. A performer improvises with a miniature skeletal version of herself. This work, both light and dark-hearted, tackles fertility, mortality, reflection, and the infinite loop inscribing parent upon child and vice versa.

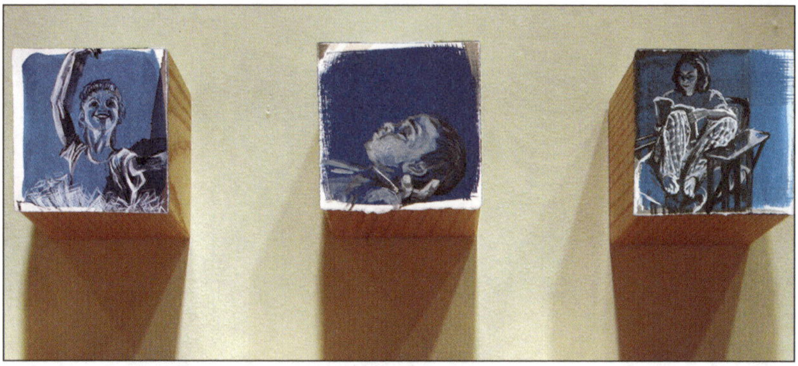

Yael Brotman, *Dreamline # 3*, 2004–07, acrylic and ink on paper on ash woodblock, 7.62 x 7.62 x 7.62 cm (each element).

In my practice, I investigate the nature of storytelling. Here, a string of small blue paintings on woodblocks creates a non-linear narrative. The images are culled from newspaper photographs and advertisements, literary sources, and my sketchbook. The juxtaposition of images is intuitive and plays with rhythmic formality versus open-ended conclusions.

Why Mothers Are Still Women

ALISON HAYFORD

TIME WAS, AS feminists of a certain age will remember, when fathers were a central part of discussions of motherhood. As the women's movement of the 1960s and 1970s tackled the issue of women's roles, it became clear that we could not discuss what women did without also discussing what men did. The feminism of the 1970s thus helped bring about a broad shift in our understanding of fatherhood, from seeing fathers primarily as sources of paychecks or castration anxieties to seeing them as—ideally, at least—co-partners with mothers in the everyday lives of families.

For many feminists, changing how men practiced fatherhood was central to women's liberation. If motherhood was a central aspect of women's lives, women could not change their lives without changing the ways they practiced being mothers; if motherhood existed in relation to fatherhood, women could not change their lives unless fatherhood changed as well. By the 1980s, the word "parenting" had come into widespread use, often as a replacement for "mothering," at least partly in recognition of the fact that not all parents are mothers. Yet after 40 years of "parenting," in many ways "parents" are still mothers, and mothers are still women. Discussions of "parenting" are most often really about the issues women face when they become mothers. Newspaper and magazine articles portray women making decisions about motherhood with little or no reference to their partners. It is as if motherhood and fatherhood have come to be seen as separate social realities rather than as mutually defining social relationships.

Narratives of motherhood in the 1970s and 1980s were not monolithic, but most understood practices of motherhood as socially constructed and relational (e.g. Chodorow; Ehrensaft; Friedan; Held; Hochschild; Luxton; Ruddick). Feminists tended to see motherhood as shaped by social orders that are male dominated or, in a literal sense, patriarchal. The ways in which women practiced motherhood were formed by the broad sociocultural contexts of mothers' lives as well as by specific family relationships. For these reasons, women had little room to make personal decisions about how they would act as mothers, and motherhood became a limiting factor in women's lives.

It was widely accepted by feminists that the liberation of women, however defined, required pulling men into the maternal order. This meant remaking masculine roles within families to incorporate basic participation in and responsibility for child care, other forms of caring work, and household work generally (Chodorow; Ehrensaft; Ruddick). The benefits were not just for women; men and children were also seen as having better lives when changes in practices of fatherhood brought men into closer relationships with their children. By the end of the 1970s, fatherhood had become an issue of public interest, not just a target for wild-eyed feminists (Gerson 1993; Hochschild; LaRossa; Toynbee).

By the mid-1990s, both fatherhood and motherhood remained objects of public concern, but the nature of public discourses had shifted. Debates over the best modes of parenting took place among women, with male voices largely absent (e.g., Peskowitz, Steiner, Warner). Even feminists increasingly treated motherhood as if women acted largely in relation to other women, not to men (e.g., Ehrenreich and Hochschild). This shift in discourse was not a direct reflection of changes in everyday life practices; if anything, the new discourses misrepresent reality. Men might not have changed their family roles as much as one might have hoped, but ideals of fatherhood have changed (LaRossa; Toynbee). Social research shows that heterosexual marriages are characterized by a good deal of negotiation about household duties and caregiving; in many households, the roles of mothers and fathers are not taken for granted and can be sources of conflict (Alstott; Bianchi *et al.*; Carey; Hochschild). We need to ask why so many popular discussions of motherhood fail to reflect the realities that social research shows are important in relations between mothers and fathers.

We can see some possible reasons for this discursive shift in a genre of motherhood narrative that emerged in the 1990s. These are books whose authors are women, most of them mothers, many of them with expertise in social science areas such as psychology or economics (Bennetts; de Marneffe; Hewlett; Lerner; Peters; Rubinstein; Smith; Williams). The genre is characterized by a combination of social scientific evidence and personal narratives—the authors' own, case histories of other people, usually women, or both. In some works, personal narratives dominate, but even in these the authors use some external evidence to validate their personal stories (Cusk; Flanagan; Krasnow; Peskowitz; Roiphe; Warner).

Narratives within this social science/memoir genre take different ideological positions on motherhood, in particular the question of whether or not mothers should be in the paid labour force. Some narratives are explicitly feminist, others are critical of feminism. What they have in common, in addition to their basic form, is the way they portray the decisions mothers make about the practice of motherhood. The social science/memoir genre frames motherhood as an essentially individual experience in which practices of motherhood are the outcomes of individual women's personal choices.

In the personal narratives that are part of this genre, women portray themselves as struggling largely alone to understand how they should perform motherhood. These authors, and the women they cite as case studies, struggle to understand the truth about what they must do to be good mothers to their children—perhaps "repressing, banishing the evil mother that lives within" (Roiphe 82) or "losing oneself, [which is], after all, what women in families do" (Lerner 54). Romantic language about mothers "falling in love" with their babies is frequent. For some women, the process of recognition involves significant inner conflict: "On some days I was so bored and frustrated that I couldn't wait to leave him. On other days, I couldn't bear to imagine life without this baby in my arms" (Lerner 54). For others, it is so sudden and complete that it is a form of a conversion experience, in which the woman suddenly realizes some truth about motherhood, changes her ways, and is "reborn at thirty-one or thirty-seven or in Tracy's case, at forty-two" (Krasnow 128).

All of the authors in this genre see the lives of mothers and fathers as profoundly different; "after a child is born the lives of its mother and father diverge, so that where before they were living in a state of some equality, now they exist in a sort of feudal relation to each other" (Cusk 5). Yet unlike authors of the 1970s and 1980s, social science/memoir authors do not focus on the reasons that men's and women's lives differ. They may accept these differences as natural and thus unchallengeable—"[W]omen miss their kids when they're at work! And men do not—they can split their lives in ways women can't." (de Marneffe, 127) Or they might assume that men cannot or will not change—the marriage in which a man carries his share of household and caring work might even be "magic" (Rubinstein 161).

For these women, awakening to truth involves struggle on multiple levels—with the self, with other people, and with social norms. The mothers in these narratives confront a variety of conflicting pressures as they discover how to practice motherhood. The central struggle involves decisions about whether or not to participate in the paid labour force. The social science/memoir genre is not marked by a single position on this issue; some of the authors advocate mothers staying at home (e.g., de Marneffe, Flanagan, Krasnow), others advocate mothers staying in the paid labour force (e.g., Bennetts, Peters), others don't take one side or the other (e.g., Lerner, Smith). What these narratives have in common is their emphasis on women's internal struggles over motherhood. Some narratives, particularly paid labour force narratives, discuss struggles that arise with husbands who don't do household work or with employers who see mothers as incompetent or with day cares that cost more than a month's wages. In the end, however, both kinds of narrative portray women's decision making (or coping) as essentially individual.

While the women in these narratives tend to find one defining truth for themselves, these truths vary from author to author. In some narratives, the truth is that women have a fundamental desire to be with their children, and to meet this desire they must stay at home with them: "I realized that for the first time in my life I was exactly where I was supposed to be. On my knees, scraping my babies' lunch off the carpet ... humbled, mercifully beaten down by children but exalted glory God, This Was It!" (Krasnow 157). In other narratives, the truth is that women have a fundamental need to stay in the paid labour force, both their mental welfare and because to leave paid work makes women (and their children) economically and socially vulnerable (Bennetts, Peters). Paid labour force narratives can be apocalyptic in their descriptions of the negative consequences for women of even short periods of withdrawal from the paid labour force. Yet for all their differences, both kinds of narratives emphasize the individual needs of women more than the needs of other family members, even children: "I needed to be her mother more than she needed my mothering" (Cusk 205).

This emphasis on women's individual needs makes these narratives both the heirs of feminism and problematic for feminism. Contemporary feminism is founded in the idea that women have a right to act and to be recognized as individuals. Contemporary feminism's fundamental claim is that women must have agency in their own lives. Social science/memoir narratives, whether stay at home or paid labour force participation, anti-feminist or feminist, all accept this claim. Women's agency is so central in these narratives that it becomes problematic for the authors to discuss the ways in which women's agency is limited, perhaps because to recognize constraints on women's agency might subvert the narratives' fundamental claims. As a result, many of these narratives mask the social and relational nature of motherhood. The emphasis on women's agency also creates a problem for these authors in dealing with the reality that the dependency of children inevitably restricts the life choices of their caregivers.

How the different narratives resolve this problem depends on the truths the authors have found find. Paid labour force narratives tend to frame household work, including caring work, as drudgery that involves no choice about whether or even how it must be done. Mothers can retain their selfhood only by staying involved in a larger world where they have options in what they do, particularly through attachments to careers. Stay at home narratives tend to frame household work, especially caring work, as a location—perhaps the only location—where a woman can develop her true self. Caring for others out of love is more personally fulfilling than paid employment can be (especially if the mother has household help to do the drudgery [Flanagan] or a breadwinner husband who takes on child care when he comes home [Krasnow]). Within these narratives, mothers' agency lies in the initial decision to stay at home with children, and the submission to children's needs that follows does not erase the fundamental individuality of the mothers who make this choice.

"Choice" is the key concept in all social science/memoir motherhood narratives. It is not uncommon for women to argue that feminism means choice, and that any choice is thus feminist—including decisions to stay home with children in a "traditional" family (Hirshman). It is authors outside the genre, who place little or no emphasis on personal narratives, who are most likely to emphasize the constraints on choice that women face (Crittenden; Hirshman; Stone) and propose social alternatives, though the issue of constraints does arise importantly for some authors within the genre (Peskowitz; Warner). A few authors see "choice" as just one more obligation that constrains women's lives (Peters; Warner).

In genre narratives, the issue isn't the nature of the choices women make, but the fact that women make choices. Thus agency takes on various meanings. For some authors, agency is an assertion of personal power—for example, stay at home authors who portray themselves as informing their husbands that they will have to be sole breadwinners because the narrator has decided to stay home (de Marneffe, Krasnow). Many narratives frame women's choices as the resistance of the individual to social pressures. For some stay at home authors, the decision to leave the paid labour force is an assertion of selfhood against feminist conformity (Flanagan; Hewlett; Krasnow). For some paid labour force authors, women's decisions to remain in the paid labour force are acts of resistance against a society that still conspires to keep mothers from full participation in the larger world (Bennetts; Gerson 2003).

Despite their emphasis on women's individual agency, negotiation is never completely absent from these narratives (e.g. Bennetts 246-266; Lerner 39; Peskowitz 227-228; Rubinstein 164 and passim). Some narratives emphasize the difficulties of getting husbands to do household work (Bennetts; Maushart; Rubinstein). Others argue that deep in their heart of hearts women really want to do household work and child care (e.g., Flanagan), though some of these authors also mention having nannies and housekeepers.

In line with the emphasis on women's agency, virtually all the narratives in this genre make women responsible for getting husbands to change, not the men themselves. If men don't change, it's because of "wives [who] permit their husbands to shirk the responsibilities of homemaking and parenting" (Bennetts 257) or women who "give and give and give some more because they know they are the only ones who will" (Rubinstein 205). Some authors see many men as almost incapable of change—in my experience women seem to have more of a connection to [housework]—and to the way that it should be done—than men do" (Flanagan 202), so that "[i]t's not that these men are cruel or incompetent or evil, it's just that they simply cannot cope; they literally can't manage" (Rubinstein 205).

Negotiations with male partners, employers, or others are present but not the focus of analysis in these texts. Instead, they emerge as backstories or as framing devices—for example, Peskowitz waits until the epilog to say "we've come together on a story about our marriage that acknowledges that his life work has been central, even if, when we met, our dream was mutuality and equality" (227), though the discerning reader has long suspected that this might be the case. This absence of analysis of the social context of individual decisions is a striking element of the social science/memoir.

Social science/memoir narratives of motherhood represent an important tendency in popular discourse. On the one hand, they reflect a legacy of feminism that enables women to claim agency and recognition in various aspects of their lives, including practices of motherhood. On the other hand, these narratives place so much emphasis on women's individual agency that they effectively remove motherhood from the realm of social relations. Thus fathers disappear from these narratives, or play minor roles, motherhood remains the realm of women, and "parenting" is not a gender-neutral term. Mothers are, indeed, still women.

[1]Paper originally presented at Association for Research on Mothering: Conference on Maternal Well-Being, Toronto, October 17, 2007.

WORKS CITED

Alstott, Anne L. *No Exit: What Parents Owe Their Children and What Society Owes Parents*. New York: Oxford University Press, 2004.

Bennetts, Leslie. *The Feminine Mistake: Are We Giving up Too Much?* New York: Voice/Hyperion, 2007.

Bianchi, Suzanne, Melissa A. Milkie, Liana C. Sayer, John P. Robinson. "Is Anyone Doing the Housework? Trends in the Gender Division of Labor." *Social Forces* 79.1 (2000): 191-228.

Carey, Anita Ilta. *Weaving Work and Motherhood*. Philadelphia: Temple University Press, 1999.

Chodorow, Nancy. *The Reproduction of Mothering: Psychoanalysis and the Sociology of Gender*. Berkeley: University of California Press, 1978.

Crittenden, Ann. *The Price of Motherhood: Why the Most Important Job in the World is Still the Least Valued*. New York: Holt, 2001.

Cusk, Rachel. *A Life's Work: On Becoming a Mother*. New York: Picador, 2001.

de Marneffe, Daphne. *Maternal Desire: on Children, Love, and the Inner Life*. New York and Boston: Little Brown, 2004.

Ehrenreich, Barbara, and Arlie Russell Hochschild. *Global Woman: Nannies, Maids, and Sex Workers in the New Economy*. New York: Metropolitan, 2003.

Ehrensaft, Diane. *Parenting Together: Men and Women Sharing the Care of their Children*. Glencoe: The Free Press, 1987.

Flanagan, Caitlin. *To Hell With all That: Loving and Loathing our Inner Housewife*. New York and Boston: Little Brown, 2006.

Friedan, Betty. *The Feminine Mystique*. New York: Norton, 1963.

Gerson, Kathleen. *No Man's Land: Men's Changing Commitments to Family and Work*. New York: Basic, 1993.

Gerson, Kathleen. "Work Without Worry." *New York Times*: 11 May 2003.

Held, Virginia. "The Obligations of Mothers and Fathers." Trebilcot, Joyce. *Mothering: Essays in Feminist Theory*. Ed. Joyce Trebilcot. Totowa: Rowman and Allenheld, 1984. 7-20.

Hewlett, Sylvia. *Baby Hunger: the New Battle for Motherhood*. London: Atlantic, 2002

Hirshman, Linda. "Homeward Bound." *American Spectator* 22 November 2005. Online: <http://www.prospect.org/cs/arti-cles?articleId=10646>.

Hochschild, Arlie Russell. *The Second Shift*. New York: Avon, 1989.

Krasnow, Iris. *Surrendering to Motherhood: Losing Your Mind, Finding Your Soul*. New York: Hyperion, 1997.

LaRossa, Ralph. "Fatherhood and Social Change." *Family Relations* 37 (1988): 451-57.

Lerner, Harriet. *The Mother Dance: How Children Change Your Life*. New York: Harper, 1998.

Luxton, Meg. *More Than a Labour of Love: Three Generations of Women's Work in the Home*. Toronto: Women's, 1980.

Maushart, Susan. *Wifework: What Marriage REALLY Means for Women.*. London: Bloomsbury, 2002.

Peskowitz, Miriam. *The Truth Behind the Mommy Wars: Who Decides What Makes a Good Mother?* Emeryville: Seal, 2005.

Peters, Joan K. *When Mothers Work: Loving Our Children Without Sacrificing Our Selves*. Reading, Massachusetts: Addison-Wesley, 1997.

Roiphe, Anne. *Fruitful: a Real Mother in the Modern World*. Boston and New York: Houghton, 1996.

Rubinstein, Carin. *The Sacrificial Mother: Escaping the Trap of Self-Denial*. New York: Hyperion, 1998.

Ruddick, Sara. "Maternal Thinking." *Feminist Studies* 6.2 (1980): 342-367. JSTOR: ITHAKA, 1980.

Smith, Janna Malamud. *A Potent Spell: Mother Love and the Power of Fear.* Mariner, 2004.

Steiner, Leslie Morgan, ed. *Mommy Wars: Stay-at-Home and Career Moms Face off on Their Choices, Their Lives, Their Families.* New York: Random, 2006.

Stone, Pamela. *Opting Out? Why Women Really Quit Careers and Head Home.* Berkeley: University of California Press, 2007.

Toynbee, Polly. "The Incredible Shrinking New Man." *The Guardian* 6 November 1987. Online: <http: // century.guardian.co.uk/1980-1989/Story/0,,110228,00.html>.

Trebilcot, Joyce. *Mothering: Essays in Feminist Theory.* Totowa: Rowman and Allenheld, 1984.

Tucker, Judith Stadtman. "The Builders of New Myths: Friedan, Feminism, and the Future." The Mothers Movement Online. March 2006. Online: <www.mothersmovement.org/features/06/03/newmyths_1.html>.

Warner, Judith. *Perfect Madness: Motherhood in the Age of Anxiety.* New York: Riverhead, 2005.

Williams, Joan. *Unbending Gender: Why Family and Work Conflict and What to do About It.* New York: Oxford University Press, 2000.

The Motherlode/Load

A Performative Praxis

PAM PATTERSON

I AM AN ARTIST who uses performative practices, enacting the body as subject. This practice is itself problematic, lacking adequate definition. Artists, viewers, and interpreters become caught in the complex engagement and representation of Self and/with Others through the corporeality of the body. It is a practice fraught with shifting meanings: emotional, political, social. As for my other defining roles, they are equally complex; I am a writer, academic, curator, educator, person with a disability, single parent, granddaughter, daughter, mother. My writing here focuses on the latter named roles, enlivened and contextualized by/through a performance practice. In my research on family, parenting, and motherhood, I have engaged with shifting perspectives relative to my family of origin, and to the families I have made and will make. It has been a lode of rich images, text, and gestures. But as I enter this next time of life, as crone, I feel the need to re-examine and discard some of this load. It has simply become too heavy to carry any longer. So, I invite you here to engage with me in a performative praxis in which the motherlode/load is richly, and perhaps rather unconventionally, used, acknowledged, held, and released.

POSITING THE MOTHERLODE/LOAD AS PROBLEMATIC

In breast cancer discussions, the right breast, some say, refers to a conflicted relationship with the father, the left with the mother. Both these relationships were certainly challenging for me. I was physically, sexually, and emotionally abused by my father. Why then did I lose my left breast? With both parents dead, the time for re-examination has come, and, with the advent of breast cancer in my body, my positing the problematic of the motherlode/load becomes imperative.

> In the night a child is screaming.... Cancer is in my head for life ... What path am I being asked to step away from on behalf of

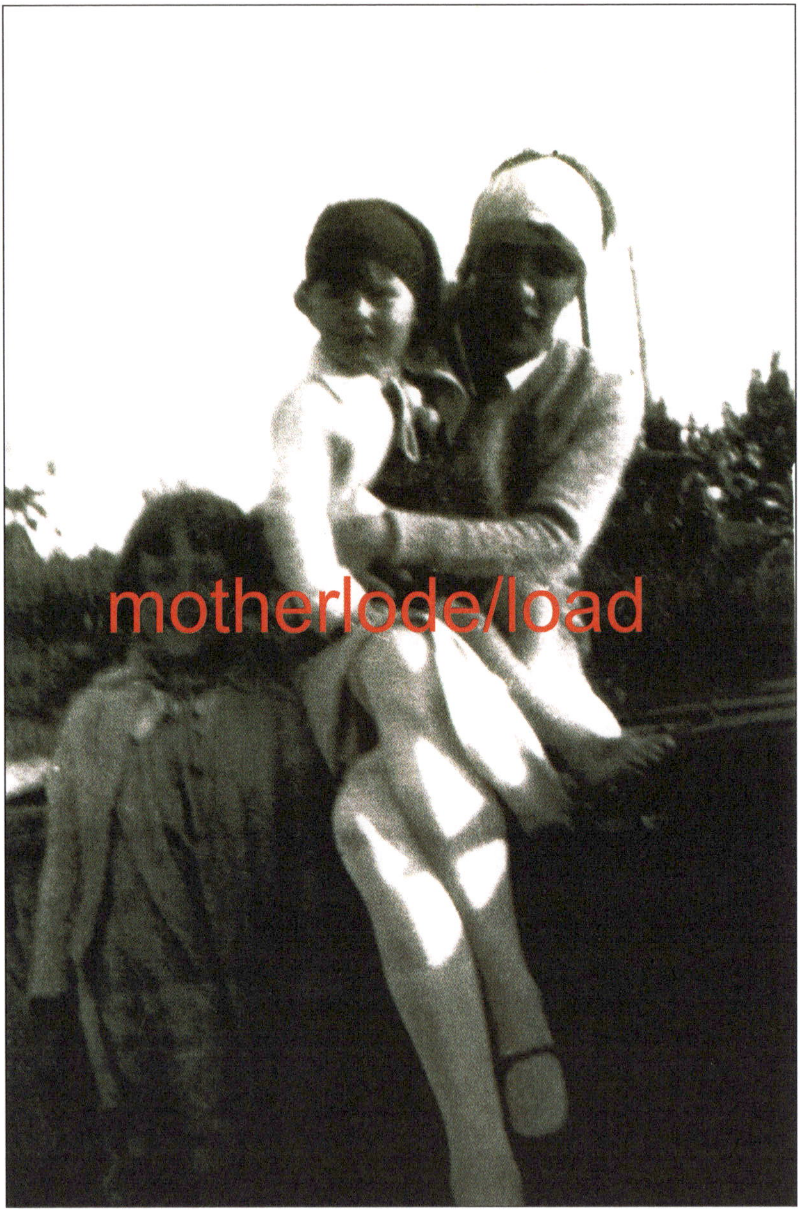

The Motherlode/load, 2003

> my life... Crossing cancer's space is a different time zone, a different space, a long breathing space in which the mind gathers its strength and takes stock of its courage. Listen, I have not lost my power... I have not forgotten who I am... Once my gods were intimates... Once I made gestures of pure exuberance... Now my hands make another body for my body... As the world reduces to a small intimate space let me suddenly have a center... Let me make a silhouette on the world... Let me stand composed before a million universes... (Patterson, Canc(H)er np).

Motherload/motherlode—various meanings resonate: motherlode as the source of all riches, the greatest find; motherload, the assumptions and expectations placed on, and named as, woman, and mother.

This juxtaposition has proved useful for me in my practices and research in and out of the academy. For the past twenty years, I have explored multi-media interdisciplinary performance as a research/learning practice. How does the speaking, feeling, woman's body, seen and experienced in performance, provide an entry point for audience? Can performance, as inter/multi-media practice, act as a research methodology as well as a presentation tool? Do performative practices generate a context for knowing? As I engage with various concerns performatively, in sounds, action, images and movement, do my participants and I come to know ourselves differently? Does performance act as a narrative or self-reflection, or is it dialogical in nature asking a response from its viewer? Does it not necessitate an alternative reading strategy to that used to read an art object? Do we assume that performance possesses, as do art objects, inherent meanings and that those who have the legitimizing aesthetic tools with which to interpret them can read easily and appropriately these meanings?

Amelia Jones and Andrew Stephenson point to the impossibility of applying such prescriptive notions of meaning to performance-oriented practices. They argue that interpretation itself is a kind of performative practice with its own modes of communication (7-8). Through performing as/in interpretation, meaning becomes a process of engagement and dwells in many places with many persons. We all engage in performative practices in doing, speaking and interpreting. In a performative praxis, works are made, read, and understood in process, open and evolving.

Here, using performative works, I re-trace and re-excavate the rich discordant place of family, mothering and the mother line. In some instances, I reflect, using narrative, on images from finished works as one interpretative strategy. In others, excerpts from performances are used, which allow for less prescribed interpretations. While this may limit the opportunities for more analytical meaning making, it provides a milieu for pleasure, and causes shifts that allow for destabilization. As practice, it invites reflection in/through a performative praxis.

BIRTH

The Birth Project was made for A Space Gallery, Toronto and shown in a second context at Gallery Gachet, Vancouver. Three mylar panels, three feet by eight feet each, display photo images of my torso at six months gestation. There are also three photo-based, framed distorted images of my torso suspended beside these panels along the wall, and photographs of my face lie on the floor staring up through plexiglass boxes. On the boxes, and drawn on the long mylar panels, are images and text that refer to herbs used before, during, and after birth: skullcap, wild red raspberry, and nettle. These dried herbs fill china teacups placed before the boxes on the floor. On either side of these cups is printed text: the text on the left is my narrative, on the right my midwife's. Each of us speaks from our own experience of my daughter's birth. The images are arranged in groupings of three, reflecting the medically named stages of birth. It seems, at first glance, a simple birth narrative. But my pregnant body is fragmented and distorted, encased in strict lines and boxes, trapped.

At the time of my daughter's birth, midwives were seeking recognition through, and in, the conventional medical system. For many of us, this shift was fraught with complexity. Would such legitimacy allow midwives to revolutionize hospital births and provide women with more choice, or would midwives become more controlled and circumscribed in their practices?

FAMILIES OF ORIGIN AND IN REPRODUCTION

After I completed *The Birth Project,* I was challenged to investigate the complexity of familial relationships. I wanted to examine the discourses, roles, and actions surrounding the family, particularly those that shaped me as mother and had formed me as child. Could I rewrite my body, the body that learned to be a girl and, later, a mother? I began to recover and recontextualize memories from both my distant and more recent past. I began to examine the ways my learning and teaching within the family was and is structured. I worked with images, sounds, and words, with actual childhood diaries and photographs taken by me and by others.

Markers from the past became even more visible once I occupied the position of mother. Once my daughter reached about three, I became aware of the responsibility I had, and the power and position I held. While I attempted to resist the location of "mother," I was very much formed by it. When I spoke a phrase a certain way, or shadowed an action of

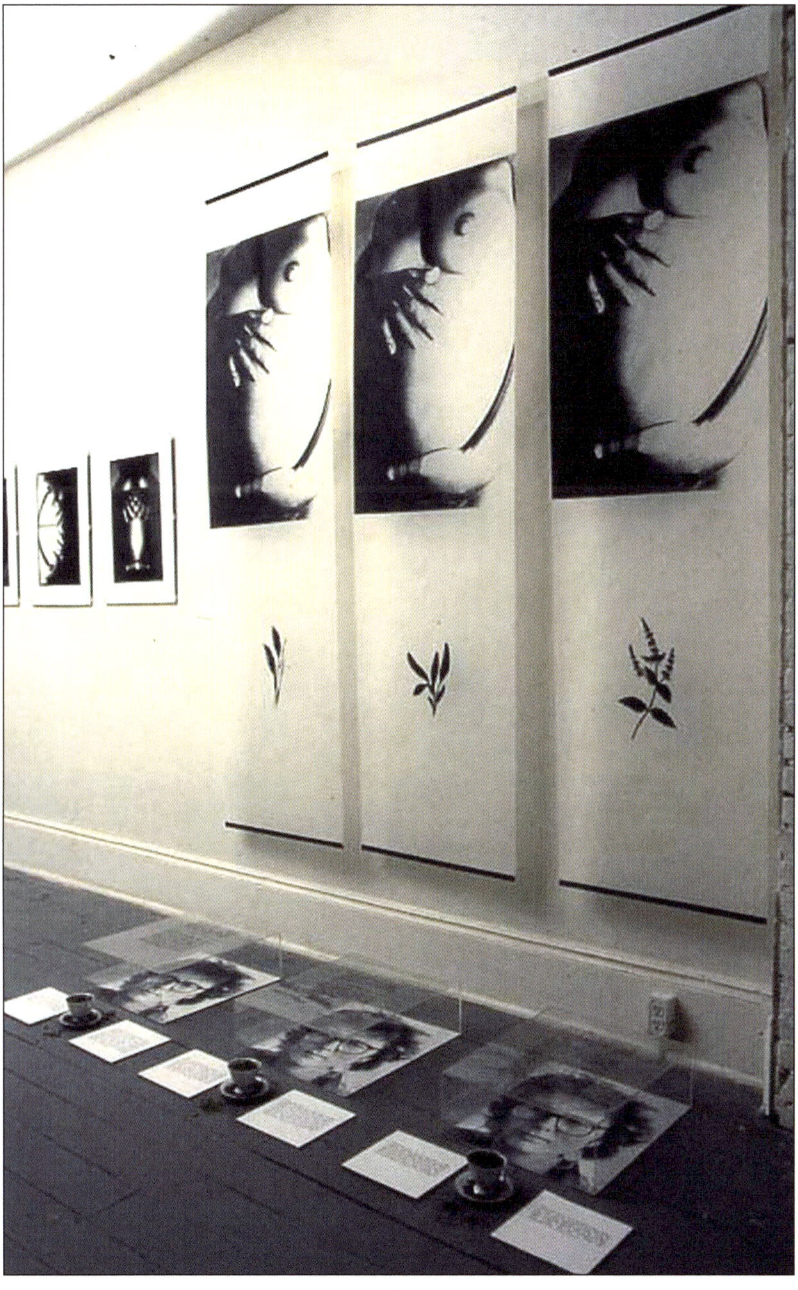

The Birth Project, 1992

my mother's, or felt the violence of my father on/in my arm, I knew such traces from my past were still active.

The writing and visual work that followed spoke of my family of origin and the family I reproduced. They were treated separately, but were not exclusive; there were overlaps. The exhibitions that used this research were loosely framed under the title *Mapping the Familial*. In these exhibitions, I attempted to demystify the monolithic family. It proved to be a tenacious and difficult task, for the family, as institution, seems to be the most natural and biological, its ideals timeless and unchanging. I struggled with the trappings of mothering: the newborn at home, the first shoes, the lunch box, the daycare. Each became resituated and framed in various contexts: my experience of the medical regulation of my child, my narrative of single parent poverty, the impact on us of a Conservative government's daycare policies, my terror of turning my exhausted rage against my child. Sitting, sometimes with other mothers, I silently acknowledged our "wars" to come. Audre Lorde wrote, "Some problems we share as women, some we do not. You fear your children will grow up to join the patriarchy and testify against you, we fear our children will be dragged from a car and shot down in the street and you will turn your backs on the reasons they are dying" (119).

> It is an old photograph, black and white, cut with scissors to frame in the centre a small child, me, about two years old. The

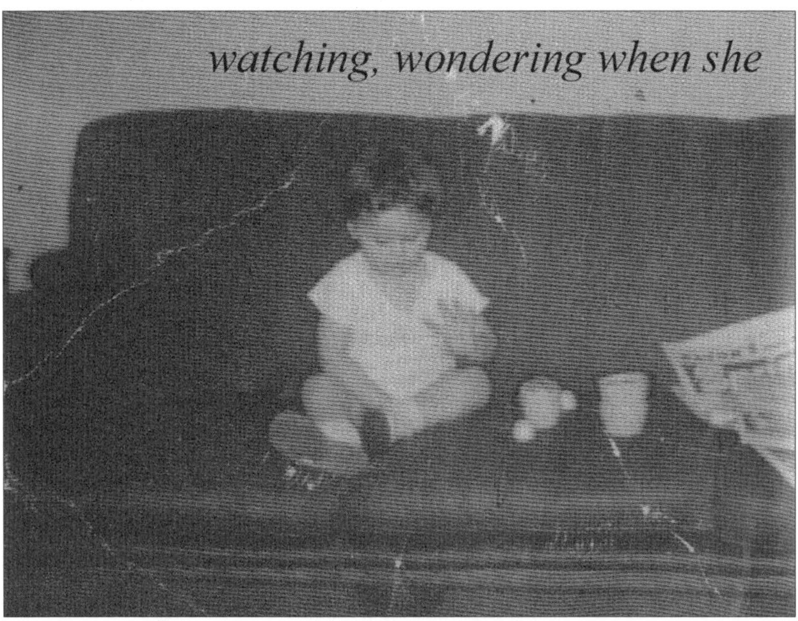

Mapping the Familial #1, 1993

> child is a girl. It is interesting that she is pictured alone. Perhaps others have been cut out of the picture. Perhaps she cut them out herself later when she recovered the picture. She doesn't remember exactly. The child seems focused on some activity hidden from our view. It is a serious business, as any creative activity will be for the years following. But, she was always aware that she was under careful scrutiny, especially by her father. Her mother always left her alone. (Patterson, Threads 13)

DEATH BY MOTHERLOAD?

In 1996 my father died, my mother in 2001.

During the 90s, I dealt with the "sins" of the father, and its impact on my own future mothering. But, as I became challenged by my own mortality, my aging body, and eventually my mother's death by cancer, a disease that later was to challenge me also, I worked deeper to excavate the motherload.

In a performance/action, *Hands on Environs*, I made at the edge of Lake Ontario, I was cold, wet, blown to the edge of the water, and deafened by the roar of the waves, wind, and rain pounding and sweeping around me. I wanted to memorialize my mother, acknowledge the ending of her breath through lung cancer, and grasp as an infant at birth for my own. As I gasped for this breath, I figuratively released my mother over the lake. Less than a year later, I was diagnosed with cancer. I had seen my grandmother and mother die of cancer. Now, I too embodied in my breast this dis/ease.

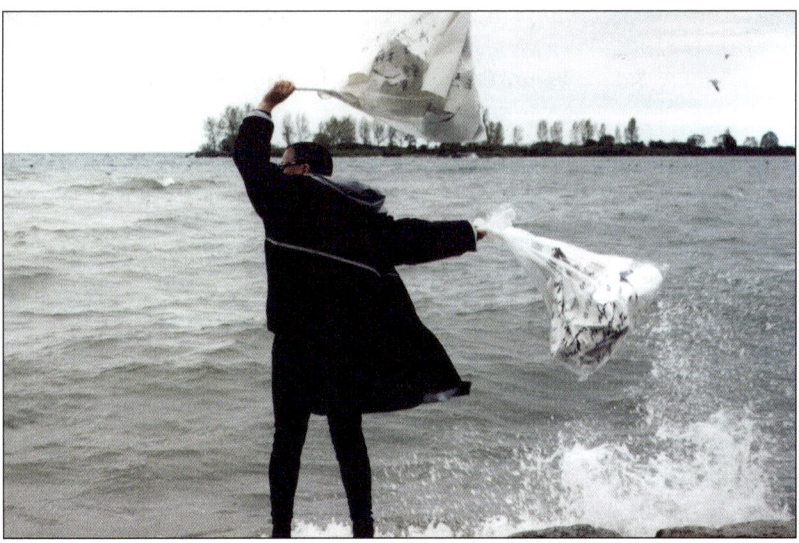

Hands on Environs, 2002

On January 7, 1880, Emile Zola finished his novel, *Nana*. His intention was to use *Nana,* in a series, to follow, scientifically, the effects of heredity and environment on a family. I used his deathbed description of his character Nana as spoken text for this performance. In his foreword, Zola theorizes woman as carrier of disease and destruction through the generations (12). Is this the woman, I ask, who bears the children, the mother?

WORKS CITED

Jones, Amelia and Andrew Stephenson, eds. *Performing the Body, Performing the Text*. London: Routledge, 1999.

Lorde, Audre. *Sister Outsider.* Freedom, CA: Crossing, 1984.

Patterson, Pam. *The Birth Project*. Patterson. *Birthtales*. A Space Gallery, Toronto, 1992.

Patterson, Pam. *Mapping the Familial*. Visual Arts Centre of Newcastle, Bowmanville, ON, 1993.

Patterson, Pam. "Threads in a Tightly Woven Fabric: An Artist's Narrative Re/Weaving." Master's paper. Ontario Institute for Studies in Education: Toronto, 1993.

Patterson, Pam. *Mapping the Familial*. Annex Art Centre, Toronto, 1994.

Patterson, Pam. *The Birth Project*. *The C.H.I.L.D. Project*, Exhibition at Gallery Gatchet, Vancouver, 1995.

Patterson, Pam. *Hands on Environs*. *Breathworks,* Waterfront Trail Artists, Toronto, 2002. 12-13.

Patterson, Pam. *Canc(H)er*. *Collisions 2006*, University of Victoria, Victoria, 2006. Performance.

Zola, Emile. *Nana*. Trans. George Holden. London: Penguin, 1972.

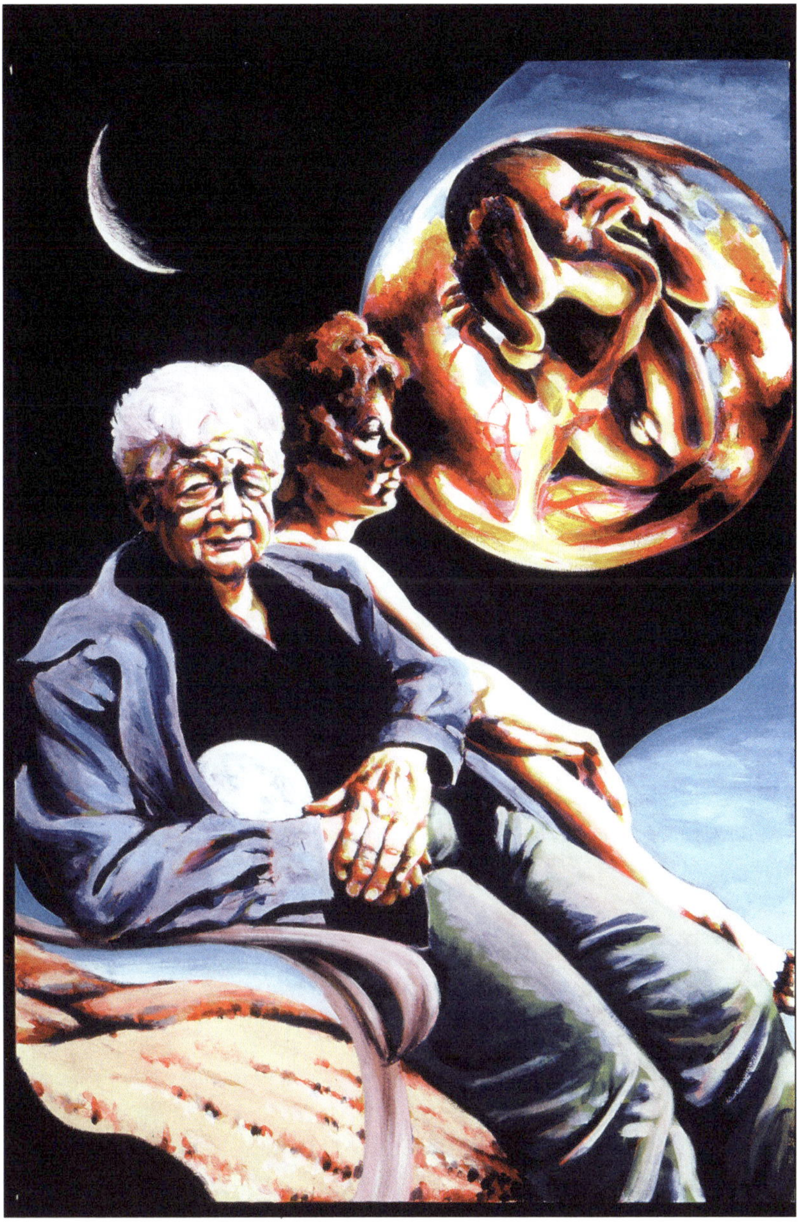

Carol Wylie, *Culmination*, 2003, acrylic on canvas, 100 x 72 cm.

This piece references generations in literal terms, but metaphorically, it's also about the cycles in one woman's life. We gather experience and wisdom, and grow older in some aspects, but if we continually seek knowledge and improvement, we perpetually end up back at the beginning of something that is new to us.

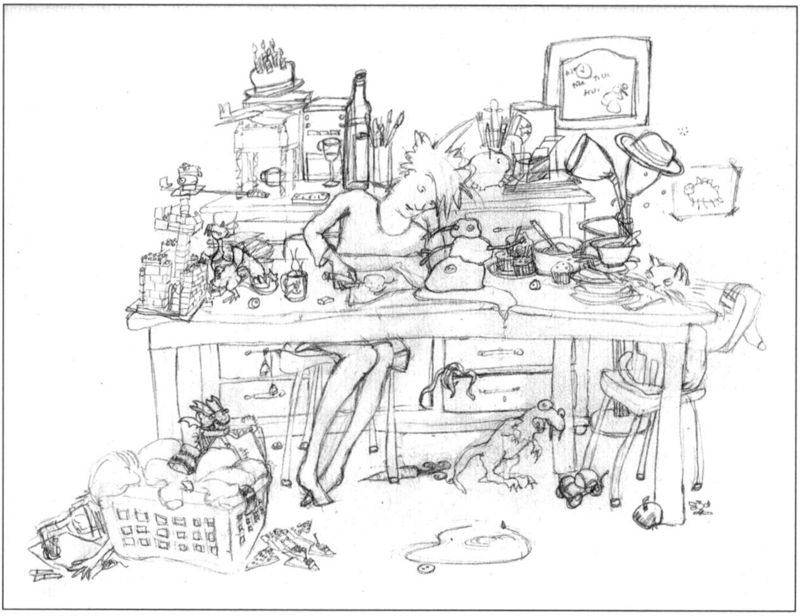

Margaret Bessai, *Self-portrait of the Artist in the Studio: It is essential, though not always easy, to draw from life…*, 2009, pencil on paper, 35.56 x 43.18 cm.

Historically, artists created "self-portraits" to practice their craft, advertise their ability, and record their place in history. Since the advent of photography, the self-portrait has increasingly become a vehicle for exploring identity. I started this self-portrait to record what I thought was a struggle for balance in my home/workplace, faithfully drawing the situation in my dining room. Upon reflection, I see no separate categories of "life" and "work" to balance. My life informs my work and my work is what I do in my daily life.

CHALLENGING

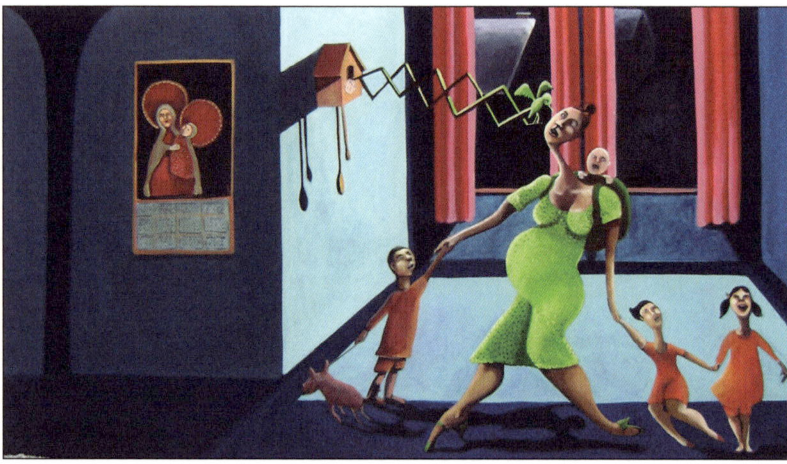

Maria Lezon, *Cuckoo Time*, 2007, acrylic on canvas, 185 x 100 cm.

This piece belongs to a series of 23 paintings titled *The Dangers of Motherhood* (2007). The work depicts the untold stories, taboo subjects and secretive ideas that cross the mind of a contemporary woman who happens to be a mother. *Cuckoo Time* reminds us of that time of the day when you just go nuts.

Devenir mère de jumelles

Toute une aventure

VALÉRIE VÉZINA

Bon matin les filles
Restez bien dans votre coquille
Jusqu'au jour dit
Où vous viendrez à la vie

Je vous vois perchées là
Votre cœur qui bat
Vos yeux qui s'ouvrent
Attendez s.v.p. que je m'ouvre.

LE SEUL MOT qui me vient en ce jour glacial, c'est «désillusion». Celle de voir mon couple tomber en miettes. Peut-on souffler sur les braises d'un amour usé par sept ans de vie commune ?

On connaît le refrain de la transformation parentale: moins de temps pour soi, moins d'intimité partagée, l'intendance qui prend presque toute la place... «Qu'est-ce qu'on mange ce soir?»; «Peux-tu acheter du pain s'il te plaît?»; «Est-ce qu'on inscrit les filles à des cours de danse ou on réessaie la natation même si l'an dernier elles n'arrêtaient pas de geindre à la fin des cours et qu'il fallait sortir de l'eau avant tout le monde ?»

Abnégation: «Sacrifice volontaire de soi-même, de son intérêt ».[1] Tiens, je pense à Patrick en écrivant ce mot. Lui ne s'exprime pas autant que moi, et je pense qu'il s'est beaucoup oublié depuis trois ans. Mais je ne voudrais pas mettre le père de mes enfants mal à l'aise avec mes confidences, alors revenons à ma maternité.

Plus jeune je me disais que la maternité allait certainement m'enrichir. Je pensais à l'expérience du lien filial, mais pas qu'à cela. À l'époque j'étais photographe et convaincue que la maternité, un jour, m'apporterait quelque chose de spécial, comme une sensibilité nouvelle qui changerait mon regard et, par-delà l'objectif, ma façon de prendre des photos.

Aujourd'hui, je constate qu'en plus de deux enfants en santé, la vie m'a donné ce cadeau inestimable, inestimable dans tout ce qu'il recèle de mystérieux et de curieux pour le commun des mortels: la gémellité. C'est fascinant, épuisant, gratifiant. Élever des jumelles, c'est multiplier par deux les moments de grâce et les difficultés logistiques.

IL Y EN A DEUX!

J'étais étendue dans une clinique de fertilité quand j'ai appris la nouvelle. (Je n'y avais pas suivi de traitement, non, ma grossesse était le fruit du hasard.) J'ai vu deux petits ronds blancs sur un écran.

«Ces deux petits ronds vont changer ta vie, mais tu n'as aucune idée à quel point».

La technicienne en échographie m'avait fait sourire en me lançant tout de go: «C'est aujourd'hui qu'on va voir s'il y en a deux». M'avait-elle devinée ou quoi? Mon ventre n'était pas si arrondi pourtant. Elle avait probablement dit cela par habitude; des grossesses multiples, elle devait en déceler souvent.

En silence, elle a fait zigue-zaguer son appareil sur mon ventre. Glisse à gauche. À droite. En haut. En bas. Encore en haut. Enfin, je l'ai vue sourire: «Oui» dit-elle.

«Oui quoi?» ai-je demandé.

«Il y en a deux!»

Patrick fixait alors l'écran, bouche bée. J'avais bien vu ces deux espèces de «tâches» blanches, je croyais que c'était la tête et l'abdomen d'un bébé. Il y en avait donc deux? Vraiment? Moi qui avais dit devant témoins, à une fête de famille quelques semaines auparavant, que je souhaitais avoir des jumeaux, je voyais mon vœu exaucé! Je n'en revenais pas.

J'ai éclaté de rire.

Il nous a fallu repasser aussitôt à la caisse pour payer le double tarif. Sans blague. Ainsi donc a commencé notre aventure—avec un supplément à payer!

Depuis ce jour-là je flotte sur le nuage maternel. J'ai rêvé de jumeaux. J'ai été enceinte de jumelles. J'ai accouché de jumelles monozygotes. Prématurées. En santé. Et j'élève deux filles, en essayant de faire du mieux que je peux.

LA GROSSESSE GÉMELLAIRE

Moi l'ex-photographe avide de nouvelles expériences, j'ai eu le privilège de voir les «photographies» de bébé numéro un et bébé numéro deux—ainsi nommés par le personnel médical—une bonne quinzaine de fois lors d'autant d'échographies. J'ai assisté semaine après semaine à l'évolution de ces deux petits êtres. J'ai développé une relation bienveillante avec quelques membres du GAR (département des «grossesses à risques») de l'hôpital Sainte-Justine. Moi la journaliste curieuse, j'ai vu une batterie de spécialistes se pencher sur mon cas. Quelle chance!

Si j'ai eu droit à un suivi médical serré, c'est parce que je souffrais du syndrome transfuseur-transfusé.[2] C'est là condition d'un placenta défectueux. Pour une raison inconnue, le placenta se met à fournir un apport sanguin inégal aux fœtus. Conséquences? Résumons grossièrement. L'un reçoit moins de nutriments que l'autre. Sa croissance stagne. L'autre se développe allègrement parce qu'il reçoit plus que sa «juste part» de nourriture, mais il présente éventuellement des problèmes cardiaques, et en occupant plus d'espace dans l'utérus, le «gros bébé» met de la pression sur le «petit».

S'il n'est pas traité, le syndrome transfuseur-transfusé s'avère mortel pour les fœtus dans 90% des cas. Ainsi donc, à 17 semaines, j'ai dû séjourner à Toronto pour être opérée[3], faute de quoi la vie des mes deux filles aurait été sérieusement compromise.

L'opération a porté ses fruits du jour au lendemain !

Pour éloigner le risque principal d'une grossesse gémellaire (un accouchement avant terme), il ne me restait plus qu'à me reposer. Du moins, c'est ce que je croyais…

Au fil des mois, j'avais pris 58 livres. À la fin du sixième, ces notes griffonnées dans mon journal auraient dû me mettre la puce à l'oreille: «J'ai une soif d'eau démesurée; je bois au moins deux litres (de liquide par jour), des jus, thé au jasmin, etc. Mes pieds sont plus gros. Je suis à l'étroit dans mes bottes! La fatigue est plus prononcée».

Dix jours plus tard, ma mère a remarqué mon visage et mes doigts boursoufflés. Lors d'un examen de routine, ma gynécologue-obstétricienne a constaté ma pression anormalement élevée et la présence de protéines dans mes urines—deux symptômes de prééclampsie. L'enflure et la fatigue ne découlaient donc pas de ma grossesse gémellaire comme je le pensais, mais de la prééclampsie. J'ai dû être hospitalisée sur-le-champ. «Mais les lits des bébés ne sont pas encore faits!», ai-je songé avec anxiété. J'accoucherais par césarienne deux jours après ce diagnostic inattendu, mais cela, je ne le savais pas encore.

Durant l'année 2005-2006, près d'un bébé sur 16 (6,1%) né dans les hôpitaux canadiens était de faible poids, pesant moins de 2 500 grammes (ou 5,5 livres), selon le Canadian Institute for Health Information (CIHI) (Lawand et Hollingsworth). Mes filles font partie de ces statistiques. Erica pesait seulement 4,08 livres à sa naissance, à 33 semaines. Charlotte, née une minute plus tard, pesait 5,04 livres.

Les deux ont eu des troubles respiratoires. Mais avec le recul, l'arrivée au monde de mes jumelles a été couronnée de succès.

Le plus difficile? Physiquement, l'installation d'une sonde urinaire. Psychiquement, cette impression bizarre, un peu irréelle, de se trouver soudainement parent sans avoir de poupon à bercer chez soi… Car leurs trois premières semaines de vie, Erica et Charlotte les ont passées à l'hôpital, d'abord à l'Unité de soins intensifs, puis à l'Unité de soins intermédiaires où on les gavait de lait à l'aide d'un tube inséré par la bouche jusque dans leur estomac. (Pour des prématurés, le gavage est moins fatigant qu'un boire au sein ou au biberon.)

De mon côté, les premières 24 heures suivant la césarienne, j'ai souffert de démangeaisons sur tout le corps à cause d'un médicament qu'on avait dû m'injecter. Alitée dans une salle sombre, placée sous la surveillance, je n'ai pu en sortir que quelques minutes pour aller voir mes enfants. Comme j'avais hâte de les prendre dans mes bras! Ce bonheur devait attendre.

Une fois transférée dans une chambre, j'étais terrorisée à l'idée qu'on retire ma sonde. Le retrait s'est finalement bien déroulé, cependant mon réflexe de miction s'est bloqué. La vessie sur le point d'exploser, je tentais d'uriner sans y arriver; la peur d'avoir mal m'en empêchait ... jusqu'à ce qu'une infirmière pleine d'empathie me propose l'idée ingénieuse de prendre un bain de siège chaud. Alléluia! Voilà sans doute une anecdote sans intérêt, sauf peut-être pour celles qui sont passées par là. Dans le même registre anecdotique, j'ai eu droit à la familiarité d'une autre infirmière qui m'appelait «Maman» à tout bout de champ. Certes j'étais devenue maman, mais pas la sienne que je sache. C'était de la petite bière tout ça.

En 2005, une bactérie mortelle circulait dans cet hôpital, causant la mort d'au moins quatre poupons. Heureusement, ni Erica, ni Charlotte n'ont été infectées.

DEUX BÉBÉS EN MÊME TEMPS ET LA LOGISTIQUE QUE CELA IMPLIQUE

Le 21 février 2005 a commencé une routine quotidienne menant le père et moi-même au chevet de nos filles dès le petit matin. Patrick partait travailler ensuite et revenait à l'hôpital en après-midi, puis une troisième fois en soirée, tandis que je me reposais pour favoriser ma production de lait. Au début, j'allais m'allonger dans une chambre louée au service d'hébergement de l'hôpital. Celle-ci a rapidement fait place à un endroit jugé plus chaleureux, situé à moins de six kilomètres de là: à la maison. Je tirais mon lait entourée de bouteilles d'eau. Cette période a été marquée par l'inquiétude (Charlotte faisait du tirage, les deux étaient suivies en cardiologie...) et l'apprentissage progressif des soins à prodiguer, comme les premiers bains, que Patrick a donnés... Le premier kangourou—l'enfant blotti entre les seins, en contact direct avec notre peau—dans une chaise berçante de fortune installée à côté des incubateurs... La première mise au sein...

Cinq jours après l'accouchement, à la mi-février 2005, la conseillère en allaitement de l'hôpital m'a prescrit huit stimulations quotidiennes au tire-lait électrique—aux 3 heures! Du 22 au 24 février, c'était aux deux heures. Ma première montée laiteuse mettra deux bonnes semaines à se produire. «Avez-vous des prothèses mammaires?», m'a demandé en désespoir de cause cette «pistonneuse» en chef. Mon air ahuri disait tout; mon corps n'était tout simplement pas prêt: «La production augmente (enfin) le 25 février 2005 (environ 30 ml). La nature fait bien les choses: ma production de lait augmente alors que je me sens un peu moins fatiguée, comme si le corps avait eu besoin de se rétablir d'abord».[4]

Les premières fois se sont ainsi succédées. J'ai ressenti une vive émotion la première fois que le personnel de l'Unité de soins intermédiaires nous a invités à vêtir nos petites d'un pyjama taille «P» («preemies»). Elles étaient reliées à leur incubateur respectif par plusieurs fils. Une fois leur état jugé suffisamment stable, libérées de ces fils, elles ont été transférées à la pouponnière. Là, quand j'ai vu le visage rougi d'un de mes bébés en train de s'étouffer après un boire trop généreux donné par l'infirmière de service, j'ai eu ma première frousse maternelle.

Enfin, il y a eu la première sortie à l'air frais, nos deux minuscules paquets emmitouflés sur la banquette arrière. «Ne roule pas vite», ai-je ordonné au papa.

Sur le chemin du retour à la maison, j'ai réalisé ce qu'était la «responsabilité parentale»: nous avions désormais deux trésors dont il fallait prendre le plus grand soin.

Mes sentiments à l'égard de Charlotte et Erica ont rapidement pris beaucoup de place, grugeant peut-être même un peu—trop?—l'espace de mes sentiments réservés à Patrick.

J'ai souvent lu que les nouvelles mères, pleines de tendresse à l'égard de leur petit et tout occupées à bâtir ce lien d'attachement si précieux avec lui, sont ainsi comblées. Sous-entendu: elles ne recherchent plus autant l'affection de leur partenaire...

Ainsi je m'attendris et je m'interroge en me relisant:

> J'adore ces instants 'bénis' où je prends l'une d'entre vous sur moi, le soir, en relaxant sur le canapé. Ou encore sur le matelas double (temporairement posé sur le sol du *den*, cette pièce dédiée à la relaxation). Charlotte, Erica, chacune se love sur ma poitrine, à plat ventre, vos mains pendent de chaque côté de moi, vous êtes complètement abandonnées, votre petite tête s'enfonçant dans le sillon entre mes deux seins. Votre respiration va et vient dans un monde imaginaire qui est le vôtre, lâchant parfois un petit murmure aigu ... comme un chat![5]

Ma «lune de miel» a duré de l'âge de quatre à six mois. Avant quatre mois, je ne me souviens pas de grand-chose. Sauf d'une impression d'irréalité («Nous avons fait ça !»), d'une grande fatigue attribuable à l'allaitement (mixte) et ... des coliques. Heureusement que Patrick se réveillait la nuit pour faire boire les petites, j'étais trop de mauvaise humeur pour bien le faire, nuit après nuit. Je lui dois une fière chandelle pour cet exploit. Quand je parlais d'abnégation....

Imaginez le lait à donner (3 500 biberons la première année!), les couches à changer, le nez à nettoyer soir et matin (prescription de la pédiatre), les suppléments de fer à administrer, les pleurs à décrypter parfois et, le meilleur, les câlins à donner. Je balançais la chaise longue du pied quand l'une pleurait, tenant l'autre dans mes bras. Pour moi, c'était très important de prendre chaque enfant durant le boire. J'ai dû abandonner mon projet d'allaiter les deux simultanément. (Oui, oui, c'est possible! Cela a l'air facile dans les livres. Seulement dans les livres.)

J'ai eu beaucoup d'aide: Patrick, mère, belle-mère, amies, grandes tantes et, dans une bien moindre mesure, l'auxiliaire du CLSC (Centre local de services communautaires) venue quelques fois chez nous pour peser les petites, stériliser leurs biberons, plier du linge. Elle m'a sensibilisée à l'importance de maintenir un horaire régulier. Cette routine quotidienne nous permettait de synchroniser autant que faire se peut les boires et périodes d'éveil. Et en échange d'un tarif horaire qui valait son pesant d'or, une puéricultrice est venue prendre le relais quelques semaines durant, de 23 heures à sept heures, deux nuits par semaine.

Le premier été des filles a été exceptionnellement chaud et je profitais des belles journées ensoleillées pour aller m'étendre avec elles au parc Laurier, majestueusement pourvu de grands feuillus sous lesquels j'étendais une couverture.

De six mois à 12 mois, je me souviens: des pleurs fréquents (dont je n'identifiais pas toujours la cause); de la volonté des deux bébés de se mouvoir, ce qui entraînait par moments leur frustration, faute d'y arriver; et d'interminables promenades avec une poussette double dans les rues et les parcs de mon quartier (pour peut-être calmer les pleurs). C'est durant cette période que j'ai trouvé Carmen, une gardienne, par l'entremise d'une petite annonce. Cette retraitée avait jadis pris soin de ses deux frères cadets, des jumeaux. Trouver une gardienne m'obsédait, aussi ai-je été soulagée de dénicher cette perle rare.

Doublement maman et heureuse de l'être, j'ai commencé à me sentir tendue au deuxième semestre de la première année, notamment chaque fois que j'entendais l'une de mes filles me réclamer du salon en pleurant, pendant que j'étais en train de langer l'autre dans la salle de bains. Des pleurs auxquels ma nature me dictait de répondre vite, mais impossible: j'avais les mains pleines. Chaque sonnerie de téléphone m'horripilait d'ailleurs pour cette raison.

Chaque enfant a besoin de sa mère, néanmoins elle ne peut se scinder!

Être parent de multiples, c'est accepter d'être unique et de n'avoir que deux bras pour s'occuper de plus que ça.

Lorsque j'allais me promener seule avec les deux, j'en emmenais une dans un porte-bébé, l'autre dans une poussette simple. Ou j'utilisais la poussette double. Ou, plus rarement, la voiture.

Être mère de multiples, c'est aussi faire le deuil d'activités banales pour d'autres mères, telle une randonnée de ski de fond. L'achat ou même la location d'un traîneau double n'en aurait pas valu la peine pour un seul hiver: traîner les deux serait vite devenu trop lourd pour moi. Je les ai bien tractées à vélo, mais avec un succès mitigé; la remorque étant basse et peu visible des voitures, il fallait être doublement prudent en ville, sans compter que mes filles, collées l'une sur l'autre, passaient leur temps à se chamailler là-dedans. Bonjour la relaxation... Et que dire des cours de natation exigeant un accompagnateur *par* enfant?

En somme, pour prendre soin de jumeaux, il faut deux choses: de l'organisation et de l'aide. Beaucoup d'aide. Paires de bras supplémentaires, entretien ménager, repas congelés, n'importe quoi! Erica et Charlotte sont allées en «escapade» chez leurs grands-parents paternels, une à la fois, puis ensemble, encore et encore. Je ne pourrais pas les en remercier assez. C'est le meilleur répit dont on puisse rêver!

LA PETITE ENFANCE DES JUMELLES, DEUX «TERRIBLE TWOS» SIMULTANÉS

À 18 mois, mes enfants ont pris l'avion avec les parents de Patrick, lui et moi, direction la Provence. Que de beaux souvenirs! «Gogoga» voulait dire «escargot». Il y avait aussi le «r» qu'elles roulaient dans «marron».... Des vacances délicieuses à tous points de vue.

Si la période suivant l'acquisition de la marche a été très joyeuse, il a fallu redoubler de vigilance. L'une pouvait capter mon attention pendant que sa jumelle faisait une bêtise, ou se blessait. Charlotte a déjà déboulé l'escalier (sans conséquence heureusement). Le parc a dû être rapproché de l'entrée afin que je puisse y déposer une petite en sécurité pendant que je détachais l'autre de son siège d'auto.

Pour éviter que la sieste ne tourne à la fête, nous devions mettre une jumelle au lit et attendre qu'elle ferme l'œil, avant de coucher sa sœur dans la même chambre. Complices, elles pouvaient discuter, sauter sur leur matelas pendant des heures, renverser de connivence leur jus, se mordre mutuellement lorsqu'elles se disputaient un jouet. Certains jours, j'avais très hâte que Carmen arrive!

Le 10 avril 2007, à deux ans, premier jour à la garderie. Ma vie a basculé. Je pouvais écrire dans un silence absolu, les enfants ayant déserté la maison. D'abord deux jours par semaine, puis trois. La fin de l'esclavage, si j'ose dire.

J'idéalisais la vie de mère à la maison. Cette vie est faite de tendres moments. De bricolages précoces. De regards charmants. De lenteur. En revanche, j'ai vécu aussi le désarroi et la colère, par exemple quand mes enfants refusaient net de faire leur sieste de l'après-midi. J'ai compris que pour favoriser leur détente, je devais faire l'effort de les emmener dehors. En dépit de cela, elles ne voulaient pas toujours s'endormir par la suite. Conséquence: je n'aurais pas les deux, trois, voire quatre prochaines heures à moi comme je m'y étais habituée. En plus j'aurais à endurer l'humeur progressivement maussade de deux trottineuses manifestement fatiguées mais refusant d'écouter leur corps (ou n'ayant pas encore développé cette capacité).

Unique solution, arrivée fin 2006: les DVDs de Passe-Partout! (Cette série d'émissions pour enfants d'âge préscolaire a été développée par le Ministère de l'Éducation du Québec.) Depuis, Charlotte est souvent tombée dans les bras de Morphée en milieu d'après-midi devant Cannelle, Pruneau et compagnie. Quant à Erica, déjà à 1 an, il lui arrivait de ronfler dans sa chaise haute avant même d'avoir avalé une bouchée de son repas. Son insatiable curiosité l'a souvent empêchée de trouver le repos. Il fallait alors cesser toute stimulation, lui infuser une bonne «dose» de calme ... par l'exemple. Pas facile.

Un jour que je devais terminer un texte dans mon bureau, à l'étage, l'une des tantes de Patrick a offert de venir les garder. Mes filles étaient tellement contentes de la revoir et de jouer avec elle qu'il était impossible d'envisager les mettre au lit à 13 heures. Vers 17 heures, n'entendant plus un bruit, je suis descendue à la cuisine. Qu'est-ce que j'ai vu ? Charlotte étendue de tout son long, sur le plancher (!), près de l'escalier menant au salon et, en contrebas, Erica, endormie quant à elle sur le sofa, immobile aux côtés de la tante en question qui m'a souri en haussant les épaules. Leur corps avait eu raison cette fois-là de leur enthousiasme délirant de jumelles.

Malgré mes bonnes intentions, je ne réussis pas toujours à être une mère calme, patiente et raisonnée. Le 2 janvier 2008, Erica tentait de passer le cordon dans les anses de sa botte d'hiver. Elle voulait bien sûr y arriver toute seule. Je l'encourageais souvent à être autonome, mais passer le cordon *correctement*—j'insiste sur ce mot parce cela dénote cet indécrottable perfectionnisme si souvent associé aux mamans d'aujourd'hui—elle n'en était pas capable... Pas encore. Et tandis qu'elle essayait, je stressais en voyant l'heure filer: «Il faut partir à la garderie, là, plus de temps à perdre!» Je me sentais pressée, il fallait en finir avec cet habillage infernal, la salopette, les bottes, le passe-montagne, la tuque, le manteau, les mitaines, sans oublier les sacs à lunch. «Maman, je veux pas mettre mes mitaines». D'accord, ne mets pas tes mitaines! Vingt minutes et une sainte colère plus tard, une fois rendues à la garderie, nous sommes descendues de voiture au beau milieu d'un banc de neige aussi haut qu'elles. Erica s'est mise à pleurnicher. Elle venait de se mouiller les mains dans la neige…

Je m'adapte peu à peu à mon rôle de mère, même si celui d'amoureuse a pris le bord. M'adapter, c'est respirer par le nez quand de tels incidents se produisent, ne plus bouillir d'impatience. Il m'arrive de crier si l'une ou l'autre de mes chéries n'obéit pas. Parfois je pleure aussi.

Vite ensuite, je reprends mes esprits et je réconforte aussitôt l'enfant grondé. Évidemment, je me culpabilise d'avoir ainsi perdu le contrôle. Je sais que de voir sa maman perdre ainsi la carte ne doit pas être très rassurant pour l'enfant, hélas! La mère est supposée être le guide, le rempart, l'exemple, la solidité, la confiance, la main tendue—pour prendre tendrement celle de l'enfant, pas la taper!

Mes filles avaient deux ans et demi quand j'ai eu le mandat de réviser la traduction française de dépliants destinés aux parents pour un organisme de la Saskatchewan. Ces textes disaient, entre autres, «réagissez et répondez calmement, gentiment et chaleureusement aux besoins de votre enfant» et «le parent parfait n'existe pas». Cela tombait tellement à propos!

Dans la voiture, après l'épisode des lacets, tout en conduisant, j'ai dit calmement à mes filles que j'étais très en colère, que je regrettais d'avoir crié. Charlotte m'a dit: «Tout à l'heure, je vais donner un bisou à maman». Cela m'est allé droit au cœur. Même pas trois ans, et elle a répondu à la violence par l'amour. De quoi me réconforter, et me déculpabiliser un peu aussi. Mais je vous entends déjà juger: ce n'est pas à l'enfant de rassurer, c'est au parent qu'incombe ce rôle. Je vous entends et je vous donne raison.

C'est ça être maman: apprendre «sur le tas», par essais et erreurs, en ne culpabilisant pas trop.

Après avoir confié mon désarroi à ma mère, chose qui m'a fait le plus grand bien ce jour-là, je me suis dit que c'était à moi d'accepter le caractère de mes filles, pas à elles de le mouler conformément à mes attentes. Et pour la petite histoire, ma belle-sœur a refilé à Erica les bottes à Velcro du cousin. (Charlotte en possédait déjà, ce qui était injuste pour Erica.)

Parfois, il ne faut pas grand-chose pour faire le bonheur d'un enfant (et de son parent), voilà l'une des leçons que j'ai apprises depuis trois ans. Par exemple, j'adore lire des histoires. De jour comme de soir, cela relaxe mes enfants. Aussi je le fais souvent. Cela m'aide à me calmer les nerfs.

Saviez-vous qu'il existe en Suède, pays considéré par ailleurs l'un des meilleurs au monde pour élever des enfants, des cours destinés aux parents qui veulent s'améliorer? La proportion de parents suédois inscrits à des classes d'éducation parentale est passée de 2% en 2004 à 7% en 2007, selon l'Institut national suédois de santé publique («À l'école des parents» 5). Ce qui motive principalement les participants ? Les disputes ou le manque d'autorité à la maison….

Des disputes, Patrick et moi en avons eu, tellement que nous nous sommes séparés avant le troisième anniversaire de notre petite famille. La communication faisait cruellement défaut entre nous deux.

Seule, je suis plus détendue avec mes filles. La routine du coucher est plutôt bien rodée. Par conséquent, elles s'endorment rapidement le soir. C'est toujours ça de gagné.

Je me réjouis de leurs progrès incomparables dans toutes sortes de domaines: le développement psychomoteur, la résolution de problèmes (elles adorent les casse-têtes) et, surtout, le langage. Elles font des phrases complètes et plutôt complexes depuis quelques mois déjà et je m'étonne presque chaque jour désormais d'un raisonnement nouveau, d'une permission gentiment demandée, avec *s.v.p.* et *merci* à la clé, ou d'un geste généreux que l'une fait pour l'autre, comme lui apporter son doudou sans que l'autre l'ait demandé.

Plus obéissantes qu'à deux ans et demi, elles se chamaillent moins. Les morsures sont depuis belle lurette terminées. Le jeu coopératif a commencé: elles négocient ensemble pour avoir le même jouet.

J'évite d'encourager la rivalité entre elles.

Chacune a ses préférences et son tempérament bien à elle. Elles ont le même ADN mais l'interprétation de cet ADN est différente, ce qui explique qu'elles n'aient pas leurs grains de beauté aux mêmes endroits, par exemple. Fait cocasse, elles ont percé leur première dent le même jour!

Au resto l'autre jour, Charlotte mangeait des sushis. Avec des baguettes! Et elle s'amusait à nourrir sa sœur... Retour d'ascenseur? En tout cas la scène m'a émue. Dans mon ventre, c'était Erica qui «donnait» de la nourriture à sa sœur.

LA « MATERNITÉ GÉMELLAIRE»

M: merveilleuse
A: aventure
T: tendresse
E: enseignement
R: réconfort
N: nourriture (dans tous les sens du terme)
I: indulgence
T: travail
É: énergivore

G: grâce
É: équipage
M: mystérieuse
E: expérience
L: lien

L: logistique
A: affection
I: individualité
R: relation impénétrable
E: enflure!

À 34 ans, je suis au mitan de la vie de ma mère, qui en a 68.

Je pense à elle. On ne peut pas faire autrement quand on entre dans le club des mamans. C'est peut-être naturel, peut-être pas, mais pour moi une chose est sûre: être maman, c'est un «métier» qui s'apprend de mère en fille.

L'autre matin, au déjeuner, j'étais abasourdie de m'entendre dire: «Un kiwi, c'est plein de vitamine C». Exactement les mêmes mots qu'elle disait en me servant une orange, ou était-ce un demi-pamplemousse? Ma mémoire me fait défaut, mais mon inconscient se rappelle, lui. Comme il se rappelle des mots doux, des caresses dans les cheveux… Ma mère enroulait une mèche autour de son doigt et tournait doucement quand je posais ma tête contre elle devant la télé. Mon inconscient se rappelle d'un amour et d'une tendresse infinies, que j'ai le bonheur de goûter encore aujourd'hui. À preuve ce courriel qu'elle vient de m'envoyer:

> Bonjour Valérie,
>
> J'espère que tu vas mieux de ta grippe. Il faut te remettre en forme au moins physiquement, si ce n'est émotivement ou affectivement.
>
> C'est bien dommage que vous vous soyez perdus de vue Patrick et toi. Il doit bien y avoir un moyen d'analyser tout ce qui vous allumait mutuellement, et qui s'est assombri.
>
> En sachant ce qui fait défaut, peut-être serait-il possible de corriger les comportements.
>
> Le pire est passé pour ce qui est des petites, elles deviennent plus raisonnables maintenant.
>
> Je pourrai aller chez toi jeudi, si cela te convient. Donne-moi des nouvelles. Bonne journée, mes bonnes pensées t'accompagnent.
>
> Michelle xx

Que puis-je ajouter à une telle démonstration d'amour maternel? Un amour disponible, généreux, réconfortant. Un amour qui fait du bien.

ÉPILOGUE

Eh bien, ce jeudi-là, ma mère a apporté le dîner. Nous l'avons mangé toutes les quatre ensemble. Erica et Charlotte étaient heureuses de revoir leur mamie Miche et je l'ai serrée fort dans mes bras sur le pas de la porte avant qu'elle ne retourne vaquer à ses occupations.

Assise dans la salle de jeux après son départ, j'étais perdue dans mes pensées, fixant les petits personnages *Little People* que mes amours avaient disposés en cercle «pour faire une ronde».

Cette entrepreneure m'a mise au monde, nourrie, éduquée, consolée, souri. Elle m'a regardée danser, patiner, plonger, elle m'a vue jouer au théâtre, encouragée à devenir journaliste. A-t-elle pensé une seconde avec amertume qu'elle manquerait ce matin un café avec une amie, une rencontre avec un client?

L'oubli de soi, dit-elle. Pour elle ... pas pour moi. N'empêche, elle m'a montré comment faire et maintenant, c'est à mon tour de transmettre à mes filles son amour en héritage.

Merci, Maman!

[1]Définition du dictionaire *Le Petit Robert.*

[2]Je renvoie les lecteurs et lectrices à l'histoire de ma grossesse compliquée, décrite en détail dans le numéro d'octobre 2007 de *Sélection du Reader's Digest.*

[3]Ce traitement, appelé foetoscopie au laser, est maintenant dispensé à Montréal.

[4]Extrait de mon journal.

[5]Extrait de mon journal.

OUVRAGES CITÉS

«À l'école des parents». *La Presse, cahier actuel* (14 janvier 2008): 5.

Lawand, Christina et Leona Hollingsworth. «Number of Low Birth Weight Babies Rising in Canada.» <http: //secure.cihi.ca/disPage.jsp?cw_page=media25jul2007_e>. 25 juillet 2007.

Bare Life ("technologies of tenderness")

SUSAN SHANTZ

AUGUST 2007. I have just returned from an international exhibition of art in Germany—Documenta 12—that occurs every five years. Ten years ago I traveled to the same art show when I was two months pregnant with my son. He is now nine-and-a-half and staying with his other mother in Vancouver. On my final day at Documenta, I climbed the hill above the baroque museum (a former castle), towards the Herkules monument at the top. I wanted to see a temporary, outdoor photo installation by American social documentary artist, Alan Sekula. Billboard-size images climbed the hill alongside the steep staircase. They were images of workers—office, blue-collar labourers. Halfway up the hill, I stopped in surprise beside one of the huge photos—it was almost identical to a small snapshot I have at home of myself and my son a week after his birth.

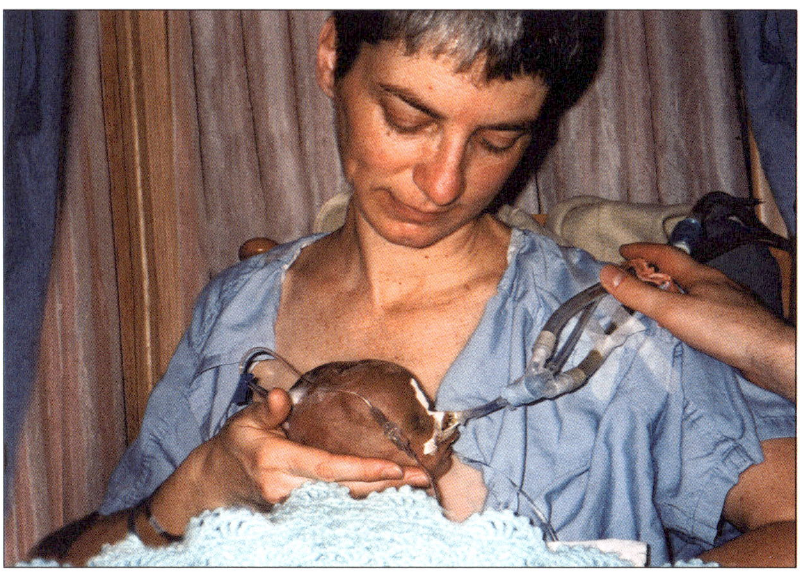

Sekula's billboard shows a Caucasian mother holding a scrawny, dark-skinned infant against her chest, the baby supported by tubes and monitors. The snapshot I have documents the first day I was able to hold my premature son after his birth by emergency caesarean, his skin darkened by the effects of extreme jaundice. After a week of incubators and oxygen, x-rays and blood tests, punctures and scans—all the technologies I had hoped to avoid with my planned home birth—I was finally able to hold my child. I held him, his other mother held him, his father held him, his grandparents and aunts and uncles held him—all those who had been called in to meet him on what was possibly the last day of his small life.

Seeing Alan Sekula's billboard photograph of another mother in a similar situation stopped me still on my ascent. In the past decade, I have never seen a post-natal photograph like my own, and certainly not this large and in such a public site. My photos, and most likely those of other mothers whose children began life in traumatic circumstances, are filed away, part of private memory, not public discourse.

The curator of Documenta 12 had posed three questions in selecting artwork for his show, the second of which was: "Life! What is bare life?" Human vulnerability was addressed by a number of artists in the exhibition, the curator's focus being on the lives of individuals (refugees, detainees) caught between political and social systems of protection. "Bare life," for me, also pointed to the state of human fragility that is birth, which, if all does not go according to our safe planning, exposes the most vulnerable human being to pain and loss.

technologies of tenderness is a body of mixed-media artwork that came about in response to the events of my son's birth and ensuing first years of life. The happy-healthy versions of mother-infant bonding that surrounded me left me feeling alienated: I had been unable to protect my son. His doll-sized hospital clothes—a sleeper, a hat, socks, mitts and diapers—were the starting point for silhouette drawings of his post-natal paraphernalia. Added to these: a miniature blood-pressure cuff and tiny hearing aids. These simplified shapes became a vocabulary of words that I used repeatedly as cut-outs—solitary holes floating in crib-sized rectangles of dark grey aluminum (*crib i-vi*), or lifting like puzzle pieces out of the grid of incubator-sized panels (*intensive care*). The small sleeper/body appears reflected in a mirror as an outline of sharp pin-points in *virtual angel.*

Pins into paper, laser saw cuts in wood and metal, holes drilled into Plexiglas, photographic contact prints of my son's day-old x-rays (*acute care*)—my art processes of marking, marring, scraping, and pressing the surfaces of materials evoke the technologies that impacted his infant body. My attempts to counter these with maternal tenderness—to touch, to hold—were also directed by the technologies of therapies— to move

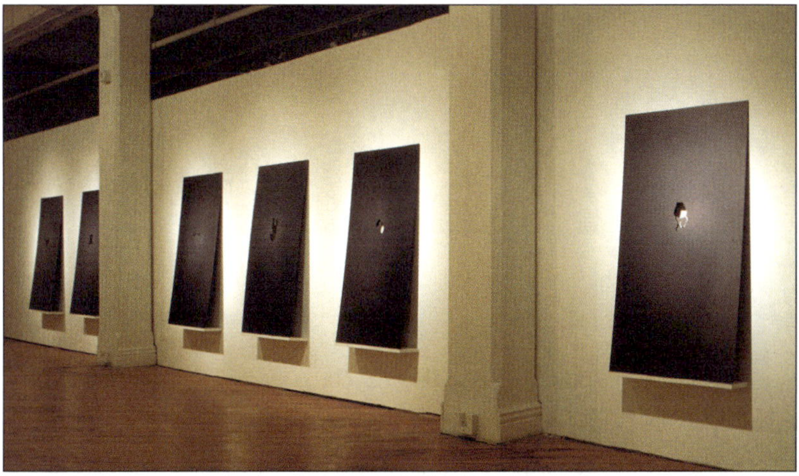

crib (i-vi), 1999, anodized aluminum, overall: 172 x 944 x 18 cm. Photo: Rory Mahoney.

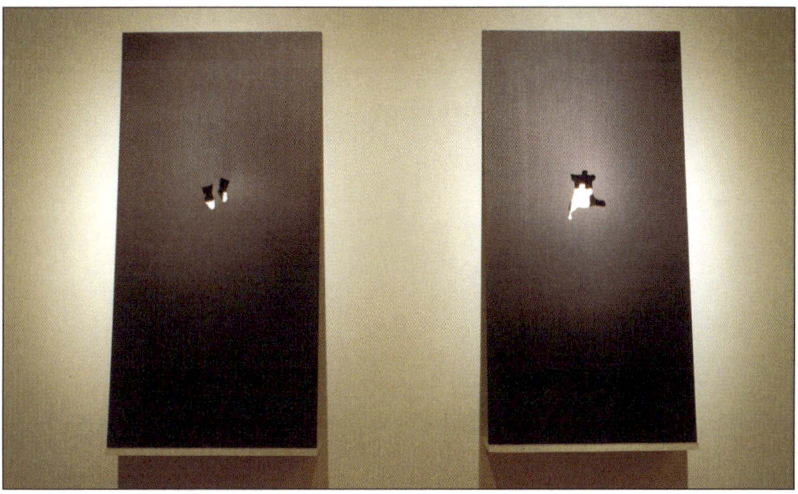

crib (i-vi), detail, 1999, anodized aluminum, each panel: 128 x 65 cm. Photo: Rory Mahoney.

his body into patterns of rolling, sitting, standing, walking, signing, and talking.

Bare life, when stripped of these natural stages of developmental progression, is exposed at its most vulnerable. The paradox of loss, but also gain (*light force*) propelled me in making this work, an attempt to speak what is largely unspeakable. My mixed-media images are abstract and evocative, while Sekula's photo is directly documentary; they are similar in making visible our potential failure to protect and preserve human life in its most vulnerable moment and the technologies of hope we hold on to in the face of fear and loss.

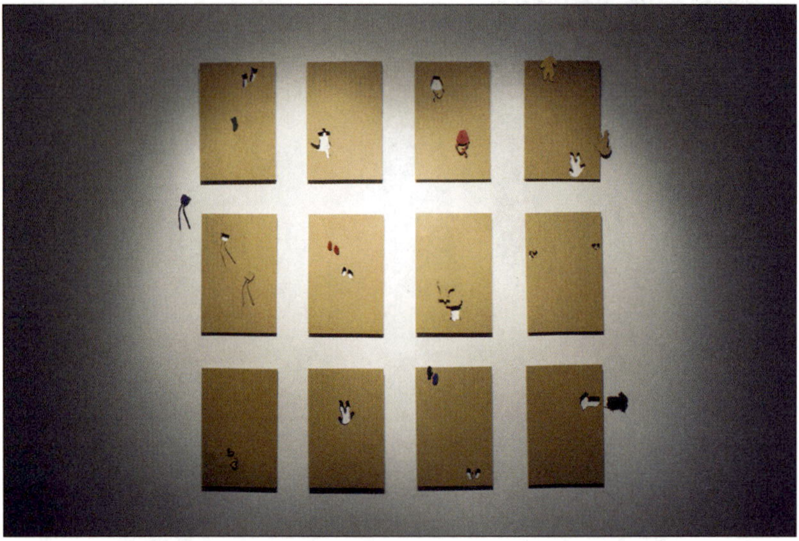

intensive care, 1999, mdf board, paint, overall: 198 x 212 x 5 cm,.
Photo: Rory Mahoney.

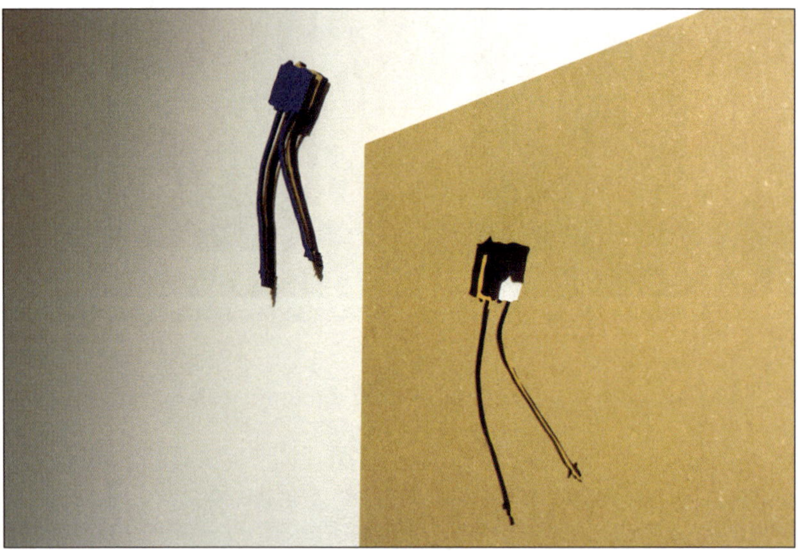

intensive care, 1999, detail, mdf board, paint, each panel: 35.5 x 54.5 x 5 cm.
Photo: Rory Mahoney.

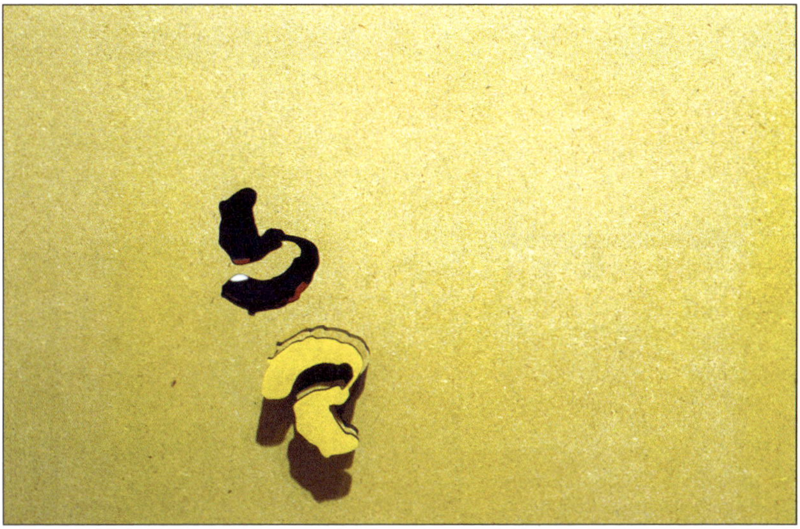

(upper)
intensive care,
detail, 1999, mdf board, paint,
each panel: 35.5 x 54.5 x 5 cm.
Photo: Rory Mahoney.

(lower)
virtual angel, 1998,
glass, mirror, metal, paper,
14.5 x 8.2 x 8.2 cm.
Photo: Rory Mahoney.

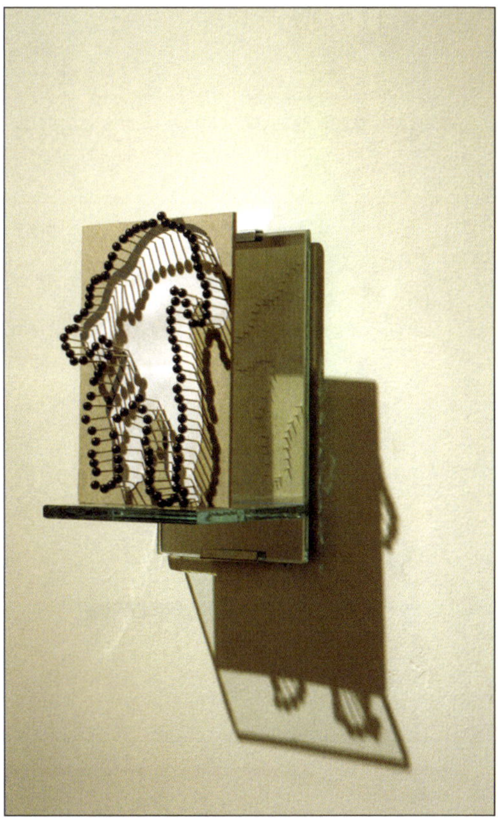

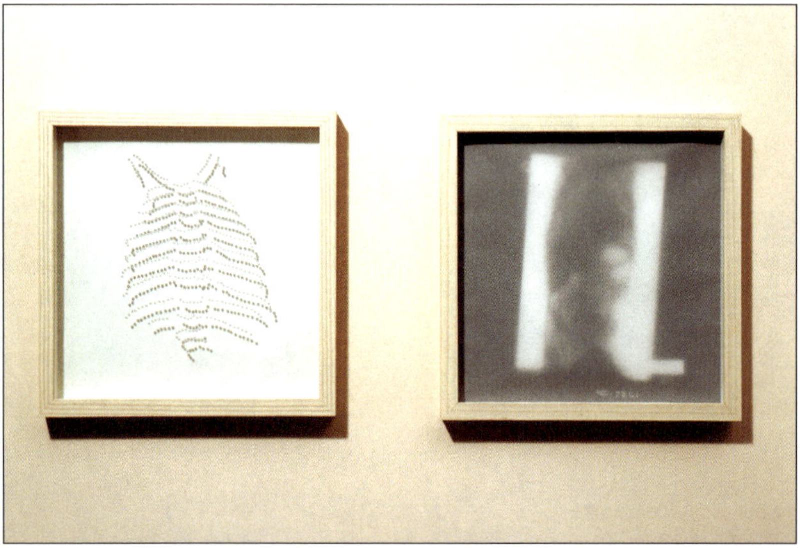

acute::care, detail, 2002, contact xrays, plexi/glass, each 28 x 28 x 3 cm. Photo: Rory Mahoney.

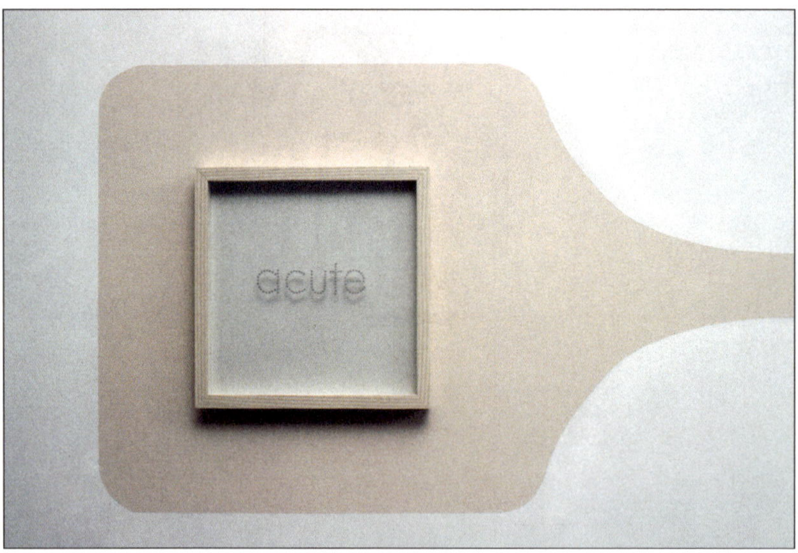

acute::care, detail, 2002, contact xrays, plexi/glass, each 28 x 28 x 3 cm. Photo: Rory Mahoney.

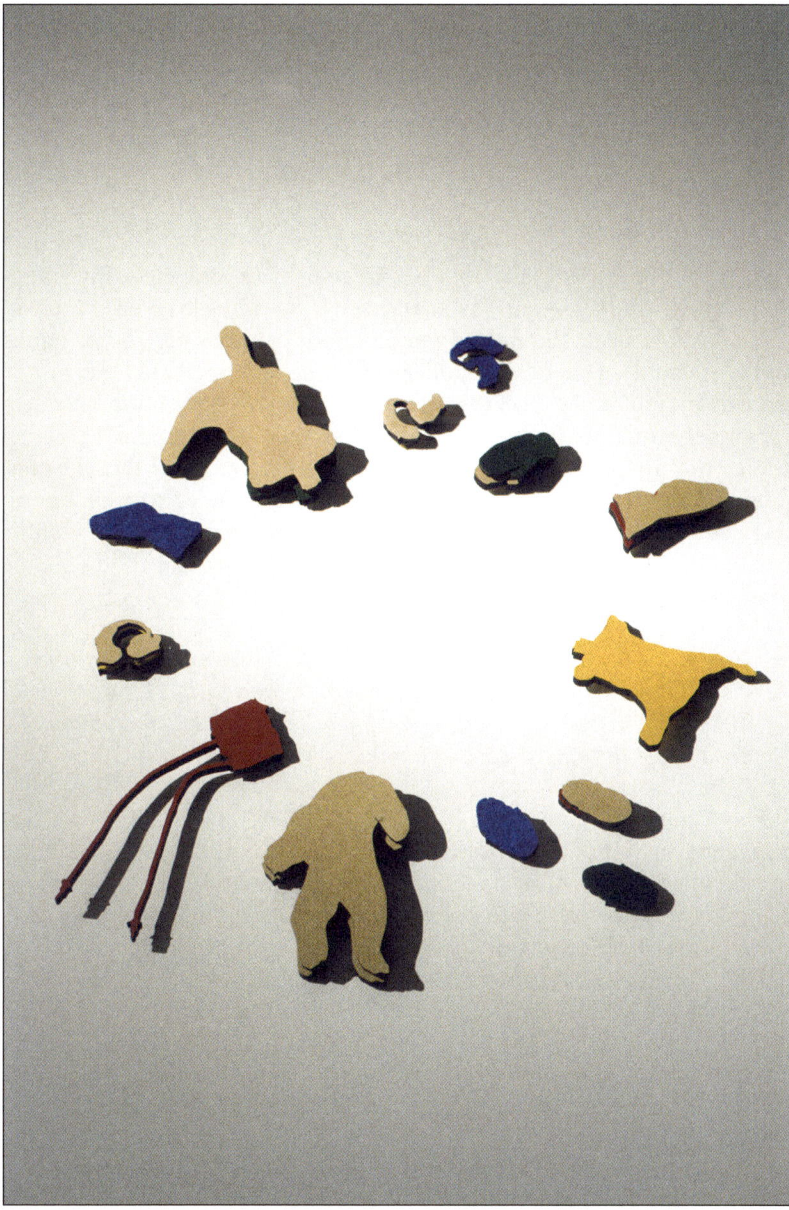

light force, 1999, mdf board, paint, 38 x 45 x 2 cm. Photo: Rory Mahoney.

Long Ago People

PAULA STROMBERG

ON MY FIFTIETH birthday, I dreamt that a little girl—my seven-year-old self—and I exchanged gifts. Standing in a Saskatchewan grain field, she passed me a grasshopper cupped in her hands and I, the adult, gave her the police emergency number 911. Her gift to me was playful and especially plentiful when you have no money. My gift to her hadn't existed when she needed it.

Why did my mother stay with a man who battered her? Did she consider the effects on her children? How have I responded to a childhood spent witnessing domestic violence? Pondering these riddles and the paths I have taken since I left home invokes a slowly-revealing child's shame that, like a melting glacier, releases its history.

> *For years beyond memory, native elders in remote communities told eerie stories about the strange netherworld of glaciers. Beneath the ice, they said, great owls slept fitfully, awakening from time to time to devour intruders.* (Pringle 57).

This is part of my story and I am ashamed. Was. Shamed. I feel frozen, struggling to respond to these questions beyond shudders, flickers. Ice shards reflect images of an alcoholic bully father and my mother who faced being kicked out with three kids she claimed she couldn't support.

"If I leave, he'll get a gun and kill us all."

That's what she whispered through swollen lips when I was seven.

From the time I was knee-high to a Saskatchewan grasshopper, I served as my mother's rescuer. As a child, I was her emotional confidante, helping set up secret bank accounts, once picking field straw out of her hair after my father pushed her out of a car into the path of a thundering train. I looked after my brothers as she recuperated from beatings. I played the anxious third corner of the triangle with my parents and, like Oedipus, I longed to kill my father and marry my martyr.

It made sense years later that I gravitated to union work. Fittingly, my first exposure was managing a woman's election campaign in 1984. She became the first female president in the union's history. Working for a union, I could help people who were shoved down, make right what was hurt, fix what I couldn't when I was little—the powerless kid who hadn't known where to begin.

My *raison d'être* was to help. I salved my ache by demonstrating for women's rights, speaking out against harassment in the workplace, and publishing stories about employment equity and pensions for women. Union work wasn't a job; it was my heart's mission.

I first honed my skills saving my mother. I remember these things as I twist in bed at night, poking at walnuts, black balls of anxiety in my gut. The finest designer silk dresses can fit inside a walnut—even when they're blood splattered. I twist hard wrinkled shells apart; the tightly rolled, compacted stuff unfurling.

Although my parents graduated only from high school, they felt a class higher than others because they were handsome, saw a dentist regularly, and dressed fashionably. They were flattered when, once, a gas station attendant in Willow Bunch, Saskatchewan mistook them for movie stars traveling *incognito*. My mother had modeled in New York, and my father was commanding in a sharp wool suit that proved his worth. The movie star story was part of family folklore—my parents had been recognized as superior beings. Yet we often lived in an old house with no electricity and no running water.

As I got older, I realized Cherie—I haven't called her Mom since I was seven—didn't care enough about my brothers or me to leave the violent marriage. Even a bird with its cinnamon heart and lentil brain chooses a safe place to build her nest. Not Cherie. Year after year, she allowed her kids to slink away as Neville—the one I don't call father—slapped and kicked her head through the drywall, stabbed his fingers into her beehive and dragged her down the hall by her backcombed hair.

She should have left Neville. They were a toxic match. Toxic mystery. Would we finish supper before Neville shoved the table over? Those years ago—my mother on whom I depended for my survival—would she be alive in the morning?

I remember her coral knit dress bunched over her pale bruised buttock as she cowered in the kitchen on her hands and knees.

I looked after my cringing mother.

She proudly tells anyone, "My daughter was an adult from the time she was three."

My aunt says that at five years old I was adamant I would never have children. I helped Cherie so I could breathe, vowed I would never be her, a wife under the thumb of he who paid the bills. Even as a young woman, I made sure to earn enough money to look after myself. I believed my feminist consciousness-raising groups in the early seventies—that money, not men, provides security and dignity. I learned not to depend on others for help.

Helping is such a faceted word. Cherie wasn't willing to leave her batterer, make a safer nest, but when I was 12, she'd stay up all night trying to help me feel better by sewing pink glass beads over hundreds of tiny pink roses on my adolescent housecoat and, when I'm 55 and she is 82, she'll still stay up late repairing holes in my sweater. Helping. Help, help ... sounds like a barking hound, yelp, yelp help.

Mothers, martyrs, who let themselves be hit—witnessing this violence makes a kid sound cold and harsh—these martyr mothers live in la-la land, denying and hiding, pulling veils over brute facts, smearing Cover Girl ivory beige over bruises. Nice lipstick smile stretching over sinking black tingling, a little kid's gloom.

Elsewhere Betty Botter bought a bit of better butter; at my house Betty Botter bought a toxic hole with a batterer at the bottom.

Get out mother or your daughter will hold you at a distance, in the refrigerator of her heart ... forever wracked that she doesn't feel much warmth toward you. Don't get me wrong. I care. Our threads of attachment are like bruised ligaments in a twisted arm and tendons in a purple neck, another quadrant of a Gordian knot.

We keep, I keep, ugly things jammed away, useless to recall, until a different kind of global warming melts the shield over the past, a history as dimly known as that of the 560-year-old hunter known as Long Ago Person Found, whose body was discovered preserved in a Canadian glacier.

> *The ancient body of the aboriginal hunter known as Long Ago Person Found was revealed in a crevasse at the foot of a melting glacier near the B.C.-Yukon borde ... headless, but otherwise preserved by the ice in the condition in which death overtook him until the receding glacier surrendered him.*

Surrender. This time, a different glacier recedes, exposing Long Ago Moose Jaw, Saskatchewan circa 1961. Images lie inside me like impacted teeth.

A very black young man is sitting beside me on the olive green Swedish modern couch in my family's house on Mercy Street. His friend, also a spectacular dark colour, is resting his pale palms on the teak arms of the matching Swedish chair. I am eleven and have rarely seen, and never spoken with, a black person.

The men's appearance in our house is disturbing. We rarely have visitors other than relatives who don't ask questions. I can't invite my friends over. It's embarrassing. Neville's a drunk. We rush to close the windows when he starts yelling, slapping, ripping off my mother's clothes, flushing her fox fur stole down the toilet—latching them tight so the neighbours don't hear. That's what a kid learns living with a mean drunk.

Once Neville dragged her out of the bathtub and locked her outside on a -50°C Saskatchewan winter night. Naked. Shapely Cherie with the eighteen-inch waist who commentated fashion shows. Bare as an icicle, she begged for blankets at the neighbour's door.

> *Some ancient bodies found elsewhere have been prepared for death, anointed, perfumed, wrapped in precious cloth, their brains drawn out of a small hole in the skull.*

Through a small hole in the skull. That is how I slowly remember these things. The two black visitors are students at the Saskatchewan Technical Institute in Moose Jaw. Although I am young, I'm a born chatterbox: the weather, the blizzard last night, where you are from, how you're enjoying the city.

They are from Nigeria and were marvelling after the blizzard left snow drifts as high as the windows on their dormitory when my father drove past. Unbelievably, he invited them home for a drink. It's about four o'clock Monday afternoon, the time period Cherie and I grimly call "the morning after the night before."

I hear my father banging cupboards in the kitchen. He's hung over.

"Guess I offered you boys beer and a sandwich. Sit-tight. Goddamn stuff's around here somewhere."

The visitors and I, flanked by brown kidney-shaped tables, continue to dredge up conversation. I smile, straining to understand their strange accents that remind me of rolling thunder. Where is my mother? Either she isn't home or she is hiding her Cover Girl bruises in the bedroom. War drums rumble. Swish, swish scours my belly as my father sweeps one slippered foot back and forth over the kitchen floor, cursing my mother for crumbs. He'll be jabbing the broom handle in her belly as soon as the guests leave.

In that scoured moment, I notice identical Jesus crosses hanging from their necks. Everyone in Moose Jaw knows these metal crosses are from the church that collects money to convert heathens. I'd opened the door often enough to Brylcreem missionaries going house to house collecting housewives' dimes and quarters to save Africa. I was eleven and barely remember the details, but I gather the visitors in their beige shirts and pressed pants are being educated in Saskatchewan so they can return to Nigeria and proselytize.

Prayers have never helped me.

Why were these people in our living room? My father's only friends were drunks, drinking buddies, and goddamn assholes. It certainly wasn't due to his milk of human kindness. He was mocking when we would drive past blacks, natives, Chinese, those stricken with acne—anyone who looked different than slim, clear-faced caucasians. If my mother protested "Oh Neville" in a shuddering tone, she'd duck her head as he raised his hand off the steering wheel. Those memories of my mother wriggle like larvae through my chest. She cowered by reflex.

"I want you to know that's not how fathers should act," my mother would whisper conspiratorially after the car ride, being careful he didn't overhear.

> *After hunters found the headless body in 1999, First Nations people cremated it and returned it to the glacier (British np). When hunters returned ... in 2003, they discovered the missing head along with several other bones had risen to the surface of the glacier.*

The head and other bones. More surfaces in my memory. When Neville invited the young black men into his car, they were wearing only thin jackets despite the crunching -20^{0} C December day. Now their jackets are draped over the back of the Swedish sofa and as I sit up straight to avoid them, I see a clump of my mother's red hair (Miss Clairol, #045 Sparkling Sherry) on the carpet under the arborite coffee table. Rigid with humiliation, I flick my eyes sideways to see if they've noticed, but, instead, the visitor beside me is gazing at one my mother's framed, technicolour Vladimir Tretchikoff pictures—Woman of the Ndebele, an African with five iron rings around her neck. It hangs in 60s splendour over our television.

A wave of something hot hovers in my chest. Neville must have pulled the clump of hair out last night. Idiots don't clean up.

Normally, looking good was important. My mother treasured appearance—beauty above all else, including good sense. "Neville is so very handsome. His nose and cheekbones are refined," she'd sigh.

Poisoned by his own suffering perhaps, Neville loved to denigrate what my mother valued. During Christmas or Easter family gatherings at our house, he would make a fine fellow of himself, jeering at her cooking show on TV, her pink cake decorated with sugared violets, or Zulu Girl's wide lips and nose in another Tretchikoff print by the dining table.

Monday late afternoon. Glacially I remember. December 1961. The two black young men seated on our green burlap Swedish modern furniture from Eaton's Department Store are staring at the kitschy Tretchikoff as if they've never seen anything like it. I sit stiff as cardboard while my father slams kitchen cupboards. He shuffles into the living room wearing a siwash sweater reeking of hangover, carrying two brown stubby bottles.

"Hey Nigeria, ya'wanna beer?" He goes back to the fridge, clanking more bottles as he calls out, "We're friends right, Nigeria?" He stands in the doorway and takes a swig of beer, tasting his tongue. "Ha ha my friends, Nigers, Nigers."

The visitors glance at each other, eyes flicking together like cold flames, heads barely turning from the Tretchikoff.

A plate crashes from the refrigerator. "This is great. You're from Nigeria. That makes you Niger niggers," my father shouts from the kitchen.

My cold horror, these images, these sounds, sprawled in the crevasse.

The men flanking me on the sofa whisper urgently in their own language, arguing perhaps. Hard as a carving, I sink through the sofa.

"More beer, yes," one calls out.

"Beers comin', you black bastards.... Hey, I can call you that—we're friends." My father guffaws with pleasure. "Wanna ham sandwich?"

Careful I am out of his sight line from the kitchen, I turn to the two guests and twirl one finger by my temple—universal school kid sign language indicating "He's off his rocker."

As fast as a blink, the young man closest to me lays his cold hand on my thigh. I remember the freeze pulsing through my dress and my nylon slip. He may as well have seized my throat. This is the first man I remember touching me.

He keeps his hand on my thigh as he speaks. I can hardly understand his foreign inflections. "We doan mind what the fool say ... beautiful yellow hair daughter. We come for sex with you, understand?"

I turn my face to his. We are nearly the same height. I know I will not call out. In this unsafe place, I will not give them away. His eyes bore into me and the cold hand tightens. I have quit breathing, caught between the bully in the kitchen who won't shut up, and the hand on my tense eleven-year-old thigh in the living room.

"Where's the goddam bottle opener?"

A drawer crashes on the kitchen floor as knives and forks clatter. Something plastic bounces several times. Neville doesn't cook. Usually my mother serves him, hunching over as she fries his T-bone steak. He sits at the chrome kitchen table drinking beer while my brothers and I choke down mustardy hot dogs, queasy with knowing that after three bottles, he's dangerous. These are my kitchen table politics.

Christians walking in thin cotton jackets become prisoner guests at -20°C, promised beer, with no money for a taxi, abused by a mean bastard. It's all his joke, bile, what else would they do?

One of the men asks me, "Sex, rape, you know this?"

Other girls would call out, shriek and run. I'm still pre-teen but I can sense why they're talking this way, with flames licking out of their heads. I shiver. The guests can tell me filthy things but they cannot do more on the Swedish sofa. Rigid as the bottom totem on an argillite pole, I understand I'm their way to spit back. My father is a creep. Perhaps pain experienced together becomes an act of union. I will never call out.

Missionary students, I too feel hate, little girl close to you in fury. Black fury. At night, the gravel crunching in the driveway means he's come home. Then he spends an hour making the bed squeak through the thin wall as he fucks her and the rest of the night pounding her head on the floor. Nausea, shame covers my child self like a snow drift. Layer upon layer. I close my eyes on the sofa and sink into a deep freeze.

Dust mites explode in a shaft of winter sun as the forced air furnace kicks in. Overheated air tickles my throat and I cough. The images, the icy hand on my thigh, the memories of the Nigerian visitors, thin jacket captives, end with me bent over my knees coughing, whooping until tears run from my bulging eyes. My lungs feel like a bag of vacuum dust.

Don't ask me what happened next. My memory of this long ago day stops here, at the edge of the receding glacier.

These moments bloom inside me like wetted tampons — slowly blooming awareness of human dignity, of one's place in the receiving line. Life. There is no where else to go until I turn seventeen and can run away.

In addition to dried berries, the stomach contents of Long Ago Person Found revealed sea asparagus although he was found far from the sea.

What goes around comes around, as they say in Saskatchewan. My father punches my mother witnessed by my brothers who then cut the heads off baby birds or kick Taco, our chihuahua, and I am the oldest so I slug my brothers. Fred, my brush-cut brother, bullied by school mates and my father, despairs of anyone ever keeping him safe and shoots himself. Fred is dead. Eric, my freckled baby brother, breaks into houses as a kid and stutters into adulthood. Later he'll be alcoholic. Marry an alcoholic.

My father slaps my thirteen-year old head, breaks my ear drum, my mother wrings her hands, hides in the bedroom.

Not looking right or left, these memories compress into a glacier. Twenty, forty years later, I am matter-of-fact, having apologized to my brother for slugging him when we were kids, become lesbian as a political choice, raised money for women's election campaigns, and written human rights stories that won awards for nineteen consecutive years.

I tried to live by the motto, "The good we wish for ourselves, we also wish for others." To me, this union principle is a call to greatness of the spirit. I wish I'd had a childhood with a similar contract.

An early day at work remains lodged in my throat. Union Representative Jackie Brown is explaining the provisions of a first collective agreement to a group of newly-unionized employees at a car rental company. I am taking photographs for the union newspaper. These people voted to form a union because of the bullying they'd endured from their employer. There are First Nations folk, Pakistanis, Somalis, Chinese, Tajikistanis, women near retirement, and from my own queer tribe, a pink pixie with ear studs and a thick moustache. Sitting in a circle on folding chairs, they stare at their knees, grow still as hunters as Jackie Brown reads the new contract aloud.

Ping, ping, ping, around the circle, I watch each person absorb how their work lives might change. My heart is full to bursting. No one looks up. I remember that moment like a quarterback who sees the world become molten, frame by frame, as she scores. With hope, I hear the refrain:

> *As we go marching, marching, unnumbered women dead. Go crying through our singing their ancient call for bread. Small art and love and beauty their drudging spirits knew. Yes, it is bread we fight for, but we fight for roses too.*
>
> —Labour movement song, "Bread and Roses" (Oppenheim and Coleman)

Unfortunately, I think that instead of "Bread and Roses," sustenance and survival seem often to be about the much nastier business of ripping and tearing, taking and being taken.

Several years ago while traveling through Namibia on a photo safari, I noticed a scuffle of dust near a waterhole. Five jackals were chasing down a small tan springbok with a white face and black ridged horns. In an effort to escape, the springbok had been leaping and zigzagging but, working as a tag team, the jackals nipped, nipped its heels until they severed its Achilles tendons. Thus crippled, the springbok sank on its haunches. I will never forget the sound of the springbok sitting there crying as jackals ate it alive—tearing chunks of flesh from its hindquarters as it cried. Life feeding on itself.

Screaming. In Africa, cradle of life, a birthplace of the human race, I was reminded survival is nuanced. Should I feel sorry for the springbok and therefore wish five jackals starve?

Elsewhere in Africa, hollow-cheeked, rake-ribbed men stare at me at a Harare vegetable market. A pot-bellied eight-year-old with a tapeworm hanging from his bum swings a machete alarmingly close to my head at a roadside stand and races away giggling when he misses. Friends with aid organizations, robbed twice in a week, learn too late of the better than one hundred percent chance of being mugged in downtown Johannesburg. Modern hunters getting food. Why not? More than a billion people in the world are starving or malnourished. Life peeled to the quick.

Taking and being taken. To me, these things are grey and black and white, turning grey again on an ever-turning wheel. At different ages, I've seen differently, wished different things for victims and victimizers, harassers and harassed.

> *Botanists studying the stomach and gut contents say the entire discovery has provided a remarkable learning opportunity.* (University of Saskatchewan)

I do not mean to forgive Cherie too easily. She chose to stay with Neville for 48 years and, as my understanding evolved, I've seen that some victims can be—are—abusers too.

> *Scientists will perform microbial DNA analysis on tissues from the hunter's body to determine how present-day bacteria have evolved from ones from the 1400s. The project is aimed at learning what diseases were present at the time.* (University of Saskatchewan)

Understanding the disease process. This may sound like heresy: Cherie never set limits, never nipped Neville in the bud, so little by spittle, blow by punch by knife cut, my father was permitted to become a monster. He became a victim of Cherie's acceptance of his behaviour. I was amazed to learn he pinched Cherie to control her reply to relatives at a party before they were married. She had many suitors. She did not have to marry him. As her fiancé, he twisted her arm. He pinched her hard; she did not cry out. He shouted. She did not say stop. She married him anyway. She had jobs. She did not leave.

He had been clear he never wanted children. She trampled on his wishes. She tricked him. She gave birth to me three years later. He never forgave her.

"I was going crazy wanting a baby," was her stunning explanation to me.

She stayed in the marriage, ignored his rules about no children and never set any of her own. He kicked her in the belly, shoved his hand in her mouth and ripped her lips when she got pregnant a second time. Cherie insists she never heard Neville say he didn't want children. She gave birth to a blue baby with a head the size of an orange. She stayed, got pregnant a third time. Neville went on an alcoholic, womanizing rampage while she was on the maternity ward delivering more of what he never wanted.

Finally, a long-time family doctor intervened, with a surprise, silent act that might be deemed malpractice today, sterilizing her on the thrice-doomed birthing table. From the children—thank you doctor. Someone needed to set a limit, but Cherie never did. Perhaps he was practising a little eugenics, halting the toxic hillbillies, preventing a fourth baby in that miserable dance, that shallow gene pool. Or was the doctor helping my father who fled each time Cherie entered the maternity ward, who went on benders, disappeared with other women for weeks, then coming home stinking to little kids who disliked him? Quite an ugly life. Perhaps the doctor saw Neville trapped in his role—a father to kids he'd never wanted to have.

> *By comparing bacteria, researchers hope to detect differences in certain genes and thus determine what environmental pressures may cause organisms to change over time.* (University of Saskatchewan)

How did my mother end up in that toxic match? Cherie was seen as a beautiful martyr, long suffering, forbearing, noble, almost holy, like our Tretchikoff print of Zulu Girl, with her primitive patience and ageless humility.

The most useful thing I learned in my life about martyrs and misery is that there are no prizes awarded for unhappiness. Until I heard this at a 12-step program for Adult Children of Alcoholics, all I had seen was my mother's perpetual subservience as if she were trying to win a sainthood prize. When you cast yourself as a victim, everyone is sorry for you. The abuser is bad and wrong, so the victim must be right.

Subservience is an immense power the victim wields. Cherie says that when Neville berated her, she would go into a trance, leave her body. She was like a cast iron stove filled with rusty water. He couldn't get beyond her wall of impassivity, so he kept on punching. She showed no need for limits. Some victims do create monsters: It's okay to shout at me, it's okay to hit me.

Who's up? Who's down? Who's the hunter, who's the hunted?

> *Various artefacts were uncovered with Long Ago Person Found. Carbon dating has shown the wooden tools to be 200 or 300 years old while the ground squirrel (gopher) robe and spruce root hat are 550 years old. The discrepancy indicates there were several events at this site ... spread out over time.* (Hunter 57)

Where does history begin? Cherie and Neville first met at a Regina church basement dance in 1946. She had come back from working in New York. Among the dancers in the basement, she noticed a green-eyed man staring at her from behind a pillar and felt weak.

Cherie told me years later her first thought was, "I could have beautiful children with that man."

My childhood fate, my brothers' fates, were doomed from that moment at the Regina church dance. Before we were born Cherie had written our script. She got her beautiful children without regard for her husband. No matter what he said or did, she would have those babies. Without regard for those babies.

For years I had nightmares that a man in a trench coat and trilby hat loomed over my baby crib wanting to kill me.

When I was an adult, Neville admitted, "I didn't want you when you were born."

I wasn't dreaming.

By transgressing his boundaries about children, Cherie set Neville up to hate me before I was born, set it up so the kids would love only her. She created Neville's alienation by making sure we were born. Of course I feared and hated him. He became a raging psychopath, the mean bastard. Our relatives and friends followed along, feeling sorry for her. Of course I wanted to kill him and rescue her.

> *Examining the old frozen remains, researchers hope to predict how disease-causing organisms may evolve in future.* (Hunter 57)

I had to slit open the belly of my childhood to finally realize that unless I changed my thinking, I might follow the same family script—I might remain a rescuer trapped in the disease process. My childhood role.

The doctor, the minister, I, many tried to help. It's easy to become a redeemer. Cherie whispered her excuses, her thanks, gave me eyelash butterfly kisses at night. Rescuing, helping by taking over, taking charge, is an easy way to feel powerful, feel some semblance of control. Some victims end up feeling powerful too, keeping the rescuer (like me) at their side, offering us a narcotic, a heady path to feeling good. Victims like her offer great emotional pull to a naive kid.

Back then, Cherie won. She drew the crowd's sympathy. Independence was less enticing than being seen as a martyr.

These are my Long Ago People. I'll never know why my mother lived that way. As a fiancée, my mother wasn't pregnant. She did not have to get married. As a new wife, she dallied childless for three years, then still chose to have babies with a man like that, a man who told her he did not want children. Stubbornly, she created the libretto, a powerful act with consequences for generations to come — but she never used her power to protect her children.

Today, she still offers no answers. The Tretchikoff pictures hang on her new walls. Her life remains a riddle. Unlike the springbok, Cherie was able to get away. Instead she stayed with Neville 48 years. He stayed with her.

They were both able to choose. Did choose.

WORKS CITED

Hunter, Troy. "They Call Him Long Ago Person Found." *Raven's Eye: The Aboriginal Newspaper of British Columbia and Yukon.* 11 December 2000. <http: //www.ammsa.com/raven/DEC2000.html>.

Ministry of Tourism, Sports, and the Arts. "Archaeology." 13 September 1999. Victoria: Government of British Columbia. <http: //www.tsagov.bc.ca.archaeology>.

Oppenheim, James and Martha Coleman [Caroline Kohlsast]. "Bread and Roses." c1910. *Songs of Work and Protest.* Eds. Edith Fowke and Joe Glazer. New York: Dover, 1973. Rpt in <http: //www.fortunecity.com/tinpan/parton/2/breadrose.html>.

Pringle, Heather. "Out of the Ice." *Canadian Geographic.* July/August 2002. <http: //www.canadiangeographic.com/magazine/ja02>.

University of Saskatchewan. "U of S Scientists to Analyze Bacterial DNA in 550-year-old Hunter's Frozen Remains." 8 December 2000. <http. www: //announcements.usask.ca/news/archive>.

Mothering Under Duress

Tuberculosis and Stigma in 1950s Rural Saskatchewan

PATRICIA MILLER-SCHROEDER

CHILDREN BORN IN the fifteen years following World War II grew up in a time of dramatic and rapid social change. These "Baby Boomers" are often spoken of as the largest and most influential cohort of people born in Canada, and thought of as a homogeneous group with iconic family experiences of the Breadwinner Family in the 1950s, and Women's Liberation, sexual freedom, and working mothers beginning in the 1960s. This is true on some levels, but on many others, the "Boomers," of which I am one, grew up and lived diverse family experiences based on gender, social class, race, ability, and many other circumstances beyond their control.

This is the story of my mother's life and her experience of motherhood in 1950s rural Saskatchewan. It is based on my recollections as her youngest child, born in 1950, when our family was experiencing a very difficult time. The story is based on my recollections, because my mother died 36 years ago, in 1971, when she was 61 and I was 21. It also includes recollections of my sisters, and published reports of aspects of life in rural Saskatchewan during this time period.

My mother, Dorothy Caroline Kilback, was born in 1910 to German immigrant parents in Melville, Saskatchewan. She was the youngest of ten children, received a grade six education, and later worked as a seamstress to help support her family. She married my father, Ralph Miller, a baker, in 1935, and raised five daughters, of which I am the youngest. My sisters are twelve, ten (twins), and six years older than me. According to my sisters' memories of the years before I was born, our family lived comfortably, although my father, for reasons I am not sure of, moved the family at least three times, each time starting up a bakery in the new town. My sisters remember living in nice houses and being accepted in the communities. My mother, who was a very bright woman despite her lack of education, kept the books and worked long hours in the bakery, both baking and serving customers. Before my sisters started school, they played in and around the bakery while my mother worked. This was all before I was born in 1950.

Things took a decidedly unfortunate turn for the worse shortly after I was born when my father contracted tuberculosis in 1951. During the first half of the twentieth century, tuberculosis was often considered a death sentence (Ott). By the 1950s, there were both drug-based and surgical treatments, and sometimes cures. However, isolation in sanatoriums for treatment was mandatory (Center for Disease Control). I don't remember my father leaving home in 1951 for the "San" near Fort Qu'appelle, since I was just a baby, but the effect must have been very traumatic on my family. It still affects my sisters to this day. The San was 100 kilometres away, but it might as well have been a thousand since we had no car and my mother couldn't drive anyway.

There has always been a stigma attached to those having tuberculosis. It appears to have been that way in the past and still is today in many countries. This resulted in those having the disease being ostracised and treated in a similar way to those having leprosy, and, more recently, HIV/AIDS (Ott). The serious consequences of stigma meant that those who were sick might not disclose their condition even to their families and friends for fear of being ostracised and shunned (Center for Disease Control). As well, the loss of income from the "Breadwinner" was also a concern in a patriarchal society that saw women and children without support from a man as a problem.

Removal of family members to Sanatoria often did not remove the stigma from their families. Instead, it resulted in the ostracism and social rejection of their children and spouses who were kept under constant scrutiny. Social distance increased dramatically. One of my sisters is still visibly upset when describing her shock and dismay at running to meet her friends on the playground shortly after our father was sent to the sanatorium, only to hear them shouting at her to stop and go away because she was "dirty" and their parents wouldn't allow them to play with her. She was ten years old at the time. Almost overnight, my mother, my sisters, and I became objects of fear, distrust, and scape-goating.

Stigma was all-encompassing and affected my family's ability to get proper housing, employment, and education, and affected how we were treated in the health and welfare systems. Saskatchewan was in the vanguard of supplying both health and social welfare benefits to its citizens but, in the early 1950s, was on the cusp of change. Although Saskatchewan had a Department of Social Welfare since the mid-1940s, its more progressive Social Welfare Act was not in place until 1959. Medicare was not introduced until 1962. Both of these came too late to affect my family's experience. As well, as social programs improved, those people living in cities and larger towns had better access than those living in rural areas (Leger-Anderson).

As it was, my mother became what was called a "straw widow" and, by default, a single mother overnight as a result of my father's removal for nearly three years. The welfare policies of the time required that all personal assets had to be used to pay living and health expenses before any government aid could be given. Accordingly, the bakery and equipment were sold, but did not provide riches since there were debts to pay and, because of the stigma that the previous owner had tuberculosis.

My mother was unable to work out of the home, due to fears of contagion, lack of education, and the motherhood mores of the 1950s since she had a very young child (me). The stigma of poverty was added to the stigma of disease. There were no food banks in rural Saskatchewan at this time, but the government social welfare department issued food vouchers, which my mother hated to cash because it reinforced and made obvious her precarious position in the community. She felt that she was under almost constant scrutiny and censure whenever she was out in public.

Under the Ideal of True Womanhood, still in place from the 1800s, a woman's most important role was to provide a safe, secure, clean, and healthy "nest" for her husband and children. Under this patriarchal ideal, my mother was obviously lacking as a wife and, especially, as a mother. Mothers were supposed to be completely self-sacrificing and forego any personal needs, and certainly personal wants, in order to be sure her children were raised properly and safely in a clean home. Mother–blaming and guilt helped enforce the rules of being a good mother. Perfect mothers meant perfect children. Perfect mothers didn't allow their children to get sick, spread contagion, live in poverty, or lack opportunities. Not being able to provide a safe and cosy 'nest" meant that a mother had failed the requirements of motherhood miserably. Therefore, my mother was a failure in the eyes of our community, of the wider society, and, not surprisingly, in her own eyes. Her guilt was even more extreme when two of my sisters were diagnosed with tuberculosis and had to depart for the "San" a year after my father did.

During this time, housing became an issue for my family. My mother had a hard time not only affording a place to stay, but also finding one where the landlord was willing to rent to us. The welfare department had to help find the places for us to rent and we moved at least four times during the years my father was away. None of the houses we lived in provided adequate living space for my mother and her five daughters.

Saskatchewan had brought in a massive rural electrification program in the 1950s and most of the homes in the urban centres had electricity although many farm and rural non-farm homes did not (Leger-Anderson). We had previously lived in town and had electricity in our home before my father became ill. Now, in our stigmatized position, we had to accept substandard housing on the outskirts of rural villages and towns. These houses were uniformly in poor condition, lacking electricity, running water, plumbing, and central heating. My mother chopped wood to burn in the wood stove, which was our only source of heat. In winter, the windows were so covered with thick ice and frost that it was impossible to see through them for months at a time. I recall watching through the open grate in the upstairs floor in the early morning while my mother, bundled in coat and scarf against the frigid air in the kitchen, would pile wood into the small stove to warm the house before my sisters and I came downstairs. Later in the day, she would go out and chop more wood to keep the stove going. She hauled water in heavy pails from a well and carried it long distance to the house. My mother also carried chamber pots used so her girls didn't have to visit the outhouse at night. She always waited until dusk had fallen to carry the chamber pots because she had been harassed and taunted by some boys once while doing this chore earlier in the day.

My mother, as our sole provider, struggled to keep her growing children fed and clothed. Prevented from participating in the paid labour force, she provided most of our food from her garden, which she planted wherever we moved. She pickled and canned vegetables and fruits for the winter. Welfare food vouchers provided some foods she couldn't grow, and there were occasional hampers of food and clothing from church groups. Still, there was often not enough food and my mother was the one who went without adequate food so her children could eat. Sometimes, she only ate the leftovers on our plates. I was too young at the time to realize why she was doing this and remember asking her why she didn't just make more food. She invariably smiled and said that she really wasn't very hungry.

My mother was, in many ways, unable to protect her children's health so she became overprotective in other ways. We received constant warnings about what was safe and not safe to do. I became timid and shy, and was aware that we shouldn't play with other children, and certainly not bring them home. As a result, I had few playmates and often lived in an imaginary world, sometimes imagining that I was a boy, Tommy, who could look after our family. My mother also felt she had to protect us from being "taken away." I remember her hiding my sister and me from ominous "others" knocking on our door. It was likely the Welfare or Health Screening people, I'm not sure which, but my mother's fear was palpable as she made us lie still behind the couch until the knocking stopped and they went away. At that point, she was very fearful of losing us.

After my father returned home, life did not really improve much. He had lost a lung and was physically weak and unable to fulfill his role as breadwinner. He either could not find work he was physically able to do, or he was still considered a threat by some of the others in the community. This was hard on his self-esteem, and he began to hide his feelings of inadequacy by drinking. This added to my mothers' burden as well.

One of my sisters was temporarily hired by the kind owner of a local restaurant who wanted to help us. The man and his family were Chinese immigrants and no strangers to discrimination themselves. My sister remembers him crying when he told her a week later that he had to let her go because people were refusing to eat at the restaurant if the Miller girls worked there.

Shortly after this, my family moved to Moose Jaw, a small Saskatchewan city 200 kilometres away, to escape the discrimination. We told no one of our past. My father eventually found work as a janitor, although he refused to eat with us or sleep in the same bed as my mother. The stigma remained in his mind until his death in 1986. I started to attend school for the first time in Moose Jaw when I was seven years old. My parents had not put me in school earlier because of the discrimination they feared I would face in the small town school. Both parents still discouraged my sisters and me from bringing anyone home. My mother continued to protect us, or as I saw it, overprotect us. She was lonely and rarely left our house, yard, or the garden that she always kept. She loved to read, but would not even go to the library. So, I would bring home books for her to read.

It was only many years later, when, as a teen-ager, I told her I would like to be a writer, that she confided in me that she had also wanted to be a writer. She had sent a story once to a magazine and been rejected. Her one attempt to have a voice was so easily silenced and was never freed again.

In 1956, the Government of Saskatchewan's Royal Commission on Agriculture and Rural Life contained a report on the home and family in rural Saskatchewan. Part of this report focused on women who were members of rural homemakers clubs in the province. Most of the women in this group were mothers in nuclear families, part of a secure social network, financially stable, and had a high school education. My mother's loneliness was worsened by her social isolation and marginalization on the outskirts of the towns as well as a fear of contagion in the community. She never belonged to homemakers' clubs or other social network in the towns or on the farms. The report did acknowledge that this group might not be representative of all rural women in Saskatchewan. However, their voices, which were the closest to the ideal of "good mothers," were the only ones focused on in the report. My mother was obviously not part of this group. She, and other mothers like her, were excluded through poverty, lack of education, and the stigma of disease.

Perhaps the telling of my mother's story today can help give her the voice she was denied in the past. Perhaps in some way she can help advocate for the support and empowerment of all mothers.

WORKS CITED

Department of Health and Human Services. Centers for Disease Control and Prevention (CDC). *Tuberculosis Behavioural and Social Science Research Form Appendix A*. Atlanta, Georgia, 2005.

Leger-Anderson, Ann. "Women of Saskatchewan—Historical Overview." *The Encyclopedia of Saskatchewan*. Regina: Canadian Plains Research Centre, 2006.

Ott, Katherine. *Fevered Lives: Tuberculosis in American Culture Since 1870*. Cambridge: Harvard University Press, 1999.

Saskatchewan. "The Home and Family in Rural Saskatchewan." *Royal Commission on Agriculture and Rural Life*. Report 10. Regina: Queen's Printer, 1956.

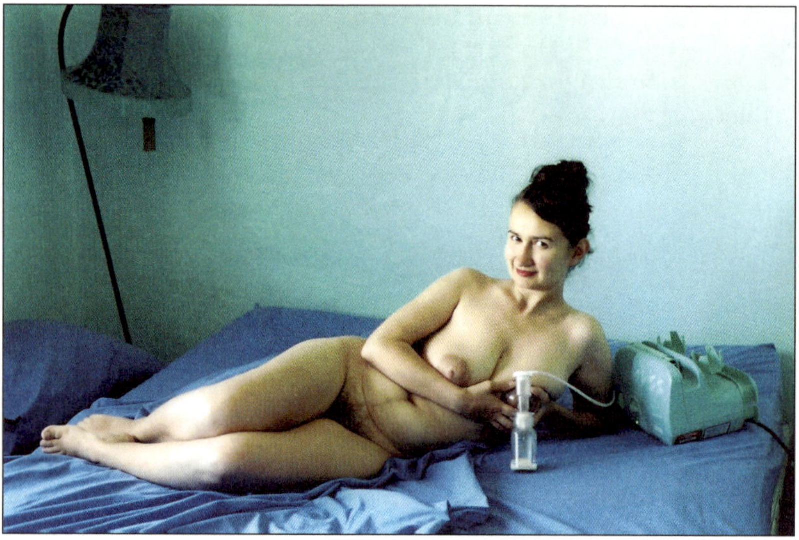

Lori Weidenhammer, *Nude with Breast Pump,* 2000, photograph, variable size.
Photo: Peter Courtemanche

When we rented a breast pump from the hospital I was amused to find that it was designed like a 1950's beauty appliance. It seemed more like something that would open to reveal hot rollers rather than a devise for suctioning breast milk. The pump's reference to the boudoir aesthetic inspired me to create a playful riff on the images of the reclining odalisques and concubines of the old masters.

Generating Economy

JODY SALERNO

I BEGAN WORKING IN social services in 1986, for the John Howard Society in a provincial halfway house. I was a COMSOC placement. What that means is that Community and Social Services offered women on, what was then "Mothers Allowance," an opportunity to enter the work force by providing employers with a financial incentive to hire us. I worked 8:00 a.m. to 4:00 p.m. and my son went to a neighbour's. I paid her one hundred dollars a week. I received two hundred and fifty dollars a week through my employment. You do the math. On that, I would have lived well under the poverty line. We had housing because I did Sex Work. I had bought a condo with the help of my "Mark" or "Sugar Daddy."

I would get up at 6:00 a.m. and prepare my son, complete with all the fixings of a fun-filled day (of which I was not a part). I would prepare food, no meat or dairy products. Nothing but the best. Toys, creative art supplies, books, including the politically correct "Heather Has Two Mommies." I would then smush him into his gear, grab the luggage, and off to the neighbour's. Thank Goddess she was in my building. She would greet him with warm fuzzies and off I would go.

I stood on the curb on Lakeshore Road at Bonneymede, in Mississauga, waiting for the Go bus to take me to Indian Road in Toronto. Ahhhhh Toronto, Land of my People. Queer folk, gurls to bois and boys to girls. I organized the office. I reminded all the clients of their appointments. I facilitated several interventions, clients angry with clients, staff angry with staff, staff angry with clients, clients angry with staff. I reminded my "superiors," top of a chain of correctional ass holes, of their meetings, prepared their reports, and made their coffee. And I earned two hundred and fifty dollars a week. I was generating the economic growth for my country. God save our Queen. You know, she's a dyke. I called my son's caregiver every couple of hours to ensure she had not self-destructed caring for my son and her two.

I would meet my "Mark," Joe, twice a week. He lived at the King Eddie, from Tuesday to Friday. He would do his business and do me. Joe bought and sold real estate. His clients would come in from all over the world, and he would grant them me, as a gift, wrapped in ribbon and eager to perform for the horny, white, rich men. I wonder how much money I made him. Sex work … present, perfect, performance—sometimes … powerful—always. In my experience, I held all the power in my work. I made all the rules. I determined when, how, and what, if anything. I had the power to cum. Earn money and cum.

Joe paid for my school, paid my rent, and took me to nice places. He worried about me like a daddy—a daddy who liked to fuck his "little girl." I loved-hated him. I made five hundred dollars for every full night I slept at the hotel with him. I would also make that same amount for every client I entertained. No taxes paid but lots of economy generated. I bought clothes and accessories, shiny things to pretty the agony of my soul. It was not the sex work that fuelled my agony, but the self-loathing adults who were unable to love themselves and, therefore, unable to love their child, me.

My son had the best of everything. No one could judge the quality of his toys, clothing, housing, or food. What my son missed in my pursuit to generate a superficial economy based on being a "good mother" was me. The kind and loving spiritual being that held, rocked, and soothed the entitled.

I have contributed to the economic generation of my country since I was fourteen years old. I earned. I spent.

Our Son is a "Q"

KATHRYN HATASHITA-LEE

"MOM, WHEN WILL I learn to read?" asked Edward, our eight-year-old son.

I wished I could give an honest answer.

Edward showed signs of suffering from a learning disability. At three years old, he needed speech therapy to correct his moderate speech delay. Remembering the alphabet frustrated him.

Edward was anxious, hyperactive, and super-sensitive, just some of many traits displayed by learning disabled children. During a snowshoe trip at age five, he bonded with a snowball. Edward smiled with pride and then cried over his friend's fragile life span. Frantically preparing a shelter for his friend was Mission One. That's another story.

Seeing my child lag behind his peers in reading disheartened both of us. Yet I knew Edward was enthusiastic about math from an early age. Although he recalled the times table or calculated simple sums slowly, math topped as his favourite subject. If only his brain and the letters on a page could pair like synchronized dance partners, then Edward could leap confidently in his reading performance. For now, Edward could not take those steps.

One educated neighbour boasted her daughter Luanne, two years older than Edward, was so advanced that the local school Edward attended was not up to her standard. Luanne wanted to learn French at a school offering a French Immersion program.

At the community Christmas dinner, this neighbour said to me with a smile, "I guess you won't consider the Early French Immersion program for Edward with all his problems!" Our neighbour's eyes widened in admiration for her Luanne as she said with awe, "Luanne is so smart...."

Smart Luanne called Edward "That Stupid Boy." In a children's courtyard, a well-behaved younger girl who occasionally stuttered dissolved into tears when darling Luanne called her stuffed animal "garbage."

The neighbour left Canada to join her next new husband. Bye-bye, Luanne. The atmosphere in the children's courtyard improved.

While reading, Edward sometimes cried if he could not sound out a word, even if he read that word many times on earlier occasions. After a spelling test, Edward forgot what he just learned. As a Grade Two student in a One/Two split, he said in a small voice, "Even the Grade One students read better than me."

As a mother, I felt clueless as Edward struggled to catch up to his classmates, while the gap between his ability and written work widened. My husband and I had no training to guide Edward through the maze of letters, sounds, and phonics that complicate and enrich our English language.

Edward could not feel the same kind of pride his classmates knew from accomplishing the next step in schoolwork. At night, it was heart-breaking to hear Edward call himself "stupid" and sob into his pillow. When I reached over to pat him consolingly on his shoulder, I tried to convince him he was anything but stupid, but to no avail.

I asked Edward's Grade Two teacher to arrange a test for learning disabilities. Halfway through Grade Three, Edward underwent a psycho-educational assessment that set the ball rolling.

During the tests, the school psychologist was a big hit with Edward. Edward told me the school psychologist "was a really nice guy." Edward even said, "I want to thank the principal for letting me have time with the guy."

The school psychologist, a genial and enthusiastic father-figure, said frankly, "Edward has a learning disability."

Edward's IQ test result profile followed a wide zigzag with peaks and valleys showing high scores in object assembly and block design, and low scores in digit span and coding. I was not surprised to see that Edward rated low in short-term memory. The psychologist said engineers and architects typically have strengths in object assembly and block design. The psychologist's report said Edward conversed on a rather mature level with adults. Yet with an IQ in the 87th percentile, Edward's reading skill remained at the Grade One level.

The school psychologist said, "We want to make school the best possible experience for Edward."

The solution: change schools.

The new school housed one special needs class, an Extended Learning Assistance Centre program taught by Ms. James, who specialized in reading skills. The Ministry of Education gave Edward a "Q" designation for learning disabled students, allowing him to enrol in this program. Like his future "Q" classmates, Edward showed a marked difference between his cognitive ability and his performance achievement. All those bright students in Ms. James' class tested at least two years behind in their reading and writing skills.

Our son joined the one in approximately five Canadians with a learning disability. As for international names, inventor Thomas Edison, statesman Sir Winston Churchill, and mystery writer Dame Agatha Christie all lived with learning disabilities. Edward and his new "Q" friends would be in good company.

Edward seemed more buoyant for the last term at his old school. On the final day Edward's teacher named him "Most Responsible Member" of his class.

When Edward heard about his acceptance at the new school, he said with confidence, "I'll be able to read!"

I felt just as excited about Edward's new educational journey as he did. As a mother of a special needs child, I felt a kinship with other parents who faced the challenge of raising one or more children with a learning disability. We knew too well what happens when attention spans, behaviour, and emotions go out of sync and make our children's moods swing with unpredictable force. I looked to the special needs teacher and teaching assistants as the strategists who will help our kids break the code.

The more my husband Roger learned about gifted-learning disabled children, the more he saw himself. In elementary school, Roger almost joined a special needs class. The learning disabled trait seemed to pass through the male line. Roger, an instrumentation technician, builds instrument panels and calibrates equipment. He tinkers with any gizmo on our kitchen table with Edward at his side. Our living room housed more disassembled computers and TVs than is considered decent.

When Roger tries to pen a letter, he asks me how to spell his sister's name. I would not trade him for a super hero.

As a wife and mother, I lived with not one, but two learning disabled males in the family. During dinner, I listened to technical jargon on circuit boards, load cells, and weigh scales; other days I explained the difference between "their," "they're," and "there" to both of my men.

On Edward's first day of class, the small yellow school bus for special needs children approached our home. I waved enthusiastically to the bus driver.

Edward said, "Man, Mom, you don't have to jump up and down!"

His class with remedial Grades Four to Seven students followed an Individual Education Plan. A modified curriculum listed certain goals and objectives for each student. Their work stressed reading comprehension, fluency, writing, and math. Even the classroom setup was different: fewer distracting papers and decorations on the wall. Carrels for each student looked like semi-private office cubicles. No stimulation overload here!

The carefully monitored progress in Edward's class proved a blessing. Having everyone in the same boat likely helped reduce anxiety and boost the children's low self-esteem. Even the small yellow school bus offered a mobile clubhouse where kids raved about electronic games on the ride home. Along with homework in math, spelling, fluency, and sequencing, each child read for twenty minutes and required a parent's signature on a reading log. I think parents should also read to their child for twenty minutes minimum and have the child sign as a witness. Reading to children should be a Commandment for parents to follow.

I looked forward to Edward's reading time just before bed. We delighted in our sense of peace and "All's right with the world" (Browning 86) feeling as we explored what other souls dreamed and dared to set in ink.

During a teachers' strike, ten-year-old Edward came to work with me. As my boss prepared materials for a health workshop, she tried to create a map for a PowerPoint presentation. The task stumped her. Edward opened a Paint software application, drew the map with all the cities, and inserted the saved file as a PowerPoint slide. At the workshop, health professionals from pharmacists to rheumatologists viewed Edward's graphic art.

As a remedial Grade Six student, Edward struggled with board games that required words to win. Still super-sensitive, he almost burst into tears as he watched a fund-raising commercial showing children suffering in Third World conditions.

On December 13th, 2006, his class participated in the "Break a World Reading Record with *Charlotte's Web*" event. They and children around the world read the endearing "Salutations" passage. Charlotte would have approved.

A "Q" child typically displays talent in one or more fields. By all means, parents, encourage that passion! Edward showed his grandmother, a stroke survivor, how to navigate her computer system, much to her relief.

In your community you could meet kids with multiple needs, "A"; visual impairment, "E"; autism, "G"; or Moderate Behaviour Support/ Mental Illness, "R" (Special). Remember that one in approximately five Canadians lives with a learning disability? You might not realize who possesses that trait. An ordinary citizen, a celebrity, or your boss could live with a learning disability. A person with disabilities contributes to the diversity of the human race. You could depend on them as much as they depend on you. We live in a world where the impact of our imperfect senses can spur research, education, and advocacy.

When a determined child receives tremendous support from great teachers and staff in a special needs program, the confidence level leaps for both generations. Parenthood gave me a chance to witness a remarkable transformation. As an eight-year-old, Edward was an anxious child who barely remembered the alphabet; as a twelve-year-old, Edward finished remedial Grade Six with Grade Seven reading comprehension.

Last September, Edward walked farther down the school hallway and joined a regular Grade Seven class. I felt sorry that he left his "Q" classmates and the small, yellow school bus.

Edward may be a "Q," but he is definitely not a quitter.

WORKS CITED

Browning, Robert. "Song from 'Pippa Passes.'" *Poems that Touch the Heart*. Ed. A. L. Alexander. New York: Doubleday, 1956. 86.

"Special Needs Category." *Vancouver School Board*. 3 Jul. 2007. </http: //www.vsb.bc.ca/vsbprograms/IEP/specialneedscategories.htm>.

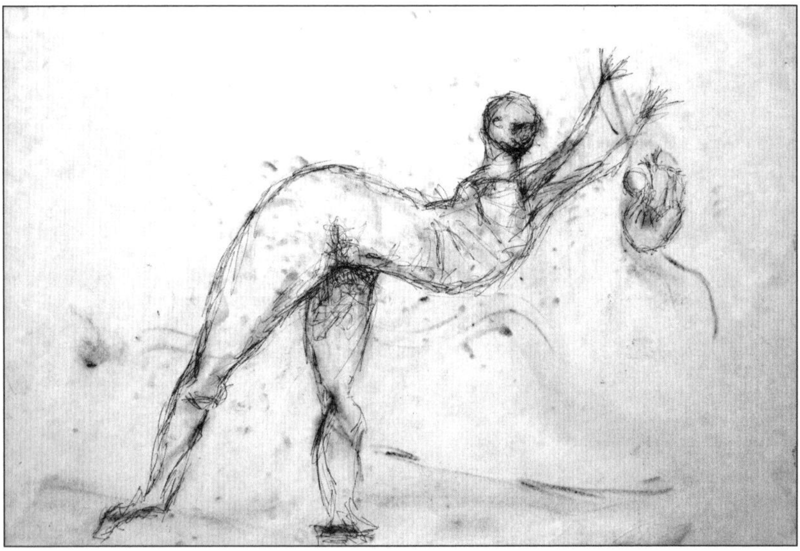

Lisa Loewen, *instinct/response,* 2007, carbon paper rubbing on layered vellum, 60.96 x 121.92 cm.

Part of the process of embracing motherhood came when I began to realize that some of our instincts are built into us in a very animalistic fashion, and others are learnt and refined through time, experience and mistakes. This piece examines the human process of failure and adaptation which I find myself constantly cycling through as a mother.

Sick Mother, No Mother

JANE ARSENAULT[1]

AT MY FIRST SESSION after my latest suicide attempt, my therapist asked me why I would do that to my sons. I replied that I felt that they were better off without me. She said that having a sick mother is better than having no mother at all. I understood, at the time, that she was trying to prevent me from trying to escape again in the near future, but I don't know that I believe that line. I have been ill my entire life as a mother—at first without really knowing it, but suspecting something was wrong. I continue to live with the chronic debilitating disease of depression, sometimes believing that I can be cured, other times knowing that I cannot. I will always be an ill mother, and, in some ways, always a mother who is more in need of mothering than able to mother, and often, a mother who is not there. Although I have grieved my mothering (or my not mothering), despised my mothering, and forsaken my mothering, I have never been able to celebrate it. I think I am only just surviving it. That's okay, because I can take it. But I worry (incessantly) on the effect of my crippled mothering on my sons, who, every day, pay the price for my illness and its manifestations, its distortions, and its limitations, and who, too frequently, have to mother me.

I enter motherhood unknowing illness

I was always dark, moody, miserable—"a witch," my mother had said. But I never realized that I was ill until my third son was born.

After the birth of my first son, I quit my job, cut off all social contact, and buried myself in the house with my baby—he was my one true love—the one who loved me even though I was dark, moody, and miserable. He needed me and I needed him.

After my second son was born, a mere fifteen months later, I was constantly fatigued, but I had two beings who loved and needed me. But they also had each other and, with surprising quickness, they became a pair, partners in crime, best friends—two beyond me.

My third son is only 18 months younger than my second son. He was born during a particularly harsh Saskatchewan winter. And he was colicky—crying four to six hours every night for the second to fourth months of his life. With three sons under three, little sleep, and no family or friends near me, I became more and more fatigued, more and more mechanical. It didn't help that I felt I had no maternal instincts.

One day I noticed the knife block on the kitchen counter…

it will never be ok i will never be okay i will never have time or space or people or even a self until i can end it as only i can end it and i have to end it there is nothing else i can do…nothing, no thing, n o t h i n g and so i must end it but i can't because i am the weakest person i know the least person i know and no one can understand what it is like because there is no like only hate and resentment and despair and pain and loneliness and fear and eternal nothingness so i must end all but i can't and that is the worst thing i can ever imagine[2]

I almost literally stopped living. I did just enough to keep the boys healthy and content—looking back, I don't know how I did that. I walked around the house in a daze, unshowered, in pyjamas, without eating, for days at a time. Often my husband would arrive home in the evening and ask what was for supper. I would not have even thought about that, except in that one second. He must have assumed that I was too busy with the boys to make supper. He never said much about it.

Within five months after my last childbirth, I was reduced to sitting in a corner of the living room sobbing, daily. My three-year-old played happily with my two-year-old and together they entertained their new playmate when he was awake, even crawling into the crib with him. They developed a taste for toast—an almost daily lunch or supper for them. My husband never said much about that either. I guess he thought women with young children act (or fail to act) this way.

When I saw the knife block on the kitchen counter, I called my doctor.

and when they tell you that it is all going to be okay they are lying because it might be okay for a day or a week or a month but in the end it is never going to be okay, never going to be not lonely never going to be something only nothing yet something very real and something very tangible and something very bad and there is no way out ever until it is done and then they tell you that if you do so you are bad because you are hurting everyone else they will be hurt and they care about you and they are better off if you are in pain and despair and longing and loneliness and they are better if you are here yet nowhere only when you are nowhere not even here and so it must be done and to hell with it all and to everyone who later will care and miss you and want to have helped you because it is already too late…

I mother with illness

Even though anti-depressants take the edge off, they are tricky, unpredictable, slow to take effect, and loaded with side effects. But, they stopped me from crying, and from wandering aimlessly, and from starving and dehydrating myself, and from my minimalist mothering.

So now mother is stoned—the chemically-enhanced mother—*vive les produits pharmaceutiques*. Besides the dry mouth and weight gain, I became hyperactive or manic or something. I did much more with my children—we sang and danced and drew and read and laughed. Our community of four, isolated and unbreakable, blossomed under the protection of my happy pills.

That's it. I'm cured. I thought. I hoped. I tried to believe. I still had the occasional dark moment—though not to the point of staring at the knife block on the kitchen counter. I still had the occasional crying jag—though usually only in association with PMS (punish my spouse; pack my suitcase). I still had the occasional bout of bulimic behaviour—though I was cooking and eating more frequently.

I should not have taken myself off the meds...

i thought it was over i went to the edge and i crawled back but it is not over and i know that it will never be over until i make it over

As my sons grew, they became increasingly aware that mommy was "sick." They noticed every time I teared up. They became the food police, constantly asking if I had eaten that day. They reported all odd behaviour to my mother 2,000 miles away and to my husband, absorbed in work and sports.

They started taking care of each other when mommy was sick. They hugged me and assured me when I was crying. They tucked me into bed and brought me crackers and water when I was exhausted. They reminded each other that if they didn't behave, mommy would be sick again. That was the worst of all. They thought they made me cry, made me tired, made me stop functioning, made me sick. I assured them that none of it was their fault, nor their father's—nobody's fault, in fact.

As older children, they occasionally were tired of my being pathetic. My oldest would warn me not to start crying AGAIN. My middle would complain that I needed to buy groceries SOMETIMES. My youngest complained that no friends were allowed to visit when I was LIKE THAT. Then they would apologize, put me to bed, feed me crackers and water, and then make themselves supper and tidy up. I imagine they must have been disgusted by me, or disappointed in me, or hated me.

I had to go back on meds—MORE meds, forever.

they are hiding and lying and believing that it is not there that all is ok that soon it will be okay and they are better off better off crying because their mother is gone and their mother will not help them that their mother has failed them that their mother is free they are better off that they no longer have to see what no one else can see that they don't have to face it or hide it or explain it or understand it as if they could and if their time comes they will follow more bravely more willingly to end what they know cannot be fixed or hidden or ended unless they end it they know they know and i wish to God that they didn't know but they know more than anyone they know

I survive (they survive) mothering with illness

As my sons entered adolescence and were more capable of understanding the nature of depression (as if anyone could understand the nature of depression) and the weirdness that comes with it (and the mania in between bouts of normalcy and depression—a mania they came to embrace), they stopped blaming themselves, their father, and even me. Perhaps they still blamed biology, or fate, or God, but they never told me.

Sometimes they put me on display like a circus freak—come and see the wild mother who acts like a kid, who is outrageous, who is comedic all the time (and often in hyperspeed). Their friends liked to hang out at our house knowing that there would always be a show, and realizing that I was barely capable (indeed, incapable) of maintaining order or discipline. (Still, no one was badly behaved or tried to provoke me.) They loved the ridiculously messy (although not *dirty*) house with barely any floor showing in any room at any given time. They loved the compulsive baking and odd cooking, snarfing whatever I had made—a dozen pies, loads of muffins, dinners of only meat, cereal at any meal except breakfast. They loved my unmotherness—my unlikeness to their mothers. They thought I was cool, wacky, unique—not sick. My sons always knew better, but pretended not to.

Then came the big bang—twelve years after the first...

i don't ask for forgiveness or understanding or sympathy or empathy or regret or love or any thing i just ask that i am allowed to be who i must be the figure falling the figure who has already fallen so short of all and so long that the top is no longer seen that the bottom is looming and yet never there i can only fall off the edge one more time

I began to lose all control. I attempted a half-assed suicide plot—pulling my car in front of an on-coming semi only to pull back into my own lane. Then I had a better plan. I would say good-bye to each member of my family and I settled on a date—August 31st, the second day of school. I felt oddly relieved.

I could get out of the mess I had made. My husband could marry a *normal* woman who could love and function. The boys would be freed from the damaging effects of crazy mother—perhaps even be rehabilitated. I could stop the cycle of normal, depressed, manic, and back again. Most of all, I could end the pain—the tangible, physical pain of my depression jail. I could escape. It was the only solution.

They really should have seen it coming. I had three traffic infractions in three days—they did take my keys away from me for the fourth day.

I would cry hysterically and then drop to the floor laughing equally hysterically. They just laughed at me and tried to convinced me that the episode was over. But they really should have noticed that I had already stopped living—I stopped eating, bathing, dressing, socializing, doing. Maybe it wasn't so obvious given their experiences with me. Maybe they just couldn't see. Maybe they just wouldn't see.

That was in 2007.

i cannot eat or sleep or breathe or think or exist this is it

I celebrate mothering despite illness

Perhaps "celebrating" is not quite the right word. But I am the mother, the woman, the person, that I am because of everything—the depression, the periods of normalcy, the mania, the death, the good and the bad.

Maybe the reason why my children and I are so close is because of our reciprocal mothering (although, I guess, since they are boys, they would father me). Maybe we are strengthened by facing this disease (because when all is said and done, that is what it is) together, head on. Maybe their remarkable emotional strength and independence comes from their premature (and unfair, I know) responsibility. Maybe they will survive and thrive in spite of me, in spite of my depression. At least I have the satisfaction of knowing that, for now, none of them exhibits the behaviours of depressions themselves, and their teachers and coaches assure me that my sons are happy and, surprisingly, quite normal.

But I still wonder about our future. I still have several years of direct parenting, and, likely, several years of offering advice (yikes) and my perspectives (warped as they may be). So, I still see the potential for causing more irreparable damage, or failing as a mother, of having them mother/father me. And what about when they are grown and have their own children—will they still feel the need to take care of me so closely—even distantly? Or will I be far enough out of my parental responsibility finally to free them? Still, I hope they will let me play with my grandchildren and I hope that they can forgive me.

I still think no parent is better than this sick parent. And there is still only one way out. But, for now, I remain.

i can see them in the hospital newborn innocent and unharmed pure and naïve and i know that this will not last because i am guilty and i am scarred and i am tainted and i know i have already hurt them and i have already abandoned them and they will end up at my side my graveside and hate me for what i have done

[1]The author is using a pseudonym.

[2]These intervals were written during actual bouts of depression, and are intended to give the reader a glimpse into the distorted logic of the author during moments of extreme despair.

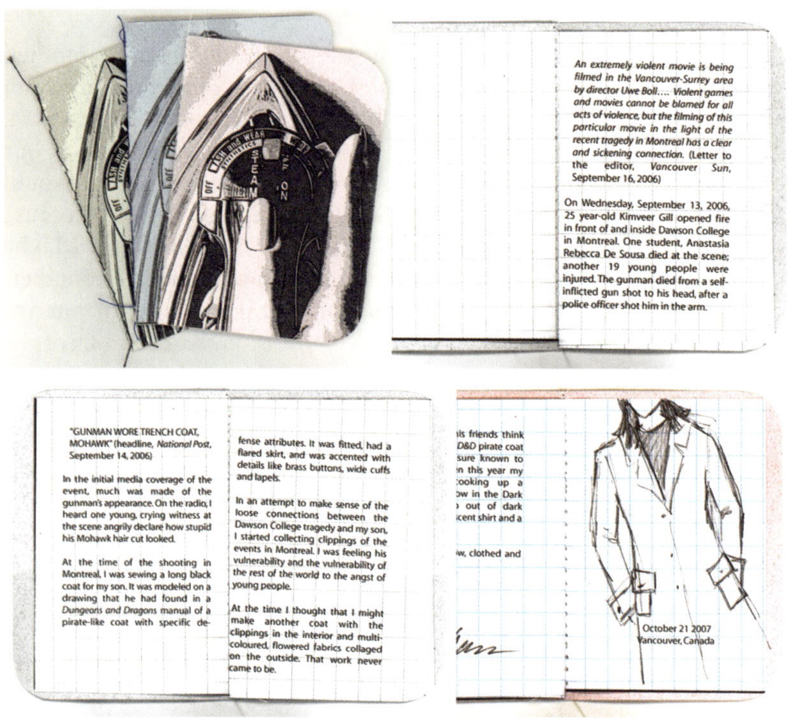

Lois Klassen, *A Personal Story About Clothing #3 - A clear & sickening connection, 2007,*
artist trading card booklet. Laser print on loose-leaf paper and card stock,
machine-sewn binding, pencil sketch, 6.35 x 8.89 cm.

A clear & sickening connection makes associations between the artist's family and details from the 2006 Dawson College tragedy. As with two others in this series of personal stories about clothing, it is a tiny book about small domestic discoveries.

Mothering in the Context of HIV/AIDS

PAMELA J. DOWNE

> *Once the fluids stopped running, I was cut loose. It was, like, nobody cared about me or my kid after I stopped breastfeeding... That's when I sunk to the low of lows. And my baby died. And they took my other children. I just got lost. I'm lost.*
>
> —"Kim" (a pseudonym), HIV-positive mother of three

"DESPITE ALL THE everyday challenges, motherhood is a source of non-stop joy," declared the popular American television talk show host, Dr. Phil McGraw, during an episode of the *Dr. Phil* show that aired in Saskatoon, Saskatchewan on June 13, 2007. As I flipped channels, this caught my attention and I stopped; this statement was very much at odds with the story that Kim, the woman whose words began this chapter, had shared so openly with me that afternoon.

At 32 years of age, Kim is an HIV-positive Aboriginal woman who moved from a northern community to Saskatoon three years ago when she was pregnant with her third child. She had regained custody of her two children, and decided to move where she might find employment and where the father of her unborn baby could not reach, threaten, or hurt her (as he had been doing). However, Saskatoon proved to be a lonely place for Kim, and she turned to the one "friend" she knew she could count on: "Lady Meth, she's always there for me, you know? Even when I know I shouldn't be doing it, Lady Meth is my best friend." Methamphetamine ("meth"), a highly addictive psychostimulant, is injected, inhaled, or, in its crystal form, smoked to achieve a "rush" that is followed by a reasonably prolonged euphoria or high. Kim had been injecting methamphetamine since early 2002, shortly after the birth of her second child, and the drug provided "a great way to bond with the baby, who cried all the time, just non-stop." The drug-induced alertness helped Kim to attend to the needs of her then five-year old daughter and her new born son, and the sense of euphoria temporarily minimized her self-doubts, concerns about money, as well as the physical and psychological effects of an abusive relationship. As in most cases, however, physiological tolerance to the drug quickly developed and Kim needed higher and more frequent doses to obtain the desired results.

Supporting what Susan Boyd and Nancy Campbell have found in their studies of women and addiction, illicit drug use was perceived by Kim to be a source of friendship and support. However, not even "Lady Meth" could offer the support Kim needed during her third pregnancy in 2005. In the course of prenatal care, an HIV test came back positive:

> *I knew that using needles was a risk ... I knew that I might get AIDS ... but I needed the drug more, and there was times when I used whatever needle I could get my hands on. I tried to clean them, you know, but sometimes I guess I just didn't do it good, and then the test said I was positive for HIV.*

As an HIV-positive Aboriginal woman living well below Saskatoon's low-income line, facing the challenges of addiction, and caring for her two children while pregnant, Kim became exhausted and despondent as she negotiated health care and social service systems that James Waldram, Ann Herring and T. Kue Young state have historically been, and continue to be, inhospitable and hostile to Aboriginal women in her situation. "It was like I wasn't just a junkie Indian mom anymore, now I was a junkie Indian mom who was dying of HIV. And I felt like all hell broke loose." Kim's HIV status marked her as a suspect mother whose seropositivity led to a series of interventions: social workers were assigned to her case, public health nurses visited, the community HIV nurse came to her door. Kim felt under siege.

After her third child was born in the fall of 2005, Kim and the baby developed serious drug-related complications. Kim started having seizures and, at one point, her oldest child found her convulsing on the bathroom floor. As traumatic as this event was, it was a turning point and Kim developed a strong and rejuvenated commitment to living a drug-free and health maximizing life. Unfortunately, for Kim, this rejuvenated commitment came too late. Her daughter's 911 call brought greater concern from Child and Youth Services. Her social workers informed Kim that her children had been in harm's way too many times, and the two older children were placed first in emergency care, and then in a more permanent foster home situation. Because Kim was breastfeeding her now three-month old baby, daily visits to her home were arranged and Kim felt disoriented and despondent by these forced changes. The public health nurse felt strongly that Kim should stop breastfeeding so as to minimize the risk of HIV transmission. It was then that Kim described seeking "the lowest of lows," and the next thing Kim remembers is being told that her infant had died from a seizure.

When she and I spoke some five months later, Kim was clearly in mourning. She mourns the absence of her children who still live in foster care and she mourns the death of her infant son. These losses are embedded in still another: the loss of formal and informal systems of support. She was "cut loose" and "got lost." Kim concluded our interview by asking rhetorically, "Why would anyone care about *me*?" Later that same afternoon, Dr. Phil's televised audience cheered loudly as he extolled the virtues and "non-stop joy" of motherhood, scolding those panelists who, despite having the courage and interest in participating in his show, did not agree with his sweeping statement. With Kim's story fresh in my mind, it became clear that she and Dr. Phil were speaking a very different language about motherhood.

MOTHERHOOD AND HIV/AIDS: OVERVIEW OF A PILOT PROJECT

Why should a discussion of mothering in Canada include an entry on HIV/AIDS? Why, given all the challenges mothers face and the questions posed to motherhood itself, should we consider, seriously and centrally, the interrelationship between motherhood and HIV/AIDS? Currently, and very significantly, the proportion of all newly diagnosed HIV infections and reported adult AIDS cases occurring in women in Canada is increasing. According to the Public Health Agency of Canada, women represent 27 percent of all newly diagnosed HIV infections, a two-fold increase from 20 years earlier. Of particular relevance to our discussion of motherhood is the fact that women of childbearing ages (17-39 years) account for 75 percent of all HIV infections among adult women in Canada, raising very serious concerns for maternal health. Seroprevalence studies indicate much higher rates of HIV infection among pregnant women living in large and mid-sized metropolitan areas, and Aboriginal women are over-represented among those diagnosed with HIV/AIDS in these urban settings. As the research of the Public Health Agency of Canada also shows, although Saskatchewan has one of the lowest HIV/AIDS rates in Canada, it also has one of the lowest male-to-female ratios of HIV (5: 1), meaning that the infection is rapidly becoming one of the most significant health concerns for women and mothers.

Despite this profile, few services are designed specifically to meet the needs of mothers living with, affected by, or vulnerable to HIV/AIDS. This may be because we know very little about the daily experiences of mothers facing HIV/AIDS. Researchers have framed and responded to the changing HIV profile with a virtually exclusive focus on pre- and perinatal transmission; and while there is no doubt that this is a critically important topic, it leaves important dimensions of the interrelationship between motherhood and HIV/AIDS unexplored. As Kim's story clearly illustrates, mothering in the context of HIV/AIDS extends beyond the pre- and peri-natal periods, with important implications for maternal wellbeing.

In January 2006, AIDS Saskatoon, the primary community-based HIV/AIDS organization in central and northern Saskatchewan, identified mothers as a significant and growing constituency among those who access their services but for whom no programs were specifically designed. To meet the needs of mothers better, AIDS Saskatoon and I embarked on a research project to generate the information that was needed for program development and service integration. Through the course of this research, I met Kim and four other women who together comprised a small sample of women who identify as mothers, who access HIV/AIDS-related services, and who are infected with, or otherwise affected by HIV/AIDS.

According to Gay Becker, narrative "is our primary means of accessing the world of bodily experience and is essential to our understanding of that experience" (26). Stories are no longer seen as the "accidental form in which data come" (Garro and Mattlingly 4) and health researchers across the disciplines now employ narrative analyses to provide important insights into medical processes and health conditions. However, listening to, and being moved by a story like Kim's is very different (though not unrelated) to analyzing it for what it tells us about the life circumstances, choices, and challenges that are made by mothers every day. Analysis requires that we centrally situate these stories in the broader contexts that give rise to them, as well as in the research context where they are shared. The former is a prairie context where HIV/AIDS is both feminized and indigenized; the latter is a research context involving an initial meeting followed by a two- to three-hour interview in which participants have the opportunity to share whatever stories they feel best reflect what it means to be a mom in the context of HIV/AIDS. Through their stories, the women emphasized repeatedly that facing HIV/AIDS posed unique and significant challenges to them *as women*. Indeed, as Erika Burger and Barbara Clow note, "[W]omen and girls are at greater risk of exposure to HIV because their bodies are different than those of males *and* because their actions and attitudes are expected to be different" (10). In sharing the insight that HIV/AIDS is gendered, the women participating in this study, spoke to the increasing feminization of HIV/AIDS.

Processes of feminization intersect with those of marginalization and racialization, as described by Denise Spitzer and Charles Briggs respectively. This has brought important information to light, such as the fact that among those living with HIV/AIDS in Vancouver, food insecurity and hunger are more likely experienced by Aboriginal women with children (Normén *et al.* 825), that Aboriginal women are more likely to be co-infected with hepatitis-C and HIV (Braitstein *et al.* 691), and that sexual violence and dislocation are common experiences in these women's lives (McKeon *et al.* 9). The feminization and indigenization of HIV/AIDS, however, have also resulted in the reiteration of "dominant representations of Aboriginal women that are deeply embedded Canadian colonial history"; these, in turn, lead to "a preference for exotic and spectacular representations of drugs, sex, violence, and crime rather than the … mundane brutality of everyday poverty" that underlies the epidemic (Culhane 594). A study of HIV/AIDS stories in Aboriginal-focused newspapers, for example, found that "although Aboriginal women were identified as being at high risk, the coverage also emphasized their lack of knowledge regarding HIV/AIDS" (Hoffman-Goetz, Friedman and Clarke 145). While misconceptions certainly exist, this emphasis on the *lack* of knowledge (rather than a differently situated knowledge) plays into discriminatory stereotypes of Aboriginal women.

For those of us interested in understanding the dimensions and diverse expressions of motherhood and mothering in Canada, picking up on these important insights and offering further inquiry into them are essential tasks.

PATTERNS AND UNANSWERED QUESTIONS

From the image-rich stories that the women shared, three important patterns emerged: oscillation in motherhood experiences; mother identities; and indigenization. The first and perhaps most apparent pattern is that there appears to be considerable oscillation between, on the one hand, positive and empowering motherhood experiences that lead to health promoting activities and, on the other hand, more negative motherhood experiences that exacerbate HIV/AIDS risks. Kim's turning point moment occurred after she suffered a seizure and subsequently recognized the danger she and her children faced. She then recast her methamphetamine use, not as the friend she once knew, but as a drug that she no longer wanted to take, and she expressed rejuvenated commitment to addiction treatment and health-generating activities. The tone of Kim's voice changed when she recalled this moment; there were fewer hesitations in her speech, stronger verbs, fewer modifiers, and a higher pitch with louder resonance. A similar tone rang through the story told by Elise, an HIV-positive, Euro-Canadian woman and mother of three. Being a role model to her daughters is a source of inspiration for Elise to "stay strong." She elaborated by telling a laughter-filled story about the last supervised visit she had with her children. Her nine-year old daughter wanted to practice "walking like mom" and the two of them choreographed a special kind of walk in which the daughter mirrored her mother. "I think of that a lot," Elise explained. "It was so much fun watching her imitate my walk. I keep thinking about that, wanting to give her good stuff, strong stuff to imitate." Motivated by that desire, Elise adamantly adheres to harm reduction drug use practices, pursues addiction treatment, and follows anti-retroviral drug therapy regimes.

For both Kim and Elise, however, positive motherhood moments were offset by the more negative experiences of custody loss and in Kim's case, the death of her infant. Just how women negotiate the swings between these positive and negative motherhood experiences in the context of HIV/AID is not fully known. Given the implications this has for health promoting behaviours and for maternal care, this is a gaping hole in the literature that is in urgent need of redress.

The second pattern that emerged in the pilot project pertains to mother identities. The literature on identity construction is massive and interdisciplinary. Scholars of motherhood—including Fiona Green, Tina Miller, and Fiona Nelson, among many others—have contributed significantly to it by exploring the ways in which women come and continue to identify as mothers, and what those identities entail. Again, though, when it comes to exploring this in the context of HIV/AIDS, scholars and advocates have been curiously quiet. This may be because, as Kim's story illustrates so well, to talk about mothers and HIV/AIDS in North America involves talking about mothers and injection drug use. For decades, there has been a persistent aversion to, and hostility toward women who have children and who use drugs. Nancy Campbell explains that, "While in the past women addicts who were pregnant or mothering were constructed as poor mothers who violated feminine norms..., in the latter decades of the century women who biologically 'reproduced' addiction played stunningly demonized roles" (138-9). These demonized roles give rise to demonized identities, and by the late 1990s addicted mothers became cast as predacious and abusive "baby killers" (Korbin 253). This abject identity not only bears down on mothers through harsh social judgment and punitive legislative control; it is also internalized with each mother acting potentially as her own harshest critic. Recall Kim's statement, "It was like I wasn't just a junkie Indian mom anymore, now I was a junkie Indian mom who was dying of HIV" and her final rhetorical question, "why would anybody care?"

Negotiating the stigmatized terrains of HIV/AIDS, addiction, and in the case of another participant in this pilot project, sex trade involvement, is different for women depending on (among other things) their custodial and residential relationship with their children. However, once again, we find little in the existing motherhood literature on the effects that full-time caretaking, non-custodial mothering, partial access, or non-residential arrangements have on the ways in which motherhood is expressed in the context of HIV/AID. The results from this pilot project suggest that maternal identities are profoundly influenced by the mother's custodial status, with custodial and full-time caregiving mothers expressing greater concern for health-promoting behaviours, and mothers with more restricted access to their children expressing greater fear for their children's wellbeing and less hope for their own future.

Third and finally, this pilot project suggests that patterns of indigenization are very significant to prairie mothers who are living with, affected by, and/or vulnerable to HIV/AIDS. Ann Silversides notes that HIV/AIDS is seen throughout prairie Canada as an "Aboriginal infection" and the Euro-Canadian women participating in this study consequently reported not only feeling at lower risk but even immune to HIV. The Aboriginal participants, on the other hand, explained that they "expected" to become infected because, as Kim put it, "AIDS is an Indian thing." With the association of Aboriginality and HIV/AIDS, Kim and Charlotte both felt that as Aboriginal women their mothering was subject to harsher judgments than White women might face. Kim felt under siege by the surveillance that followed her HIV test, and Charlotte recounted an incident when a stranger in a shopping mall accused her of giving her children fetal alcohol syndrome. "If that woman had known I was at risk for AIDS," Charlotte explained, "I bet she would have hit me! But she would never know that the kids got grandmas and aunties and lots of love."

Kim Anderson persuasively argues that Aboriginal motherhood—though definitely fragmented by nation, community and broader colonial context—has never been subject to the same privatization that Shari Thurer claims characterizes British, French and colonial maternity. Instead, Anderson argues that motherhood in Aboriginal communities is more collectivist, with other mothers (grandmothers, extended kin, and neighbours) participating actively in the nurturing, mentoring and care of children. While extreme caution must be taken not to reproduce misleading dichotomies of collectivism and individualism, and we should always keep in mind that "Native women have definitely been caught up in the 'history and ideology' of patriarchal western motherhood" (Anderson 761), there is now a growing body of literature that attests to the material, discursive and ideological differences that separate Aboriginal from Euro-Canadian motherhood (Bédard). However, just how these differences manifest themselves in the contexts of HIV/AIDS, and particularly in contexts of indigenized HIV/AIDS, remain unknown and unexamined.

CONCLUSION

For scholars of motherhood and mothering in Canada, Kim's story and the shifting profile of HIV/AIDS should be compelling reasons to explore how the oscillation between positive and negative mothering experiences, mother identities, and indigenization affect maternal health and care. With the establishment of the Association for Research on Mothering in 1998, a flurry of activity has ensued in bringing together scholars, activists, practitioners, community leaders, and mothers to explore dimensions of what it means to be a mother in all regions of Canada. Opening and pursuing a discussion of what it means to be a mother in Canada facing HIV/AIDS is an important contribution to this task because I firmly believe that Kim deserves an answer to her question, "why would anybody care?"

WORKS CITED

Anderson, Kim. "Giving Life to the People: An Indigenous Ideology of Motherhood." *Maternal Theory: Essential Readings*. Ed. Andrea O'Reilly. Toronto: Demeter, 2007. 761-81.

Becker, Gay. *Disrupted Lives: How People Create Meaning in a Chaotic World*. Berkeley: University of California Press, 1997.

Bédard, Renée. "An Anishinaabe-kwe Ideology on Mothering and Motherhood." *"Until Our Hearts are on the Ground": Aboriginal Mothering, Oppression, Resistance and Rebirth*. Ed. D. Memee Lavell-Harvard and Jeannette C. Lavell. Toronto: Demeter, 2006. 65-75.

Boyd, Susan. *Mothers and Illicit Drugs: Transcending the Myths*. Toronto: University of Toronto Press, 1999.

Briggs, Charles L. "Communicability, Racial Discourse, and Disease." *Annual Review of Anthropology* 34.1 (2005): 269-91.

Burger, Erika and Barbara Clow. "From Recognition to Action: Gender-Based Analysis and Mainstreaming in HIV/AIDS." *Research Bulletin of the Centres for Excellence for Women's Health* 5.2 (2006): 10-11.

Braitstein, Paula *et al.* "Differences in Access to Care Among Injection Drug Users Infected Either with HIV and Hepatitis-C or Hepatitis-C Alone." *AIDS Care* 18.7 (2006): 690-93.

Campbell, Nancy. *Using Women: Gender, Drug Policy, and Social Justice*. New York: Routledge, 2000.

Culhane, Dara. "Their Spirits Live with Us: Aboriginal Women in Downtown Eastside Vancouver Emerging into Visibility." *American Indian Quarterly* 27 (2003): 593-606.

Garro, Linda and Cheryl Mattingly. "Narrative as Construct and Construction." *Narrative and the Cultural Construction of Illness and Healing*. Ed. Mattingly and Garro. Berkeley: University of California Press, 2000. 1-49.

Government of Canada. *HIV and AIDS in Canada: Surveillance Report to June 30, 2006*. Ottawa: Surveillance and Risk Assessment Division, Centre for Infectious Disease Prevention and Control. Ottawa: Government of Canada, 2006.

Green, Fiona. "Feminist Mothers: Successfully Negotiating the Tensions

Between Motherhood as 'Institution' and 'Experience'." *Mother Outlaws: Theories and Practices of Empowered Mothering*. Ed. Andrea O'Reilly. Toronto: Women's, 2004. 31-42.

Hoffman-Goetz, Laurie, Daniela B. Friedman, and Juanne N. Clarke. "HIV/AIDS Risk Factors as Portrayed in Mass Media Targeting First Nations, Métis, and Inuit Peoples of Canada." *Journal of Health Communication* 10.2 (2005): 145-62.

Korbin, Jill. "'Good Mothers,' 'Baby Killers,' and Fatal Child Maltreatment." *Small Wars: The Cultural Politics of Childhood*. Ed. Nancy Scheper-Hughes and Carolyn Sargent. Berkley: University of California Press, 1998. 253-76.

McKeon, Iris *et al.* "Sexual Violence and Dislocation in Women's Acquisition of HIV in Manitoba." *Research Bulletin of the Centres for Excellence for Women's Health* 5.2 (2006): 8-9.

Miller, Tina. *Making Sense of Motherhood: A Narrative Approach*. Cambridge: Cambridge University Press, 2005.

Nelson, Fiona. "Motherhood as Culture: Rituals and Rites of Passage." *Motherlife: Studies of Mothering Experience*. Ed. Vangie Bergun and Jeanne VanderZalm. Edmonton: Pedagon, 2007. 83-100.

Normén, Lena *et al.* "Food Insecurity and Hunger Prevalent Among HIV-Positive Individuals in British Columbia Canada." *Journal of Nutrition* 135.4 (2005): 820-25.

Silversides, Ann. "Complex and Unique HIV/AIDS Epidemic among Aboriginal Canadians." *Canadian Medical Association Journal* 175.11 (2006): 13-59.

Spitzer, Denise. "Engendering Health Disparities." *Canadian Journal of Public Health* 96.S2 (2005): 78-96.

Thurer, Shari. *The Myths of Motherhood: How Culture Reinvents the Good Mother*. Boston: Houghlin, 1994.

Waldram, James, Ann Herring, and T. Kue Young. *Aboriginal Health in Canada: Historical, Cultural and Epidemiological Perspectives*. Toronto: University of Toronto Press, 2006.

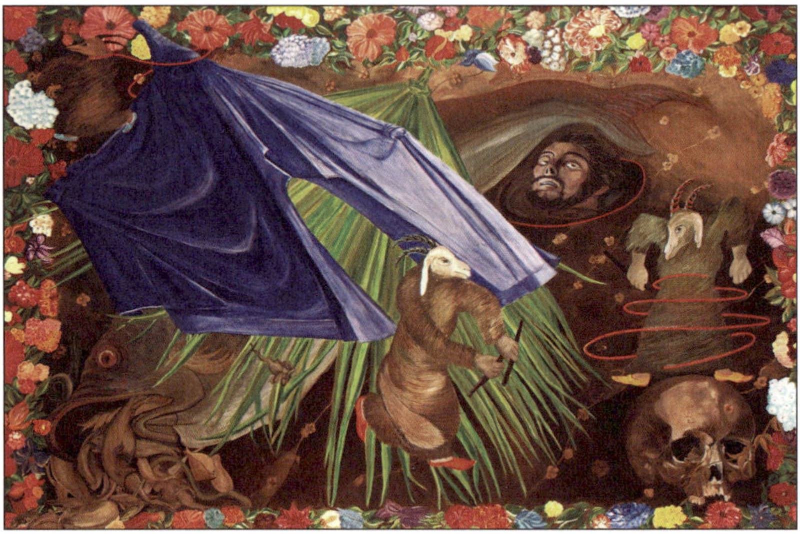

Sylvat Aziz, *Mother of all Postcards (or the Haha behind the Bush)*, 2004-05, oil/pigment on canvas, 396.24 x 518.16 cm.

The work targets the dominant paradigm necessary for the western masses to stay ignorant or, euphemistically, innocent. It portrays the relentless compulsive consumption of the first world on the resources and survival of the "other" as "mothering," or an enforced dependence that maintains the current 'desirable' global economic order.

Fetal Alcohol Spectrum Disorder

Mothering the Child Who "Can't"

HELEN HOY

As parents, our job is to snatch our children from the path of an oncoming train. We've come to realize that our daughter is *the train.* —Mother in Guelph FASD support group

ONE DAY, WHEN my daughter Elizabeth was eight years old, I said to her crossly, with inappropriately elevated vocabulary (we had no idea of her problem; she now has the usual FASD[1] verbal expressiveness and difficulty with verbal comprehension), "This impertinent talk is going to stop right now." Characteristically, she retorted at once, "No, it's not." Then, quite uncharacteristically, she paused, reflected for a moment, and added, "It should.... But it's not going to." Fetal Alcohol in a nutshell.

When Elizabeth was twelve years old (still no diagnosis, but we were beginning to think fetal alcohol), she and I were at a therapy session at the Community Mental Health Clinic. I had posted short maxims for her on the refrigerator (invitingly entitled "Tips for Teenagers"), illustrated with stick figures (not prohibitions with "don't," but instructions in the positive, as recommended for children with FASD). But I had no idea whether she was taking them in or able to remember them. "Let's ask Elizabeth," said the therapist. Too bashful to speak out directly, Elizabeth leaned forward to whisper one example to me. "'Hands off other people,'" she quoted, while at the same time dabbing a black line on my face with her magic marker.

My daughter was diagnosed at age thirteen with Alcohol-Related Neurodevelopmental Disorder (ARND), which falls under the umbrella term Fetal Alcohol Spectrum Disorder. In the five years since then, I've been a desperate/grateful member of the Guelph Fetal Alcohol Spectrum Disorder parent-support group, sharing the stories and strategies, anguish and laughter of parents with children damaged by alcohol before birth.[2]

Donna Debolt, an FASD consultant in Lethbridge, has described the characteristics presented by caregivers of alcohol-affected children, and, more specifically, has enumerated the losses we caregivers experience, losses producing the grief, the frustration, the resistance to suggestions, or the apparent craziness we may exhibit. Debolt lists such losses as loss of dreams, of shared milestones, of a sense of competence, of financial resources, of a balanced family system, of family and friends' support, of independence, of privacy, and ultimately of our children themselves (also in Buxton 261). Using evidence from my own mothering and that of the other mothers I have encountered, I want to expand the subjective side of FASD mothering. And the mothering I've observed, in almost every instance, has been a different, as well more as intensive, version of the parenting provided by fathers, mothers acting as the co-ordinators of their children's care.

One of the encouraging changes advocated for FASD caregivers is a shift in thinking and expectations, from perceiving a child who *will* not, a bad child engaged in wilful misconduct, to recognizing a damaged child who *cannot* (Malbin np), cannot learn from consequences, read social cues, predict effects, recognize similarities and generalize, interpret sensations of pain or temperature, perform executive functions of planning and breaking tasks into steps, maintain attention, draw inferences, handle money and time, regulate emotion, control impulses, retain and access information consistently, or think well abstractly. That change in expectations, and the shift from useless behaviour modification to modifications of the child's environment, reducing demands and stresses, simplifying her physical and mental world, helped save my family and me, once we recognized that Elizabeth had FASD. We put her in a private school, for kids with learning disabilities, with smaller classes, short assignments, repetition, immediate follow-up, and controlled social interactions. We eliminated punitive consequences and the emotional escalations they produced. We talked less and more briefly. We anticipated the stress of transitions, hunger, lack of movement, fatigue, menstruation, illness, and over-stimulation. We demanded less of Elizabeth, while keeping her occupied and supervised as much as possible. I wrote her daily notes about her successes. And her behaviour improved.

Now, however, as she turns eighteen, I'm facing the other side of that mantra: "It's not that they won't; it's that they can't." She really *cannot* break down good resolutions into the steps needed to realize them, being at her place in the evening in order go to school the next morning. She cannot learn, from experience, that if she hangs out with street kids, she will get entangled with the law. She cannot resist the immediate gratification of a drug or an exciting new friend or a party. She has little recognition of the stages and reciprocality of relationships, making instant "best friends," draping herself over the boy she just met, assuming that someone is safe because he's known to someone else she has just met through the internet. She cannot use the rational part of her brain to counter the adrenaline rush of a teenage drama, a friend with a bloodied nose, with a police charge, with a romantic crisis. And she cannot appreciate the extent of her deficits and vulnerabilities or accept help for them. Now that she has shrugged off the structures created for her by her family, her school, and the supportive residence she lived in for half a year after refusing the rules of home, I can see how much her successful path was the product of those invisible fence-rails. The absence of the "external forebrain" (Sterling qtd. in Buxton 109) that we, and others, provided shows just how poorly her own forebrain serves her.

MY CHILD ISN'T SO DIFFICULT: WHY AM I HAVING SUCH A HARD TIME?

In talking about children with FASD, I never know whether to shock listeners with the horror stories—and I have a number —or to stress the apparent ordinariness of such children. With an estimated one in one hundred Canadians affected by prenatal alcohol poisoning, you all have met many and not even known it (most of them undiagnosed and unaware of why they are having such difficulties). Alcohol-affected children have been described as verbal "savants," who, because they talk well, are mistakenly assumed to think well (Lutke and Antrobus 63). One of the challenges of this syndrome is having a child perceived by many as "normal." On the same day, I have had one of my sisters say, "I don't see anything wrong with Elizabeth," and "You let her talk to you like that!" at once denying the difficulty *and* criticizing my failure to handle it well. So, mothers simultaneously feel overcome by the extremity of raising such a child and apologetic about flagging under challenges similar to those faced by many parents of difficult children and teenagers, not to mention addicted, bipolar, physically disabled, schizophrenic, suicidal, or technologically-dependent children. What differentiates FASD mothering from the mothering of the ordinary, difficult child are the intensity, relentlessness, and intractability of the behaviours, the unlikelihood that behaviours will respond to the usual interventions, and the lack of hope for a future reprieve.

"INDUSTRIAL-STRENGTH TRAFFIC ON DOMESTIC-STRENGTH BRIDGES" (DEBOLT)

Bonnie Buxton, in *Damaged Angels*, replaces the roller coaster, as a metaphor for life with a child with FASD,[3] with the constantly spinning kaleidoscope (264). I might suggest the tilt-a-whirl. Everything can be upside right one moment, then you're fitting an apparent rape into your day and unsure even whether it's an emergency, or a confabulation, or an instance of spin control. Conversely, a seeming crisis can prove to be premature. How can I join the long-planned, summer women's week at a cottage, when Elizabeth, who has taken an unauthorized two-night absence, on top of a two-week suspension of privileges from Wyndham House, is likely to return angry and ready to sabotage her stay there, and my partner may over-react to whatever happens? Then, the week proves uneventful, with no trouble at her residence and an actual improvement in their father-daughter relationship. Or Elizabeth comes home for a visit. Though I know that, for her, taking money is like a hungry person's taking food, when I discover ten dollars missing from the purse I've hidden in a closet, I feel surprisingly unsettled and hurt to think that "I'm feeling homesick" may simply mean "I need a chance to find and take some money."

So, disequilibrium is a persistent feature of FASD mothering. The one predictable feature is that you can count on change. When Elizabeth's needs or wants are met, when her world has been stable for a while, when she's not stressed, not over-stimulated, not trying to impress peers, and not in social conflict, she can be a warm, funny, smart, and gentle girl. She wants to please and be loved, and there are moments when we get painful glimpses of the person she could have been, if her brain had not been poisoned with alcohol before birth. Indeed, the differences in behaviour from one period to another can be so great that, even after diagnosis, the temptation of denial can loom again. I've tried to persuade myself from time to time that Elizabeth's diagnosis was based on assessments at a time when wrong medications and withdrawal from other medications were exacerbating her symptoms. It only takes one new moment of driven behaviour to correct that self-deception.

FASD keeps you off-balance, blindsiding you. "I have trained myself to have no expectations at all," one mother in our group says. "It hurts too much. Something goes well, then it all comes crashing down." While you are working against a deadline on funding for her group-home stay (with its structured expectations), your child phones that she's dropping out of her credit-recovery summer course—an automatic disqualification for the home—later the same day that she's moving to another city. Near midnight, she's moving home, surrendering her bed. Then she poses a choice: she'll go to Jake's, whoever he is, or she'll stay at Wyndham House, but not go to school the next day, in either case, disqualifying herself for the group home—all this in a state of agitation that makes problem-solving temporarily futile. You live with the knowledge that any success is provisional, that brain damage may sabotage whatever promising arrangement is currently in place, that you cannot necessarily imagine the direction from which trouble will strike.

The inconsistencies can be concurrent too. I can come home from a parent-support meeting where Elizabeth's improvement is held up as a hopeful example, or from a talk for FASD Day[4] about challenges of parenting, ending, "Yes, Elizabeth is a success, so far," and slump at facing the daily on-going grind of her behaviours, her increasingly angrier demands and denunciations. Or I read a report on what keeps adolescents with FASD in school—friendships and parental interventions—based, in part, on a lengthy interview with me and a short one with her, when it looks as if my own child is in the process of dropping out after all, despite my interventions.

The mother of a child with FASD is frequently caught between contradictory self-critical emotions, especially because, unlike most disabilities, FASD is not responsive to traditional methods of parenting: expecting experience to teach, applying consequences, letting children learn from their mistakes, building independence. You can trust no parenting advice from those inexperienced with fetal alcohol. So, while seeking information, you approach Explosive Child parenting groups, the John Howard Society, AlAnon, and the like, sceptically having to ask, "Yes, but does this apply? Does it work the same for the child with FASD?" The commonplace assumptions of parenting culture cannot guide you, but will indeed betray you. "Without identification or diagnosis, parenting a child with FAS/FAE is like trying to find your way around Denver with a road map of Cincinnati," writes Diane Malbin. "It's a good map—it worked in another city, and some of the streets have the same name, but they just dead-end or don't go where you expect" (np).

Even with FASD guidelines, you are often unsure if you are being over-controlling, over-permissive, over-protective, over-restrictive, over-suspicious, over-critical, over-forgiving. You blame yourself simultaneously for catastrophizing and playing ostrich, for having excessively low expectations and not making sufficient allowances, for berating the child about what is not her fault and not holding her accountable. This is the definition of parenting, admittedly, but it is magnified by FASD and by the paucity of models for this kind of parenting. Because every alcohol-affected child has been damaged prenatally at different moments and to differing degrees, none of us mothers knows exactly where on the spectrum of capability our own child lies, what exactly is reasonable to expect from her, or when. On that, even parent-support groups have limited ability to help. And because, as I see it, the developing adolescent brain already has much in common with FASD,[5] the challenge of differentiating brain damage from everyday non-compliance in adolescence becomes more confounding. (Imagine facing a lifetime with an erratic, moody, reckless, volatile, and hapless teenager.)

The drug-and-alcohol counsellor I consult thinks I may be enabling Elizabeth, by being in touch on a daily basis, while the FASD mantra is to maintain the emotional connection at all cost. My son reports that his girlfriend thinks Elizabeth is spoiled: she's just stolen and sold dozens of his

DVDs, yet is being driven to (therapeutic) horse-riding lessons. Simultaneously, I'm feeling guilty about having forbidden her access to the house, because of the thefts, and so denying her Thanksgiving dinner. Has the alcohol been watered down? Is money missing from the car ashtray, my purse? Has the outdoor key been taken, the house entered? Has she been selling her "lost" bus passes for drugs? Are the straws in her backpack for snorting cocaine? Why has she chosen to sit in the car rather than accompany me into a store? I feel simultaneously naïve/stupid/credulous for not suspecting and suspicious/unfair/paranoid for suspecting. I feel guilty for having my twelve-year-old (psychologically speaking) daughter living on her own, when my goal all along was to keep her in a safely structured environment at least until her mid-twenties. Yet, at the time, I could do nothing to prevent her departure. If motherhood, as my sister argues, is the exercise of feeling bad about oneself, then mothering with FASD is that in spades.

Mothering a child with FASD produces chronic arousal, and, because it is chronic, affords only glacial recovery: anticipating rules you never thought you'd need to make (the china cabinet off-limits for hide-and-seek), ferreting out the source of the current agitation (a quarrel at school concealed from you), taking care not to set your child up by leaving tempting possibilities in her path, containing your own hurt and anger and disappointment and anxiety, flinching at the step on the stairs or the ring of the phone, awaiting the next demand, meltdown, or disaster (suspension from the school bus, the visitation from schoolmates' angry parents, expulsion from summer camp over sex with another camper). You live under siege. You keep your wallet in a fanny pack or the car trunk, your keys on a chain around your neck (even into the shower), your alcohol in a locked bedroom cupboard, and your telephone under a pillow. Or your phone has blocks on three-way and long-distance calling, last-caller I.D., and 1-900 numbers. You try to collect addresses of new friends, for future disappearances. You plan activities in a vain attempt to keep your child safely occupied. In his interviews with FASD families, Patrick Morrissette identifies seven predominant themes, the first of which is that of constant vigilance (np). Not surprisingly, every period of respite is too short, so that, instead of welcome relief, your first emotion is tense anticipation of your child's return. Raising a child with FASD is an ongoing assault on your limbic system, with bursts of cortisol (the fight-or-flight hormone) linked by relentless stress.

I'm not a medical doctor, but I believe that this state of chronic arousal endangers the physical health of FASD mothers. "Long-term potentiation" describes the tendency of the over-stimulated synapses of the amygdala (the emotion centre of the brain and part of the limbic system) to react more readily than usual ("Amygdala" np; Ratey 190-93).[6] One of the reasons I knew I needed to consider a medical leave from work was the state I found myself in, many months after a debilitating crisis with Elizabeth, a crisis during which the others in the family left the house nightly, to provide her fewer targets to rage against, and waited for a signal that she was finally in bed. Even after her condition improved, I reacted with all the galvanized intensity of those earlier days to any minor flare-up on her part. And the hypersensitivity persisted, as I kept waiting for it to subside. High levels of cortisol associated with chronic stress produce impaired cognitive function, sugar imbalances including hyperglycemia, reduced bone density, decreased muscle tissue, raised blood pressure, compromised immunity, inflammatory reactions, and increased abdominal fat—along with impulses to eat more and to eat carbohydrates ("Cortisol" np). I spent years seeing neuropsychologists and other specialists for the deterioration of my memory, attentiveness, and cognitive functioning in the period before my stress leave. Almost every one of the other impacts has affected either my partner or me, despite an otherwise healthy regimen.

Secondary disabilities for alcohol-affected youth include disrupted schooling, addictions, sexual misbehaviour, trouble with the law, mental health disorders, confinement or incarceration, and difficulty with employment and independent living (Streissguth 108-110). There are secondary or indirect disabilities for caregivers as well. At the grief session at the Beyond Diagnosis conference in Toronto, a facilitator, Diana Fox, proposed that fetal alcohol creates ADHD-like symptoms in caregivers. I would go further and argue for the infectiousness of fetal-alcohol characteristics generally: the irritability, low frustration tolerance, inattentiveness, comprehension problems, short-term memory loss, emotional volatility and reactivity, and sleep disorders. Moreover, the precautions of life with FASD compound life's complexities: having no money for parking because of keeping few coins in the car; being unable to offer friends a drink without going upstairs to the bedroom; failing to answer the phone, from your son with an injured hip, because you've already spoken twice that evening to your daughter; being locked out of the house because you have removed the hidden outdoor key....

Debilitating projections into the future foolishly pile dreaded imagined calamities onto the day's burden. It makes little sense to dread, simultaneously, that your child will be dead and that she will live with you forever, but you do that. Even so, you are still not ready for the predicted developments when they happen in your own family: the emergency-room call about alcohol poisoning, the arrest for being found asleep in a stolen car while the others shoplift, the forearm slashed to the bone.[7] However difficult the early years, your child then seems more ordinary, not of the same order as the deviant teenagers you are hearing about, and, in any case, others' children with FASD seem more dysfunctional and impossible than your own—while other members of the group feel the same way about yours.

Hindsight will bring a different perspective, making earlier anguish seem excessive and naïve. Parents will be in tears over six–year-olds not meeting academic milestones, while those of us past that stage urge avoidance of homework and delaying of school progress, aware of harder disappointments ahead. A parent may complain of a child's needing to find more highly skilled work, when, in others' eyes, holding down a job at all has come to seem an achievement. My crises over Elizabeth's botching of her Wyndham House stay now seem turbulence over the inevitable. And I fear that in the future I may wonder, by comparison, why I felt so distressed over Elizabeth's current choices. So mothering such a child means acclimatization over time to norms you would have found intolerable earlier. In the meantime, though, you experience each new loss, each poor outcome, each bad choice, each narrowing of possibilities with the heartsickness of the uninitiated.

All this happens, of course, alongside the usual crises of life. Will she flare up at your mother's wake? Can she be left alone, while you deal with mismanagement of your father's estate now that he has Alzheimer's? Will she become unmanageable on the plane, during the trip you must take? In our small group, most of us are on some form of anti-depressant or anti-anxiety medication.[8] And I haven't even explored the strain on spousal relationships, the marriage or partnership breakdowns, or the painful cost to other children without FASD, who resent the special treatment of their sibling and the loss of parental attention, who stop bringing their friends home. The challenge of alcohol-affected children exacerbates differences in parenting approaches as well. My group keeps a lengthy, sometimes amusing list, "It Might Be FASD If . . . ," now some twenty-five pages long. One of the most poignant entries, for me, reads, "It might be FASD if once you had a typical family, and then your husband left, and then your other son left, and now you live alone with your child who has FASD." Nor have I mentioned adoption breakdown, and the heartache and guilt of deciding that you can no longer parent this damaged child and survive.

Ann Waller writes, "In 1995, FAS*FRI [Family Resource Institute] documented that the large majority of (one or both) parents of these children had been so extremely stressed and depressed that they had thoughts of suicide. (Subsequent surveys had similar results)" (qtd. in McKinney, Le Fever, and DeVries 138). Such information should not be a consolation, but, to me, it is. I have discovered what the seemingly pedantic psychological term "suicidal ideation" is all about, when independent of any conscious intent, your mind keeps elaborating the details of plans that could stop the pain. I take comfort, too, in a disability spokesperson on CBC radio, speaking of an elderly B.C. couple who had killed themselves and their disabled adult son, when they could find no prospect of care for him after their death. She said that all parents of disabled children have had such thoughts, and, though she may have been over-generalizing, her willingness to articulate a taboo subject is reassuring for me. I have wondered sometimes why I'm trying to protect Elizabeth from dangers rather than welcoming them—except that they might be damaging *without* being fatal. Early on, after the diagnosis, I told a therapist that I could imagine taking care of a Down's Syndrome child or a dying child less painfully than one with FASD, whose destruction (worse than mere death) I could anticipate while being unable to intervene in any meaningful way. I am haunted too by the possibility that Elizabeth may bear an alcohol-poisoned child or even a healthy one to be harmed by inadequate or disrupted care. "No more damage!" is my cry. And I have said to myself, "Dead is easier. At least, then her chance to be hurt and to hurt others is over." So, no, mothers dealing with FASD are not always a pretty sight.

As this might suggest, one of the losses I have felt in mothering Elizabeth is the alcohol-produced assault on the mother-child bond. Although she was not one of those alcohol-affected babies hypersensitive to touch or averse to cuddling (indeed, she could apply her body deliciously to every square millimetre of one's torso, shoulder and neck, and did so for years), mothering Elizabeth has been an exercise in managing her behaviour.[9] This was so constant and tiring, from so early on, that, combined with the adversarial tinge to such wariness, it drained emotional energy from my relationship with her. This sense of the job outweighing the joy persisted until Elizabeth was about nine, when she and I were able to find a common interest in (of all things) consignment-clothes shopping. In addition, I discovered early that she was a visual and kinaesthetic learner (a temperamental difference possible in any parent-child pairing but exacerbated by the FASD impairment of her verbal-processing and abstract-thinking abilities). As a verbal and intellectual being, I found myself shut out of so much I had hoped to offer her, not just the dream of mother-daughter confidences but, more painfully, the hope that my experience and knowledge could aid her in navigating a world made all the more dangerous by her disability. Much of what I have to share, she is unable to receive, and, in fact, experiences as an unpleasant bombardment of words. The pleasures of mothering, of feeling and expressing affection,[10] are often shouldered out of the way by the work—the emotional agility, the advocacy, the interventions—and by the emotional chaos and tension of FASD life. "Do not be deceived by the false promises so freely given by the agencies that tell you, 'All the children need is consistency in a loving and nurturing home. Take our special needs children and we will give you all the help you need'...Until you need it!" (Hardy qtd. in McKinney, Le Fever, and DeVries 137; ellipsis in original).

Thus far I have spoken about daily life with FASD, but that is only half the story for mothers. Jason Brown and Lisa Bednar, interviewing parents with alcohol-affected children, found that the one theme not included in the usual literature was the challenging lack of respect from professionals (np). Here's one parent from our group:

> Raising a child with FASD will destroy you. It will destroy your self; it will destroy your future; it will destroy your hopes for a relationship with that child. And trying to get help from social services is just as bad. It's like being in a relationship with an FASD child: social services can't hear anything you say, they can't understand complex ideas, they perseverate, they say they're sorry and do the same thing again, they have black-and-white thinking, they don't learn from consequences. Having an FASD child and dealing with social services is like having wasps in your hand. You never know when one or the other will sting you.

Interviewing adoptive and foster mothers of older children with FASD, Holly Gammon found that major stressors came from "systemic barriers" in the "medical, educational, judicial, child welfare and adult services" (46), the last of these the only one I have yet to run afoul of.

Since Elizabeth was a pre-schooler, I have dealt with child psychiatrists, psychologists, developmental pediatricians, school IPRC committees, and social workers, with West End Crèche Child and Family Clinic (Toronto), Upper Grand River School Board, Mother-Risk (Hospital for Sick Kids, Toronto), Family and Children's Services (Guelph), Youthdale (Toronto), and Community Mental Health Clinic (Guelph)—including their Children and Family Intensive Services and their Mobile Crisis Intervention team— among others. The process of seeking help has often resembled a lengthy wait in line, before finally reaching what proves to be an empty room. I was given unhelpful diagnoses and inappropriate recommendations—"wait and see"; "she's not ADHD [and so there's nothing to be done]"; "try a behavioural programme of operant conditioning" (an inappropriate treatment for FASD); "she is a spirited child"; "it must be a learning disability; see your school board"; "it's not a learning problem; see the mental-health clinic"; or "a complex and confusing case" (even after FASD was raised as a likelihood).

Most workers, including supposed FASD specialists, from whom we received such nuggets as "well then, if she's an affectionate child, she probably doesn't have it," and "be glad she doesn't have FASD, because there's nothing you can do about it" (these, while unaware that their own psychologist had already identified Elizabeth as ARND), in fact, were uninformed or misinformed about fetal alcohol. The long sought-after diagnosis itself came with no offer of further support. One mental health worker at least candidly acknowledged that I already knew, after a few months' research, four times as much about FASD as she did. A co-ordinator at Elizabeth's supportive residence, after complaining on separate occasions that she was feeling manipulated and that Elizabeth was using her FASD as an excuse, responded to my fetal-alcohol information by twice stating, "I know about FASD 100%." My encounters with service providers have often felt as stressful, enraging, painful, and demoralizing as the task of trying to raise a brain-damaged daughter.[11]

I am a university professor, by temperament and by training inclined to research, to seeking out knowledge. My partner and I even knew personally Michael Dorris, author of *The Broken Cord*, the first popular book on the syndrome. Yet, until I connected with a parent-support group, everything I heard about FASD led me to believe that there was virtually no information available on the subject, and that, in any case, such information would be pointless, because nothing could be done. Fetal Alcohol Syndrome Assistance and Training (FASAT Ontario, as the group was then known) and its parenting workshops proved otherwise. Only in the parent-support group did I get the detailed and informed knowledge that I needed. In fact, as with many in the group, I reached the diagnosis before professionals did and then fought for it. Social-service agencies, by contrast, undermined me, often by assuming a parenting problem and compounding that by offering harmful, old parenting advice. "When I think back to raising Colette," Buxton writes, "what was hardest was not Colette's difficult behaviour, but the uninformed arrogance and denial of many professionals who shifted the blame to us" (107). "Are you kidding?" bursts out a mother at our recent group meeting, "Someone told you about Children with Severe Disabilities payments? No one told me a thing that I was entitled to!" No wonder Donna Debolt describes caregivers dealing with FASD as resistant to suggestions, in conflict with other adults, convinced that "nothing will work," seemingly crazy, and representing our previous attempts to find help as damaging (another potentially unflattering description that I found comforting, for its validation of the desperation I felt). I remember thinking what a wild impression I must have been making, as I glared in rage and despair at a psychologist and a social worker offering me only another psychological report, when my household faced a nightly onslaught from a frantic, screaming thirteen-year-old. Jan Lutke and Tina Antrobus assert, "[A]ll [families with FASD] know and understand pain on a level most people would find intolerable.... And in the end, *each one* comes to the end of the road. There is no safety net" (69). Family and Children's Services did refer a number of prospective adoptive parents to the parents' workshop I co-facilitated at the Guelph "FASD through the Life Cycle" conference (October 26, 2006). I look forward to the day when the "parent-expert" will be a valued and primary member of any FASD service team for his or her child.[12] Still, even if service providers become more aware and qualified (and better funded), raising alcohol-affected children will remain a grinding business. No advice, after all, can offer what we really need: a means to undo our children's brain damage. FASD is a parenting challenge that refuses to go away.

I won't end on that note. The laughter that bursts from our parenting-group meetings, often when the revelations are at their most anguished, is intense, and intensely healing. So are the friendships with other mothers, the startling recognitions of commonalities, the shared specificities of our children's behaviour, the proffering of parenting ideas grounded in knowledge of this syndrome, the emotional bonds with people with whom I might otherwise have no connection. We exchange perplexities and shameful moments. We celebrate our children's accomplishment. We cheer on a mother in her struggle to provide her daughter with the protection of a tubal ligation and share the sense of loss that entails.

I have learned things I never expected to learn: that pepper spray on a wall cannot be painted over, that anti-psychotics are used as mood stabilizers, that chewing on drinking straws keeps you from grinding your teeth while on Ecstasy, that local pawnshops warehouse new purchases for a month in case they've been stolen, that you can shoot a flame across the kitchen by spraying and lighting Pam. I have also learned that there *is* such a thing as post-traumatic growth. I have learned, by necessity, to balance my life, to breathe, to be mindfully in the present, to distract my amygdala with mental puzzles, to parent as a team, to replace prohibitions with instructions, to speak less, to resist projecting into the future, to recognize silence as companionable, to put my painful experience to broader positive use in the community, to give up controlling what I cannot, to pair stress with extra sleep, to find creative outlets, and to build a network of support. I feel no need for romantic obsession as a means of feeling deeply, of having my heart torn open. Mothering an alcohol-affected child has dredged my heart. It is not the method I would have chosen for myself, and I would wish it on no one. But, as a therapist said to one mother in my group, about her daughter, "You have found yourself a Zen Master."

[1]Fetal Alcohol Spectrum Disorder is the overarching classification for the diagnoses of Fetal Alcohol Syndrome (FAS), Partial FAS (pFAS), both characterized by facial anomalies along with other damage, and what used to be called Fetal Alcohol Effect (FAE) or Alcohol-Related Neurodevelopmental Disorder (ARND), involving the same neurological damage as FAS but without the cautionary external evidence.

[2]Most of the families in my parent-support group are adoptive families, mostly white (though a number have Black, Native, Asian, or mixed-race children) and many affluent. If families with these social privileges and resources are as stressed as they are, the circumstances for alcohol-dependent or recovering alcoholic parents and even more so those with FASD themselves, those poor, marginalized, or isolated, are inevitably even grimmer.

[3]Buxton writes, "[O]ne day things are terrible: we are floating between anger and frustration and sobbing. A day later this person can be an absolute delight, and all of a sudden we are back into denial.... You have to accept the roller coaster" (260).

[4]September 9, the ninth day of the ninth month.

[5]See Nora Underwood for an overview of adolescent prefrontal cortex development and related development in executive function—planning, judgment, impulse control, and the understanding of consequences (all areas of deficit in children with FASD), of teenage circadian brain rhythms, sleep deprivation, and memory loss, and of the testosterone-stimulated swelling of the amygdala, centre of emotions, in both sexes. On the gradual activation of the frontal cortex to permit cognitive processing of emotion in teens, see Ratey (234).

[6]See also Ratey, on the "overly efficient neural pathway from the amygdala to the sympathetic response" (173), in hyper-aroused people.

[7]Some of my examples come from other members of my parent-support group, here, and occasionally elsewhere.

[8]"I can't help feeling that somebody else's drinking decisions are going to lead to my having to take medications I would rather not even consider," one group member emailed me in frustration.

[9]I had to laugh when one doctor-therapist, despite my suggestion of FASD, proposed that perhaps we'd been liberal, *laissez-faire* parents whose *new* curbing of adolescent independence was provoking a defiant reaction from Elizabeth. Knowing nothing of FASD recommendations, we knew enough from Elizabeth's earliest behaviours to set firm guidelines, eliminate exceptions, maintain structures and consistency, and shun precedents, to "manage" her. I even carried her in and out of buildings past age four rather than deal with the consequences of setting her loose (an anticipatory form of preventative parenting).

[10]Missing the natural, easy forms of affection, I recently gave my daughter a fuzzy, powder-blue scarf, explaining that this was a more obvious way of showing my love than my past four days' work on her disability application; she was put out that I didn't say the obligatory "I love you" when we parted moments later.

[11]When I made this statement in a brief address at a Guelph FASD conference, in October of 2006, there was an audible gasp from the audience (largely service providers, with some family members). I was surprised

at the surprise, having come to treat this as commonplace in talks with FASD or disability activists.

[12]In fact, after that conference, I had a phone call from a worker who'd carried my comments back to one of our mental-health-care facilities, proposing that we meet and follow up on my experience of frustration with service providers.

WORKS CITED

"Amygdala." Wikipedia. 23 August 2006. <http: //en.wikipedia.org/wiki/Amygdala>.

Brown, Jason and Lisa M. Bednar. "Challenges of Parenting Children with a Fetal Alcohol Syndrome Disorder: A Concept Map." *Journal of Family Social Work* 8.3 (2004): 1-18.

Buxton, Bonnie. *Damaged Angels: A Mother Discovers the Terrible Cost of Alcohol in Pregnancy.* Toronto: Knopf, 2004.

"Cortisol." *Wikipedia.* 23 August 2006. <http: //en.wikipedia.org/wiki/Cortisol>.

Debolt, Donna. Oral Communication. Fetal Alcohol Spectrum Disorder Training Day, Owen Sound, Ontario, 20 September 2002.

Dorris, Michael. *The Broken Cord.* New York: HarperCollins, 1989.

Fox, Diana. Personal Communication. FASD: Beyond Diagnosis Conference. St. Michael's Hospital, Toronto, 24 Sept. 2005.

Gammon, Holly. "Fetal Alcohol Disorders, Stress, and the Female Caregiver." *Envision* 1.2 (2002): 43-53.

Lutke, Jan and Tina Antrobus. "Fighting for a Future: FASD and 'The System': Adolescents, Adults and Their Families and the State of Affairs." Proceedings from a Two-Day Forum: June 19 and 20, 2004. Surrey, British Columbia: FASD Connections. 20 Dec. 2004. <www.fasdconnections.ca>.

Malbin, Diane. *Fetal Alcohol Syndrome, Fetal Alcohol Effects: Strategies for Professionals.* Centre City, MN: Hazelden, 1993.

McKinney, Victoria, Linda La Fever, and Jocie DeVries. *Nurture: The Essence of Intervention for Individuals with Fetal Alcohol Syndrome.* Lynnwood, WA: FAS Family Resource Institute, 2005.

Morrissette, Patrick J. "Fetal Alcohol Syndrome: Parental Experiences and the Role of Family Counsellors." *Qualitative Report* 6.2 (2001). <www.nova.edu/ssss/QR/QR6-2/morrissette.html >. 20 March 2006.

Ratey, J. J. *A User's Guide to the Brain.* New York: Pantheon, 2001.

Streissguth, Ann. *Fetal Alcohol Syndrome: A Guide for Families and Communities.* Baltimore: Paul H. Brookes, 1997.

Underwood, Nora. "Your Teenager's Mind." *Walrus* 3.9 (2006): 48-56.

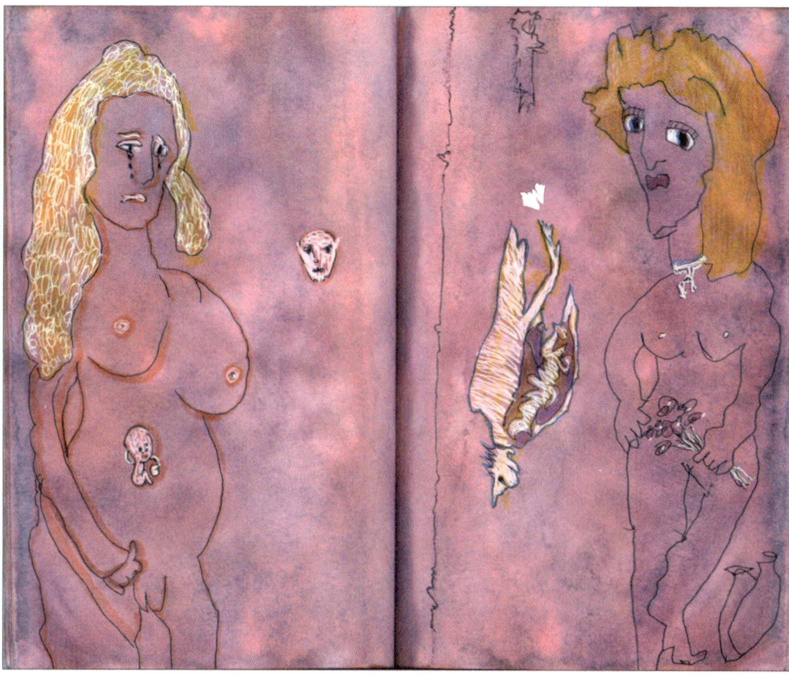

Grace Rose Holyer, *Grandma, Go Home*, 1999,
mixed media on paper (two pages from Artist's Book), 15.24 x 20.32 cm.

Sometimes young children form an attachment to their mothers and do not like interference from others. My grandson often told me to go home when I was visiting my daughter. This passed as he got older. The drawings in this book reflect my subconscious emotions about rejection and attachment.

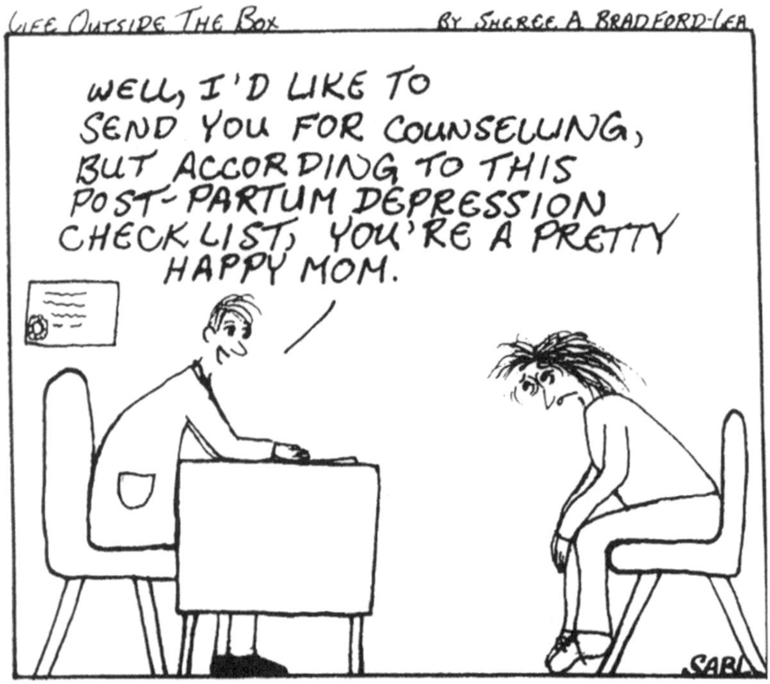

Sheree Bradford-Lea, *Happy Mom*, 1999, paper, 12.07 x 13. 34 cm, (including *Life Outside The Box* title).

The cartoon was donated for use as part of a lecture given to nurses and midwives in the Ottawa area to educate them about post-partum depression, 1999. *Happy Mom* has appeared in: *Hip Mama: The Parenting Zine,* Issue # 39, 2008; and *Homebase: A Forum for Mothers,* Issue 57, Fall 1999, p. 39.

Five Daughters and a Ph.D.

Pinay and Mothering in Canada

GLENDA LYNNA ANNE TIBE BONIFACIO

FACILITATING LECTURES, NEWSPAPER profiles, and interviews seem ordinary among academics. I would no doubt be writing about this if the subject of the lectures or profile pertains simply to an issue of interest in the community. Surprisingly, the subject of this "public" interest since I moved to Alberta is not related to my research and teaching areas but to my reproductive achievement of having five daughters while completing a Ph.D., and then working full time at the university as a relatively new immigrant in Canada.

I do not consider myself an anomaly in the academe, although I was made aware that I am after completing my doctoral studies in Australia in 2003. In that one sunny day in Wollongong, south of Sydney, my supervisor received the completed dissertation and, after browsing through the pages, learned for the first time that I have five children to whom I dedicated my three years of study. With a sense of disbelief as to what I have been through to finish my degree in a foreign country, my supervisor informed almost everyone in the hall at that time about her "discovery."

Moving to a medium-sized city in southern Alberta to teach in the Women's Studies Program at the University of Lethbridge in 2005 made me look back to what transpired in Australia two years earlier. As a new faculty member joining the university, I guess it was routine that somebody from the information services would interview me and get to know my research agenda and teaching specialization. None of the information that I had shared came out to attest to my professional qualification. Instead, the local newspaper ran a profile and highlighted my having five daughters (Schurtz A2). From then on, I am often introduced by my colleague in this manner: "This is Glenda and she has five kids." Of course, my departmental affiliation comes either before or after my name.

Should I justify? This is the question I ask myself having been made aware that in Canada, as well as in Australia, having five children, all daughters, amidst academic work is an anomalous combination and is becoming part of my identity. I have been asked twice to talk about balancing work and family in a regular course in Psychology, and I anticipate more to come as I currently hold the most number of children among academics at the University of Lethbridge. As I met new students, young women, potential mothers, and requests for interviews about my life, I started to think about how all this started. Not that I am going back to when I first met my husband, but to personally question what I did that made others ponder my life, particularly my attaining the highest degree in the university while rearing five daughters away from the support of my family. Or, does it matter?

In this personal approach to a scholarly discourse on mothering, my discussion starts with the context of mothering from where I originally came, the Philippines, and situates the cultural roots of mothering practice. The experience of migration to Australia and Canada demonstrates how the culturally-prescribed norms of mothering are negotiated in various spaces. Examining my work in Canadian academia as a full-time faculty member and an immigrant mother of five daughters presents the challenges of having the best of both worlds. As a conclusion, I offer my views on the discourse of balancing work and family and reframe its populist version into one that allows women to embrace the notion that both can be empowering, instead of a source of deficiency.

PINAY AND MOTHERING

Mothering is a practice that finds its roots in culture (Thurer 334). There are different ways of performing this socially prescribed role for women in many communities and one that is complex to define (Nakano Glenn, Chang, and Forcey 2). As bearers of children and nurturers of the family, motherhood depicts the single most important role for women within patriarchy. Nancy Chodorow notes, "[W]omen's mothering is a central and defining feature of the social organization of gender and is implicated in the construction and reproduction of male dominance itself" (9). Although motherhood and mothering emanate from the same gender role, there is a difference between the two. The former refers to the institution that aims to subject women's reproductive abilities under male control while the latter suggests female-centered practices and experiences of care and nurturing (O'Reilly 2).

Sara Ruddick argues that "maternal thinking" is cultivated by motherhood that produces its own truths centered on "attentive love" (119). Maternal work incurs three demands: "preservation, growth, and social acceptability" (17). Mothers act on these demands and demonstrate culturally-variable practices towards their children. Social acceptability foregrounds training children on normative group values, which is considered the "central challenge of mothering" (104). Mothering occurs daily, on the second, and that it requires our complete attention—physically, mentally, and emotionally. This, according to Ruddick, is the discipline of mothering.

For women in the Philippines, colloquially referred to as *Pinay* either in singular or plural, the primacy of motherhood in their lives by the patriarchal state intertwined with a strong Catholic dogma since the 16th century has been socially ingrained. Religion and education effectively transmitted Castillan values into the lives of the *mujer indigena* (indigenous woman) demonstrated in the adage that "woman are made to weave, to give birth, and to weep" (Mananzan 22). While mostly observed among women of the upper class in close association with the colonizers (Santiago "Rebirthing" 114), the ordinary woman had to combine the rigours of work in the agricultural field with mothering as an accepted mode of providing care and sustenance to the family. The integrated sphere of economic contribution and maternal duties are visible aspects of mothering in today's *Pinay* in the Philippines and those who join their *kababayan* (compatriots) as the most mobile and widely dispersed migrant workers in the world (Piper 3).

Like others before me, I learned about the practice of mothering from my mother, grandmother, and a number of auntie-mothers while growing up in the Philippines. My mother worked before she got married and continued to do so until she opted for early retirement to pursue her dream of administering her own nursery school. She was in no way different from other mothers I know of from my classmates in grade school. While she worked the whole day from 8:30 in the morning until 5:00 in the afternoon as a teacher and later as staff of a college counselling program, my mother would often come home during her lunch breaks to check on our food or what was going on at home in a time when telephones were usually found only in offices or grocery stores. I also witnessed her indulgence in church-related activities, which became an important aspect of her social life.

The tide of modernization and infusion of western ideals into Philippine society as a result of its postwar neocolonial relations with the United States did not alter the prescriptive role of women as mothers first. More than half of the working population in the Philippines are women and mothers, and their double burden of having to care for their families while undertaking paid employment is often shared by women in other parts of the world. Catholicism has also entrenched the ideology of the self-sacrificing mother, her reward becoming great in the afterlife.

My mother and her running a household while I was growing up largely looms in my memory. Up to now, although gradually shifting with the feminized labour migration, Filipino women are still expected to command the domestic sphere with little expectations of their husbands to help them in household chores. Income from paid work and the extensive kinship network often enable working mothers to hire domestic helpers to live with the family. This practice creates a pattern of subordination of women by women based on class and the performance of expected norms of motherhood becomes possible, especially "keeping an orderly household" (Santiago "Roots" 169). If the mother is not able to find a hired help, then other women in the family unit, depending on the level of confidence, are sourced out to assist her temporarily.

Raising a child is a social responsibility. As the saying goes, it takes a community to raise a child. In the Philippine context, the community often refers to the large extended family network that usually lives close together or in contiguous areas to watch each other's children. Families rely on their own kinship and affective associations in the absence of a day-care system in the country. Family helpers accompany children as young as four-years-old to start private nursery schools in urban areas. The shared collective endeavour to nurture children among Filipino families has now become a source of strength for many women forced to take on overseas work to survive in an ailing economy.

Although preservation of children through provision of basic needs and a better future is now foremost in the minds of Filipino working mothers, the growth and rearing of children according to standards of society are reinforced in schools and in churches, especially among the predominantly Catholic families. Mothering places emphasis on the value of education through undertaking early child education out of their own pockets. In a class-based society like the Philippines, the education of children is a vital component of mothering for upward mobility.

Bringing up morally-upright citizens with a keen sense of the virtues of obedience, respect, and conformity to established mores at home and in society is shared by patriarchal institutions. Typical mothering practices, Joyce Trebilcot notes, "perpetuate hierarchical social arrangements in a variety of ways" (1). Although there is separation of church and state in democratic Philippines, practices inside the classroom belie secularization. In public schools, such as those I attended, the morning program starts with a prayer or a silent pause. Many schoolchildren today, as in the past, also participate in local religious festivities in honour of the town patron saint. The seemingly unified directives for nurturing children along the accepted social activities from the school to the family provide a schema for mothers. My mother, through her own example, made us all attend Sunday mass or go to church at least once a week. By doing this weekly ritual, I am said to be following the right path to godliness.

Mothering as a practice in the Philippines does not only involve the routine activities of preparing healthy food in a clean house, attending school meetings, ensuring safety and other related activities, but also the spiritual and moral growth of children. Understanding what is right and wrong in the eyes of the law and in religion appears to be an emphasis in my upbringing. But I learned early on that my mother prefers that I keep straight with the teachings of the Church because that would make me a better citizen. A syncretic law and moral argument finds present value in my mothering in a world inundated by senseless disregard for respect of human dignity.

Since I found my mother's liberality rewarding, I tend to follow those practices that allow for individuality and responsibility to my own daughters. However, an involved spouse made a lot of difference in my mothering. I could say that men are capable of the same commitment to "mother" children and, in my case, shared parenting "challenges a universal structure in the organization of gender" (Ehrensaft 43). Modern fathering, Susan Chase and Mary Rogers argue, does not only involve providing finances but also "reordering priorities and making a commitment to physically and emotionally care for children" (105). In a way, my mothering is assisted with fathering and this mutuality contributed significantly in our sojourn to foreign lands.

MOTHERING AND MIGRATION

Migration is a life-altering phenomenon. We move away from the familiarity of our own support system and face myriad challenges in the host society. Living in another culture with different ways of mothering inevitably touches a chord in our own understanding of mothering. In a span of five years since we left the Philippines in 2000, my five daughters found themselves living in two countries, first in Australia and then in Canada. It is through our migration to these Western societies that my practice of mothering comes into question.

Unlike many *Pinay* in the global labour diaspora forced to leave their children behind, I left the Philippines under an Australian scholarship that allowed me to bring my family. Contrary to all advices of leaving my five daughters behind while I pursue further studies, my husband and I decided that it would be best if we all stayed together despite perceived difficulties. We set out to live like any other ordinary family in the West, that is, without hired help and on our own.

Migration offered an opportunity to critically examine myself as a mother and appreciate this role in my own terms. Without anyone to whom to be compared except myself, I felt a different sense of being as a mother, of knowing my children better as they grow up, of loosening myself with mistakes in cooking, and, more importantly, the realization that seeking normalcy in work and family relations is not an individual pursuit but arises from the contribution of every member in the social unit. While I miss the familiarity of home, the best years of mothering occurred outside of my own national borders, contending the challenges of mothering daughters in a society whose ideals of femininity and womanhood are quite different than those from where I came.

With a teaching position in one of the campuses of the University of the Philippines, my role as a mother was overshadowed by professionally-related activities that would determine the pay scale under a politically-charged campus. As long as I had a reliable person to take my place with my children, usually my mother, I took off island-hopping to attend conferences and meetings. Mothering, it seemed, co-existed with the economics of the profession. Because everyone appeared to be doing what I was doing in the Philippines, I thought my mothering was sufficient.

One time at a pharmacy in Australia with my health card number to buy a prescription drug, the female receptionist looked at me in awe after scanning the names in the card. Then she shouted, "Oh, my God! This little lady has five daughters!" I was shocked by the public introduction and did not fully comprehend the meaning of her ecstasy. My second daughter laughed at it because she just met a classmate with seven siblings. From then on, the pharmacist appeared interested in how my kids were doing every time I handed her a prescription.

How are my kids doing? I admit this question resonated while I was immersed in my doctoral studies. Like other international students with limited financial resources, I simply brought my youngest child to the university after her four-hour day care thrice a week was over. We just walked to school for ten minutes, holding hands along the crosswalks, having light refreshments upon reaching the university, and going to the library or to our shared offices to use the computers. This we did for a year until she entered kindergarten. The other four daughters were in Grade 8, Grade 6, Grade 4, and kindergarten at that time.

Preparing children for school is a daily mothering activity. Fetching kids from school and making sure they do their homework is routine. However, I realized that this is not enough. I met many mothers in Australia and Canada who, as a norm, bring their children to after-school programs, especially related to sports and dance, with hefty price tags. Like many immigrant mothers in the settlement period, these normal childhood activities did not find urgency in our weekly budget. I cannot describe how I felt at an interview with the teacher of my youngest child whose summer journal indicated that her fun activity was going to the library with mom complete with stick-like caricatures of us holding hands.

Getting by through the years in Australia until I submitted my dissertation, and then immigrating immediately and permanently to Canada involved lengthy conversations with my growing children. Sometimes questions about race and differences with mainstream children of Anglo-European descent pushed me to justify my mothering practices, especially my decision about no-sleepovers in other houses except their own. As a rule, sleeping is a highly personalized activity shared with families we trust. This level of trust was absent for us as new immigrants and required time to develop. Changing residences and schools four times in two years upon arrival in Canada made this rule hardly bendable.

Because my frame of mothering is rooted in my own culture, I am reminded of raising good daughters both in mind and in spirit. While I consider myself a feminist, the ritualized tradition of attending church bridges the vital aspect of my own culture to my children in Canada. I find that this ceremony connects them with their own community in the Philippines and the sense of cultural disjuncture is somewhat addressed in case they would go back home. But, understanding the difficulties faced by my children in making friends in their new schools, I discovered that it is awfully painful to "mother out" their loneliness or isolation. Sometimes I blame myself for the decision to migrate and uproot them away from the comfort of an extended family network. Going back home in the summer of 2007, my children, now between the ages of 10 and 20, expressed that I made the right decision. In the years before, I used the formal avenues in school to complain about bullying and cogently manifest the ways to face this issue or, as Patricia Hill Collins explains, "equipping children with skills to confront" (322), if not "to challenge systems of racial oppression" (322). Living as outsiders is a struggle my daughters and I tread daily and, while we meet friendly faces along the way, the genuine acceptance of immigrants as equals in all aspects of Canadian life remains veiled.

Western societies like Canada and Australia tend to embrace ideals of femininity and womanhood through the pervasive influence of popular media. The sexualization and commodification of the female body (Bordo 1993; Fausto-Sterling 2000) with the perceived "ideal look" touch deep in my relations with my daughters. As a fourth grader, my daughter's incessant request to "do something about her moustache" is appalling, yet understandable, relative to my own experience. At her age in the Philippines, I know that combing is part of hygiene and that's it! The social pressure to "look normal" amongst her friends is, for me, ridiculous, but also a wake-up call that mothering racially-defined daughters is about teaching them to be comfortable in their own bodies.

Migration altered our ways of life. Away from the cultural conventions of motherhood of my own country, I define my mothering practices in different spaces mindful that within these spaces my daughters traverse as well. To substitute the concept of the "feminine" to "mother," using the words of Jane Evans Braziel, "the spatial and material demands revaluations, not only of time, but also of generation, motion, and temporality as central to language and to constructions of knowledge" (104) about mothering today and tomorrow. Mothering involves a continuous process of negotiating with new modes of social relations brought about by migration, with our children, and with the society of which they became part. In each step we enhance our capacities to begin anew.

MOTHERING IN CANADIAN ACADEMIA

I often ask myself, had I been a stay-at-home mom would I receive the same queries about mothering five daughters? Not that those women who do to stay at home and look after their children deserve less notice. Rather, the question reflects my increasing interest in the personal politics of migration and mothering in diaspora. Times have changed that women now have more spaces to talk about their quotidian lives. In particular, motherhood and mothering find scholarly merit since the publication of Adrienne Rich's *Of Woman Born*. Combining work in the university with an above average number of children in Canada is, according to my colleagues, a statistical improbability. I have to admit though that, with limited professional interactions, I have never made acquaintance with an academic with the same number of children in Australia or in Canada. But I know there are others out there.

Academic work is rigid. In Canada and elsewhere, tenure and promotion are dependent upon meeting certain standards of performance that vary according to discipline and the interpretations of these standards by select adjudicating committees. A pre-tenured faculty is in a precarious situation in which non-performance equals rejection from a privileged corps. Based on the rigid system of tenure and promotion mainly institutionalized through male practices, it seems that mothering is incompatible with full-time academic work, or to even aspire to do so.

But mothering, in my experience, *is* compatible with academic work. Regardless of the number of children one would bring to this world or care for, academic work is one of the best options for mothers and women. In my case, as well as for others, it took a much longer time to start a Ph.D. and get a tenure-track position in a predominantly white western academia (not to mention the intervening factors of pregnancy during probationary years that slow down the permanency route). However these hurdles come to play in our desire to be more than mothers, a work that we love to do is worthwhile.

Academic work promotes independence of thought in a chosen field of study and offers women that immeasurable opportunity to explore different subjects that may one day be the topic of discussion with children. Since I am with the Women's Studies Program, I find the information not only useful to my students but also to my five daughters. I feel morally obliged to share new information that may affect their views on life. Teaching students who are of the same age as my daughter connects me to their generation, allowing me to understand them better. A case in point: my hype about wearing different coloured socks as laziness only to find out that some students love them too.

While academic work is rigid, mothering is more than work. Like other immigrant mothers placed in a social milieu quite different from where and when they were brought up, academic work becomes the facilitative mechanism of bridging potential generational conflict with my daughters. Teaching in Canada opens an objective examination of my ways of mothering often questioned by my daughters seeking their own spaces of identity in their adopted country.

A happy balance?

I started teaching right after graduation from university. Teaching two courses in *Comparative Politics in Asia* to students, the majority of whom were my friends and the rest of whom I was familiar with in varied campus activities, made a huge impact on my decision to take on an entrance scholarship to a masters program after my wedding. Academic work offered me a subliminal reality of the indomitable urge to change society, ideally starting with myself and then to others, my daughters included. Combining academic work with mothering five daughters as an immigrant, however, raises questions of balancing the two.

The popular version of balancing work and family in the West is that a woman happily take on both paid work and maternal duties. Work and family become the two variables in constructing the balance paradigm. Ann Crittenden shows in her study that motherhood and career involve such humungous responsibilities that many American college-educated women are opting to stay at home (17). Academic work, in theoretical terms, is different from the regular 9-to-5 employment or its variations because of the opportunity to teach at certain times with prior consultation with department heads. Other schedules for research and service are individually determined. However, the apparent flexibility in the university is not usually an advantage for women academics as the culture of this type of work makes parenting or mothering contentious (Bassett 1-16).

I acknowledge the difficulty of mothering and work in the academe: the times I literally change the clock to rush a chapter, the 18-hour vigil to complete a thesis, burnt food while thinking about a research grant application, covered pajamas with my husband's jacket to fetch the children at the bus stop, seating my child at the back of the row with the stern order to be quiet, and too many more to mention. Looking back at these instances, I would not change my career a bit. Academic work is fairly rewarding financially, keeps me in touch with the younger generation, offers opportunities to challenge hegemonic life discourses in an atmosphere of freedom, respect, and collegiality, and, more importantly, empowers my mothering practice.

As new technologies are developed to facilitate learning and communication for our students at the university (such as the use of WebCT and email exchanges), I employ the same strategy to convey my feelings to my daughters when talk is emotionally charged. Letting go of my eldest daughter became easier as she eloquently discussed her position in a lengthy email. I would darn well use Facebook if I had to.

I do not subscribe to the "balance" paradigm, of putting academic work and family work at the same level of attention. This suggests that working "X" number of hours and mothering for the same "X" number of hours yields a balance. In reality, this does not exist. I argue that the notion of balance is a mathematical construct applied to complex lives (work plus family equals...). If we bend the answer, the equation shows a human face. Being involved with work and family is an intrinsic aspect of modern life, and the balance pendulum should not be constructed in divisible spheres or measured externally among working mothers.

External bases for balancing work and family refers to those criteria and norms to be considered productive in the workplace defined by male values. According to Suzanne Cox, professional integrity is "evaluated by colleagues adopting a traditional model of assessing scholarly productivity" (228). In contrast, I opt for an internal basis of balance and the ways in which women engage with it in their own individual abilities of negotiating two conflicting spheres. Balance is, essentially, a matter of perspective of our ever complex lived realities, and the recognition that only humans have the simultaneous capacity to engage in rational activity with emotional tasks such as mothering.

The sense of balance between work and family is finding a holistic sense of who we are. Work and family, or mothering with work, is part of our lives that many cannot do without. While there could be no "balance" *per se*, it mirrors the attempt to find meaning in our involvement with these two. We need work in order to survive, contribute to sustain our families, as well as look after ourselves in retirement. And, as an immigrant, I have no one else to turn to except my own share of the economic basket to continue a modicum way of living. Being a *Pinay* working mother in the university is part of who I am now in Canada. Having five daughters would not in any way change the way I am, although I am gradually shifting my modes of mothering as the years go by.

WORKS CITED

Bassett, Rachel Hile. "Introduction." *Parenting and Professing: Balancing Family Work with an Academic Career*. Ed. Bassett. Nashville: Vanderbilt University Press, 2005. 1-16.

Bordo, Susan. *Unbearable Weight: Feminism, Western Culture, and the Body*. Berkeley: University of California Press, 1993.

Braziel, Jane Evans. "Being and Time, Non-Being and Space... (Introductory notes toward an ontological study of 'Woman' and *chora*)." *Belief, Bodies, and Being: Feminist Reflections on Embodiment*. Ed. Deborah Orr, Linda Lopez Mcallister, Eileen Kahl, and Kathleen Earle. New York: Rowman and Littlefield, 2006. 103-25.

Chase, Susan and Mary Rogers. *Mothers and Children: Feminist Analyses and Personal Narratives*. New Jersey: Rutgers UP, 2001.

Chodorow, Nancy. *The Reproduction of Mothering*. Berkeley: University of California Press, 1978.

Collins, Patricia Hill. "Shifting the Center: Race, Class and Feminist Theorizing About Motherhood." *Maternal Theory: Essential Readings*. Ed. Andrea O'Reilly. Toronto: Demeter Press, 2007. 311-30.

Cox, Suzanne. "Living and Teaching Developmental Psychology in a Liberal Arts Setting: A Blending of Mothering Roles." *Parenting and Professing: Balancing Work with an Academic Career*. Ed. Rachel Hile Bassett. Nashville: Vanderbilt University Press, 2005. 225-30.

Crittendon, Ann. *The Price of Motherhood*. New York: Henry Holt, 2001.

Ehrensaft, Diane. "When Women and Men Mother." *Mothering: Essays in Feminist Theory*. Ed. Joyce Trebilcot. New Jersey: Rowman and Allanheld, 1983. 41-61.

Fausto-Sterling, Anne. *Sexing the Body: Gender Politics and the Construction of Sexuality*. New York: Basic, 2000.

Mananzan, Mary John. "The Filipino Woman: Before and After the Spanish Conquest of the Philippines." *Essays on Women* (Rev ed). Ed. Mananzan. Manila: The Institute of Women's Studies, St. Scholastica's College, 1987. 6-35.

Nakano Glenn, Evelyn, Grace Chang, and Linda Rennie Forcey. *Mothering: Ideology, Experience and Agency*. New York: Routledge, 1994.

O'Reilly, Andrea. "Introduction." *Mother Outlaws: Theories and Practices of Empowered Mothering*. Ed. Andrea O'Reilly. Toronto: Women's Press, 2004. 1-28.

Piper, Nicola. "International Migration and Gendered Axes of Stratification." *New Perspectives on Gender and Migration*. Ed. Piper. New York: Routledge, 2008. 1-18.

Rich, Adrienne. *Of Woman Born: Motherhood as Experience and Institution*. New York: Norton, 1986.

Ruddick, Sara. *Maternal Thinking*. Boston: Beacon, 1989.

Santiago, Lilia Quindoza. "Roots of Feminist Thought in the Philippines." *Review of Women's Studies* 5.2 (1996): 159-72.

Santiago, Lilia Quindoza. "Rebirthing *Babaye*: The Women's Movement in the Philippines." *The Challenge of Local Feminisms: Women's Movement in Global Perspectives*. Ed. Amrita Basu. Boulder: Westview, 1995. 110-28.

Schurtz, Delon. "Glenda tackles women's issues at home and also at the U of L." *Lethbridge Herald*. 26 August 2005, A2.

Thurer, Shari. "The Myths of Motherhood." *Maternal Theory: Essential Readings*. Ed. Andrea O'Reilly. Toronto: Demeter, 2007. 331-44.

Trebilcot, Joyce. "Introduction." *Mothering: Essays in Feminist Theory*.

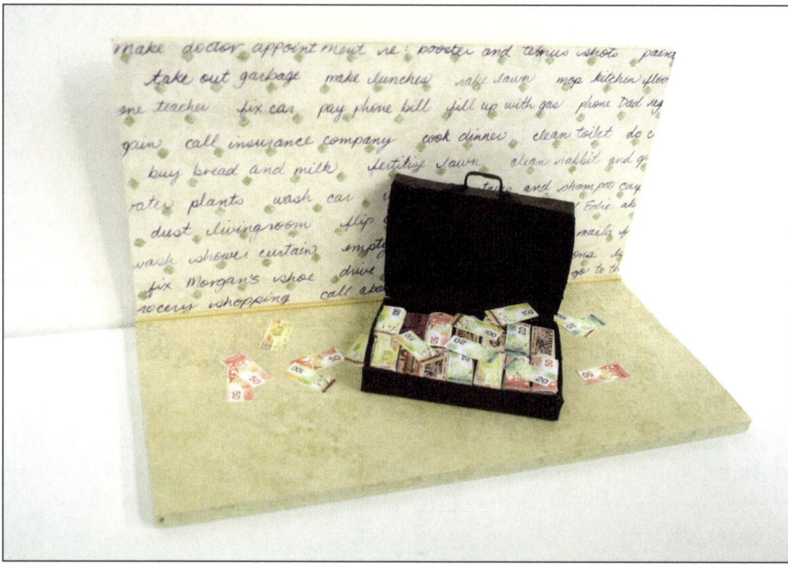

Sylvia Ziemann, *Unpaid Work: What's it Worth?* 2008, wood, paper, paint, wallpaper, 12.70 x 12.70 x 20.32 cm.

In *Unpaid Work,* I was interested in the tremendous amount of labour women do as mothers and home keepers. In most cases, this work is under-appreciated, unnoticed, and not considered "real" work since it does not generate income. If women were paid for their time, I wondered, how much revenue would that yield?

Othermothering

Parenting Across International Borders

NATALIE M. WARD

SINCE THE ACKNOWLEDGEMENT in the 1970s that women were migrating as independents and not just as dependants, there has been a growing focus on issues specific to the female experience of migration. Between the early 1970s and 1980s, when men still dominated the flow of migration, the traditional ideological foundation of the family remained stable. Migration did not question the division of labour in the family, as husbands continued to sustain family life economically while mothers reproduced it. However, there has been a substantial increase in the emigration of women during the last two decades, primarily for economic reasons, which has led to changes in these family arrangements (Parreñas *Servants* 144).

Dubbed "transnational motherhood" by Pierrette Hondagneu-Sotelo and Ernestine Avila, these migrant women work as foreign domestics caring for the homes and children of families in industrialized societies while their own children remain in the country of origin (Hondagneu-Sotelo 24; Parreñas *Children* 13, 23). The situation of migrant mothers is particularly interesting because they must adapt to their new surroundings, while maintaining a relatively stable relationship with their family at home. Likewise, those family members who remain in the home country must simultaneously adapt to their absence (Hondagneu-Sotelo and Avila 562: Parreñas *Servants* 122).

It is within this context that the "problem" of the broken home (Parreñas *Servants* 144) or the "crisis in the domestic sphere" (Arat-Koc 34) has become a widespread issue. Transnational households have come to signify the disintegration of family values and the destruction of the moral fabric of many societies because they do not conform to dominant cultural notions of a typical nuclear family (Parreñas *Servants* 109; *Children* 30).

Public policy and cultural values in Western society support biological parents as the primary caregivers for children. It is within this framework that migrant mothers are criticized. They are acting against the ideal of the western "good mother" by working and leaving their children at home. In doing so, they are breaking up the sacred family arrangements that are to be disrupted only for the most desperate reasons. Moreover, we cannot imagine a mother willingly leaving her child.

This article argues that mothers who leave their families at home while they migrate to find wage labour abroad are redefining perceptions of motherhood. I maintain that these women are not abandoning their families or responsibilities. By leaving their families and migrating, domestic workers are redefining the way motherhood is conceptualized in both sending and receiving societies. My objective is to highlight both the active role migrant women play in defining their own roles and the limits of their agency.

ASSUAGING THE DEMAND FOR AFFORDABLE CHILD CARE

In any society, raising children is work that requires a tremendous expenditure of manual, mental, spiritual, and emotional energy. The high costs of regulated day care and the difficulty of finding subsidized day-care spaces, combined with rigid hours (typical day-care centres operate Monday-Friday 9:00 to 5:00) make it difficult for parents, especially those who work irregular hours (Bakan and Stasiulis 308). Migrant women are a potential solution to this problem.[1] They are often available to live directly in the home, allowing parents increased affordability[2] and flexibility.[3]

Canadian immigration laws[4] and the job characteristics of paid domestic work, particularly live-in work, impose transnational motherhood on migrant women who have children of their own (Hondagneu-Sotelo 50, 51; Fincher *et al.*72). The long hours inherently required of domestic workers does not offer the flexibility required by a mother intent on raising her children (Chang 13; Hondagneu-Sotelo 24). It is common today for many domestic workers to care for the homes and children of families in industrialized societies while their own children remain in the country of origin (Hondagneu-Sotelo 24; Parreñas *Children* 13, 23). This arrangement signals new international inequalities of social reproduction and the creation of the transnational family[5] (Hondagneu-Sotelo 24).

MOTHERING ACROSS BORDERS

Transnational mothers are actively developing new strategies that are born out of the financial need to provide for their family. They seek to prevent the need for migration in future generations by allowing their children to obtain better education (Parreñas *Servants* 124; *Children* 56). For the most part, mothers justify their decision to leave by highlighting the markedly visible material gains they can provide their family, including better nutrition, clothing, and schooling (Hondagneu-Sotelo and Avila 562: Parreñas *Servants* 122). By operating with this mindset, mothers can rationalize the need to sacrifice intimate familial bonds for the collective family's material well-being and, as such, transnational mothers are able to rely on commodities to establish concrete ties with their families (Momsen 302; Parreñas *Servants* 123-24).

Instead of berating themselves, many mothers manipulate their vision of motherhood to enable themselves to participate as they would if they were home, recognizing the quality rather than quantity of time spent with their children as being especially important. Motherhood involves not only a duty to provide money for the children, but also to provide them with guidance and direction, something that money alone cannot do. In this way, they continue their motherly role not only by communicating through calls, letters, photographs, and telegrams, but also by physically traversing the borders if they can afford to return for a visit[6] (Hondagneu-Sotelo and Avila 564). For these transnational mothers, the meaning of motherhood is different than if they were involved in daily care. Rather than merely replacing their care giving with breadwinning, the migrants are expanding the concept of motherhood to include breadwinning and care giving that may require long-term separation (Hondagneu-Sotelo and Avila 562).

Whatever the merits of migration, migrant mothers often wonder if it is worth the cost. They accept their position as a necessary responsibility to their relatives, while acknowledging the painful costs of their actions experiencing the absence of domestic family life as a both physical and mental loss (Hondagneu-Sotelo and Avila 552). The absence of daily interactions denies familiarity and creates a void in parent-child relations. Migrant mothers often battle with the grief imposed by constant reminders of their children and the strain of living on their own in a strange place. The pain of family separation is further intensified by the care giving tasks in domestic work. Taking care of children is not so simple when one cannot "take care" of one's own family. Emotional strains of transnational parenting include feelings of anxiety, helplessness, loss, guilt, and loneliness. For them, missing their children's youth is a great loss, which sadly turns into a deep-seated regret over the emotional distance it has caused the family (Parreñas *Servants* 121). These migrant women are trapped in the contradiction of being physically separated while having to give in to the family's dependence on the material rewards granted by this separation. While they may long to return home to be with their children, their family's dependence on their earnings makes this desire problematic (Parreñas *Servants* 119-20).

As migrant mothers wrestle with the contradictions between their current situation and traditional gender roles, they find themselves devising new emotional strategies. To reduce the longing for their own children, some workers develop strong ties with the children for whom they are caring (Hondagneu-Sotelo 26). Not all workers do, but many criticize what they perceive as their employers' neglectful parenting. Typically, they blame biological mothers for hiring domestics in order to gain more leisure time for themselves. Transnational mothers indulge in the rhetoric of comparative mothering highlighting the sacrifices that they make as poor, legally disenfranchised, racially subordinate working mothers that set them in contrast to what they perceive as substandard mothering provided by their privileged employers. In response, transnational mothers construct new measures to gauge the quality of their mothering. By setting themselves against the negative models of mothering that they see in others, especially the models that they can closely scrutinize in their employers' homes, transnational mothers redefine the standards of good mothering on their own terms. At the same time, selectively developing mother-like ties with other people's children allows them to enjoy the affectionate, face-to-face interactions that they cannot experience on a daily basis with their own children (Hondagneu-Sotelo 26-27).

STRAIN AT HOME

Tensions are also evident in the home country (Hondagneu-Sotelo 26). Expectations caused by encultured gender roles are also causing the children stress as they come to realize their mothers are not fulfilling the culturally-defined maternal roles. Children of migrant fathers are not as likely to doubt the motives for parental migration as are those children of migrant mothers (Parreñas *Servants* 132; *Children* 64). Examples given in Rhacel Salazar Parreñas' work with children in transnational families show that children recognize the economic contributions their mothers are making, but do not accept it as appropriate care. Children still hold their mothers responsible for traditional care responsibilities of nurturing the family, holding on to traditional perceptions as fathers as breadwinners (Parreñas *Children* 60, 124). Fathers can effectively establish their love and support simply by sending monthly remittances, but mothers must maintain the most intimate involvement in their lives, making meeting the standards of care almost impossible to attain (Parreñas *Children* 127).

For children left behind in the Philippines, staying together and keeping the family whole is more important than achieving material security. Parreñas has identified three central conflicts plaguing the relationships between migrant mothers and the children whom they have left behind in the Philippines. First, children tend to disagree with their mothers that commodities are sufficient markers of love. Second, they do not believe that their mothers recognize the sacrifices that they as children have made toward the successful maintenance of their families. Finally, while they appreciate the efforts of migrant mothers to create "bridges" of affection and care, they still question the extent of these efforts (Parreñas *Servants* 132). Parreñas tempers this argument by claiming that these children can make such sweeping claims about maternal presence being more important than money because the material security provided by migrant parents affords them the luxury of demanding greater emotional security. She concludes that it would be highly unlikely that impoverished children would make similar demands (Parreñas *Servants* 132). She has also noted that children receiving adequate care sometimes still view themselves as not receiving enough, or satisfactory care simply because it is not done directly by their biological mothers (Parreñas *Children* 140).

DISCUSSION

Transnational motherhood contradicts the dominant discourse of motherhood. The general perception is that a caring mother should be at home with her children, not on the other side of the world working. Umut Erel argues that conceptions of mother as primary carer is a "class-specific ethnocentric construction" in which neither the working-class nor the wealthy mothers who have nannies conform (Erel 132-33; Lan 12). The pressure exerted upon mothers regarding the need for a mother's physical presence in her child's life in order to create healthy development holds women singularly accountable for their child's development (Erel 132-33).

It is interesting to note that while mothers who leave the home to support their children are viewed as bad mothers, the same criticism is not levelled at fathers (Swift 104). Various studies suggest that a large proportion of fathers do not provide for their children financially, take little responsibility for childcare, and are not involved in disciplining children. They take little interest in their schooling or general well-being, and may gamble the remittances, or take a mistress (Le Roux 190; see also Constable; Erel; Lan; Parreñas; Paz Cruz; Romero; Silvera).

If the father is not working in the paid economy and the mother has to leave home in order to support the family, she is criticized in her home country for taking on a male role. The father, however, is not criticized for failing to conform to his traditional gender role (Swift 103). Parreñas argues that the emotional insecurity that migrant's children feel, even with the presence of fathers, suggest that fathers have failed to respond equally to the efforts of mothers to sustain the family economically. She considers this unsurprising as many of the migrants in her study attributed their migration to their husband's irresponsibility. Many children often have fathers who are physically present but emotionally absent[7] (Parreñas *Children* 99). The question, then, is whether fathers are able to provide the maternal love missing in the lives of children if women are capable of assisting them with their ideologically prescribed role as income-provider (Parreñas *Servants* 147). I suggest that in situations where the father is actively involved in the care of his children, the love of a father is sufficient to make up for the lack of maternal love, i.e. in the form of the mother's physical presence. Likewise, it must be noted that by presuming that maternal love is somehow superior to paternal love, researchers are proliferating the perception that parenting is somehow divided along gender lines.

The problem Western critics have with migrant mothers is not that they leave, but that their departure disrupts the notion of family and breaks with a particular idea of motherhood. In the Western view of family as a primordial structure, disrupting such a "sacred" institution is distinctly discouraged. As ideological constructs of feminine identity are modeled from mothering and caring roles, the independent migration of women constitutes a direct liberation from traditional duties and roles (Parreñas *Servants* 63).

Migrant domestic workers highlight the theoretical discord between the categories of work and home, contesting the "naturalness" of mothering, the gendered nature of this role, and the power structures that surround it (Gamburd 195, 196; Parreñas *Children* 57). Gamburd notes that new consciousness of women's roles and personal identities make women more critically aware of the gender hierarchies, class differences, and the international relations of power with which they live (Gamburd 195, 196). One could even suggest that through migration and performing their traditional roles for wages, women are obtaining their freedom from culturally-bounded roles at home. Women are allowing themselves the opportunity to step away from their prescribed role at home and reinvent themselves on their own terms. While away from home and not integrated into their place abroad, women are offered the chance to redefine themselves within the structure of the host society. Migration also creates the opportunity for women to explore themselves and decide what image they want to portray and how they want to be viewed.

Far from abandoning their families, these women have taken it upon themselves to fulfill a "male role" while maintaining their previous role as mother and wife. As the ways women demonstrate their love and caring for their children are transformed through migration, the social valuations of the worth and meaning of mothering is reconfigured. Evolving roles and behaviours conflict with existing values, ideals, and habits of family life, both challenging and reinforcing more established thinking about motherhood, gender hierarchies, personal identity, and women's work (Gamburd 179).

Tizard argues that the separation of the mother and her children is not necessarily traumatizing when they are taken care of by a good and trustworthy caregiver (136). Migrant mothers are not causing irreparable harm by migrating; they are instead breaking free of inflexible norms and causing people to confront what they believe the correct role for women should be. Critics often fail to realize that while migrants are changing and adapting to their new role in the receiving country, the family left behind undertakes a similar reconfiguration. Children adapt to not having their mothers home. Although they may not find the situation the most ideal, it is functional. By viewing migrant cultures as though they were similar to our own, western critics often fail to realize the fundamental differences in family structure that can allow women to leave their families, knowing that they are in capable hands and are benefiting from the money remitted.

The negativity associated with transnational motherhood is easily interpreted as abandonment as the women leave their families behind. Female migrants rely on extended kin to care for their children, while extended kin raise their standard of living with the financial support provided by migrant workers. The persisting cultural value of familism assists in the formation of transnational households as much as the structural forces of globalization propel it (Parreñas *Servants* 113). Transnational households would not be able to form without the cultural values of mutual obligation and collectivism in the extended family (Parreñas *Servants* 108).

[1]The extent to which childcare is degraded as gainful employment betrays the real value of mother's work as is demonstrated by the low wages received by domestics (Bakan and Stasiulis 307; Parreñas 25; Stiell and England 43; Thurer xix).

[2]In 2006, Canadian families were allowed to deduct $7,000 per child under the age of six from their taxable income (Canada).

[3]According to a survey conducted by INTERCEDE, a Toronto organization for domestic workers rights, only thirty-five percent of live-in domestics worked a regular workweek. Forty percent work 45 to 50 hours, eighteen percent work 50 to 60 hours, and six percent work more than 60 hours a week. The survey found that a high percentage of domestics who perform overtime work are not compensated with legally mandated rates ($11.63 in 2007) or time off (Arat-Koc 233). A live-in domestic worker in Ontario who works a 44-hour week (no overtime) takes home a monthly net pay of $882.21 (INTERCEDE).

[4]In the early 1950s, pressure from Canadian employers and British Caribbean governments led to the execution of agreements between Canada, Jamaica, and the Barbados that became known as the Caribbean Domestic Scheme. Under this program single, healthy women between the ages of eighteen and forty with no dependents and at least an eighth-grade education were admitted to Canada as landed immigrants

on condition that they remain in live-in domestic service for at least one year (Macklin 16).

After a brief period of relatively open migration for domestic workers, the Canadian government instituted a system of temporary work visas for domestic workers in 1973. The visas allowed the holder to remain in Canada only as long as she was employed as a domestic worker. The visas could be renewed annually but the domestic worker had no genuine prospect of converting her status from visitor to immigrant and ultimately to citizen (Macklin 17).

The Foreign Domestic Movement (FDM) Program replaced the Caribbean Domestic Scheme in 1982. Having a spouse and/or dependants made women less attractive candidates for admission to the program and ultimately for immigration (Macklin 20).

The current federal legislating governing the recruitment of domestics is the Live-in Caregiver Program (LCP). The LCP, developed in 1992 to replace the Foreign Domestic Movement Program, defines a caregiver as those who care for a child or an elderly or disabled person in the home of their employer. Applicants to the program are required to meet certain educational and employment standards in order to be accepted. Upon completion of 24 months of work within three years, the caregiver may apply for permanent resident status. Canadian law requires foreign domestics have a full-time offer of live-in employment prior to entering the country. For their first two years in Canada, the domestic is granted only temporary status, subject to employment termination, at which point the work permit is withdrawn (Bakan and Stasiulis 309).

[5]By "transnational families" I mean families whose core members are located in at least two nations, as defined by Parreñas (*Servants*).

[6]This type of mothering is referred to as "intensive mothering" by Sharon Hays, who defines it as care from afar while overcompensating for physical absence (cited in Parreñas *Children* 103).

[7]As described by one of Parreñas' informants, Isabelle Tirador, "It's annoying. I cannot help but feel resentful, because I feel abandoned. It's because my father is here but he does not care. He does not support us, especially when it comes to school.... My mother is the one who is far away but she is the one who is close" (Parreñas *Children* 99).

WORKS CITED

Arat-Koc, Sedef. "Immigration Policies, Migrant Domestic Workers and the Definition of Citizenship in Canada." *Deconstructing a Nation: Immigration, Multiculturalism and Racism in '90s Canada*. Ed. Vic Satzewich. Saskatoon: Fernwood, 1992. 229-42.

Bakan, Abigail B. and Daiva Stasiulis. "Making the Match: Domestic Placement Agencies and the Racialization of Women's Household

Work." *Signs* 20.2 (1995): 303-35.

Canada. Revenue Canada. *Child Care Expenses Deduction for 2006*. 1 August 2007. Online: <http: //www.cra-arc.gc.ca/E/pbg/tf/t778/README.html>.

Chang, Grace. *Disposable Domestics: Immigrant Women Workers in the Global Economy*. Massachusetts: South End, 2000.

Constable, Nicole. *Maid to Order in Hong Kong: Stories of Filipina Migrant Workers*. Ithaca: Cornell University Press, 1997.

Erel, Umut. "Reconceptualizing Motherhood: Experiences of Migrant Women from Turkey Living in Germany." *The Transnational Family: New European Frontiers and Global Networks*. Ed. Deborah Bryceson and Ulla Vuorela. New York: Berg, 2002. 127-46.

Fincher, Ruth, with Lois Foster, Wenona Giles, and Valerie Preston. "Gender and Migration Policy." *Immigration and Refugee Policy: Australia and Canada Compared*. Ed. Howard Adelman, Allan Borowski, Meyer Burstein and Lois Foster. Toronto: University of Toronto Press, 1994. 148-86.

Gamburd, Michele Ruth. "Nurture for Sale: Sri Lankan Housemaids and the Work of Mothering." *Home and Hegemony: Domestic Service and Identity Politics in South and Southeast Asia*. Ed. Kathleen M. Adams and Sara Dickey. Ann Arbor: University of Michigan Press, 2000. 179-205.

Henshall, Janet. "Maids on the Move." *Gender Migration and Domestic Service*. Ed. Janet Henshall Momsen. New York: Routledge, 1999. 1-20.

Hondagneu-Sotelo, Pierrette. *Domestica: Immigrant Workers Cleaning and Caring in the Shadows of Affluence*. Los Angeles: University of California Press, 2001.

Hondagneu-Sotelo, Pierrette and Ernestine Avila. "'I'm Here, but I'm There': The Meanings of Latina Transnational Motherhood." *Gender and Society* 11.5 (1997): 548-71.

INTERCEDE: For the Rights of Domestic Workers, Caregivers, and Newcomers. How to Calculate Your Pay Worksheet. 15 June 2007. <http: //www.intercedetoronto.org/>.

Lan, Pei-Chia. "Maid or Madam? Filipina Migrant Workers and the Continuity of Domestic Labor." *Gender and Society, Global Perspectives on Gender and Carework* 17.2 (2003): 187-208.

Le Roux, Tessa. "'Home is Where the Children Are': A Qualitative study of Migratory Domestic Workers in Mmotla Village, South Africa." *Gender Migration and Domestic Service*. Ed. Janet Henshall Momsen. New York: Routledge, 1999. 179-90.

Macklin, Audrey. "On the Inside Looking In: Foreign Domestic Workers in Canada." *Maid in the Market: Women's Paid Domestic Labour*. Ed. Wenona Giles and Sedef Arat-Koc. Halifax: Fernwood, 1994.

Parreñas, Rhacel Salazar. *Children of Global Migration: Transnational Families and Gendered Woes*. Stanford: Stanford University Press, 2005.

Parreñas, Rhacel Salazar. *Servants of Globalization: Women, Migration and Domestic Work*. California: Stanford University Press, 2001.

Paz Cruz, Victoria and Anthony Paganoni. *Filipinas in Migration: Big Bills and Small Change*. Manila: Scalabrini Migration Center, 1989.

Romero, Mary. *Maid in the USA*. New York: Routledge, 2002.

Silvera, Makeda. *Silenced: Talks with Working Class Caribbean Women about Their Lives and Struggles as Domestic Workers in Canada*. Toronto: Sister Vision, 1989.

Stiell, Bernadette and Kim England. "Jamaican Domestics, Filipina Housekeepers and English Nannies: Representations of Toronto's Foreign Domestic Workers." *Gender Migration and Domestic Service*. Ed. Janet Henshall Momsen. New York: Routledge, 1999. 43-60.

Swift, Karen J. *Manufacturing "Bad Mothers": A Critical Perspective on Child Neglect*. Toronto: University of Toronto Press, 1995.

Thurer, Shari L. *The Myths of Motherhood: How Culture Reinvents the Good Mother*. New York: Houghton Mifflin, 1994.

Tizard, B. "Employed Mothers and the Care of Young Children." *Motherhood: Meaning, Practices and Ideologies*. Ed. A. Phenix, with A. Woollett and E Lloyd. London: Sage, 1991.

L'adoption d'un enfant en provenance d'un orphelinat chinois

L'expérience de l'attachement selon la perspective des mères adoptantes québécoises

CLAUDINE HOULE

DES STATISTIQUES DE la dernière décennie sur la situation de l'adoption internationale au Québec démontrent que près de 43% des enfants adoptés proviennent de la Chine (Secrétariat à l'adoption internationale). Face à un phénomène social d'une telle envergure, il est légitime de s'interroger sur l'intégration de ces enfants dans la société en général et dans leur famille. Cette intégration est principalement assurée par une garantie de sécurité ressentie par l'enfant dans sa relation avec une ou des «personne(s) significative(s)». Ainsi cette sécurité se développe par l'attachement qui est le lien profond et durable entre un enfant et une personne significative, souvent la mère selon la littérature (Bowlby 350-373, 229-270).

Par ailleurs, l'engagement et la complémentarité de la mère et du père, auprès de l'enfant, favorisent le développement du lien d'attachement sécure et ce, autant pour la famille biologique (Bell *et al.*, «Mothers' and Fathers' View» 179-200), que pour la famille adoptante (Juffer et Van Ijzendoorn 2501-2515). L'écart entre les deux types de famille s'est atténué pour mettre l'emphase sur des liens fondés sur un projet parental réfléchi, engagé et véritable (Ouellette et Belleau 9-26) et l'investissement personnel dans le rôle parental (Bell *et al.*, «Lien parent-enfant» 32-36; Hopkins-Best 44; Levy 67-108).

Cet article porte sur une recherche qualitative réalisée auprès de trois couples québécois ayant chacun adopté une petite fille chinoise afin de cerner le phénomène de l'attachement dans le contexte de l'adoption internationale. Il comprend deux parties. Dans la première partie, le cadre conceptuel ainsi que la méthodologie de l'étude sont présentés. Puis, dans la seconde partie, les résultats des entretiens sont analysés et particulièrement la dimension de la relation mère-fille.

PRÉSENTATION DE L'ÉTUDE

Une adoption réussie exige que l'enfant adopté s'attache à sa nouvelle famille. Le parent adoptant disposerait de trois façons pour développer l'attachement sécure chez l'enfant adopté soit; 1) la proximité (l'interaction positive parents-enfants); 2) la réciprocité (le cycle répétitif et évolutif); et 3) la réclamation mutuelle.

La *proximité* assure la protection et la réduction de la détresse chez l'enfant qui, dès sa naissance, démontre une compétence de partenaire actif à rechercher la proximité de la mère par ses pleurs (Bowlby 229-270; Van Egeren *et al.* 684-697). Dans le contexte de l'adoption, l'enfant qui a vécu un séjour en orphelinat a souvent connu la négligence dans les soins. Cette négligence entraîne le développement de comportements passifs dans l'interaction avec les autres (Bowlby 229-270; Zeanah 42-52).

La *réciprocité dans un cycle répétitif et évolutif* est gouvernée par deux mécanismes en constante activation (Bowlby 350-373; Fahlberg 33; Van Egeren *et al.* 684-697) qui sont: 1) l'éveil, généralement initié par l'enfant qui exprime un inconfort; il s'accompagne d'un besoin d'action; et, 2) la relaxation, souvent amenée par la mère lorsqu'elle répond aux besoins de l'enfant par le maternage dans la routine au quotidien. Cette réciprocité influence la nature de la relation et représente aussi un facteur à considérer dans le développement favorable de l'attachement et de la santé mentale future de l'enfant (Bowlby 350-373; Zeanah 42-52). Dans le contexte de l'adoption, l'enfant qui a vécu les facteurs de négligence et le manque d'interactions sociales dans les orphelinats après son abandon vit un départ défavorable. Suite à l'adoption, cet enfant, qui vit la réciprocité, réalise que ses parents adoptants représentent un modèle de soins consistant dans ses interactions parents-enfant et ses réponses adoptées; apprend de nouvelles stratégies d'adaptation; et développe de la sécurité (Shapiro *et al.* Chapitre 5).

La *réclamation mutuelle* permet la création d'une identité familiale (Fahlberg 37; Levy 140). Ainsi, le parent accepte l'enfant comme sien, comme membre de la famille, et l'enfant accepte l'adulte comme son parent et se sent comme un membre de la famille.

Selon Kirk (1-203), l'intégration de l'enfant nouvellement adopté représente la tâche principale de tous les parents adoptants. Dans sa *théorie du destin partagé,* Kirk (1-203) relie les différentes dimensions de l'expérience de la famille adoptante et suggère des besoins particuliers. Dans cette enquête, trois éléments de cette théorie sont retenus soit: la reconnaissance de la différence, la révélation et l'empathie. Dans la *reconnaissance de la différence*, le parent reconnaît sa position parentale d'adoptant et mise sur cette reconnaissance des différences pour bâtir sa relation avec l'enfant. La *révélation* est l'engagement du parent adoptant à parler de l'adoption à l'enfant et ce, le plus tôt dans sa vie. Ainsi, l'acceptation du passé de l'enfant souvent inconnu favorise la capacité de partager son destin. Enfin, le parent adoptant *empathique* peut comprendre le vécu du parent de naissance qui abandonne son enfant, en se connectant à sa propre peine reliée au deuil de la parenté biologique. Cette empathie place le parent adoptant en disponibilité pour aider l'enfant dans sa quête d'identité face à son abandon et à son adoption, sans se sentir menacé dans son rôle de parent (Cohen *et al.* 441-456; Nickman *et al.* 987-994). Paradoxalement, l'enfant adopté vivant le destin partagé se sent plus ancré dans sa famille adoptante et ce, malgré le fait qu'il puisse ressentir des incertitudes à différentes étapes de sa vie.

Dans la présente étude, le modèle de Calgary est le transporteur de l'attachement. Le modèle de Calgary de Wright et Leahey (1-347) mise sur l'importance de l'engagement à long terme selon lequel chaque membre de la famille organise sa vie en fonction des autres. Ce modèle permet une représentation claire de la famille et reconnaît les forces et les défis de la famille. Il facilite aussi la synthèse de la collecte des données par le Modèle de Calgary relatif à l'évaluation de la famille (MCEF) qui comprend trois dimensions de la famille: la structure, le développement et le fonctionnement.

La *structure* permet de tracer la configuration de la famille et d'apprécier la qualité des liens entre les membres de la famille et les suprasystèmes représentant la famille élargie et l'environnement.

Le *développement* permet de situer le stade de vie où se retrouve la famille. À chaque stade du développement de la famille se rattachent des responsabilités, des tâches et des liens affectifs. Le processus de transition affective qui caractérise le stade vécu par les parents adoptants à l'étude est l'acceptation de nouveaux membres dans la famille. Les tâches qui y sont spécifiques sont: 1) l'adaptation du système conjugal à l'arrivée de l'enfant où le couple doit préserver l'espace essentiel à chacun des membres de la famille, à sa relation de couple et à ses rapports sociaux; 2) le partage des tâches relatives à l'éducation des enfants, à la recherche de ressources financières et à l'entretien de la maison qui exige que le couple fasse des choix judicieux; ainsi que 3) le réajustement des relations avec la famille élargie.

Le *fonctionnement* est de deux types: instrumental et expressif. Le *fonctionnement instrumental* évalue les activités de la vie familiale. Cette dimension est particulièrement importante dans les situations de transitions de la vie. Le *fonctionnement expressif* apprécie, entre autres, les différentes dimensions de la communication incluant l'attachement ainsi que les croyances dans la famille.

Enfin, Wright *et al.* (40-43) définissent une croyance comme une conviction de la vérité, d'une réalité subjective qui influence le fonctionnement de la personne et qui teinte sa façon d'être et de voir le monde. Une croyance facilitante contribue à l'élaboration des solutions à des problèmes. À l'opposé, une croyance contraignante apporte de la souffrance et nécessite une intervention.

L'étude se propose de comprendre l'expérience de la famille adoptante, particulièrement à partir du récit que se font les parents 1) des stratégies développées pour favoriser la proximité, la réciprocité et la réclamation mutuelle; 2) des perceptions des stratégies pour permettre de vivre le destin partagé dans le type de famille qu'ils ont formé; et 3) des croyances facilitantes qui aident les nouveaux parents adoptants à recréer l'attachement. Les trois dimensions du MCEF permettent d'évaluer l'attachement et ce, en se basant sur le cadre conceptuel à l'étude, adapté du Modèle de Calgary, des théories de l'attachement et de certains éléments du destin partagé dans le contexte de l'adoption internationale.

Au cœur du cadre conceptuel à l'étude se trouve le *fonctionnement expressif*: la proximité, la réciprocité et la réclamation mutuelle, composantes essentielles du développement de l'attachement, dans le cas de l'adoption internationale. De plus, la représentation que les parents adoptants se font du destin partagé, particulièrement en ce qui concerne la reconnaissance de la différence, y compris l'empathie face à la mère de naissance, et le fait de parler de l'adoption, y apparaît aussi. Ce fonctionnement expressif est tributaire de deux autres niveaux représentés par les deux cercles environnants: la structure interne, externe et contextuelle de la famille et la structure instrumentale de la famille.

Le cercle immédiat entourant ces composantes essentielles du développement de l'attachement (*fonctionnement instrumental*) est constitué par les parents adoptants pour la première fois, l'enfant adopté en provenance d'un orphelinat chinois, les rôles parentaux et les croyances qui habitent les nouveaux parents adoptants. Enfin, le *maternage dans la routine au quotidien* s'y retrouve. Ces composantes permettent d'évaluer les stratégies utilisées auprès de l'enfant nouvellement adopté, autant par la contribution de la mère adoptante que par celle du père adoptant.

Enfin, le cercle externe, constitué à partir du génogramme et de l'écocarte, représente la *structure interne, externe et contextuelle* de la famille adoptante. La perméabilité des différentes dimensions du cadre conceptuel permet l'influence mutuelle entre les différents niveaux du cadre conceptuel.

Dans la présente enquête, une approche qualitative inductive phénoménologique est privilégiée pour mieux comprendre le phénomène de l'adoption selon le point de vue des personnes qui en font l'expérience (Fortin 140).

Pour le recrutement, le Centre local de services communautaires (CLSC) du Lac Saint-Louis est l'organisme qui a démontré un intérêt pour le projet et son équipe d'adoption internationale a pu trouver trois familles qui répondaient aux critères d'inclusion. Le CLSC du Lac Saint-Louis offre des services d'accompagnement en adoption internationale sous forme de groupe, de consultation individuelle et de visite à domicile sur demande lors de l'arrivée de l'enfant.

Une rencontre de deux heures a eu lieu au domicile des participants. L'entrevue semi-structurée sur un enregistrement audio, le génogramme et l'écocarte font partie des stratégies phénoménologiques choisies. Les divers moyens proposés pour la collecte et l'analyse des données ont respecté les règles générales d'éthique. La retranscription intégrale du verbatim a permis l'obtention des données brutes, soit la perspective des nouveaux parents du développement de l'attachement, à partir desquelles l'analyse des données a été possible selon l'approche phénoménologique.

RÉSULTATS DE L'ÉTUDE

Dans cette section, les résultats, soit les 12 thèmes qui se dégagent de l'analyse des entrevues sont présentés et ce, en lien avec le cadre conceptuel de l'enquête et avec les autres éléments qui ont émergé de l'analyse des données. L'échantillon représente six participants qui sont fictivement identifiés comme les couples Claude et Pauline, Daniel et Catherine, et Serge et Sylvie. L'âge moyen des mères est de 38 ans et celui des pères est de 36 ans. Les parents parlent couramment le français et habitent la région de Montréal. Les trois couples sont parents par adoption pour la première fois d'une fille provenant d'un orphelinat chinois: Marie, Clothilde et Jeannette, respectivement. L'âge moyen des enfants à l'adoption était de 12 mois. Les trois enfants ont fait un séjour en orphelinat depuis leur abandon, quelques jours après leur naissance jusqu'à l'adoption. De plus, elles présentaient toutes un retard dans leur développement selon la perspective des trois couples. Enfin, les trois familles entretiennent des rapports harmonieux avec la famille élargie qui semble avoir bien accueilli l'enfant. Par ailleurs, les nouveaux parents sont satisfaits de leur réseau de soutien.

Dans le premier thème *(la vision stigmatisante de la société québécoise face à l'adoption internationale)*, les six participants reconnaissent que la société québécoise semble manifester une volonté pour accepter les différences dont l'adoption. Mais en réalité, elle démontre peu d'ouverture face à ces différences. Malgré une plus grande ouverture face aux différences, il demeure une vision stigmatisante de la société québécoise face à l'adoption. Ainsi, considérant qu'un consensus existe pour les six participants, cet élément a été ajouté au cadre conceptuel final, le rendant plus près de la réalité des trois familles.

Les trois thèmes dégagés de la section du fonctionnement instrumental touchent: le rôle des parents en pré-adoption (la préparation); le rôle des parents adoptants en post-adoption (s'accorder le droit d'être parents ou *entitlement*); et le maternage dans la routine au quotidien.

En pré-adoption, le parcours des trois couples dans la *préparation* à l'adoption (deuxième thème) démontre un projet parental réfléchi. Les six participants sont d'accord sur le fait que leur agence d'adoption et particulièrement le CLSC du Lac Saint-Louis offrent des informations précieuses aux futurs parents adoptants pour les préparer au voyage en Chine, à leur nouveau rôle de parents et à l'importance d'avoir des attentes réalistes à l'égard de l'enfant qui leur sera confié.

Le troisième thème de l'*entitlement* a été abordé unanimement par les six participants. Claude et Pauline croient que l'adoption est une voie qui leur permet de devenir parents. Daniel et Catherine croient que la responsabilité parentale est présente peu importe comment la famille s'est formée. De plus, ils croient qu'être parent a un impact positif sur la légitimité du lien pour l'enfant. Serge et Sylvie ont fait le choix réfléchi de devenir parents par l'adoption. Ainsi, considérant l'importance donnée à cette dimension de s'accorder le droit d'être parent par les nouveaux parents adoptants, elle a été ajoutée au cadre conceptuel final comme thème émergeant.

Le quatrième thème concernant le *maternage dans la routine au quotidien* permet de découvrir comment le maternage influence positivement l'attachement ainsi que l'unanimité de cette croyance autant chez les mères que chez les pères de l'étude. Claude et Pauline expliquent que le rôle des nouveaux parents adoptants est d'établir des routines pour donner un cadre à l'enfant. Ces routines sont des réseaux de communications parents-enfant. Selon eux, l'attachement a lieu si les bonnes choses sont faites au bon moment. De leur côté, Serge et Sylvie se sont accordés le temps d'être à l'aise avec les soins à l'enfant dans l'intimité de leur foyer. La complémentarité du couple se conjugue au quotidien pour relever les défis. En effet, la routine permet de gérer les problèmes de sommeil chez l'enfant sans briser l'attachement qui se crée. Daniel et Catherine abondent aussi dans ce sens. Il s'est créé un petit rituel matinal impliquant toute la famille qui favorise le contact physique, le plaisir et la douceur. Selon Catherine:

> *À tous les matins de la première année, j'ai donné un biberon à Clothilde dans mon lit. Cette attention plus particulière a été faite sans tenir compte de son âge mais pour le plaisir de se rapprocher… Daniel se levait pour le préparer et l'emmener dans le lit avec ma tasse de café.*

En bref, les trois couples se sont assurés de prodiguer eux-mêmes tous les soins nécessaires à leur enfant pour s'assurer de la reconnaissance de leur rôle de parent par l'enfant et ainsi favoriser l'attachement.

Comme mentionné plus haut, le fonctionnement expressif explore les mécanismes mis en place plus particulièrement par les mères pour favoriser l'attachement de l'enfant et le destin partagé dès le début de la relation. Le thème sur le premier moment en Chine introduit cette partie et est suivi par les thèmes touchant la proximité, la réciprocité et la réclamation mutuelle.

De façon unanime, pour les trois mères, le *premier moment en Chine* avec leur fille (cinquième thème) s'est déroulé beaucoup mieux que dans leurs attentes; les trois enfants ont peu réagi dans ce moment de transition important dans leur vie. Les mères ont vécu des émotions différentes les unes des autres. Pauline s'est sentie sans contrôle et a rapidement réagi en révisant les étapes à suivre pour toutes les situations reliées aux soins à l'enfant, qu'elle avait préparées au préalable, pour composer avec cette situation stressante. De son côté, Catherine a laissé son cœur prendre le contrôle par le toucher et par le chant. Quant à Sylvie, celle-ci a pu promouvoir, en ce premier moment, une valeur importante dans son rôle de mère: le calme. De plus, elle a été témoin d'une brève interaction entre une nounou de l'orphelinat et Jeannette lui permettant de construire une croyance facilitante remplie d'espoir, à l'effet que Jeannette aurait pu développer un attachement, même faible, à une personne significative durant son séjour à l'orphelinat. Pour Sylvie:

> *Elle [la nounou] a commencé à faire des «guili-guili» à Jeannette. Jeannette s'est mise à rire... Alors là, j'ai vu la vraie Jeannette... Là, j'ai réalisé parce que nous étions avant sur notre nuage, on pensait que cela se passait bien car elle nous regarde ... Juste de voir qu'elle était sur le choc (avec nous) était pour moi un bon signe... J'étais contente aussi, de voir qu'elle a eu un lien important avec une personne significative car c'est quelque chose que l'on s'est fait dire que c'est important qu'elle ait connu cela au moins une fois dans sa vie, la possibilité d'attachement.*

En somme, le premier moment en Chine a été jugé important pour les nouvelles mères en terme d'émotions et de la concrétisation du projet d'être parents, quoique les émotions des mères sont plus variées entre elles que pour les pères. Considérant l'importance accordée à cette dimension comme thème émergeant, elle a été ajoutée au cadre conceptuel final.

Dès le premier contact et au retour de Chine avec sa nouvelle famille, les trois filles démontraient des comportements passifs dans les interactions mère-enfant. Les trois mères de l'étude ont eu la possibilité de vivre pleinement la *proximité* par leur choix de prendre un *congé parental* (sixième thème) pour s'occuper de leur fille. Pauline raconte avoir eu besoin de ce temps pour mieux connaître sa fille. Elle a pu passer d'un mode de survie visant à s'assurer que les besoins de son enfant étaient comblés, à un style de vie plus adapté et ce, par l'effet de la proximité. Catherine précise la nécessité de doser l'ardeur de l'amour et des émotions du nouveau parent pour aider l'enfant qui vit, elle aussi, un moment de transition important:

> *Ne pas l'étouffer.... L'enfant ne nous connaît pas. L'enfant est dans une période de mutation, de grands changements, de tension, elle ne comprend pas ce qui se passe, alors cela peut la stresser. Alors, il faut y aller très doucement.*

En bref, les mères ont su tirer avantage du congé parental pour apprendre à mieux connaître leur fille et à développer leurs habiletés maternelles ce qui confirme le thème de la proximité mère-fille favorisée par le congé parental.

Chacune à sa façon dans la *réciprocité*, les mères semblent avoir un style dans leurs échanges avec leur enfant. Elles partagent toutes un *sentiment de responsabilité* important (septième thème) qui teinte leur approche auprès de l'enfant. Ainsi, Pauline n'a pas hésité à réviser ses priorités face à l'esthétisme de la maison pour le mieux-être de la relation mère-fille. Pauline a le souci de rester en contact avec les réactions de Marie, de l'accompagner dans les moments d'angoisse et de prévoir l'imprévisible. De son côté, Catherine s'implique entièrement dans son rôle et concentre toute son attention sur Clothilde et oublie Daniel pour un moment. Pour sa part, Sylvie reconnaît vivre des inquiétudes comme toutes les mères; elle explique que l'approche du parent adoptant exige de la prudence car laisser pleurer un enfant adopté n'a pas le même impact que pour un enfant non-adopté:

> *Lorsque l'on est arrivé ici avec Jeannette, on n'a pas été comme les parents qui viennent d'avoir un bébé de façon naturelle. C'est différent quand un bébé pleure, ils ne se disent pas comme je l'ai fait: « Si on la laisse pleurer, elle ne nous aimera plus».*

Aurement dit, les propos des trois mères reflètent leur souci de composer avec la délicate balance de la singularité de l'enfant et d'éviter de stigmatiser leur fille en attribuant constamment les défis parentaux à l'adoption. Il ressort que leur sentiment de responsabilité face au bien-être de leur enfant et leur investissement important dans le rôle de mère se retrouvent aussi dans la littérature chez les nouvelles mères biologiques.

Dans le huitième thème de la *réciprocité dans un cycle évolutif* est abordée la délicate question de *la discipline*. Dans le contexte de l'adoption cette intervention parentale face à l'enfant qui bâtit son attachement représente un défi. En effet, la réciprocité dans le cycle évolutif de l'attachement est un bel exemple de représentations du changement dans les comportements de l'enfant et dans les conduites de la mère. Malgré des nuances, les trois mères sont plus craintives que les pères face à l'impact de la discipline sur l'attachement de l'enfant. Pauline conclut positivement l'interaction coercitive, démontrant sa sensibilité maternelle et ne laisse plus la culpabilité prendre la place sur le bon sens:

> *J'ai parlé beaucoup avec les parents et ils me faisaient toujours le reproche de me dire que ce n'est pas parce que ta fille a été adoptée (qu'elle peut faire ce qu'elle veut sans conséquence). Là je me suis dit: «Non, on ne peut pas accepter cela».... Des affaires que je peux juste repousser plus loin, je le faisais.... Quand on va discipliner Marie, on prend la peine à la fin de dire: «Marie, on t'aime».*

Pour sa part, Catherine applique simplement des conséquences aux comportements inappropriés de Clothilde:

> *On lui donnait du « time out » comme on dit en anglais. On lui dit que l'on n'est pas d'accord... On lui dit comment les choses doivent se faire... On compte jusqu'à trois de temps en temps pour qu'elle le fasse.*

Quant à Sylvie, elle est présentement au stade d'intégrer le principe de discipline et de trouver son style dans la préservation de sa sensibilité maternelle:

> *Je pense que c'est bon et j'essaie de faire des limites mais je trouve cela difficile car je ne veux pas briser le lien d'attachement.... Veux ou veux pas; il faut dire non, et sans être bête il faut être plus sec; et ne pas être maternante; et douce; et ne pas être à l'écoute à 150%. Quand je cuisine, je lui ai répété: «Maman cuisine et je l'emmène ailleurs». À force de le dire, elle a compris. Je me dis que c'est bon.*

En somme, il est important d'insister sur la capacité autant des mères que des pères adoptants à bien différencier un comportement relié au contexte des enfants adoptés, de celui relié à l'enfant comme être unique. Enfin, il faut souligner le souci du parent adoptant de conclure l'interaction de façon positive en reconnaissant le malaise de son enfant et en le réconfortant par ses contacts pour compléter le cycle éveil relaxation (Bowlby 350-373).

De façon générale sauf pour Pauline, il semble que dès qu'ils ont eu leur enfant dans les bras, les trois mères l'ont reconnu instantanément comme étant leur enfant malgré qu'elles ne connaissent pas ses habitudes. Le thème sur le premier moment en Chine semble en lien avec ce neuvième thème de la *réclamation mutuelle*. Plusieurs parents parlent «de tomber en amour» avec leur enfant au premier regard comme pour la majorité des parents de l'enquête. De son côté, Pauline n'a pas vécu la réclamation immédiatement. Ce besoin de connaître l'autre, vécu par Pauline, se retrouve dans les écrits et est essentiel pour développer un sentiment d'appartenance à la famille. Cela ne diminue en rien la profondeur du lien, ni les efforts investis pour créer la relation, comme le démontrent ses propos:

> *Non, ça s'est vraiment fait avec le temps passé avec elle. Je n'ai pas senti un moment, ou un événement ou elle m'a dit maman et j'ai craqué. [Maintenant] quand je regarde Marie dans les yeux, elle est ma fille.*

Par ailleurs, cette réclamation mutuelle s'étend au regard que porte la famille élargie des trois couples sur l'enfant. Ainsi, considérant l'importance accordée à cette dimension de la *réclamation mutuelle par le regard de la famille élargie* pour les parents de l'étude, elle a été ajoutée au cadre conceptuel final comme élément émergeant du contexte.

Dans ce dernier segment du fonctionnement expressif est abordé le thème du destin partagé et de son impact sur l'attachement selon les propos des trois familles.

Une première stratégie parentale reliée au destin partagé (dixième thème) est de parler de l'adoption en adaptant les propos à l'âge de l'enfant par divers moyens tels les photos et les livres. La discussion est ouverte et adaptée à l'âge de l'enfant. Elle inclut ces sujets au quotidien par le biais des photos, des histoires ou des livres pour éviter que l'enfant découvre les enjeux de son adoption par des étrangers.

Une seconde stratégie de la *reconnaissance de la différence* dans la famille adoptante a un effet thérapeutique très réparateur pour atténuer l'effet des pertes citées précédemment pour toute la famille. Catherine vit l'abandon de sa fille, par sa mère de naissance, avec une grande tristesse. Ainsi, l'influence de ce mode de la reconnaissance l'aide à composer avec ses souffrances et à trouver des solutions pour aider sa fille. Par sa détermination, Pauline a su transformer une croyance contraignante sur les raisons ayant motivé la mère de naissance à abandonner Marie en une croyance facilitante apportant de la compassion à l'égard de cette femme. Cette découverte faciliterait ses conversations sur le sujet avec sa fille:

> *Je n'en veux pas à cette femme-là [qui] m'apporte un bonheur que je ne pouvais pas avoir mais il y a toujours ce questionnement sur le pourquoi ... J'ai compris finalement, je me suis dit que cette femme-là ne voulait pas probablement laisser Marie.... C'est de la compassion. Je me dis: «Wow, c'est courageux de vivre avec cela, et elle fait passer les besoins de sa famille avant les siens».... Je voulais écrire une lettre à sa mère. Je ne l'ai pas fait encore, je voulais attendre d'avoir plus de bagages.... Mais s'il y a quelque chose que je peux faire pour retrouver cette femme-là pour qu'elle sache que Marie va bien, je ne sais pas comment ... pour qu'elle se dise: «J'ai fait la bonne chose».*

Figure 1: Le cadre conceptuel final adapté du Modèle de Calgary et des théories de l'attachement et du destin partagé

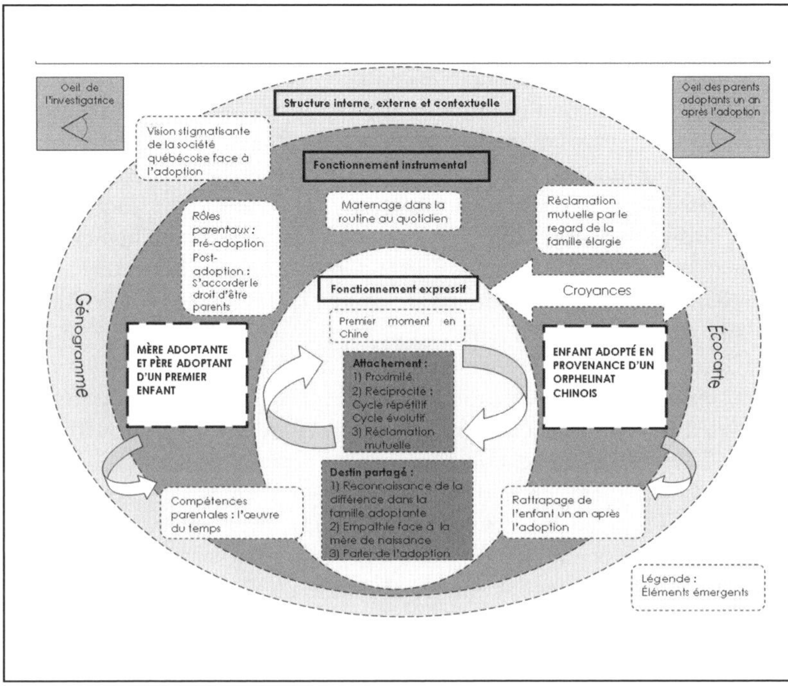

Quant à Sylvie, elle démontre aussi cette ouverture pour les parents de naissance de Jeannette. Sylvie conclut toujours ses interactions lorsqu'elle parle avec *empathie* des parents de naissance avec Jeannette tout en la rassurant sur la permanence de sa présence. Car le sujet de l'abandon attriste Sylvie:

> *Je lui dis souvent que je vais être là toujours. J'essaie de lui parler de ses parents chinois car quand elle aura des questions par rapport à cela, elle n'ait pas peur de nous en parler.... J'ai de la difficulté à lui parler de son abandon ... quand je pense à moi qui viens d'une grosse famille.... J'essaie d'en parler avec elle pendant qu'elle est jeune ... qu'elle ne doit pas sentir que je deviens triste un peu quand j'en parle mais à force d'en parler, pour moi cela va devenir plus naturel.*

Il est rassurant de voir l'engagement des mères et des pères à appliquer la théorie du destin partagée dans leurs conduites parentales. En effet, malgré certains propos des parents qui reflètent à l'occasion leur inconfort à le faire, ils persévèrent dans cette approche pour le mieux-être de leur enfant.

L'avant-dernier et onzième thème touche la *compétence parentale (l'œuvre du temps)*. Spontanément, les six parents ont parlé de leurs bons coups et de l'importance de les reconnaître. Le succès dans l'intégration de leur fille donne un sentiment de compétence parentale à ces nouveaux parents adoptants. Finalement, ils ont pu se dire: «Je suis un bon parent». En somme, autant les mères que les pères, chacun à leur manière ont démontré une grande habileté à mobiliser leurs ressources internes pour la résolution des problèmes au quotidien. À titre d'exemple, ils ont déployé tous les moyens pour permettre à leur enfant de créer l'attachement et de déployer sa singularité. Cette compétence parentale représente un élément émergeant, qui a été ajouté au cadre conceptuel final, comme résultante de l'attachement pour les parents adoptants de l'enquête.

Le dernier et douzième thème concerne le *rattrapage de l'enfant un an après son adoption*. De façon unanime, les six participants croient que leur fille a développé un attachement sécure, a démontré un rattrapage dans son développement, et a démontré sa réclamation mutuelle de ses parents. Ces éléments étant des prédicteurs, ils permettent de croire en la présence de l'attachement sécure de leur enfant, un an après son adoption. Ce rattrapage des enfants représente un élément émergeant et a été ajouté au cadre conceptuel final, comme résultante de l'attachement.

CONCLUSION

La présente étude contribue à l'enrichissement des connaissances sur l'attachement dans la famille adoptante au Québec. Les quatre forces de cette enquête sont commentées: 1) la perspective de la mère et du père enrichit la vision systémique de l'attachement et de la complémentarité de chacun des parents; 2) la réclamation mutuelle dans un cycle évolutif comme composante importante de l'attachement dans le contexte de l'adoption; 3) la pertinence de la théorie du destin partagé et son intégration dans les programmes d'adoption comme celui du CLSC du Lac Saint-Louis; et 4) le paradoxe de la faiblesse de l'échantillon.

La faiblesse principale de cette enquête est l'homogénéité et le petit nombre de participants. Cette faiblesse s'explique par le choix des participants à l'étude qui s'est fait par le biais de la collaboration unique du CLSC du Lac Saint-Louis. Paradoxalement la faiblesse de l'étude est aussi une force. En effet, l'étude a permis de démontrer la pertinence de la préparation reçue au CLSC participant et du suivi des familles adoptantes et ce, par le succès des trois familles à développer l'attachement. Ce succès inviterait le CLSC du Lac Saint-Louis à passer à l'évaluation des interventions spécifiques auprès des familles adoptantes qui participent aux programmes offerts en adoption internationale.

L'expérience d'adoption des trois familles de l'étude a démontré que l'adoption est une intervention efficace pour le rattrapage du développement de leur enfant. L'adoption est une expérience unique pour les nouveaux parents qui accueillent un enfant qui a déjà quelques pages écrites à son histoire de vie. Ainsi, l'attachement se tisse par le maternage dans la routine au quotidien ainsi que dans la complémentarité de chacun des parents en accordant une place à toutes les dimensions de l'expérience de l'adoption pour bâtir une relation permanente fondée sur le destin partagé.

Spécifiquement, l'engagement des mères adoptantes québécoises semble similaire à celle des mères biologiques, à cela s'ajoutent les défis spécifiques reliés aux enjeux de l'adoption afin de recréer l'attachement dans le respect de l'individualité de l'enfant.

Mes remerciements à Marie Hatem pour son accompagnement et ses précieux conseils lors de la rédaction du texte.

OUVRAGES CITÉS

Bell, L. *et al.* «Lien parent-enfant à la période périnatale: Évaluation et intervention». *Perspective Infirmière* 1.6 (2004): 32-36.

Bell, L. *et al.* «Mothers' and Fathers' View of the Interdependence of Their Relationships with Their Infant: A Systems Perspective Bowlby on Early Family Relationships». *Journal of Family* 13.2 (2007): 179-200.

Bowlby, J. «The Nature of the Child's Tie to his Mother». *International Journal of Psycho-analysis* 36 (1958): 350-373.

Bowlby, J. *The Role of Attachment in Personality Development and Psychopathology*. Madison: Int. Univ. Press, 1989.

Cohen, N. J., J. C. Coyne et J. D. Duvall. «Parents' Sense of 'Entitlement' in Adoptive and Non-adoptive Families». *Family Process* 35 (1996): 441-456.

Fahlberg, V. I. *A Child's Journey through Placement*. Indianapolis: Perspectives Press, 1991.

Fortin, M. F. *Fondements et étapes du processus de recherche*. Montréal: Chenelière Éducation, 2006.

Hopkins-Best, M. *Toddler Adoption: The Weaver's Craft*. Indianapolis: Perspectives Press, 1997.

Juffer, F. et M. H. Van Ijzendoorn. «Behavior Problems and Mental Health: Referral of International Adoptees: A Meta-Analysis». *JAMA* 293.20 (2005): 2501-2515.

Kirk, H. D. *Shared-Fate: A Theory and Method of Adoptive Relationship*. Indianapolis: Ben-Simon Publications, 1984.

Levy, T. M. *Handbook of Attachment Interventions*. San Diego: Academic Press, 2000.

Nickman, S. L. *et al.* «Children and Adoptive Families: Overview and Update». *Journal American Academy of Child and Adolescent Psychiatry* 44.10 (2005): 987-994.

Ouellette, F.-R. et H. Belleau. «L'intégration familiale et sociale des enfants adoptés à l'étranger: recension des écrits». *Rapport de recherche sociale* (RS-2406 094). INRS, 1999.

Secrétariat à l'adoption internationale (Gouvernement du Québec, Ministère de la Santé et des Services Sociaux). *Statistiques: Adoption.* Ottawa: Canada, 2001.

Shapiro, V., J. Shapiro et I. Paret. *Complex Adoption and Assisted Reproductive Technology: A Development Guide to Clinical Practice. Chapter V on International Adoption and Family Formation.* New-York: Guilford Press, 2001.

Smit, E. M. «Unique Issues of the Adopted Child: Helping Parents Talk Openly and Honestly with their Child and the Community». *Journal of Psychosocial Nursing* 34.7 (1996): 29-36.

Stams, G. J. J. M. *et al.* «Attachment-Based Intervention in Adoptive Families in Infancy and Children's Development at 7: Two Follow-up Studies». *British Journal of Developmental Psychology* 19 (2001): 159-180.

Van Egeren, L. A., M. S. Barratt et M. A. Roach. «Mother-Infant Responsiveness: Timing, Mutual Regulation, and Interactional Context». *Developmental Psychology* 37.5 (2001): 684-697.

Wright, L. M., W. L. Watson et J. M. Bell. *Beliefs: The Heart of Healing in Families and Illness.* New York: Basic Books, 1996.

Wright, L. M. et M. Leahey. *Nurses and Family: A Guide to Family Assessment and Intervention.* Philadelphia: F.A. Davis Company, 2000.

Zeanah, C. H. «Beyond insecurity: A Reconceptualization of Attachment Disorders of Infancy». *Journal of Consulting and Clinical Psychology* 64.1 (1996): 42-52.

Representing Maternal Ambivalence

A Process of Surrender and Withdrawal

ELIZABETH MACKENZIE

MY PRACTICE AS an artist has been deeply affected by my role as a mother. I have often felt that my greatest struggle was negotiating the conflicts between my children's developing sense of self and my individuality as expressed within my practice as an artist. It would be an understatement to say that my needs and desires have not always been congruent with those of my children.

The following text was presented as an artist talk I gave in 1999.[1] *These kinds of presentations give artists the opportunity to describe some of the conditions surrounding their production as artists. With two young children (aged eleven and four) the demands of mothering posed a significant threat to my practice, so this talk describes the strategies I developed that allowed me to fulfil the roles of both an artist and mother. It also describes a number of artworks that address the maternal ambivalence I've experienced within this complicated circumstance.*

My daughters have grown up since this text was written, and so my strategies have changed. Where once I tried to escape my predicament, these days I surrender to them more readily, since the necessity has become less of an obligation. As the vicissitudes of growing up take my daughters further away from me, I see the value of remaining a fixed point within their navigations. As they mature and our relationship takes on greater intellectual dimension, I trust the passion and complexity of my experience as an artist will inspire them in their own struggles to live lives of commitment and engagement.

I am an ambivalent mother. This may be the same as saying that I am a bad mother. I admit that I find it difficult to do what I want to do, while tending to the needs of my children. How is it possible to maintain a sense of self, a creative self, while nurturing parasites whose presence invades and disrupts all of the circumstances once believed necessary to produce art?

Since I had my first child more than eleven years ago, I've struggled with how to maintain my practice as an artist while meeting the needs of my children. Along with the work I've produced, I've also written about artist-mothers.[2] Rather than recognizing more and more similarities between myself and other artists who mother, I've come to appreciate how each woman's circumstance is unique, and therefore the decisions she makes (or, sometimes those that are made for her) as how to proceed as an artist are individual as well.

My strategy, as an artist, as a mother, is to alternate between surrendering to and withdrawing from the circumstances of maternity. First, I'll discuss the terms of my surrender.

The most significant aspect of this surrender is the sharp decrease in my production as an artist. Claiming an identity as an artist is generally predicated on the production and exhibition of artwork. So, to give up all or part of your production, even for a short time, can be pretty devastating. At the same time as I'm redefining the terms of maternity for myself, I'm also having to redefine what an artist is. Sometimes it's simply an act of faith. My surrender can also be represented by my preoccupation with the subject of maternity within what work I do produce.

Representations of maternity both fascinate and repel me: I am intrigued by a circumstance in which the boundaries of inside and outside, self and other, dissolve. Such representations of maternity delivered by mainstream North American culture are consistently fraught with ambivalence and anxiety. While mothers may be romanticized as nurturing and self-sacrificing, they are also demonized as overpowering and destructive. Although these oppositions are useful in articulating the constructed nature of the role of mothers in our culture, they still have a tremendous impact upon how I define myself in relation to this role. I have always considered maternity another form of women's sexual exploitation. It's damned hard work that women usually get stuck with. Unfortunately, not having children doesn't let you off the hook either. Often women wonder if they should, if they could, when they can, why they can't, or why they didn't.

My preoccupation with maternity first manifested itself explicitly within a piece I produced years before I had children. "Taking Care" was a large-scale work produced for a group show in 1984.[3] Within this piece, which followed the birth my best friend's son, I questioned the possibility of a woman having a life beyond her role as a mother. I drew a vast but helpless baby that loomed over images of a woman and man struggling with issues of parental responsibility. Off to one side, a woman with the camera stands for me, the artist, an interested onlooker on the drama of maternity. Even then, I felt it was crucial for mothers to create spaces for themselves outside of their domestic environment. In retrospect, I realize I was also trying to make a space for myself in my friend's dramatically altered life.

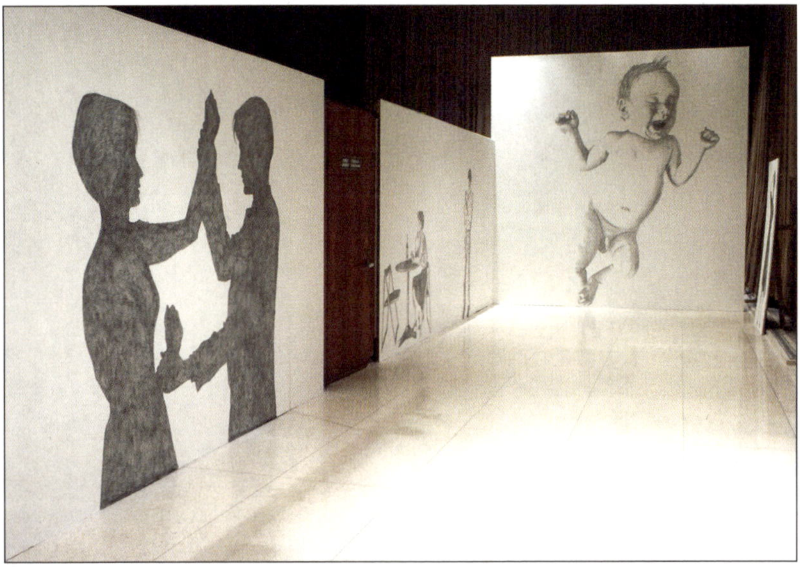

Taking Care, 1984, installation view, graphite on constructed walls and drywall panel.

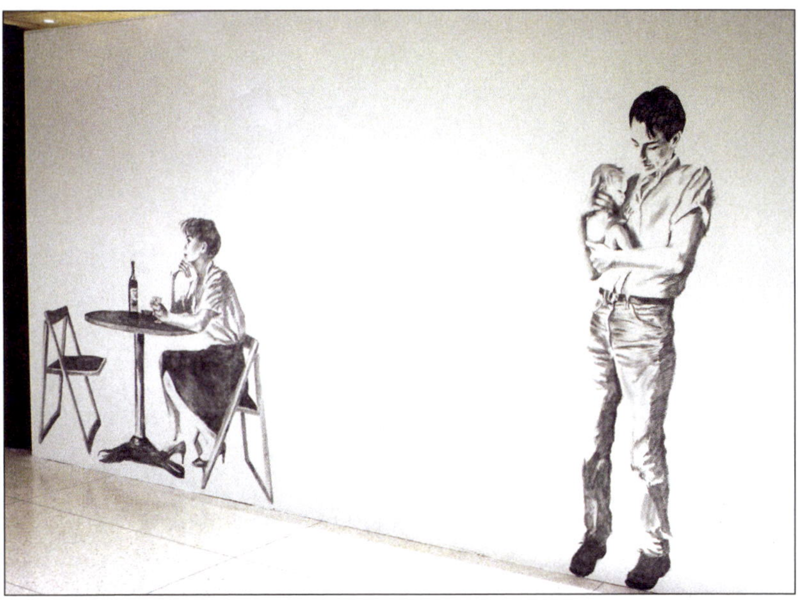

Taking Care, 1984, installation detail, graphite on constructed walls and drywall panel.

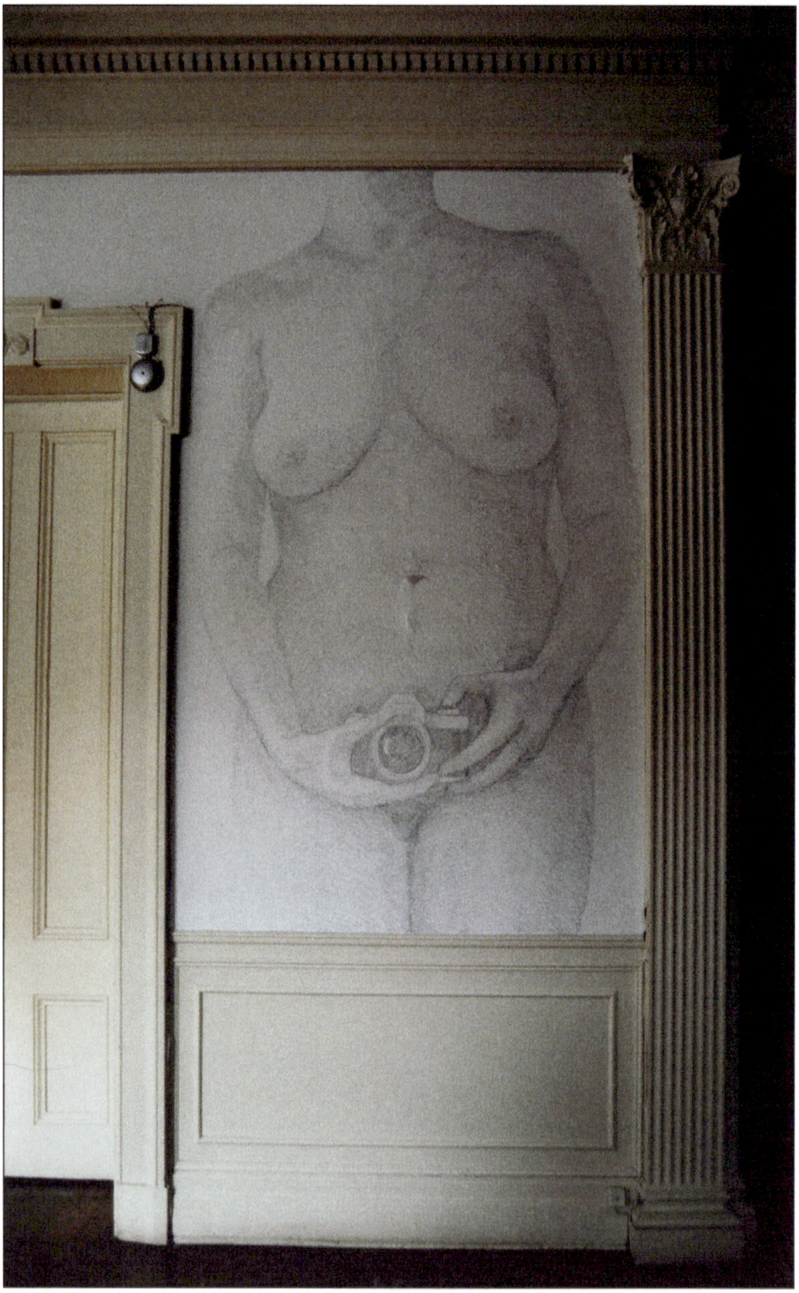

Baby Food, 1989, installation details, graphite on existing walls.

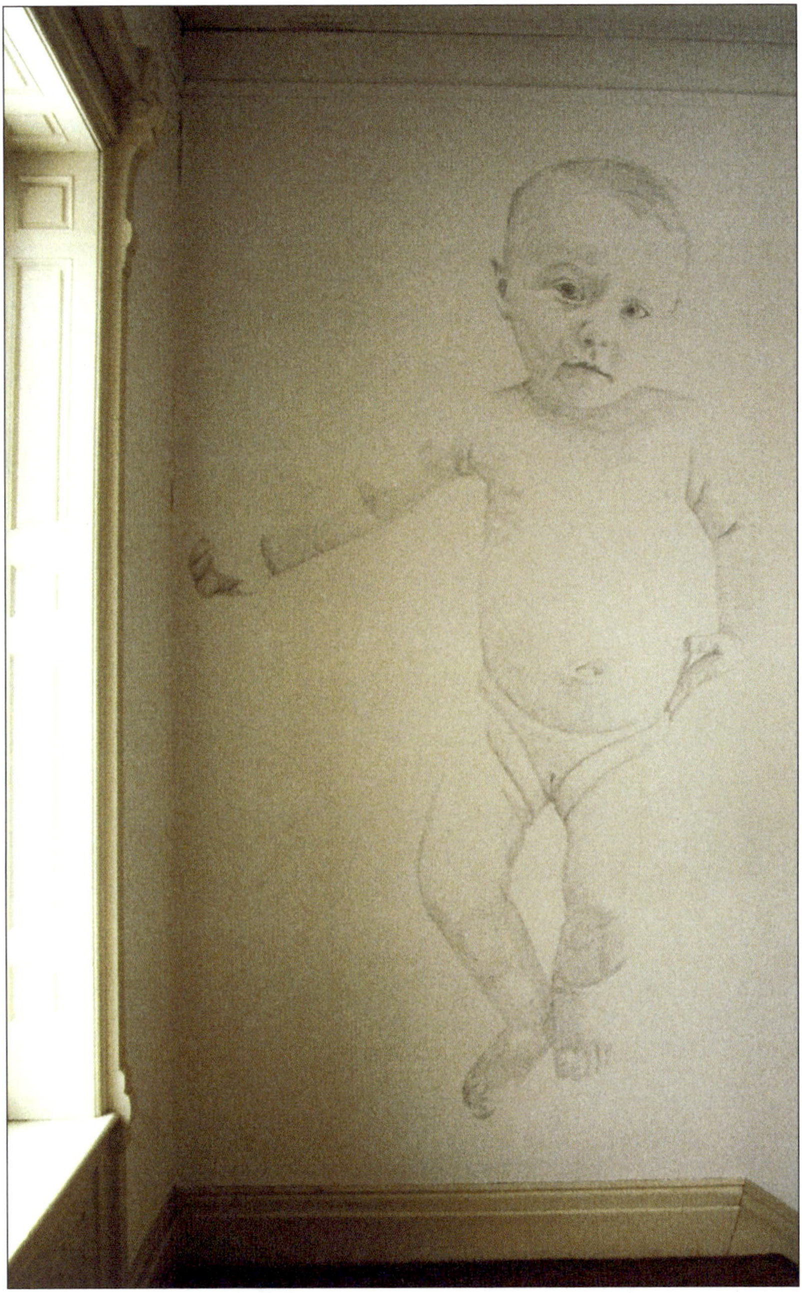

Baby Food, 1989, installation details, graphite on existing walls.

Four years later, in 1988, I gave birth to my first child. When she was eight months old, I installed "Baby Food" in a group exhibition about mothers and daughters.[4] This piece describes my anxiety about my ability to nourish my daughter, as I struggled with both breast-feeding and art making.

The installation "With Child," produced for a group show in Calgary in 1991,[5] portrays some of the conflicts of over-identification and self-immolation that were raised for me within the dyads of pregnancy

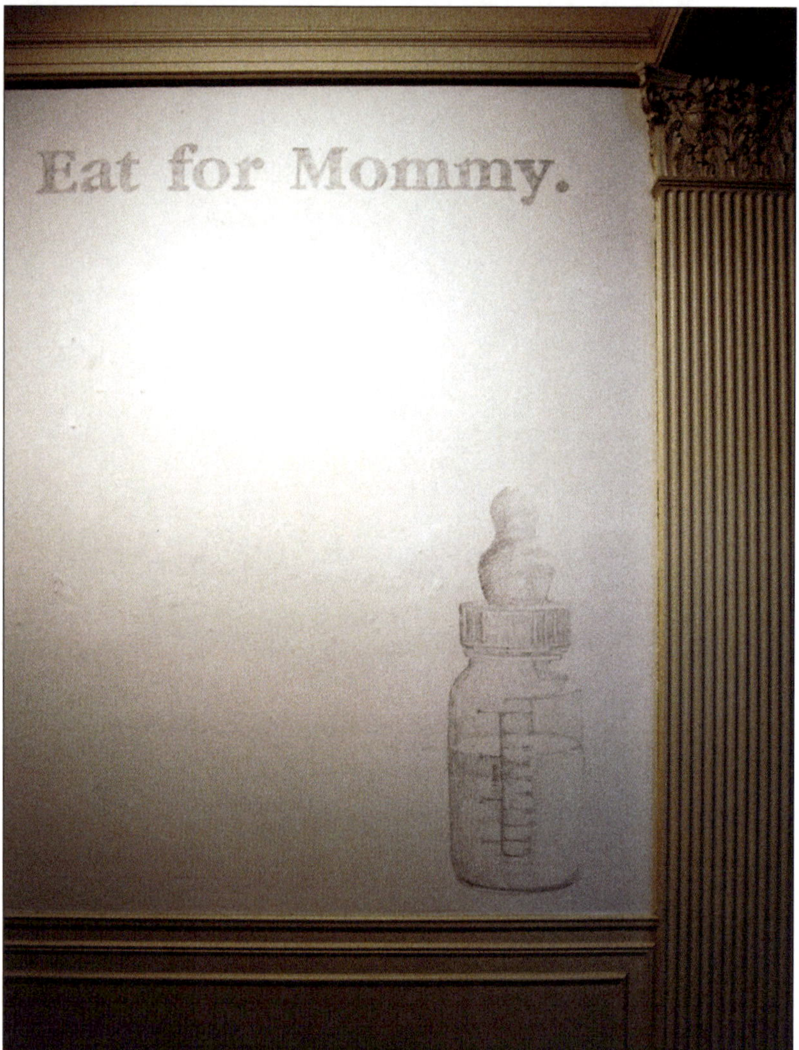

Baby Food, 1989, installation detail, graphite on existing walls.

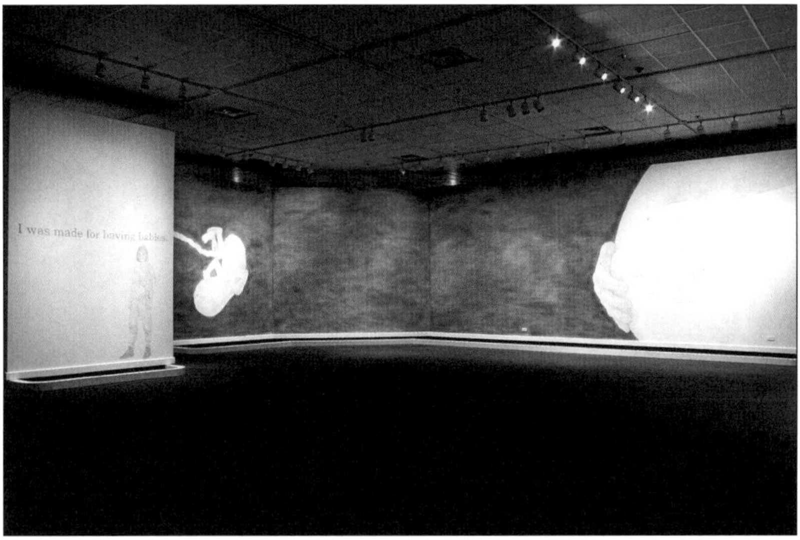

With Child, 1991, installation view, graphite on existing walls.

and maternity. I was fearful that my child had become, even before birth, an autonomous creature I would never be able to encompass and keep safe. This combination of images on a long wall produces an impossible representation that has become increasingly normalized: we see a pregnant body as well as what is inside the body. Although I was thrilled to become a mother, I was horrified by the loss of boundaries I experienced. Both my body and my psychic space were invaded.

In 1991, I also began graduate studies at the University of Saskatchewan. I wanted to review my ten-year practice as an artist as well as continue to investigate representations of pregnancy. The thesis I developed, "Spacemen and Invisible Women," examined popular representations of pregnancy that obliterated the pregnant woman, and represented the fetus (or embryo) as a tiny self-sufficient space traveler, floating in a black void. My 1993 graduating exhibition, "Invisible/Stranger/Mine,"[6] examined maternal erasure and the cult of fetal personhood within a number of related works.

The installation "Radiant Monster," completed in 1996, was shown in a number of different contexts.[7] Once again, this work represents the ambivalent feelings I've experienced in response to real and imagined pregnancies and children. I wanted to express a continuum between the desire and the anxiety that the contemplation and experience of maternity evokes. Not surprisingly, reproductive technologies that offer new choices to infertile women, and increase the opportunity for interventions during pregnancy and birth, extend and exaggerate our relationship to our reproductive capacities.

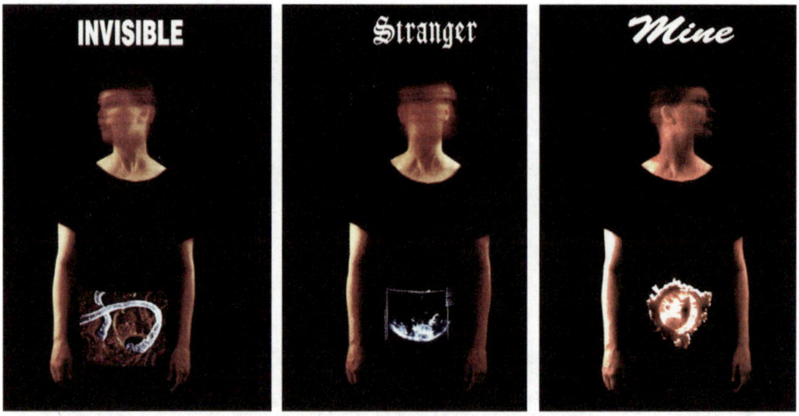

Invisible/ Stranger/ Mine, 1992, cibachrome prints,
each: 53.34 x 63.50 cm, overall: 63.50 x 170.18 cm.

Within contemporary images of pregnancy, the focus has gradually moved from the pregnant woman to the unborn fetus. Once the domain of right-to-lifers, graphic images of embryos and fetuses appear regularly within popular culture. Increasingly, the needs of the fetus are detached from the needs (and desires) of the pregnant woman.

Hands outstretched, holding, releasing or displaying something have been recurring images within my work. Within "Radiant Monster," the image of a hand within the doorway of the structure stands for the body, without specificity of a face, it represents an exchange with the outside world. The hand simultaneously grasps and relinquishes a phantom child (represented by a fetal ultrasound), which, to my mind, functions as a succinct representation of parenting.

I'm intrigued by the relationship between the fetal ultrasounds and parenthood itself; they're both about projection, desire, anxiety, and confusion. Most pregnant women routinely undergo ultrasounds. Within this circumstance, attention moves away from the pregnant woman towards the monitor, a mapping of the woman's interior landscape. What is inside is displayed as something that is outside; our relationship to pregnancy is simultaneously ruptured and repaired by technology. Representations of fetuses are illusions forged for practical purposes. I was interested in reappropriating these images for myself, both as an artist and as a mother.

The "Radiant Monster" installation included a series of seven phrases representing the ambivalence I have experienced in relation to maternity: Invisible/Stranger/Mine; This/Radiant/Monster; Her/Dreaded/Beloved; That/Enchanting/Tyrant; Our/Dangerous/Angel; These/Dazzling/Fictions; Adorable/Demon/You. I've always been interested in the problem of adding words to images. The specificity of words can often overpower

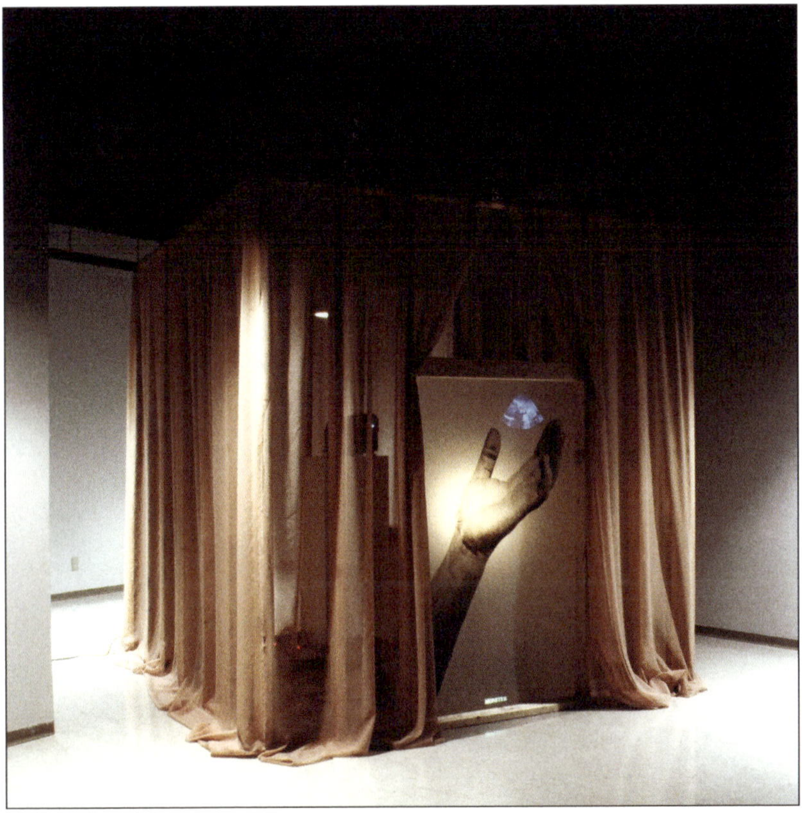

Radiant Monster, 1996, installation view, lumber, fabric, photograph on mylar, fetal ultrasound video, 35 mm slides, slide projectors, slide dissolve unit, intra-uterine sounds audio loop, tape player, speakers, a/v cart, speakers, clip-on light, 244 x 244 x 244 cm (overall).

images, and over determine how the images function. My goal is to use words to help locate the viewer within a realm of thought processes, without constraining their interpretation.

When I designed the wooden armature for this installation, I was thinking about a number of things. I wanted it to be seen as a construction in process, always incomplete, an idea of a room rather than an actual room. I thought about the room as a skeleton, a room where the body is surveyed, a prison, a hospital, a temple (a home for a goddess or god, who is not actually present), a tomb, a womb, and a bed. The image of the hand and the projections are suspended in the doorway of the room, at the threshold, in the liminal state between two places.

The sheer fabric that covers the room is a skin, a veil, a penetrable barrier between what is outside and what is inside. It covers, while it reveals, it softens, it protects, and it evokes a domestic space traditionally associated with the feminine. The sound that viewers heard as they

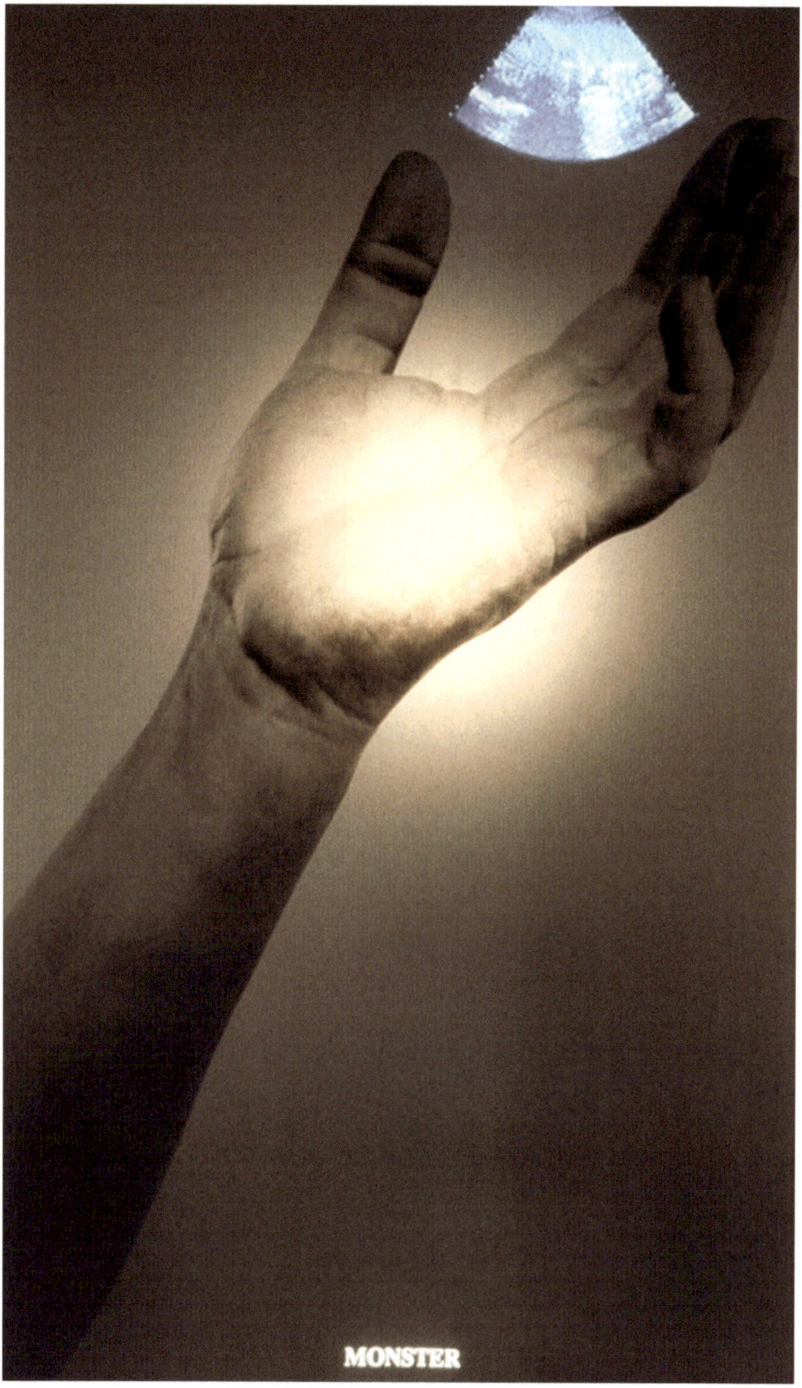

Radiant Monster, 1996, installation detail.

stood near the installation was from a recording produced by an obstetrician: the sounds created by blood moving through the main arteries of a pregnant woman. This is what it sounds like inside the body of a pregnant woman. This recording, and other contraptions that produce similar sounds, are sometimes used to soothe newborn babies. To my mind, the interior workings of the body sound like the engine room of a steam ship.

Earlier, I spoke about my strategy of alternating between surrender and withdrawal from the circumstances of maternity. While surrender is about transforming my practice as an artist and allowing myself to examine this circumstance more closely as a subject within my work, withdrawal is basically about disappearance. By removing images of my (maternal) body from my recent work, I am following the simple and expedient strategy I've developed within my home life: whenever possible, after a particularly difficult time as a mother, I leave. This is the best possible way for me to deal with the irritability, frustration, and ambivalence I experience as a mother. My absence from my children, from my home, gives me the opportunity to reclaim that part of my identity that exceeds my role as a mother. When I leave my children, for an hour or for days, they become responsible for maintaining an image of me, holding a place for me, in my absence. Their imagination and the traces of my presence that remain assist them in this project. My absence allows them creative possibilities that would not be possible if I were present.

This is what I hope to do within my work: invite the viewer to construct a maternal image from the traces I provide, as well as from their own imagination. The maternal becomes what is there and what is not there, a representation forged from two or more perspectives, provisional, incomplete and contingent, a presence marked by a (partial) absence.

[1]This talk was presented at the School for Contemporary Art, Simon Fraser University, Burnaby, B.C., October 20, 1999.

[2]I co-wrote a column about artist-mothers, "First Person Plural," with artist Martha Townsend in Mentoring Artists for Women's Art's (Winnipeg) bi–monthly newsletter from 1997 until 1999. This project culminated with a symposium for artist–mothers in Winnipeg in 2000.

[3]Dessin-Installation-Drawing-Installation, curated by Diana Nemiroff at the Saidye Bronfman Centre, Montréal, Quebec.

[4]Mothers of Invention, curated by Jo Anna Isaak at the McNeil Gallery, Philadelphia, PA and Hobart and William Smith Colleges, Geneva, New York.

[5]"The Embodied Viewer," curated by Vera Lemecha at the Glenbow Museum, Calgary, Alberta.

[6]At the Snelgrove Gallery, University of Saskatchewan, Saskatoon, Saskatchewan.

[7]In the group exhibition Fertile Ground, curated by Jan Allen at the Agnes Etherington Art Centre in Kingston, Ontario in 1996; as a solo show at the Photographers Gallery in Saskatoon, Saskatchewan in 1996; and as a solo show at Gallery 1.1.1., organized by the University of Manitoba and Mentoring Artists for Women's Art (MAWA) in Winnipeg, Manitoba in 1998.

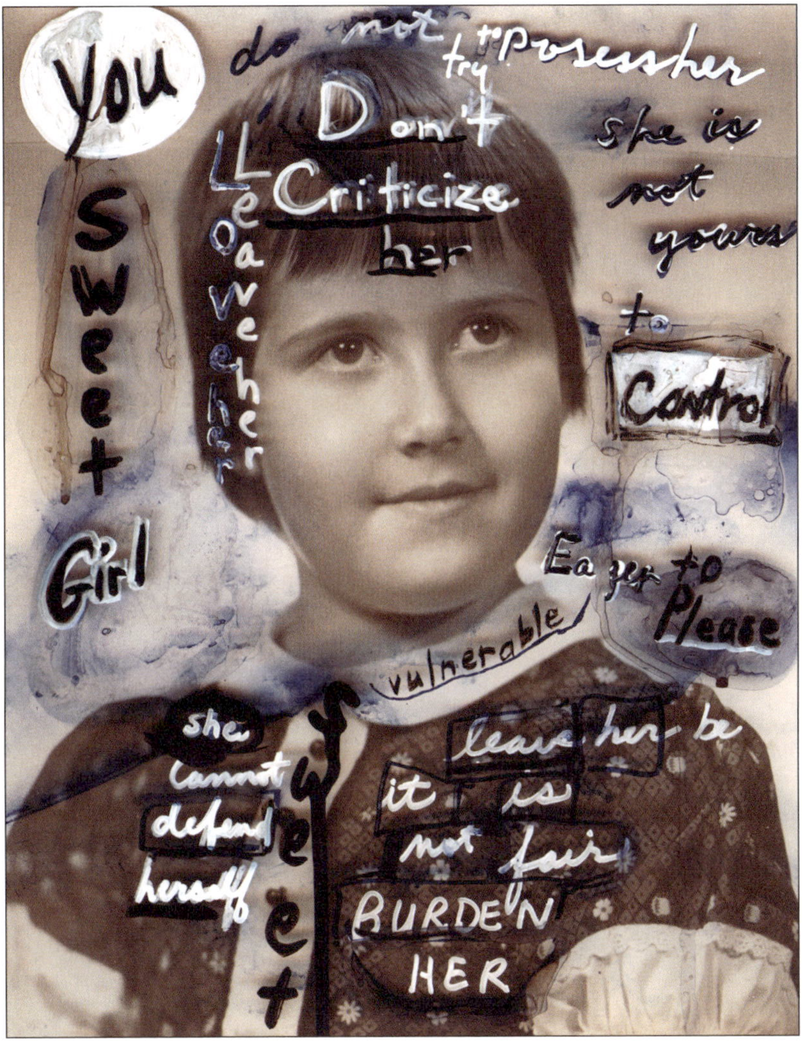

Leesa Streifler, *Parenting Revisited: Portrait at Five Years*, 2008,
chromogenic print, 38.1 x 30.5 cm.

This piece is part of a series on parenting titled *Parenting Revisited*. In this series, text has been superimposed over childhood photographs of myself. My intention was to challenge, from my vantage point as a mother, parenting ideas that were popular when I was growing up in the 1960s.

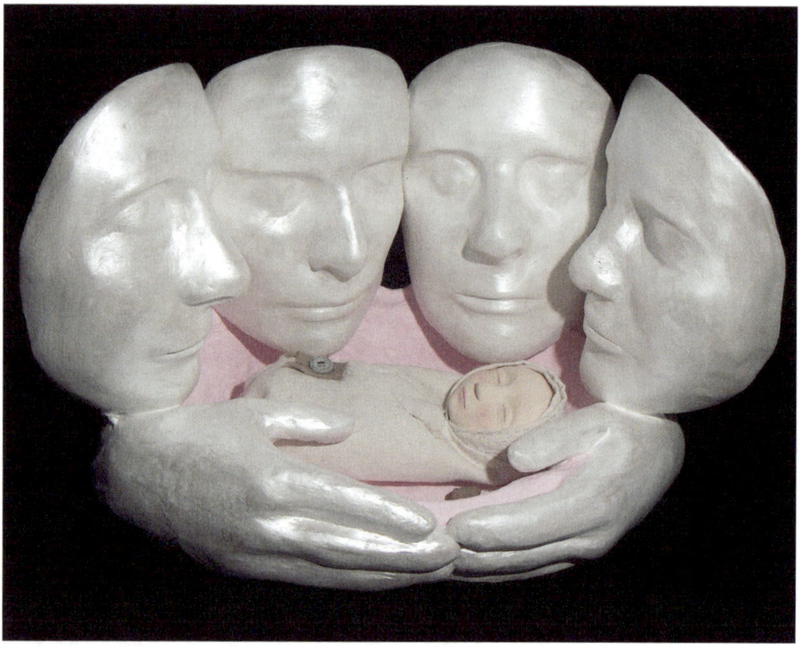

Patrice Keats, *Restitution,* 2003, plaster, clay, fabric, stone, 34 x 35 cm.

This plaster-based sculpture represents four mothers who lost a child through violence. The sculpture reflects the union of these women as a protective force and antidote to the violence and abuse of children. The child in the centre is protected by the conviction and strength of the women's solidarity.

SUPPORTING

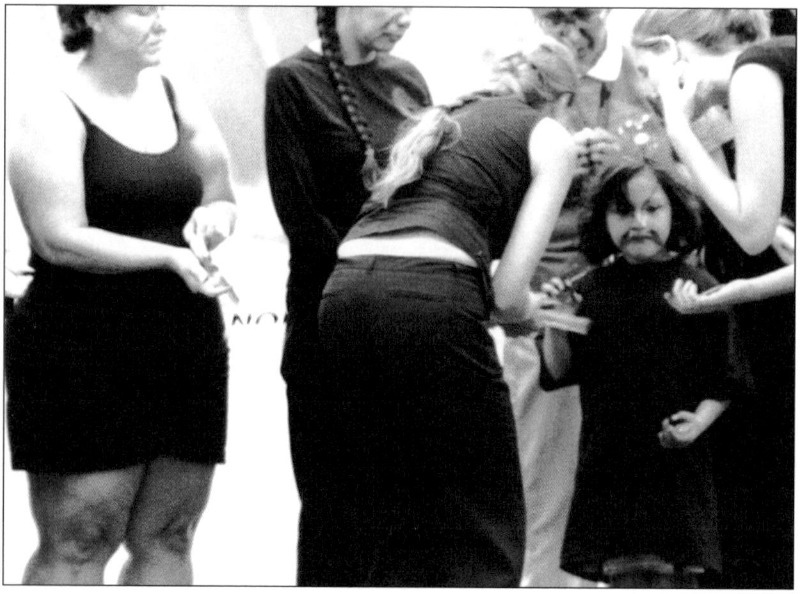

Dianne Hancherow Anderson, photo documentation of *Project X* performance, July, 2006.
Photo: Jody Hancherow.

Project X was a series of site-specific public art performances undertaken for community empowerment and to show support for the families of missing women in our province. Executed with all women, pictured above is the artist Dianne Hancherow Anderson, her daughter Anna Hancherow, and Pauline Muskego, the mother of missing Daleen Bosse, and Faith Bosse, Daleen's daughter, in Saskatoon, Saskatchewan on July 28, 2006.

Voices from Moon Lodge

ELDER BETTY MCKENNA, MARY HAMPTON, CARRIE BOURASSA, KIM MCKAY-MCNABB, AND ANGELINA BAYDALA

WOMEN, ROAD TRIPS and stories, Mary, Carrie, Kim, and Angelina load into a car in Regina, Saskatchewan and travel across the land to visit with our Kookum, our Grandmother Elder Betty McKenna.The four of us are academic women; all of us are mothers. One of us is a Métis woman (Carrie) and one is a First Nations woman (Kim); two of us are non-Aboriginal women of Polish ancestry (Angelina and Mary). All of us seek a richer meaning in the value and power of Mothering. We sit in Kookum's living room and listen to stories that make us proud to be women. Four granddaughters, we sit with our Grandmother and listen to the Teachings of the Old Ones as they were lived by our Grandmother. We have heard of the Moon Lodge where women gathered during their Moon Time (menstrual cycles) and wish to learn more about this. We digitally record these stories and hope to some day share them with others. Questions and conversations weave together, but we have distilled our inquiry (the italicized questions that follow) and presented Kookum's words as she told them (the stories that follow). We will share with you here traditional stories told to us by an Anishnabe Elder who was raised with the experience and the teachings of the Moon Lodge.

Kookum, what is the Moon Lodge?

Elder Betty: What was practiced in the Moon Lodge was that all girls could go. Anybody who's menstrual in the family went in all at the same time. But there were always other women out there. If you had pregnant mothers that didn't go to the Moon Lodge, they could stay out there and cook and do the things they had to do to keep things going. What we used was moss. Then we had to give that moss back to Mother Earth. You cut the moss and then there was actually a ceremony we did to give the moss back to Mother Earth. In the Moon Lodge, you're preparing yourself, you're being taught all those things, all those components that you have to go through in life, if your life is going to be ending at the age of eighty or ninety or something, you have to look at all those things that you're going to encounter in life. In that Moon Lodge, you're preparing your body, knowing that you've got to go through birth and that you've got to go through menopause. Those are the sacred things that women go through.

What are the Moon Lodge teachings?

Elder Betty: When women are in that Moon Lodge, you learn about how the concept of Grandmother Moon is so vital. Grandmother Moon is the next light to the sun, right? We need Grandmother Moon just as much as we need the sun. Grandmother Moon is so powerful that the water will rise up and follow her. The women had all that knowledge and it was passed from the Grandmother to mother and to daughter to granddaughter, aunty to niece. But very rarely did it ever go out to the males because the males lead a different life. It's also important to know that your energy at the Moon Time is powerful. We think of ourselves as a connection to that Mother Earth, that we are a product of Mother Earth; we come from her, we go back to her.

When we take care of ourselves the proper way, then we have to realize that the gift that is given by the Creator is so special and so unique that we can't violate that gift. So when you're around somebody else's sacred objects or you go to the drum or you go to the powwow, you're violating your gift. You're violating what the Creator gave you, that specialness the Creator gave you. You're saying, "I only want the specialness when I want it." That's what you're saying to the Creator. "It's only going to be special to me when I want it. Right now it doesn't fit." But the Creator made a pact with woman from the beginning of time, from the time Sky Woman fell. Woman would have an important part to play here on earth and we're just letting it slide when it's not convenient.

Once women go through the teachings of the Moon Lodge, they would not be promiscuous. From the time when you enter the Moon Lodge to when you go out as a grandmother, menopausal, in that length of time the gift is that you are the doorway and there's that ceremony of through the doorway that you are told: "You are now the doorway between that world and this world." Our belief is that our ancestors are there waiting for the baby and to push them through the doorway. You wouldn't abuse it; you don't want to go out and be promiscuous, or do anything to violate the sacredness of that doorway because your ancestors are watching. You're watched all the time. You want them to think well of you and be praying for you, not thinking that you're blind or not listening to the teachings. The only thing between death and bringing life is you. In the sweat lodge, when we think of going back into the mother's womb, one of the important designations is a doorkeeper. I don't even think women know that we're the doorkeepers. That whole meaning behind the sweat lodge and the meaning behind the moon lodge and what it is to the women is how that time is really important.

What is the meaning of some protocol that Aboriginal Peoples observe when a woman is on her Moon Time?

Elder Betty: Up until then (first Moon Time), you had free reign to ask anybody anything, up until you hit that time, that Moon Time. As a little kid, you could ask any question of anyone. After that there were protocols you had to follow. You don't participate in pipe ceremonies. You don't participate in sweat lodges. If your food was brought to you then you could cook your own food, but you weren't allowed to go out and work in the garden or prepare anybody else's food.

It's that you have to respect who you are and your gift. That gift is so powerful at that time that, in order to respect it and other people, don't be around their sacred things because you take their power away. You just suck that power, taking it at that point in time. That's why we say Moon Time. Like with Grandmother Moon, the water rises up and follows her. The same thing happens with women and the Moon Time. They pull the energy like that. The Moon Time is a great energy pull; they're pulling energy into themselves at that time.

During the Moon Time we wear skirts, and we're taught to wear skirts at that time, especially during certain ceremonies, to get that connection again with Mother Earth. You can always get it through the skirt. The reason we wear fringes is to let you know "those are our roots." Fringe skirts, fringe jackets, fringe shawls, anything fringe signifies our roots are from Mother Earth. As women, we are, in a sense, a smaller version of Mother Earth; we give life, we work, and protect.

How did the Moon Lodge teachings prepare girls for their first Moon Time?

Elder Betty: You were then considered a young woman. You weren't a child. We consider every time you have a period as cleansing. You're going through that whole process of cleansing; in fact, some Saulteaux people won't sweat because they say as long as we're going through our periods, we cleanse every month. The thing that you have to do, and it's part of going into that Lodge, the Moon Lodge, is to learn from the Grandmothers and why they're called a Grandmother. Because it was a big deal to become on your time. You'd come back from the lodge and people would say, "She was on her first time! Look at that now." Keeping that place in between that world and this world, it's special. Men can't say there's a divine time for them. Men don't have it like women do. I think that maybe what a person has to do with young people is have them look forward to having the Moon Time. That this is a big event and if other people in their lives make it a big event it will be a big event. If people celebrate that beginning in a young girl's life, that young girl isn't going to follow the norms that her peers do. She will be a leader amongst her peers instead of following what they do, when you teach them that their living now is a sacred thing. And they're taught that, and they believe that; they will keep it sacred. So I believe that that's one of the essential things to do for young girls and even teens who have already gone through it. They can always benefit from knowing what really women are on the Earth. And we're a reflection of the Creator, each and every one of us.

How did the Moon Lodge teachings prepare women for childbirth?

Elder Betty: These are also the things that come back to you to do when you are having that baby. When you're in labour, you do the whole thing again. You were practicing the whole time you were in the Moon Lodge. It's just natural. You find your own place in that. That's what you're learning through the whole process of how your body works and how to be comfortable with it, how to be comfortable with your body and how to respect that and to know that it's a gift. It's not given to man. It's only given to women. You have to learn how to work with it, live with it, and appreciate it. There were exercises we actually did to tell you this is the bottom of what I later learned is called the pelvic floor; it's kind of like if you were to stop mid-stream when you're going to the bathroom. Those were the muscles. They would also teach you to feel the muscle contractions in your tummy. Then, for the very first time, you can feel them more than any other time. We were told that those are the muscles that have to stretch and move because when you are going to be a mother those are the muscles that stretch and move and move the baby out. If you had an arm and you tied it up and never used it, what would happen to your arm? It would be useless. We have to start using what we have long before.

Our bodies are smart. We have to learn our bodies are smart and to learn to relax and trust our bodies to be smart, instead of trying to control the body with what we're thinking. We would learn to do the right kind of breathing, and with those chants that we used to do you'd have to breathe in through the nose and go out "Ahhhh." These actually helped your stomach relax and it helped to let oxygen into your blood at the time.

See, that's another thing too. I know our people didn't treat this [pregnancy] as an illness where in today's society, you're looked on as ill. That's why you go to a hospital. What do you go to the hospital for? You're sick, right? Like there isn't a place that is separate and away from hospital that says this is run just by women; this is our birthing centre. You know, and that would be totally different then having a room on the floor of a hospital. That says: this is women's health.

For instance, this is one of the things you heard is the stories from the grandmothers and the aunties and mothers of what people go through, what they can expect. And generally these women are having huge families. I came from a family of ten. So, you know that they certainly had a lot of experience; sometimes they've had as many as 21 children. So you get someone who has had 21 kids and they're talking about childbirth, they probably have a lot of knowledge, with 21. (Laughter) And so those were some of the things that you will learn.

For instance, somebody who is having heavier and heavier babies. I can remember this one particular woman who was having children. She had a huge family and she was a very heavyset woman. But her babies were getting successively heavier each time she had one. And my mother saying, "There must be something wrong with her. She wouldn't be having big heavy babies." This woman apparently had been diabetic. But nobody knew at that time; it wasn't picked up by anybody cause a lot of time they just have them at home, eh? I think it's all the growth hormones in the foods that the mother is having. We even have vegetables now that have growth hormones, and the meat, you know, all the cattle everything is vaccinated, buffalos. And giving birth hormones to speed up their process so they can go through the slaughtering thing a lot faster because of consumerism. And before, you know, we didn't have that.

Were there teachings that assisted with women's physical health?

Elder Betty: One of the things about being in the Moon Lodge is that when we went into the Moon Lodge, you had to envision what you look like inside. You have to envision it being healthy, clean because that's what it's like, the inside of a shell. We had to envision everything smooth and healthy and always visualizing that there were no restrictions there, there's always lots of blood flow to the area.

When you went to the Moon Lodge, there was no such thing as PMS. There wasn't. When we went to the Moon Lodge there was a big box that would have smooth rocks. You'd warm them and hold them against your tummy so you didn't have cramps. It's so common that a person has cysts on their ovaries. And as long as it's not growing to the size of a basketball and it's not cancerous, and they can tell you that without taking that cyst off, you can actually use creative visualization to shrink that cyst. When you got cramps it was because you were starting to restrict the blood flow. You had to learn to relax.

What about Two-Spirited (gay/lesbian) people? Did they also have teachings?

Elder Betty: In the Moon Lodge is also when we all took the teachings of the two-spirited people. It's like a circle and if you are half that circle, there's that part in the middle, there's a space in the middle, and the Creator said male on this side, female on that side, and he split that circle. The ones in the middle are the two-spirited people because they are both spirits. That's how we learned that the two-spirited people were extremely gifted. Most of them had second sight, and they came with many different gifts. They weren't viewed as flawed members of society but as great gifts from the Creator because the Creator gave that two-spirited nature to them, not man or woman. They carry both.

It's because you realize most of the two-spirited people are not going to ever give birth to children. So when you have a segment of your population that's not ever going to give birth, they still have to be honoured for their life experience and what they've gone through; therefore they were given that title of Grandmother. That's why they said, you know, our Aunties, and when we said *Aunties* they usually were, a lot of times they were the unmarried women in the community. They were *Aunty*, you know. And those women who were two-spirited, when they hit menopause, they are called Grandmother too.

What do the Moon Lodge teachings say about menopause and about growing older?

Elder Betty: The thought behind women who are menopausal, in the western sense, is that there's a loss for them. For Aboriginal people, we have a gain, a gain. We've become Grandmother Moon. We have become so powerful that when we come into a house or a place of young women, we can pull those young women into unison on their periods. Like attracts like, so the Grandmother has already got to that space in time where water will rise and follow her. That's why we have the Grandmothers come into Moon Lodge because then when we inhabit a place anybody who is going to menstruate, aunties and cousins and all those who are in their Moon Time, we get them all together. This is how the Moon Lodge wasn't occupied everyday of the week. Everybody would congregate together and within a day, or even hours of one another, they'd all start.

When you look at menopause as something you dreamed of, a pinnacle in the life of women, then they feel they've reached a pinnacle at menopause. This is opposed to a loss. It's a big difference in how you view yourself and how you feel about yourself.

That's what brings us to why when you hit menopause you are called a Grandmother. So it's not like in the western world, where you have to produce children for you to be called Grandmother. It's when you're menopausal you're a grandmother. You didn't have to have had children to be called *Kookum*. Everybody was a Grandmother that hit that time.

What about mothering?

Elder Betty: There were teachings that women are the doorway to that other world, that although we are that doorway, the teaching was that there's not necessarily always going to be a spirit step through that doorway for everyone. That is determined by the Creator. About other children that are born to parents who don't want them, and they could use a parent. Our people were adopting children long before adoption in the Western world was even thought of. That was common practice, that a child was a gift to the whole community. And everyone accepted that gift when it came. And if a child is a gift, then that gift could be shared, and there were children that were taken and raised by aunties and uncles and a child always had a parent. And it didn't have to be the ones who brought you into this world. They were either their sisters' children or nieces' children or cousins' children. They were their parent for however long they needed it.

Back then you're going to become a woman very early. So once that happens and you move into the Moon Lodge with the women and start having to go to the Moon Lodge with the women. Well, most of those young girls had babies very young. And so they really wanted to still be out there with their man, whether it's canoeing or trapping somewhere... they would follow the man, wherever they went, hunting or trapping or whatever. And the first-born would be given to the mother [Grandmother] to raise because they were still relatively young themselves. They were still babies really themselves. So that's where the practice came from, that was normal, to give your first child to the parents.

Did the teachings assist men, too?

Elder Betty: The men's teachings were that they respected the women going into the Lodge on their Moon Time. During the Moon Time, I think the men saw themselves as privileged that they helped out. There were a lot of teachings, too, around how you treated your brothers and uncles and your dad and male relatives. I think it benefited the men as well. Certain codes that you had to know about were taught, like when you got married to respect your father-in-law; you didn't speak directly to your father-in-law. You spoke to your husband if you wanted the message to go to your father-in-law. You never approached him, and vice-versa with your husband. He'd approach you to go to your mom, or he would go to maybe your sister. He would never approach her directly. Those are teachings that we had. My teaching is now finished for my son because once my son hit 13, that's it, he learns now from his dad and it's supposed to be other male family members who teach, not his mother. You have your boy till he gets to that age.

What they always said was: "You know the women were the ones who had that knowledge from Mother Earth, Grandmother Moon."

And they always said about men was: “Let them go hunt ... don’t let them worry about things that women took care of.” Women take care of some important things and I guess hunting was a very a tough job back then. And it was also dangerous. It is just like it is now days too. I’ve known a lot of people who go out hunting and don’t come back. It is not something just in the past. It’s still a reality today. I know lots of men who shoot themselves and don’t come home.

Do you think we need the Moon Lodge today? How would it help us?

Elder Betty: Oh yeah, it is different now. Everything now is geared towards men’s teachings. Everything has to come from the male. You see what I found was, in this society nowadays, they make girls somehow believe they’re like a boy with something missing. And treats them as such. And I mean they’re always even told you’re weaker than males. That, by golly let’s see a male give birth. (Laughter) You know.

If you have the teachings of the sacred gift of being between the worlds, well you just don’t abuse it and go out like I see a lot of young girls do. We have too many young mothers at 13, 14. Nowadays what we have is there’s things that young girls are indulging in that is causing that [diseases, infertility] to happen. Number one is having sexual relations too young and multiple sex partners, is causing the highest rate for young girls is this thing called Chlamydia. And that’s preventing them from having that spirit step through the doorway. So you start that young, you know, you figure by the time they are eighteen, nineteen years old, how many partners they may have. Somewhere in there the teachings of how to be able to connect to your spirit instead of letting your, there’s a word for it, this energy that runs through a young person’s body that causes them to decide (finger snaps) like that. They need to do this instead, saying, “Well, no, wait a minute, I got to distance myself here. I got to do something else.” So, for a number of reasons, I think the teachings were there for people so that they didn’t leave out any point of choice for themselves.

CONCLUSION

As listeners of Elder Betty’s experience, we’ve come to a new and sacred understanding of our bodies, our sexuality, and our mothering. We are inspired to communicate the spirit of these ancient teachings to build healthy, strong communities of women and men, mothered and able to mother. We hope that her words also resonate deeply within you and that you will reflect upon her teachings. These teachings are meant to be shared as well as to encourage dialogue about our sexuality and womanhood. It is also important to note that these teachings cannot be described as generalized experience for all Aboriginal Peoples; these teachings are told from stories by an Anishnabe Elder who was raised with the experience and the teachings of the Moon Lodge. Each one of us, no matter who we are or where we come from, can learn from these words of wisdom.

The authors thank Maureen Lynn for her assistance with this work. Funding from the Luther College President's Research Fund helped support this research.

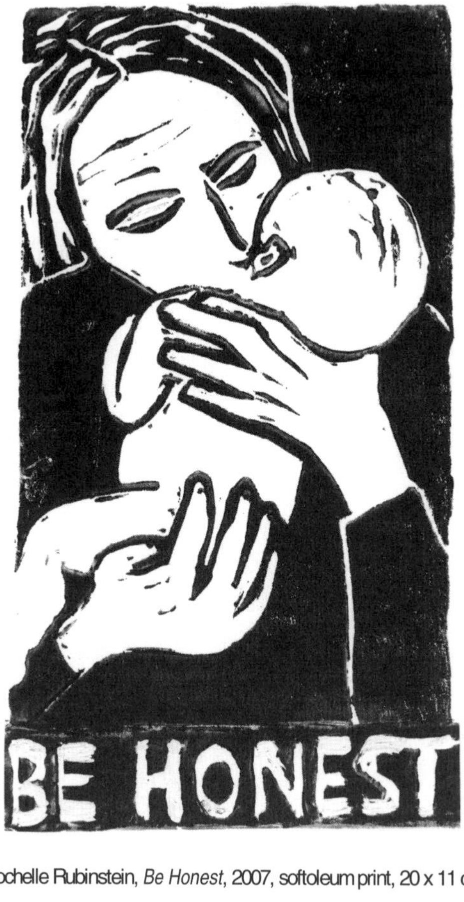

Rochelle Rubinstein, *Be Honest*, 2007, softoleum print, 20 x 11 cm.

Be Honest belongs to a series inspired by two phrases frequently used by my friend, Eva, a psychiatrist: be honest and don't blame. The imagery and text of my simple block prints deal with repression, projection, bullying, and familial relations.

Les services de garde de jeunes enfants au Canada Anglais et au Québec

JOCELYNE PRAUD ET ISLA DOWLING

> C'est un fait indéniable: la vaste majorité des mères canadiennes d'aujourd'hui travaillent. Plus de 65% des femmes qui ont des enfants de moins de trois ans travaillent à l'extérieur du foyer. Et 75% des femmes qui ont des enfants d'âge préscolaire ... font aussi un travail rémunéré. Or, en dépit de la demande non équivoque ... seulement 16% des enfants du Canada avaient accès à des services de garde réglementés en 2004 (Byers citée par le Congrès du travail du Canada 1).

CETTE ÉTUDE PORTE sur les services réglementés de garde d'enfants d'âge préscolaire (de zéro à cinq ans) qui sont offerts à temps partiel ou à temps plein, soit en milieu familial, soit en milieu collectif.[1] Au Canada, ces services «réglementés» doivent respecter les règles (relatives par exemple à la santé, la sécurité et le ratio enfants/éducatrices) établies par la province ou le territoire où ils opèrent et sont payants. En 2004, les parents résidant au Canada Anglais déboursaient chaque mois de 482 $ au Nouveau-Brunswick à 783 $ en Ontario pour un enfant de zéro à 17 mois, de 380 $ à Terre-Neuve et au Labrador à 662 $ en Colombie-Britannique pour un enfant de 18 mois à trois ans, et de 360 $ à Terre-Neuve et au Labrador à 577 $ au Nunavut pour un enfant de trois à cinq ans (Canadian Broadcasting Corporation). De plus, depuis la fin des années 1960, les provinces et les territoires accordent des subventions seulement aux familles à faible revenu qui remplissent leurs critères particuliers d'éligibilité.

Partout au Canada excepté au Québec, «la garde des enfants [est] typiquement conçue comme étant un service d'aide sociale»[2] (White et Friendly 6). Au lieu d'un réseau «universel», c'est à dire financé par des fonds publics et de ce fait accessible à tous les parents canadiens quelque soient leurs revenus[3], on trouve un amalgame de services dont l'abordabilité, la qualité et l'accessibilité varient grandement selon les provinces et les territoires, ce qui a des répercussions considérables sur les mères de jeunes enfants. Même si les pères d'aujourd'hui s'occupent beaucoup plus de leurs enfants qu'auparavant, le plus souvent ce sont les femmes qui interrompent leurs études ou bien s'arrêtent de travailler à la naissance d'un enfant. En 2004, 60% des enfants canadiens d'âge préscolaire étaient gardés par un parent (Cool), vraisemblablement la mère dans la plupart des cas. Il est donc indéniable que l'absence d'un réseau universel adéquat de services de garde restreint les opportunités des femmes canadiennes et contribue à perpétuer les inégalités économiques et sociales existant entre les femmes et les hommes. Cependant, la situation n'est pas la même partout au Canada. En effet, depuis la fin des années 1990, le Québec dispose d'un réseau universel de services de garde ne coûtant que cinq $ (et maintenant sept $) par jour.

Notre analyse, qui repose essentiellement sur des documents des gouvernements fédéral et québécois, des rapports d'organismes canadiens soutenant le développement des services de garde ainsi que des statistiques, comprend deux parties. Dans un premier temps, nous examinons les services de garde existant au Canada Anglais et, plus particulièrement, les initiatives lancées par les gouvernements fédéral et provinciaux de la Seconde Guerre mondiale à nos jours. Puis, nous portons notre attention sur le réseau québécois.

LES SERVICES DE GARDE AU CANADA ANGLAIS

En vertu de l'Article 92.7 de la Loi constitutionnelle de 1867, les provinces sont responsables de «l'établissement, l'entretien et l'administration des hôpitaux, asiles, institutions et hospices de charité»[4] (*The Constitution Act, 1867*), autrement dit de la mise en place, la gestion et la prestation des services de santé et de bien-être. Bien que la Loi constitutionnelle de 1867 identifie les services sociaux comme relevant du palier provincial, le gouvernement fédéral a joué un rôle majeur dans l'établissement de ces services. En effet, à partir des années 1970, ce dernier a cofinancé divers services sociaux avec les provinces afin d'assurer une certaine équité à tous les citoyens canadiens. Cependant, la première fois que le gouvernement fédéral alloua des fonds spécifiquement pour les services de garde de jeunes enfants fut durant la Seconde Guerre mondiale.

En 1942, pour pallier à la pénurie de main-d'oeuvre et encourager les femmes à travailler dans les industries de guerre, le gouvernement fédéral proposa un accord aux provinces, le *Dominion-Provincial Wartime Day Nurseries Agreement* (DPWDNA). Selon cet accord, la moitié des coûts associés à la mise sur pied de services de garde serait prise en charge par le fédéral et l'autre moitié par le provincial. Seuls l'Ontario et le Québec, les deux provinces les plus industrialisées du pays, signèrent l'Accord. Quoique ces services de garde s'adressaient principalement aux femmes travaillant dans les industries essentielles de guerre, telles que les manufactures de munition et d'armement, un quart des places disponibles étaient réservées aux femmes travaillant hors de ces industries. Puis, à partir du mois de mai 1944, toutes les femmes qui travaillaient eurent accès à ces services (Pierson 53, 55). Une fois la guerre finie, le gouvernement fédéral abolit l'Accord, les femmes et les enfants rentrèrent à la maison et les hommes reprirent leurs emplois.[5] Autrement dit, le DPWDNA permit la mise en place temporaire d'un réseau universel de services de garde en Ontario et au Québec visant surtout à répondre aux besoins ponctuels du gouvernement fédéral.

Il fallut attendre la fin des années 1960 et, plus précisément, la création du Régime d'assistance publique du Canada (RAPC) en 1966, pour que des fonds fédéraux puissent être alloués à des services de garde. Le RAPC était un programme fédéral ayant pour objectif de créer des programmes d'assistance sociale et de services sociaux à coûts partagés. C'est ainsi que le RAPC permit le cofinancement par le fédéral et les provinces ou les territoires des frais de garde encourus par les familles nécessiteuses ainsi que la création de quelques garderies publiques sans but lucratif. Comme Beach et Friendly le font remarquer, la plupart des fonds générés par l'entremise du RAPC servirent à financer les subventions aux familles à faible revenu plutôt que l'établissement de garderies publiques (3). En bref, la garde des jeunes enfants était avant tout perçue comme un service d'aide sociale destiné aux plus démunis et non pas comme un service universel auquel tous les parents devaient avoir accès.

Dans les années 1990, l'établissement d'un réseau universel de services de garde au Canada semblait particulièrement utopique. Le gouvernement conservateur de Brian Mulroney puis le gouvernement libéral de Jean Chrétien décidèrent que la meilleure façon de combler le déficit fédéral était de réduire les dépenses sociales. En 1990, le premier annonça que sa contribution annuelle au RAPC n'augmenterait que de 5% dans les trois provinces les plus riches du Canada (l'Ontario, l'Alberta et la Colombie-Britannique). Cinq ans plus tard, le second abolit le RAPC et ses règles ainsi que le Financement des programmes établis concernant les soins de santé et l'enseignement postsecondaire et remplaça ces deux programmes de transfert par un nouveau mécanisme de financement général, le Transfert canadien en matière de santé et de programmes sociaux (TCSPS). La création du TCSPS s'accompagna aussi d'une baisse de sept milliards $ sur deux ans, ce qui conduit les provinces à sabrer dans leurs dépenses d'aide sociale aux individus et aux familles démunis (Conseil canadien de développement social).

À partir des années 2000, le Canada étant maintenant dans une ère d'excédents budgétaires, de nouvelles initiatives de financement des services de garde furent lancées par les gouvernements fédéral, provinciaux et territoriaux. Au mois de septembre 2000, ces derniers (excepté le gouvernement du Québec) annoncèrent la mise en place de l'*Accord sur le développement de la petite enfance* (ADPE).[6] L'ADPE identifiait quatre domaines d'action soit: «promouvoir la santé des femmes enceintes, des nouveau-nés et des jeunes enfants; améliorer l'aide aux parents et aux familles; améliorer le développement des jeunes enfants, les soins qu'ils reçoivent et leur capacité d'apprentissage; renforcer le soutien communautaire» (Gouvernement du Canada). Dans le cadre de l'Accord, le gouvernement fédéral s'engageait à transférer 2,2 milliards $ sur cinq ans par le biais du TCSPS afin de soutenir les investissements dans les programmes et les services provinciaux et territoriaux relatifs au développement de la petite enfance (Gouvernement du Canada). Trois ans plus tard, les ministres fédéral, provinciaux et territoriaux responsables des services sociaux approuvèrent le *Cadre multilatéral pour l'apprentissage et la garde des jeunes enfants* (CMAGJE) qui visait à améliorer l'accès à des services de garde et des services éducatifs réglementés abordables et de qualité. Dans cette optique, le gouvernement fédéral prévoyait d'allouer 1,05 milliard $ sur cinq ans par l'entremise du TCSPS (Secrétariat du Conseil du Trésor du Canada). Enfin, en novembre 2004 et février 2005, les ministres fédéral, provinciaux et territoriaux responsables des services sociaux s'entendirent sur les quatre principes—la qualité, l'universalité, l'accessibilité et la contribution au développement de l'enfant—devant guider le développement d'un nouveau réseau national d'apprentissage et de garde des jeunes enfants au Canada. Le 29 avril 2005, le Manitoba fut la première province à signer un accord de principe avec le fédéral (Beach et Friendly 4; Friendly et Ferns 1). À la fin de l'année 2005, toutes les autres provinces (sauf le Québec) conclurent des accords de principe avec le gouvernement fédéral (Friendly et Ferns 2).[7] Les parents canadiens pouvaient enfin se permettre de rêver à l'établissement prochain d'un réseau universel de services de garde. Le rêve fut de courte durée.

En mars 2006, seulement deux mois après son arrivée au pouvoir, le gouvernement conservateur de Stephen Harper annonça que ces accords ne seraient pas ratifiés et que les ententes de financement sur cinq ans expireraient au printemps 2007 (Georgetti). À leur place serait instaurée la Prestation universelle pour la garde d'enfants (PUGE) visant à «appuyer [les] choix [des familles canadiennes] en matière de garde d'enfants par l'entremise d'un soutien financier direct» (Agence du Revenu du Canada). La PUGE consiste à verser 100 $ par mois pour chaque enfant de moins de six ans à toutes les familles canadiennes quelque soient leurs revenus afin de les aider à défrayer leurs frais de garde. On peut se demander dans quelle mesure cette prestation universelle, mais aussi imposable au parent ayant le plus faible revenu, aide véritablement les familles canadiennes. En effet, si l'on se reporte aux frais de garde cités dans l'introduction, on ne peut que conclure que la PUGE représente seulement moins d'un quart des dépenses de garde encourues chaque mois pour chaque enfant et probablement moins quand certains prestataires de services de garde en profitèrent pour augmenter leurs tarifs.[8] Autrement dit, la PUGE offre une bien maigre subvention aux parents et ne fait rien pour améliorer l'abordabilité, l'accessibilité et la qualité des services de garde. En bout de ligne, la PUGE est un obstacle majeur à l'établissement d'un réseau universel de services de garde au Canada puisqu'elle monopolise les fonds publics qui pourraient être investis directement dans les services de garde existants ou à venir.

Sans un appui financier conséquent et constant du fédéral, il est extrêmement difficile pour les provinces et les territoires de faire de réels progrès dans ce domaine. Récemment, le Congrès du travail du Canada évalua les performances des gouvernements fédéral et provinciaux (excepté celui du Québec) à partir de diverses données publiques concernant l'abordabilité (soit le coût des services de garde), la qualité (soit les salaires du personnel des services de garde) et l'accessibilité (soit la création de places). Alors que le gouvernement fédéral recevait une note d'échec (E), le Manitoba recevait la meilleure note, soit un B+, et la Colombie-Britannique un D- (Congrès du travail du Canada). Dans un entretien que Martha Friendly accordait à la revue *SIPP Policy Dialogue*, elle aussi soulignait la bonne performance du Manitoba surtout en matière d'accessibilité et de qualité et la contrastait avec celle de la Saskatchewan. Bien que ces deux provinces des Prairies ont une démographie et une population enfantine semblables, le fait qu'en 2005-2006 le Manitoba alloua presque quatre fois plus que la Saskatchewan, soit 86,3 millions $ contre 22,8 millions $, aux services de garde réglementés explique en grande partie leurs différentes performances (Friendly citée par Bell 5-6). En outre, Friendly décrit les services de garde saskatchewannais comme étant parmi les plus «sous-développés au Canada en ce qui concerne la qualité, le financement et l'accès» (Friendly 14).[9] Quant à la Colombie-Britannique, elle recevait un D- à cause du coût croissant de ses services de garde, des bas salaires versés au personnel et du manque de places autorisées (Marshall 6).

Bien que la mise sur pied, la gestion, la prestation et la réglementation des services de garde incombent aux provinces, il est indéniable que le gouvernement fédéral a exercé une influence importante sur le développement de ces services. S'il n'existe toujours pas de réseau universel de services de garde au Canada Anglais, c'est en partie à cause du gouvernement fédéral et des diverses initiatives qu'il a lancées au cours des six dernières décennies. En effet, le DPWDNA (1942-1945), l'ADPE (2000-2007) et le CMAGJE (2003-2007) auraient pu éventuellement aboutir à l'établissement d'un réseau universel, mais ils furent abandonnés quelques années après leur lancement. Quant au RAPC (1969-1995) et au TCSPS (1995-2004), ils servirent principalement à financer les subventions allouées aux familles à faible revenu. Comme il est noté plus haut, bien qu'universelle, l'impact de la PUGE sur l'accessibilité aux services de garde est discutable. Toutefois, la situation est bien différente au Québec, la seule province à s'être dotée d'un réseau universel de services de garde. En effet, en 1997, le Québec élimina progressivement les subventions aux familles les plus démunies et les remplaça par un réseau universel de services de garde ne coûtant que cinq $ par jour par enfant. C'est sur ce réseau que nous portons maintenant notre attention.

LES SERVICES DE GARDE AU QUÉBEC

L'histoire des services de garde québécois consiste en trois grandes phases. De 1858 à 1969, il s'agit surtout de services d'aide sociale que des organisations religieuses et charitables offraient aux familles pauvres. Puis de 1969 à 2000, ces services, qui relevaient toujours de l'aide sociale, étaient en partie subventionnés par des fonds fédéraux et provinciaux et régis par le gouvernement québécois. Enfin, à partir de 1997, on assiste à la mise en place graduelle d'un réseau universel.

Les toutes premières garderies québécoises virent le jour au dix-neuvième siècle à Montréal. Entre 1858 et 1922, les «salles d'asile» créées par les Sulpiciens et gérées par les Soeurs grises accueillirent près de 60 000 enfants âgés de trois à sept ans. En 1887, le Montreal Day Nursery ouvrit ses portes grâce aux subventions d'organisations charitables. À partir de 1922, reconnue comme étant une institution d'assistance publique, cette garderie anglophone reçut des subventions du gouvernement québécois (Société Radio-Canada 1). Le DPWDNA permit la mise en place de six garderies publiques à Montréal durant la Seconde Guerre mondiale (Collectif Clio 388-389). Cependant, les garderies établies au Québec durant les années 1950 et 1960 étaient surtout des garderies privées à but lucratif qui n'étaient ni subventionnées, ni réglementées par le gouvernement (Société Radio-Canada 1).

La Révolution tranquille, le mouvement de modernisation et de sécularisation qui balaya le Québec à partir de 1960, remit en question le rôle prédominant que L'Église catholique jouait dans la vie des citoyens et permit à l'État québécois de lancer d'importantes réformes sociales et économiques. En ce qui concerne les services de garde, les années 1970 virent une plus grande implication non seulement gouvernementale, mais aussi citoyenne. Dès la création du RAPC en 1969, le gouvernement québécois accorda des permis aux garderies qui opéraient déjà dans la province et subventionna des services de garde dans certains quartiers déshérités de Montréal. Puis, entre 1971 et 1973, grâce à des subventions que le Ministère fédéral de la Main-d'oeuvre et de l'Immigration accordait à divers projets de création d'emplois, 70 garderies sans but lucratif furent établies au Québec. Toutefois, la plupart d'entre elles durent fermer leurs portes lorsque le Ministère retira ses subventions.

La fermeture de ces garderies déclencha un mouvement de mobilisation à travers la province, le Comité de liaison des garderies populaires, qui réclamait que les garderies soient désormais financées de façon permanente par le gouvernement québécois. Trois grandes centrales syndicales ainsi que plusieurs associations féministes appuyèrent publiquement les revendications du Comité de liaison des garderies populaires (Société Radio-Canada 2; Fédération des femmes du Québec). Au mois de juin 1974, Lise Bacon, la Ministre d'État provinciale aux Affaires sociales, présenta un plan, qui visait principalement à accorder des subventions (d'un maximum de cinq $ par jour par enfant) aux familles à faible revenu et aux mères sans conjoint. Le plan Bacon, qui prévoyait aussi des subventions de démarrage de 5 000 $ aux nouvelles garderies, suscita de nombreuses critiques parmi ceux qui revendiquaient l'établissement d'un réseau universel de services de garde financé par le gouvernement. En dépit de ces critiques, le gouvernement libéral adopta le plan Bacon (Société Radio-Canada 2; Collectif Clio 489).

Après l'arrivée au pouvoir en 1976 du Parti québécois (PQ), qui avait inscrit le développement d'un réseau de garderies publiques à son programme électoral, d'importants jalons furent posés pour l'avenir des services de garde québécois. Tout d'abord, Denis Lazure, le nouveau Ministre aux Affaires sociales, lança un programme de financement qui accordait des subventions directes aux garderies. C'est ainsi que la part du budget provincial consacrée aux garderies plus que doubla entre 1978 et 1980 de 7,2 millions $ à 16,2 millions $ (Société Radio-Canada 3). Puis, en 1979, afin de coordonner et de promouvoir le développement des services de garde de jeunes enfants, le gouvernement créa l'Office des services de garde à l'enfance, un «organisme public dont le mandat était d'identifier les besoins en matière de garde à l'enfance, de planifier leur développement en harmonie avec les autres politiques familiales du Québec, de les réglementer et d'en assurer la qualité» (Tougas 2). Quatre ans après sa création, les chiffres publiés par l'Office indiquaient clairement qu'un changement radical de politique était nécessaire: les 26 393 places reparties dans 560 garderies collectives et 1519 garderies familiales reconnues pour une population totale de 282 499 enfants ne répondaient qu'à 13% des besoins (Société Radio-Canada 3). Il fallut cependant attendre le retour des péquistes au pouvoir en 1994 pour qu'un changement de cap ait lieu.

En janvier 1997, Pauline Marois, la Ministre péquiste de l'Éducation, annonça une nouvelle politique familiale visant à assurer un meilleur équilibre entre vie professionnelle et vie familiale. Dans le cadre de cette nouvelle politique, trois mesures principales étaient proposées: une allocation unifiée pour les enfants des familles à faible revenu; des services de garde et des services éducatifs stimulants; et un nouveau régime d'assurance parentale. Pour ce qui était des services de garde et des services éducatifs, le gouvernement prévoyait l'instauration de la maternelle à plein temps pour les enfants de cinq ans ainsi que l'implantation progressive de services de garde à tarif unique, soit cinq $ par jour pour les enfants âgés de moins de cinq ans (Gouvernement du Québec «La politique familiale»).[10] Au mois de mars 1997, Marois annonça la création de Centres de la petite enfance, des organismes privés à but non lucratif devant être gérés par un conseil d'administration formé majoritairement de parents et chapeautant des services de garde éducatifs en milieu collectif et en milieu familial pour une contribution parentale de cinq $ par jour par enfant et proposa aux garderies à but lucratif de se convertir en organismes privés à but non lucratif afin de pouvoir elles aussi offrir des services de garde éducatifs à cinq $ (Gouvernement du Québec «Pauline Marois»).[11] Ces Centres de la petite enfance sont tenus de fournir aux jeunes enfants sous leur responsabilité les soins de base favorisant leur santé et leur sécurité ainsi qu'un environnement stimulant privilégiant leur plein épanouissement. En somme, l'objectif du gouvernement péquiste n'était pas de créer un simple réseau de services de garde, mais plutôt un réseau de services de garde éducatifs de qualité destiné à préparer les jeunes enfants à la scolarité (Tougas 6; Jenson 55).

Les mesures concernant les enfants des milieux défavorisés démontrent que la réforme visait bien tous les enfants québécois quelque soit leur milieu social. Ainsi, les assistés sociaux pouvaient envoyer leurs enfants de plus de deux ans dans un service de garde collectif ou familial gratuitement pendant 23 heures et demi chaque semaine. S'ils étaient inscrits dans un programme d'employabilité, ils avaient aussi la possibilité de défrayer leurs frais de garde supplémentaires. Quant à ceux ayant droit à l'Aide aux parents pour leurs revenus de travail, ils pouvaient aussi recevoir une subvention de trois $ par jour et donc voir leurs frais quotidiens de garde réduits à deux $. La réforme prévoyait aussi que les enfants de quatre ans des quartiers déshérités de Montréal pourraient fréquenter la pré-maternelle à mi-temps ainsi que des services de garde éducatifs gratuitement (Jenson 54-55).

De 1997 au début des années 2000, alors que le gouvernement québécois mettait sur pied un réseau universel de services de garde, on put constater de nettes améliorations, surtout en ce qui concerne l'accessibilité et l'abordabilité. Entre 1997 et 2001, le nombre de places disponibles aux enfants de zéro à quatre ans passa de 82 302 à 139 683 (Friendly *et al.* 71), ce qui permit à la fréquentation d'augmenter de façon significative. Ainsi, de 1995 à 2003, la proportion des jeunes enfants québécois étant inscrits dans un service de garde tripla de 11% à près de 35%, soit le double de la moyenne canadienne, et la garde des enfants par les parents diminua de 56,1% à 33,1% (Daoud 2). De plus, au début des années 2000, plus de 98% des parents québécois envoyaient leur enfant de cinq ans à la maternelle à temps plein même si ce n'était pas obligatoire

(Tougas 7). Enfin, du fait des services de garde à coût fixe, en 2002, une famille québécoise payait 1 400 $ par an par enfant, soit deux fois moins que dans le reste du Canada et deux fois et demi de moins qu'une famille ontarienne (Daoud 2).

Néanmoins, la création d'un tel réseau rencontra aussi des écueils. Victimes de leur popularité, les services de garde à cinq $ ne furent pas en mesure de répondre à la demande massive de places, ce qui allongea les délais d'attente. D'après Friendly *et al.*, plus de 85 000 enfants se trouvaient sur une liste d'attente en 2000 (71). En outre, le fait que 54,5 % des heures de garde étaient utilisées par des familles gagnant plus de 60 000 $ par an semblait indiquer que le nouveau réseau profitait avant tout aux familles aux revenus moyens et supérieurs (Société Radio-Canada 5). Enfin, entre 1997 et 2003, la facture publique des services de garde plus que quintupla de 239 millions $ à 1,3 milliard $ (Société Radio-Canada 5). Peu de temps après son élection au printemps 2003, le gouvernement libéral de Jean Charest déclara qu'il prendrait d'importantes mesures pour réduire cette facture et freiner le développement du nouveau réseau. En juin 2003, en dépit de la manifestation et de la pétition de plus de 100 000 signatures organisées pour réclamer la protection du réseau universel, le gouvernement annonça que le budget des services de garde serait coupé de 25 millions $ par an et que la contribution parentale passerait de cinq $ à sept $ (Friendly *et al.* 71).[12]

Une décennie après le lancement de ce réseau universel de services de garde, quel bilan peut-on en faire? Puisque l'abordabilité des services de garde pour les parents n'est plus à démontrer même après l'augmentation de 2003, considérons des données récentes sur la facture publique de ces services, le nombre de places réglementées et d'enfants d'âge préscolaire ainsi que les salaires et qualifications du personnel des services de garde afin d'en évaluer le coût, l'accessibilité et la qualité. En 2005-2006, les dépenses du Québec relatives aux services de garde réglementés pour les enfants de zéro à quatre ans s'élevaient à 1,5 milliards $ (Friendly *et al.* 68). Selon l'Organisation de coopération et de développement économique (OCDE), en proportion de son produit national brut, le Québec dépensait presqu'autant que la Finlande, deux fois plus que le Royaume-Uni et cinq fois plus que le reste du Canada (Perreault). En 2005, on comptait 200 105 places réglementées pour 236 900 enfants de zéro à quatre ans qui avaient une mère qui travaillait (Friendly *et al.* 60, 66). Même si il n'y a toujours pas assez de places réglementées et que les listes d'attente demeurent une réalité surtout pour les parents vivant dans les grands centres urbains de Montréal et Québec (Gagnon et Croteau), le réseau paraît répondre aux besoins d'une majorité des parents et des enfants. Pour ce qui est de la qualité, rappelons que d'emblée l'éducation de la petite enfance a été une composante clé de la réforme de 1997. D'autre part, les mesures prises quant aux qualifications et aux salaires des employés des Centres de la petite enfance et des garderies privées semblent indiquer que le gouvernement provincial a pour priorité d'offrir des services de garde éducatifs de qualité aux familles québécoises. Ainsi, depuis le 31 août 2006, les Centres de la petite enfance et les garderies ont cinq ans pour s'assurer que les deux tiers de leur personnel obtiennent un diplôme collégial ou universitaire en Éducation de la petite enfance (Friendly *et al.* 73). De plus, entre 1998 et 2002, les salaires des éducatrices et des aides-éducatrices de la petite enfance progressèrent de 12,49 $ de l'heure à 17,30 $ de l'heure (Daoud 3). Cependant, d'après Québec-emploi, en 2005 leur revenu annuel n'était que de 23 000 $.

Certes, le réseau québécois coûte cher, mais il est aussi abordable, accessible et axé sur la prestation de services de garde éducatifs de qualité. D'ailleurs, il est indubitable que le réseau de services de garde a aussi eu un impact positif sur l'emploi des femmes. Entre 1994 et 2002, la proportion de mères qui travaillaient augmenta de 21% au Québec, contre seulement 9% dans le reste du Canada (Boileau). Le fait que d'après l'OCDE, la proportion de femmes avec enfants de moins de trois ans qui ont un emploi à temps plein est 34% plus élevée au Québec que dans le reste du Canada renforce l'argument selon lequel le réseau de services de garde a favorisé l'emploi des mères (Perreault).

CONCLUSION

En 1995, soit 25 ans après que la Commission royale d'enquête sur le statut de la femme au Canada fit plusieurs recommandations relatives à l'établissement d'un réseau national de services de garde, Condition féminine Canada déclarait qu'un tel réseau n'existait pas (Status of Women Canada 5). Treize ans plus tard, force est de constater qu'un tel réseau n'est toujours pas en place. Au Canada Anglais, où les services de garde sont généralement associés à l'aide sociale, on trouve un amalgame de services dont l'abordabilité, l'accessibilité et la qualité varient selon les provinces et les territoires où ils se trouvent. Toutefois, depuis 1997, le Québec, avec son réseau universel de services de garde éducatifs abordables, accessibles et de qualité, se démarque des autres provinces.

Comment se fait-il qu'un tel réseau ait pu voir le jour au Québec mais pas au Canada Anglais? Diverses raisons d'ordre historique, culturel et politique apportent des éléments de réponse. Premièrement, du fait de sa langue et de sa culture françaises, le Québec est plus à même de se tourner vers l'Europe, où plusieurs pays, dont la France et la Suède, disposent de services de garde éducatifs universels et de qualité. Les provinces anglophones, quant à elles, sont plus à même de se tourner vers les États-Unis, où, à l'instar du Canada Anglais, les services de garde laissent à désirer (Human Early Learning Partnership). Deuxièmement, les valeurs collectivistes et étatistes paraissent plus solidement ancrées au Québec que dans le reste du Canada. En effet, les francophones du Québec se voient comme étant une collectivité linguistique et culturelle qui a pu survivre et prospérer sur le continent nord-américain en se serrant les coudes. De plus, à partir de la Révolution tranquille, l'État québécois a lancé d'importantes réformes sociales et économiques qui ont donné aux Québécois le sentiment d'être «Maîtres chez eux» et qui leur ont permis d'apprécier le rôle de l'État. Il n'est donc pas surprenant que la réforme lancée en 1997 par le gouvernement péquiste, qui s'apparente à des valeurs collectivistes et étatistes, reçut immédiatement les suffrages des familles québécoises. Le fait que de telles valeurs soient peut-être plus contestées au Canada Anglais et que la garde des enfants soit considérée avant tout comme étant la responsabilité individuelle des parents plutôt que la responsabilité partagée des parents, de l'État et de la société explique en partie pourquoi un réseau universel de services de garde n'existe toujours pas au Canada Anglais. Troisièmement, comme nous l'avons souligné plus haut, en fin de compte, c'est un gouvernement provincial doté d'une volonté politique ferme de changer de cap qui donna naissance aux Centres de la petite enfance et aux garderies à cinq $. Les efforts que le gouvernement provincial suivant déploya au début des années 2000 afin d'enrayer le développement du populaire réseau de services de garde n'ont pas vraiment abouti. Le réseau québécois de services de garde à coût fixe n'est pas prêt de disparaître.[13]

Au Canada Anglais par contre, les perspectives d'avenir des services de garde de jeunes enfants ne sont pas encourageantes. Tout d'abord, la PUGE, l'innovation du gouvernement conservateur de Stephen Harper, qui a été réélu l'automne dernier, constitue un obstacle majeur à l'établissement d'un réseau universel puisqu'elle monopolise les fonds publics qui pourraient être investis directement dans les services de garde existants ou à venir. De toute façon, comme les conservateurs l'ont clairement signifié avant et durant la campagne électorale, la mise place d'un tel réseau ne fait pas partie de leurs priorités et ceci encore moins depuis que l'économie mondiale est en récession. En effet, le plan d'action économique présenté dans le budget fédéral de 2009 prévoit d'importantes dépenses en matière d'infrastructure et de réduction d'impôts et donc un déficit de 33,7 milliards $ pour l'année en cours et de 29,8 milliards $ pour l'année suivante afin de relancer l'économie canadienne (Ministère des finances du Canada). Cependant, comme le remarque le Syndicat canadien de la fonction publique, ce budget « ne contient rien pour la mise en place d'un programme progressiste d'éducation de la petite enfance et de services de garde à l'enfance » (Syndicat canadien de la fonction publique). Or, à l'orée du vingt-et-unième siècle, il est grand temps que les gouvernements fédéral, provinciaux et territoriaux fassent preuve de volonté politique et mettent sur pied un réseau universel de services de garde éducatifs abordables, accessibles et de qualité. Il est indubitable qu'une telle réforme profiterait aux enfants et aux parents, favoriserait la pleine participation des mères à la vie économique et sociale du pays et aiderait à relancer l'économie du pays.

Un grand merci au Dr. Karl A. Henriques pour ses excellents commentaires.

[1]Notre étude ne considère pas les arrangements informels et non réglementés auxquels bon nombre de familles canadiennes sont obligées d'avoir recours. En effet, selon Julie Cool, en 2004, plus de 80% des enfants canadiens d'âge préscolaire étaient gardés soit à la maison par un parent (60%) ou par quelqu'un d'autre (6%), soit à l'extérieur du foyer familial par un membre de leur famille (7%) ou une gardienne non réglementée (15%).

Les lecteurs remarqueront que nous employons le terme «services de garde» plus souvent que celui de «garderies» dans le texte. Cela tient au fait que depuis l'implantation en 1997 d'un réseau universel de services de garde de jeunes enfants au Québec, dans cette province, le terme garderies fait référence aux garderies privées qui ne sont pas chapeautées par un Centre de la petite enfance et qui sont à but lucratif. Les garderies privées qui sont sans but lucratif et dont le conseil d'administration ne comprend pas une majorité de parents, telles que par exemple celles affiliées à une église, sont aussi considérées comme étant des garderies (Friendly *et al.* 65). En conséquence, dans le texte, le terme garderies désigne les services de garde offerts en milieu collectif excepté dans la seconde partie concernant le Québec où, à partir de 1997, il désigne seulement les garderies privées.

[2]Notre traduction.

[3]Définition de la Child Care Advocay Association of Canada.

[4]Notre traduction.

[5]Le DPWDNA prit fin à l'automne 1945 au Québec et au printemps 1946 en Ontario (Pierson 56, 60).

[6]Bien que le gouvernement du Québec ne signa pas l'ADPE, 71,6 millions des fonds de l'ADPE lui furent attribués (Friendly et Beach 65).

[7]Le Québec, qui avait déjà un réseau universel de services de garde en place, voulait que l'équivalent financier du programme lui soit versé sans reddition de comptes (voir «Ottawa créera un réseau de garderies»). Éventuellement, le Québec et le gouvernement fédéral signèrent un accord (plutôt qu'un accord de principe) afin d'appuyer les investissements dans le réseau québécois (Friendly et Ferns 2).

[8]Sur l'augmentation des frais de garde suite à l'instauration de la PUGE, voir De Souza.

[9]Notre traduction.
[10]Les enfants de quatre ans devaient être les premiers à bénéficier des services de garde à cinq $ en septembre 1997. Suivaient ensuite ceux de trois ans en septembre 1998, ceux de deux ans en septembre 1999 et enfin ceux d'un an en septembre 2000 (Gouvernement du Québec «La politique familiale»). Du fait de leur popularité, le gouvernement ouvrit les services de garde à coût fixe à tous les groupes d'âge (de zéro à douze ans) en 2000 (Tougas 8).
[11]En ce qui concerne la distinction à faire au Québec entre les Centres de la petite enfance et les garderies privées, se reporter à la note 1. Depuis 2006, ce ne sont plus les Centres de la petite enfance mais les Bureaux coordonnateurs de la garde en milieu familial qui gèrent les services de garde en milieu familial. En 2005-2006, on comptait 1 004 Centres de la petite enfance, chapeautant 1 306 services de garde en milieu collectif et 13 776 en milieu familial, et 612 garderies privées (Friendly *et al.* 66).
[12]Le gouvernement avait aussi l'intention d'améliorer le financement des garderies privées et ainsi d'encourager la création de places dans ces dernières plutôt que dans les Centres de la petite enfance (Friendly *et al.* 71).
[13]En ce qui concerne l'impact des cultures politiques européennes, nord-américaines et québécoises sur les politiques sociales lancées en Europe, en Amérique du Nord et au Québec, voir l'excellente étude de Théret.

OUVRAGES CITÉS

Agence du revenu du Canada. «La Prestation universelle pour la garde d'enfants». <http:// www.cra-arc.gc.ca/bnfts/uccb-puge/menu-fra.html>. 20 août 2008.

Beach, Jane et Martha Friendly. «Child Care Fee Subsidies in Canada». Toronto: Childcare Resource and Research Unit. <http://www.childcarequality.ca/wdocs/QdD_FeeSubsidies_Canada.pdf>. 20 août 2008.

Bell, Patricia. «Investing in Childhood Education and Care: Questions for Martha Friendly». *SIPP Policy Dialogue* (printemps 2008): 5-7.

Boileau, Josée. «À démontrer». *Le Devoir* 3 février 2006. <http://www.ledevoir.com/2006/02/03/101239.html>. 29 août 2008.

Canadian Broadcasting Corporation (CBC). «Day Care: Cost to Parents». *CBC News Online* 9 février 2005. <http:// www.cbc.ca/news/background/daycarecosts.htm>. 19 août 2008.

Collectif Clio. *L'Histoire des femmes au Québec depuis quatre siècles*. Montréal: Le Jour, 1992.

Congrès du travail du Canada. «Le gouvernement fédéral obtient un E pour la garde des enfants». 12 juin 2008. < http://congresdu travail.ca/node/2763>. 19 août 2008.

Conseil canadien de développement social. «Quel avenir pour le Canada? Il est temps de débattre du Transfert social canadien». 8 avril 2004. <http://www.ccds.ca/francais/ip/ts/ts.htm>. 30 août 2008.

Cool, Julie. «Child Care in Canada: Regulated, Unregulated, Private or Public». Bibliothèque du Parlement. Service d'information et de recherches du Parlement. 3 juin 2004. <http: //www.parl.gc.ca/information/library/PRBpubs/prb0418-e.htm>. 19 août 2008.

Daoud, Marc. «Les garderies publiques: un succès pour la collectivité». Institut de recherche et d'informations socio-économiques. <http://www.iris-recherche.qc.ca/publications/le_systeme_de_garderies_.pdf>. 10 février 2008.

De Souza, Michael. «Day-care fee hikes may erase benefit of child-care funds». *The Star Phoenix* 1er juillet 2006. <http://www.canada.com/saskatoonstarphoenix/news/national/story.html?id+dfa81dcc-4459-47f5-8ec5-42...>. 20 août 2008.

Early Learning and Child Care Research Unit. «When Walking Hasn't Worked, It's Time to Run: Evidence-based and Community-driven Advice on Child Care». Human Early Learning Partnership, University of British Columbia, août 2006. <http://www.earlylearning.ubc.ca/documents/2006/RandP_ChildCare_Highlights_Aug_06_Final.pdf>. 29 août 2008.

Emploi-Québec. «Éducateurs/éducatrices et aides-éducateurs/aides-éducatrices de la petite enfance (4214)». <http://imt.emploiquebec.net/mtg/inter/noncache/contenu/asp/mtg122_statprof_01.asp?cregn=QCandPT1=3andlang=FRANandPorte=1andprov=FPTandPT3=9andpro=4214andPT2=17andPT4=53andcmpregn=QCandmsta=1>. 29 août 2008.

Fédération des femmes du Québec. «Prise de position de la FFQ sur les garderies (1974)». <http://www.cybersolidaires.org/histoire/docs/1974b.html>. 29 août 2008.

Friendly, Martha. «Early Learning and Child Care in Saskatchewan: Past, Present and Future». *SIPP Public Policy Paper* 36 (octobre 2006).

Friendly, Martha *et al. Early Childhood Education and Care in Canada 2006*. 7ème édition. Toronto: Childcare Resource and Research Unit, juin 2007. <http://www.childcarecanada.org/ECE2006/pdf/ECEC06_QC.pdf>. 29 août 2008.

Friendly, Martha et Jane Beach. *Early Childhood Education and Care in Canada 2004*. 6ème édition. Toronto: Childcare Resource and Research Unit, mai 2005. <http://www.childcarecanada.org/ECEC2004/index.html>. 10 février 2008.

Friendly, Martha et Carolyn Ferns. «Briefing Notes: The State of the National Child Care Program and Provincial/Territorial Contexts, March 2006». 14 mars 2006. <http://www.childcarecanada.org/pubs/pdf/BN_StateNatCCProgram3_06.pdf>. 18 août 2008.

Gagnon, Katie et Martin Croteau. «cpe: une révolution victime de son succès». 2 septembre 2007. <http://www.cyberpresse.ca/article/20070902/CPACTUALITES/709020423/1028>. 29 août 2008.

Georgetti, Ken. «Jeunes parents au Premier ministre Harper: honorez les ententes sur les garderies». 8 mars 2006. <http://action.clc-ctc.ca/fr/jeunes_parents_au_Pr>. 18 août 2008.

Gouvernement du Canada. «Accord fédéral-provincial-territorial sur le développement de la petite enfance: rapport sur les activités et dépenses du gouvernement 2000-2001». Fiche d'information. Novembre 2001. <http://www.socialunion.gc.ca/ecd/ecd-back201101_f.html>. 20 août 2008.

Gouvernement du Québec. «La politique familiale: les enfants au cœur des choix du gouvernement». 23 janvier 1997. <http://www.meq.gouv.qc.ca/cpress/cpress97/c970123.htm>. 29 août 2008.

Gouvernement du Québec. «Pauline Marois annonce les récentes décisions du gouvernement en matière de politique familiale». 20 mars 1997. <http://www.meq.gouv.qc.ca/CPRESS/CPRESS97/c970320.htm>. 29 août 2008.

Jenson, Jane. «Family Policy, Child Care and Social Security: The Case of Quebec». *Changing Child Care: Five Decades of Child Care Advocacy and Policy in Canada*. Sous la dir. Susan Prentice. Halifax: Fernwood Publishing, 2001. 39-62.

Marshall, Jenn. «City's Child Care Can't Meet Demand». *Nanaimo News Bulletin* 26 juillet 2008: 6.

Ministère des finances du Canada. « Le budget de 2009: le Plan d'action économique du Canada ». 27 janvier 2009. <http://www.fin.gc.ca/n08/09-011-fra.asp>. 31 août 2009.

«Ottawa créera un réseau de garderies avec les provinces». *Le Devoir* 3 novembre 2004. <http://www.ledevoir.com/2004/11/03/67640.html>. 20 août 2008.

Perreault, Mathieu. «Les garderies québécoises louangées». *La Presse* 30 novembre 2007. <http://www.mri.gouv.qc.ca/fr/_scripts/Atualites/ViewNewQcNews.asp?ID+601andMenu+defaultandlang=f>. 29 août 2008.

Pierson, Ruth Roach. *'They're Still Women after All': The Second World War and Canadian Womanhood*. Toronto: McClelland and Stewart, 1986.

Secrétariat du Trésor du Canada. «Cadre multilatéral pour l'apprentissage et la garde des jeunes enfants». <http://www.tbs-sct.gc.ca/rma/eppi-ibdrp/hrdb-rhbd/dep-min/hrdc-rhdsc/elcc-agje/description_f.asp>. 20 août 2008.

Société Radio-Canada. «Un Québec fou de ses garderies». 18 janvier 2007. <http: //archives.radio-Canada.ca/societe/famille/dossiers/1699/>.10 février 2008.

Status of Women Canada. *The Royal Commission on the Status of Women: An Overview 25 Years Later.* Ottawa: SWS, 1995.

Syndicat canadien de la fonction publique « Le budget fédéral 2009 et l'éducation de la petite enfance et garde à l'enfance». 25 janvier 2009. <http: //scfp.ca/garde-a-l-enfance/a4988732f06d1f>. 31 août 2009.

Théret, Bruno. *Protection sociale et fédéralisme: L'Europe dans le miroir de l'Amérique du Nord.* Québec: Les Presses de l'Université de Montréal, 2001.

Tougas, Jocelyne. «La restructuration des services éducatifs et de garde à l'enfance au Québec: les cinq premières années». Document hors-série 17. Toronto: Childcare Resource and Research Unit, mars 2002. <http://www.chilcarecanada.org/pubs/op17/op27FR.pdf>19 août 2008.

White, Linda et Martha Friendly. «Early Learning and Child Care Governance». *Discourse* 17.1 (automne 2007): 6-7.

Le soutien aux mères étudiantes universitaires au Québec

DOMINIQUE TANGUAY

IL EST POSSIBLE depuis plusieurs années déjà d'observer une diversification de la population étudiante au Québec, ce qui laisse penser qu'un nombre grandissant d'étudiantes et d'étudiants pourrait assumer des responsabilités parentales. Selon le Conseil national des cycles supérieurs (CNCS) (4-5), 40% des étudiants québécois des cycles supérieurs inscrits à temps partiel et 20% de ceux inscrits à temps plein ont une ou des personnes à charge.

Les études quantitatives déjà réalisées tendent à démontrer que les femmes sont plus nombreuses que les hommes parmi les étudiants universitaires qui ont des enfants.[1] Des avis et des mémoires témoignent des problèmes rencontrés par les mères étudiantes universitaires dans leur parcours.[2] Il est indéniable qu'une fraction des étudiants universitaires sont des pères, mais il semble que les mères sont plus nombreuses et éprouvent des difficultés à combiner leurs rôles de vie. C'est pourquoi cet article se limite à la situation des mères étudiantes universitaires.

Or, les universités québécoises ont-elles vraiment pris conscience des besoins des étudiantes qui sont mères? Quelles sont les mesures mises en place pour faciliter la conciliation études-famille? La recension des écrits en vue de ma thèse de doctorat m'a amenée à contacter les universités québécoises, les associations étudiantes, ainsi que divers organismes québécois et canadiens et certains ministères québécois dont les mandats sont liés à l'éducation postsecondaire ou à la famille, dans le but de dresser un portrait de la conciliation études-famille au Québec.

Bien que plusieurs mesures s'adressant à l'ensemble de la communauté universitaire peuvent se révéler précieuses pour les mères étudiantes—pensons notamment aux banques alimentaires—cet article se restreint aux mesures institutionnelles et gouvernementales destinées spécifiquement aux parents étudiants et se divise en trois sections: les services de garde, le soutien financier et les initiatives institutionnelles.

LES SERVICES DE GARDE

Le Québec s'est doté en 1997 d'un vaste réseau public de Centres de la petite enfance (CPE), lesquels offrent des places subventionnées à sept $ par jour par enfant. Une telle mesure sociale, qui place le Québec dans une position enviable par rapport aux autres provinces canadiennes, peut permettre aux mères étudiantes de poursuivre leurs études en confiant leur enfant à un service de garde abordable et de qualité. Cependant, l'accessibilité et la flexibilité ne sont pas toujours au rendez-vous.

Une enquête de Force Jeunesse, un regroupement de jeunes travailleurs et d'associations voué à l'amélioration des conditions de travail, sur les services de garde dans les universités québécoises trace un portrait plutôt sombre de la situation. Quelques universités ne disposent d'aucun service de garde (ni CPE ni garderie privée) (3); certaines se contentent de référer les mères étudiantes à des services à l'extérieur de l'université (6). La plupart des universités n'ont qu'un seul service de garde. L'Université Laval et l'Université du Québec à Montréal, avec chacune trois CPE, possèdent les services les plus développés (4-5).

Toutefois, la présence d'un service de garde sur le campus n'en garantit pas l'accès. Un seul CPE réserve la moitié de ses places aux enfants des étudiants (Force Jeunesse 4) et quelques CPE en milieu universitaire accordent la priorité aux enfants d'étudiants (4-7). Parmi les pratiques restreignant l'accès, il convient de noter que certains services de garde limitent leur offre aux enfants dont au moins un parent est étudiant à temps plein, imposent des frais pour l'inscription sur la liste d'attente, exigent que cette démarche se fasse en personne ou que le parent étudiant ait en main sa confirmation d'inscription, ce qui pose problème aux futures étudiantes, à celles qui n'habitent pas à proximité ou qui ne peuvent se déplacer durant les heures d'ouverture (2). L'Université Laval, identifiée comme offrant le plus vaste service de garde parmi les universités québécoises avec ses trois CPE totalisant 181 places, ne comble pas la demande. Dans sa *Plateforme de revendications*, l'Association des étudiants de Laval inscrits aux études supérieures (AELIES) souligne l'insuffisance de ce service car les listes d'attente contiennent environ 1 200 noms (13). Il est possible que plusieurs noms apparaissent sur les trois listes, mais même en supposant que ces listes soient identiques, il y aurait deux fois plus d'enfants en attente qu'il n'y a de places disponibles.

Les haltes garderies, qui offrent des services de garde de courte durée ou de façon ponctuelle, sont rares sur les campus québécois. Une exception: le Baluchon, la halte garderie de l'Université de Montréal, réservée aux enfants des étudiants et dont le financement provient principalement de la Fédération des associations étudiantes, reçoit une trentaine d'enfants par jour et cherche à se relocaliser afin de doubler ce nombre. Chaque enfant peut fréquenter la halte garderie jusqu'à concurrence de six demi-journées par semaine (Gariépy *et al.* 35). En novembre 2007, les membres de la CADEUL, association étudiante du premier cycle de l'Université Laval, ont accepté lors d'un référendum de verser cinq $ par session pour la mise sur pied d'une halte garderie, qui sera, selon toute vraisemblance, la seconde en milieu universitaire au Québec (Laverdière).

Les haltes garderies représentent une alternative très intéressante aux CPE, particulièrement pour les mères étudiantes à temps partiel. Les CPE accordent la priorité aux enfants inscrits à temps plein, puisque leur financement est calculé en fonction du taux de fréquentation. Comme les listes d'attente des CPE sont plutôt longues, les chances d'obtenir une place à temps partiel sont minces. Les mères étudiantes qui souhaitent effectuer un retour progressif aux études tout en se consacrant à leur enfant se retrouvent parfois dans l'obligation de l'inscrire à un CPE à temps plein, afin de sécuriser une place, même si leur besoin n'est qu'à temps partiel. Une halte garderie à temps partiel répondrait donc mieux aux besoins de ces mères étudiantes qu'un CPE. De même, les couples étudiants qui planifient leur horaire de façon à ce que l'un des parents puisse assurer la garde des enfants bénéficieraient des services des haltes garderies pour les périodes occasionnelles où les deux parents sont absents.

Il est possible d'identifier plusieurs limites des services de garde actuels. Les heures d'ouverture varient en général entre 7 heures et 18 heures. Or, l'horaire des cours universitaires se prolonge jusqu'à 21 heures 30, ce qui pose problème particulièrement aux mères monoparentales et à celles dont le réseau de soutien ne peut prendre le relais. Les cours du soir occasionnent donc des frais supplémentaires dans le cas où ces étudiantes doivent faire appel à une gardienne à la maison. Dans le cas où un cours obligatoire est offert le soir, il y a peu d'alternatives car il est difficile, sinon impossible, de le reporter à une session ultérieure. Les travaux d'équipe se réalisent aussi souvent en soirée ou durant la fin de semaine, périodes pendant lesquelles les services de garde ne sont pas en opération.

Également, les services de garde existants ne sont offerts qu'aux enfants d'âge préscolaire. Aucune information n'a été trouvée sur les services de garde après l'école offerts en milieu universitaire pour les enfants fréquentant l'école primaire.[3] La journée d'école primaire se termine en général entre 14 heures 30 et 16 heures, ce qui signifie que les mères étudiantes ne sont pas toujours disponibles pour accueillir leurs enfants à la sortie des classes. Il en va de même pour les journées pédagogiques, pendant lesquelles les enfants d'âge scolaire ont congé alors que les mères étudiantes ont cours, ce qui peut poser des défis logistiques. Aucun service de garde d'urgence, par exemple pour assurer une présence pendant quelques heures lorsqu'un enfant est malade, le temps d'un cours ou d'un examen, n'a été répertorié dans les universités québécoises.

Les mères étudiantes canadiennes et américaines dénoncent fréquemment le coût des services de garde comme étant un frein à la poursuite des études (Bassett; Stalker et Prentice). Une enquête d'Arnaud Sales *et al.*, réalisée avant la mise sur pied des CPE, affirmait que les étudiants québécois avec enfants consacraient 10,7% de leur budget aux frais de garde (264-265). Il est possible que la portion du budget dédiée aux frais de garde ait diminué depuis ce temps grâce aux places subventionnées à sept $ dans les CPE. Le problème du coût semble donc moins urgent que celui de l'accessibilité dans le contexte québécois. Les CPE ont de longues listes d'attente et le nombre de places, particulièrement en milieu universitaire, est insuffisant pour répondre à la demande. Les haltes garderies représentent une alternative intéressante, car elles peuvent accueillir des enfants sur une base occasionnelle ou à temps partiel, mais une seule halte garderie est en opération. Quant aux services de garde s'adressant aux enfants d'âge scolaire, ils sont inexistants. Les mères étudiantes doivent donc se fier aux services offerts en milieu scolaire ou sur leur réseau social si elles ne peuvent être présentes à la maison en fin de journée et durant les journées pédagogiques.

LE SOUTIEN FINANCIER

L'Aide financière aux études (AFE), programme géré par le Ministère de l'éducation, du loisir et du sport, comporte quelques mesures à l'intention des mères étudiantes qui présentent une demande d'aide financière. Ces mesures incluent entre autres le report du remboursement des prêts lorsque l'étudiante doit interrompre ses études pour la naissance d'un enfant[4], la création du statut d'étudiante « réputée à temps plein » pour les étudiantes à temps partiel qui ont des responsabilités familiales[5], l'inclusion des frais de garde dans le calcul de l'aide accordée, la prolongation de la période d'admissibilité à des bourses de deux sessions pour les mères étudiantes et la prise en compte de la situation familiale dans l'admissibilité au programme de remboursement différé de la dette pour cause d'insuffisance de revenu (CFS, *Maintenir* 37-38). Ces mesures témoignent d'une certaine volonté de l'AFE de prendre en compte la situation particulière des mères étudiantes qui présentent une demande d'aide financière et vise à favoriser leur persévérance aux études.

Toutefois, des critiques sont adressées à l'AFE. Entre autres, les limites posées en fonction de l'âge des enfants sont perçues comme injustifiées ou arbitraires, puisque ces derniers demeurent légalement à la charge de leurs parents jusqu'à 18 ans et dans la réalité parfois au-delà de cet âge (CFS, *Maintenir* 39-41). Certains frais (dont les frais de dentiste et de lunettes) sont exclus des dépenses admissibles dans le calcul de l'aide attribuée, mais ils sont importants et incontournables (42). Les pensions alimentaires, versées pour répondre aux besoins de l'enfant, sont comptabilisées dans les revenus de la mère étudiante qui a la garde, à l'exception d'une exemption de 100 $ par mois (43). Cette pratique est dénoncée puisqu'elle accentue la précarité financière de la mère étudiante et affecte sa qualité de vie et surtout celle de son enfant (CNCS 25-26; CFS, *Étudiante* 51-52; MEMEQ 13). Finalement, les montants de dépenses admissibles sont les mêmes pour tous les étudiants, avec ou sans enfant. Alors qu'il est commun pour les étudiants sans enfant de vivre en colocation, cela se révèle plus difficile pour les mères étudiantes. Les frais partagés en colocation, dont les frais de téléphone, d'électricité et de chauffage, sont alors totalement à la charge des mères étudiantes. Elles constatent donc un écart entre les dépenses prévues par l'AFE et leurs dépenses réelles, ce qui fait en sorte que l'aide financière qui leur est accordée est insuffisante (CNCS 26-27; CFS, *Étudiante* 50).

Le Régime québécois d'assurance parentale (RQAP), en vigueur depuis janvier 2006, a été élaboré dans une optique d'inclusion de toutes les travailleuses, salariées et autonomes, et des pères, qui disposent maintenant d'un congé de paternité. Or, les mères étudiantes n'ont pas directement accès à ces nouvelles mesures. Le RQAP n'est accessible qu'aux étudiantes qui occupent un emploi, car il est nécessaire d'avoir obtenu un revenu assurable de 2 000 $ au cours de l'année précédente pour y être admissible. Certaines situations, comme l'inscription dans un programme d'études intense ou la présence de plusieurs enfants à la maison, empêchent parfois les mères étudiantes d'occuper un emploi durant l'année scolaire et d'atteindre 2 000 $ de revenu assurable, ce qui les prive des prestations du RQAP. De plus, les bourses d'excellence ne sont pas reconnues comme des revenus assurables aux fins du RQAP, ce qui implique que l'étudiante boursière doit occuper un emploi autorisé dans le cadre de sa bourse afin de pouvoir être admissible à des prestations du RQAP.

Il convient de souligner que plusieurs organismes subventionnaires prévoient désormais un congé parental rémunéré pour les boursières et boursiers, en général d'une durée d'une session (CFS, *Les études* 20-21). Bien que le congé soit court, sa rémunération permet à l'étudiante boursière qui devient mère de prendre un répit des études et de profiter de quelques semaines avec son poupon tout en disposant d'un revenu. Or, ce privilège n'est pas commun: seulement 25% des étudiants diplômés québécois bénéficient d'une bourse d'excellence (CNCS 5).

Les bourses offertes par les universités et les fonds de soutien offerts dans certains programmes de deuxième et troisième cycles, comme les bourses des organismes subventionnaires, sont généralement réservés aux étudiants inscrits à temps plein. Les mères étudiantes inscrites à temps partiel en sont donc privées. En ce qui concerne les fonds de soutien, plusieurs programmes accordent un congé de maternité, en n'incluant pas dans le calcul des sessions d'admissibilité les sessions sans inscription suite à la naissance d'un enfant. Cependant, de retour aux études, les mères étudiantes doivent poursuivre leur cheminement au même rythme que leurs collègues. Lorsque les responsabilités familiales freinent la progression, l'étudiante peut perdre un ou des montants versés par le fonds de soutien si elle ne complète pas les étapes du programme dans les délais prescrits, ce qui affecte particulièrement les mères étudiantes disposant de maigres revenus.

Une initiative de l'Université de Montréal mérite toutefois d'être soulignée: le Rectorat et la Faculté des études supérieures offrent, depuis 1998, une bourse de 3 000 $ à chaque doctorante qui donne naissance à un enfant, de façon à permettre un congé de maternité d'une session (Gariépy *et al.* 35). Cette mesure, unique au Québec selon nos informations, témoigne d'une réelle prise en considération des réalités vécues par ces étudiantes et constitue certes un atout pour les mères qui y ont accès.

En dépit des récents efforts du gouvernement québécois pour mettre en place des mesures facilitant la conciliation travail-famille, il demeure plusieurs lacunes dans les programmes de soutien financier touchant les mères étudiantes. Bien que quelques mesures visent à reconnaître la situation des mères étudiantes, elles sont oubliées par le RQAP qui s'adresse seulement aux travailleuses et leur situation particulière n'est pas toujours bien prise en compte par l'AFE, ce qui peut expliquer la précarité financière et le sentiment d'invisibilité dénoncés par plusieurs mères étudiantes (CSF, *Étudiante*, *Maintenir*; MEMEQ). Celles qui ne sont pas récipiendaires d'une bourse et dont l'entourage ne peut les appuyer financièrement durant leurs études se retrouvent donc devant deux avenues: l'endettement, par l'entremise de l'AFE et des prêts personnels, ou l'occupation d'un emploi, qui accentue la pression sur les horaires déjà chargés des mères étudiantes.

LES INITIATIVES INSTITUTIONNELLES POUR LES MÈRES ÉTUDIANTES

Le Conseil du statut de la femme note que chaque université québécoise devrait adopter une politique déterminant les règles relatives aux congés parentaux pour tous ses étudiants (*Les études* 21). Seule l'Université de Sherbrooke a déjà inséré un congé parental dans son Règlement des études, en donnant droit à une interruption des études allant jusqu'à 24 mois aux étudiants parents (Gariépy 36). Dans les autres universités, certaines politiques départementales existent, mais la règle demeure la négociation au cas par cas auprès des directions de département et des professeurs, ce qui n'assure pas un traitement équitable, entre les programmes d'études et dans le temps, de toutes les mères étudiantes.

Dans un avis portant sur les mères étudiantes, le Conseil du statut de la femme a répertorié certaines pratiques mises en place par les établissements québécois d'enseignement secondaire et postsecondaire. Une seule université figure dans la liste: l'Université du Québec à Chicoutimi, qui maintient un contact téléphonique avec ses étudiantes qui interrompent leurs études pour la naissance d'un enfant et offre son aide dans la recherche d'une place en garderie. Cet établissement dispose également d'un salon d'allaitement (*Étudiante et mère* 105).

Deux autres universités disposent d'un salon d'allaitement. Depuis septembre 2006, l'Université Laval offre aux nouvelles mères un espace où elles peuvent se retirer pour nourrir leur poupon, résultat d'un projet du Bureau d'entraide en nutrition. En avril 2007, l'Université du Québec en Outaouais s'est aussi dotée d'un salon d'allaitement, cette fois grâce au travail de deux étudiantes en sciences infirmières (« Les étudiantes »).

Peu d'universités québécoises disposent de résidences pouvant accueillir des familles. Le logement est un poste de dépense important, particulièrement pour les mères étudiantes disposant d'un maigre budget qui ne peuvent toujours se permettre d'avoir un appartement près de l'université, où les prix des loyers sont plus élevés. Dans cette situation, elles doivent demeurer en banlieue où les prix des loyers sont plus bas, ce qui implique cependant des frais de transport. Les résidences étudiantes pour des familles seraient donc une alternative de choix pour les mères étudiantes. Plusieurs étudiantes américaines et canadiennes ont témoigné de l'impact positif de leur passage dans des résidences universitaires familiales: elles y ont trouvé des consoeurs avec qui partager la garde des enfants, une façon de faciliter la logistique des travaux d'équipe, un réseau de soutien lors de situations imprévues et un environnement convivial pour elles et leurs enfants (Bassett; Stalker et Prentice). L'offre de résidences étudiantes pouvant accueillir des familles est primordiale, considérant les lacunes actuelles et les bénéfices qui découlent de ce service pour les mères étudiantes et leur famille.

Les contacts avec d'autres étudiantes qui vivent la même réalité sont importants aux yeux de plusieurs mères étudiantes. Quelques universités ont un regroupement d'étudiants parents, dont l'Association cigogne à l'Université de Montréal (Gariépy *et al.* 35) et l'Association des parents étudiant ou travaillant à l'Université Laval (APETUL)[6], né de la volonté des mères étudiantes de se réunir afin d'offrir un lieu de rencontre et de partage des expériences et des informations, ainsi que d'assurer la visibilité et la représentation des étudiants parents sur le campus et auprès des instances universitaires. Par exemple, l'APETUL a mis sur pied un bazar où les parents étudiants peuvent se procurer des articles pour enfant à prix réduit et se départir des jouets et vêtements qui ne sont plus utilisés par leurs enfants, ainsi qu'un site Internet où il est possible d'afficher des petites annonces contenant conseils, objets recherchés ou à vendre, activités familiales gratuites, etc. Ces groupes peuvent entretenir des liens plus ou moins étroits avec des associations étudiantes—par exemple pour obtenir du financement—et peuvent même établir des partenariats avec des organismes communautaires sans lien avec l'université. Ils constituent une forme de soutien institutionnel, même si l'institution n'en est pas l'instigatrice.

QUE CONCLURE?

À la lumière de ces informations, il apparaît que les universités et le gouvernement québécois ont pris conscience qu'une fraction des étudiantes sont aussi mères puisque certaines mesures ont été mises en place pour faciliter la conciliation études-famille. Cependant, des lacunes importantes persistent. Les CPE peuvent se révéler particulièrement précieux pour les mères étudiantes, mais le nombre de place en milieu universitaire est insuffisant. Des services de garde flexibles, pour répondre aux besoins à temps partiel ou occasionnels, sont aussi nécessaires pour permettre à toutes les mères étudiantes de poursuivre leurs études. Peu de programmes de soutien financier sont offerts aux mères étudiantes à temps partiel et certaines dispositions de l'AFE pourraient être modifiées de façon à mieux prendre en compte la situation des mères étudiantes. La précarité financière a un impact sur la qualité de vie des mères étudiantes et de leur famille et peut mener à l'endettement et à l'abandon des études. Quant aux initiatives institutionnelles, elles demeurent restreintes pour l'instant.

Malgré ce constat peu réjouissant, il convient de tenter de situer ces conclusions dans le contexte canadien. Le Québec dispose d'un vaste réseau de CPE dont le coût des places est très abordable par rapport aux services présents dans les autres provinces canadiennes. L'enquête *Le prix du savoir 2004* de la Fondation canadienne des bourses du millénaire nous permet de dresser quelques comparaisons. Les droits de scolarité applicables au Québec sont les plus bas au Canada (119). Les coûts reliés à la location d'un appartement et à l'achat de nourriture y sont relativement bas en comparaison avec le reste du Canada (139, 149). Il semble également que l'aide financière prévue par l'AFE pour les étudiantes et les étudiants universitaires qui ont des personnes à charge est plus généreuse que celle prévue dans les autres programmes canadiens (209). Il serait donc possible de penser que les mères québécoises disposent de certains avantages économiques dans leur expérience de la conciliation études-famille par rapport à leurs consoeurs canadiennes.

En ce qui a trait aux mesures institutionnelles, bien qu'aucune recherche visant à présenter l'état de la situation des mesures offertes par les universités canadiennes n'ait été répertoriée[7], il semble, selon des témoignages de mères étudiantes (Stalker et Prentice), que certaines mesures s'adressant aux ménages étudiants, comme les résidences étudiantes pour les familles, les bourses d'études pour parents ou les congés de maternité, seraient plus développées dans les autres provinces canadiennes qu'au Québec.

La période des études ne se limitant plus au passage précédant l'insertion professionnelle mais survenant désormais tout au long de la vie, la proportion de mères étudiantes universitaires est appelée à se maintenir, sinon à augmenter, ce qui devrait inciter les universités et les gouvernements, au Québec comme dans le reste du Canada, à s'intéresser aux conditions de vie des mères étudiantes et à revoir leurs politiques, leurs programmes et leurs services, de façon à s'adapter aux besoins et aux contraintes de ce segment de la population étudiante.

[1]Parmi les études présentant des données sur les parents étudiants québécois, notons AELIES, *Analyse socio-économique* 19-21; Fondation canadienne des bourses du millénaire, *Faire place* 51-53; Gariépy *et al.*; Pageau et Bujold 25; et Sales *et al.* 142.
[2]Parmi ces mémoires et avis, notons ceux produits par le Conseil national des cycles supérieurs, le Conseil du statut de la femme (CSF), la Fédération étudiante universitaire du Québec (FEUQ) et le regroupement Mères et ménages étudiants du Québec (MEMEQ).
[3]Il convient toutefois de rappeler que les écoles primaires peuvent organiser des services de garde après les classes.
[4]Le Ministère de l'Éducation, du loisir et du sport assume alors les frais d'intérêt encourus sur la dette, pour une période maximale de trois trimestres, qui peut débuter au trimestre où l'étudiante atteint 20 semaines de grossesse.
[5]Le statut d'étudiante « réputée à temps plein » signifie que l'étudiante qui est inscrite à la moitié d'une charge à temps plein peut, en raison de ses responsabilités familiales, bénéficier du programme d'aide financière, habituellement réservé aux étudiants à temps plein (CSF, *Maintenir* 37).
[6]Le site web de l'APETUL procure davantage d'information sur les activités de cette association. 3 avril 2007 <http://www.apetul.asso.ulaval.ca/accueil.html>.
[7]Le Georgian College Institute of Applied Research and Innovation a publié une étude dans laquelle il présentait une vue d'ensemble des catégories de mesures s'adressant aux étudiants avec personnes à charge recensées dans un échantillon d'établissements d'éducation postsecondaire canadiens et américains. Bien que cette étude ne constitue pas un état de la situation précis, elle présente un éventail de mesures déjà élaborées qui peuvent aider les parents étudiants à concilier famille et études.

OUVRAGES CITÉS

Association des étudiants de Laval inscrits aux études supérieures (AELIES). *Plateforme des revendications électorales de l'AELIES: Comité d'élection du recteur*. Québec: Université Laval, 2007. <http://www.aelies.ulaval.ca/documents/pforme2007.pdf>. 16 août 2007.

Association des étudiants de Laval inscrits aux études supérieures (AE-

LIES). *Analyse socio-économique sur les membres de l'AELIES*. Québec: Université Laval, 2006.

Association des parents étudiant ou travaillant à l'Université Laval (APETUL). Québec: Université Laval, 2007. <http://www.apetul.asso.ulaval.ca>. 3 avril 2007.

Bassett, Rachel Hile, sous la dir. *Parenting and Professing: Balancing Family Work with an Academic Career*. Nashville: Vanderbuilt University Press, 2005.

Conseil national des cycles supérieurs. *Conciliation des études et de la famille: une lourde tâche pour les étudiants-parents*. Montréal: CNCS-FEUQ, 2002.

Conseil du statut de la femme (CSF). *Étudiante et mère: un double défi. Les conditions de vie et les besoins des mères étudiantes*. Québec: CSF, 2004.

Conseil du statut de la femme (CSF). *Les études, l'enseignement et la recherche universitaires: enjeux émergents pour les femmes. Mémoire à la Commission parlementaire sur la qualité, l'accessibilité et le financement des universités*. Québec: CSF, 2004.

Conseil du statut de la femme (CSF). *Maintenir le soutien financier aux études et s'adapter aux nouvelles réalités*. Québec: CSF, 2004.

Fédération étudiante universitaire du Québec (FEUQ). *Améliorer les conditions de vie des étudiantes mères: les ressorts d'une plus grande égalité entre les sexes. Mémoire déposé dans le cadre des audiences publiques de la Commission des affaires sociales de l'Assemblée nationale du Québec*. Montréal: FEUQ, 2005.

Fondation canadienne des bourses du millénaire. *Faire place aux différences: l'éducation postsecondaire parmi les Autochtones, les personnes handicapées et les personnes ayant des enfants*. Montréal: Fondation canadienne des bourses du millénaire, 2005.

Fondation canadienne des bourses du millénaire. *Le prix du savoir 2004. L'accès à l'éducation et la situation financière des étudiants au Canada*. Montréal: Fondation canadienne des bourses du millénaire, 2004.

Force Jeunesse. *Situation dans les Centres de la Petite Enfance des Universités du Québec*. Montréal: Force Jeunesse, mars 2002. <http://www.forcejeunesse.qc.ca/PDF/tableau%20CPE%20universitaires%20final.doc>. 9 février 2007.

Gariépy, Geneviève *et al*. *Connaître les parents-étudiants de l'UQAM. Réalités, besoins et ressources. Première partie*. Montréal: Institut de recherches et d'études féministes, Services à la vie étudiante de l'UQAM, février 2007. <http://sve.uqam.ca.etudes-familleéRapports-parents-etudiants-premiere-partie.pdf>. 15 octobre 2007.

Georgian College Institute of Applied Research and Innovation. *Étudiants avec personnes à charge: pratiques courantes dans les établissements d'enseignement postsecondaire du Canada et des Etats-Unis*. Montréal:

Fondation canadienne des bourses du millénaire, 2005.

Laverdière, Simon. « Pas un sou de plus pour la CADEUL». *Impact Campus* 4 décembre 2007. <http://www.impactcampus.qc.ca/actualites/20071204/003412.html>. 2 février 2008.

«Les étudiantes de l'UQO auront leur salle d'allaitement ». *Le Droit* 3 avril 3007. <http://www.cyberpresse.ca.article/20070403/CPACACTUALITES/704030335/1028>. 4 avril 2007.

Mères et ménages étudiants du Québec (MEMEQ). *Revendications sur la situation des mères étudiantes et des ménages étudiants du Québec. Document préliminaire*. 2004. <www.antipatriarcat.org/memeq.pdf>. 9 août 2007.

Pageau, Danielle et Johanne Bujold. *Dis-moi ce que tu veux et je te dirai jusqu'où tu iras. Les caractéristiques des étudiantes et des étudiants à la rescousse de la compréhension de la persévérance aux études*. Québec: Université du Québec, Direction du recensement étudiant et de la recherche institutionnelle, 2000.

«Régime québécois d'assurance parentale ». *Emploi et solidarité sociale Québec* 2007. Gouvernement du Québec. <http://www.rqap.gouv.qc.ca>. 4 avril 2007.

Sales, Arnaud *et al. Le monde étudiant à la fin du XXe siècle. Rapport final sur les conditions de vie des étudiants universitaires dans les années quatre-vingt-dix*. Québec: Ministère de l'éducation; Montréal: Département de sociologie, Université de Montréal, 1996.

Stalker, Jacqueline et Susan Prentice, ed. *The Illusion of Inclusion: Women in Post-Secondary Education*. Halifax: Fernwood, 1998.

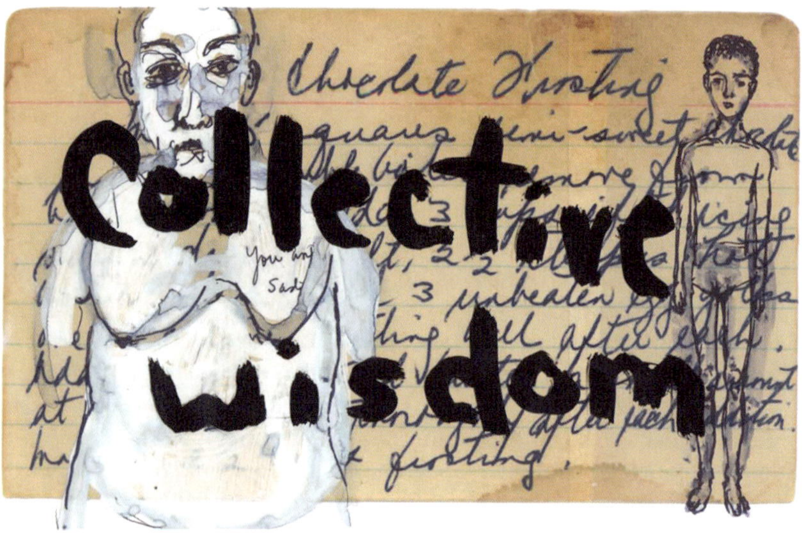

Leesa Streifler, *Collective Wisdom* (from *Her Domain: A Recipe Card Project*), 2006, chromogenic print, 68.58 x 96.52 cm.

This piece reflects on the collective wisdom and experience that informs and supports mothering practice. It acknowledges the bond between mothers as we support and nurture each other on our individual, yet connected paths as mothers.

The Division of Childcare Tasks in the First Year

Pre-natal Intentions and Post-natal Reality

LYNN LOUTZENHISER, PHILLIP R. SEVIGNY, AND MAUREEN THOMPSON

HISTORICALLY, WOMEN HAVE been expected to take primary responsibility for meeting the needs of family members, in general, and children, in particular. There is reason to believe, however, that in recent decades there has been increased support for egalitarian models of parenting where parenting responsibilities are equally shared between women and men (Cabrera, Tamis-Lemonda, Bradley, Hofferth, and Lamb; Gaetner, Spinrad, Eisenberg, and Greving; Julian; Milkie, Bianchi, Mattingly, and Robinson). For example, in a large-scale telephone survey, Melissa Milkie *et al.* found that two-thirds of parents support the view that caring for children should be shared equally between mothers and fathers. This may reflect a general decrease in the rigidity of gender roles, as reflected in women's increased participation in the paid labour force, as well as evidence that increased father involvement in parenting contributes to desirable child outcomes (Bryant; Gaunt; Sanchez and Thomson). However, despite the apparent support for a more equal distribution of childcare duties, research demonstrates that women perform the bulk of child related duties in the family, regardless of their paid employment status (Flouri; Pleck; Pleck and Masciadrelli). Thus, the actual division of labour in contemporary families continues to reflect more traditional, rather than egalitarian, gender roles (Sanchez and Thomson).

Researchers attempting to explain the discrepancy between favourable attitudes towards egalitarian parenting and actual parenting behaviours have focused on societal and economic barriers toward equality, as well as gender ideology (Deutsch; Ishii-Kuntz and Coltrane; Renk *et al.*). The assumption underlying this discussion is that even if women (and men) go into parenting intending to have a relatively egalitarian split in the division of childcare duties, this does not occur due to societal factors and gender ideologies. However, researchers' conceptualizations of this subject may distort or obscure the findings. More specifically, researchers may have failed to take into account a discrepancy between attitudes and behaviours. The social psychological Theory of Planned Behaviour (TPB) (Ajzen), an extension of the Theory of Reasoned Action (TRA) (Fishbein and Ajzen), argues that it is behavioural intentions, and not attitudes, that are the most immediate determinants of behaviour. In studies of the division of childcare duties, few researchers have directly asked parents about their intentions regarding the division of childcare duties within their own families. Instead, researchers have focused on the relationship between parents' attitudes in general toward "ideal" or egalitarian parenting models and their subsequent parenting behaviours (Fish, New, and Van Cleave). Thus, the finding that attitudes and behaviours toward the division of childcare duties are inconsistent may, in part, reflect limitations in data collection since parents are not usually asked about their intentions to share childcare duties in their own families.

It is possible that while individuals may hold favourable attitudes toward egalitarian parenting models, they may also intend to divide the duties in a manner inconsistent with this attitude within their own families. From the TPB perspective, in order to develop a comprehensive understanding of the division of childcare duties in Canadian families, researchers need to assess parents' intentions to share childcare duties and then examine whether these intentions are related to their subsequent behaviours. In this research, we further our understanding of the division of childcare duties between mothers and fathers by asking first-time, expectant parents to report on their intentions regarding this division of labour, and then comparing these intentions to their actual division of labour during their infants' first year of life. We also examine the division of childcare duties in families with toddlers, to develop a better understanding of changes in the division of these duties as children age. In this article, we explore the following questions:

1) Do first-time Canadian expectant parents intend to equally share childcare responsibilities once their babies are born?
2) What is the relationship between prenatal intentions regarding the division of childcare responsibilities and actual division of childcare responsibilities at three-months and twelve-months post-partum?
3) Does the division of childcare responsibilities significantly change from infancy to the toddler period?

METHOD

Participants and Procedures

This paper draws on data from two separate studies of mothers and fathers with young children. Participants in Study 1 were couples enrolled in a longitudinal study examining the transition to parenthood, who participated in three data collection periods (Phase 1, third trimester of pregnancy, Phase 2, three-months post-partum, Phase 3, twelve-months post-partum). In this study, the average age for mothers was 28.7 years (range 18 to 40 years) and for fathers was 30.8 (range 19 to 57 years). These couples were well educated (79.2% had some post-secondary education), with the majority reporting a combined family income of over $69,000. In terms of employment, all of the mothers were home full-time with their infants and receiving maternity benefits at three-months post-partum. At the one-year mark (the end of paid benefits), the majority of mothers (69.2%) were employed outside of the home, working an average of 33.4 hours a week. For fathers, most of them were employed in full-time employment at three-months post-partum, and all were employed in full-time employment when their infants were one-year of age, working an average of 40.6 hours a week. In Study 2, participants were parents of first-born toddlers (average age 27.4 months; range 18 to 35 months). The average age for mothers was 33.1 years (range 23 to 43 years) and fathers was 34.1 years (range 28 to 47 years). These participants were also well educated (89% had some post-secondary education), and had moderate to high levels of family income (78.8% with a total family income of over $60,000). In addition, almost all of the fathers (93.5%) were employed in full-time paid work, working an average of 41.9 hours per week. By comparison, 77% of the mothers were employed in paid work, working an average of 32.8 hours per week.

For each of the three phases in Study 1 (prenatal, three-month, and one year), as well as for Study 2, couples participated in interviews during which they were administered a modified version of the "Who Does What?" questionnaire to assess responsibility for childcare duties (Cowan and Cowan).

MEASURES

Responsibility for childcare

Responsibility for childcare duties was assessed using a modified version of the "Who Does What" questionnaire (Cowan and Cowan). During the prenatal interview, couples were asked how they intended to divide responsibilities for ten childcare duties that reflect various aspects of caring (e.g., "bathing," "dressing," and "going on outings") when the baby was born. During the post-natal interviews for Phase 2 and 3, two additional items, "play with the infant," and "buy clothes and toys for the infant" were added to the ten items asked in the prenatal period, bringing the total number of childcare duties assessed to 12. In Study 2, two additional items were added: "staying home when the child is sick," and "plans activities." Couples were asked to report on who was actually completing these duties, and their responses were coded on a five-point Likert Scale, with 1 = "always mom" (mothers performing the task 90-100% of the time), 2 = "mostly mom" (mothers performing the task 61-89% of the time), 3 = "about equal" (mothers performing the task 40-60% of the time), 4 = "mostly dad" (mothers performing the task 11-39% of the time), and 5 = "always dad" (mothers performing the task 0-10% of the time). In Study 2, mothers and fathers completed this questionnaire separately, so their scores were averaged together on each of the 14 items. For each of the time periods, responses were summed and then divided by the total number of responses to create an average childcare responsibility score. Lower scores on this measure indicate greater maternal responsibility for childcare duties, while higher scores indicate greater paternal responsibility for childcare duties.

RESULTS

Do first-time expectant parents anticipate childcare duties to be equally shared between them once their babies are born?

Table 1 presents the means and standard deviations for each of the childcare duties, as well as the total childcare responsibility scores for each of the time periods. In terms of prenatal expectations, "bathing the baby" was the only childcare task that, on average, expectant parents anticipate would be shared ($M = 3.09$). In terms of responsibility for the entire range of childcare duties, expectant couples viewed these duties as primarily the responsibility of the mother ($M = 2.15$, $SD = .31$).

What is the relationship between prenatal expectations of division of childcare duties and postnatal division of childcare duties at three-months and twelve-months post-partum?

To explore the relationships between couples' prenatal expectations of the division of childcare duties and the actual postnatal division of childcare duties, a repeated measure Analysis of Variance (ANOVA) was conducted on the longitudinal data from Study 1. The results indicated a statistically significant difference across the three time periods (F (2, 128) = 9.32, $p < .001$), with couples during the prenatal period expecting childcare duties to be more shared than they actually were when their infants were three months of age ($p < .01$). By the time infants were one year old, childcare duties were more shared than they had been when the infants were three-months old ($p < .001$) and did not statistically differ from their prenatal expectations. However, at each of these time periods childcare duties were reported to be primarily the responsibility of the mother.

Table 1: *Descriptive data for the study variables*

Item	[a]Time 1 prenatal Mean (S. D.) Range	[a]Time 2 3 months Mean (S. D.) Range	[a]Time 3 12 months Mean (S. D.) Range	[b]Time 4 18—35 months Mean (S. D.) Range
Dressing	2.12 (.79) 1.0 - 3.0	1.76 (.78) 1.0 - 3.0	2.32 (.92) 1.0 - 4.0	2.39 (.83) 1.0 - 4.5
Feeding	1.23 (.51) 1.0 - 3.0	1.47 (.77) 1.0 - 3.0	2.46 (.75) 1.0 - 4.0	2.53 (.75) 1.0 -4.0
Diapering/ Toileting	2.53 (.62) 1.0 - 3.0	2.26 (.71) 1.0 - 3.0	2.55 (.61) 1.0 - 4.0	2.75 (.42) 2.0 - 4.0
Bathing	3.09 (.76) 1.0 - 5.0	2.10 (1.12) 1.0 - 5.0	2.55 (1.17) 1.0 - 5.0	2.73 (1.04) 1.0—5.0
Put to bed	2.71 (.76) 1.0 - 5.0	1.97 (1.07) 1.0 - 5.0	2.51 (1.20) 1.0 - 5.0	3.05 (.87) 1.0 - 5.0
Attend to at night	1.99 (.88) 1.0 - 5.0	1.57 (.95) 1.0 - 5.0	2.05 (1.12) 1.0 - 5.0	2.89 (.89) 1.0 - 5.0
Take on outings	2.81 (.43) 1.0 - 3.0	2.50 (.71) 1.0 - 3.0	2.49 (.77) 1.0 - 5.0	2.72 (.47) 1.5 - 3.5
Play	--	2.68 (.55) 1.0 - 4.0	2.86 (.43) 2.0 - 4.0	3.06 (.40) 2.0 - 4.0

Stay home when child is sick	--	--	--	2.29 (.86) 1.0 - 4.0
Arrange appointments	1.36 (.76) 1.0 - 5.0	1.28 (.89) 1.0 - 5.0	1.22 (.62) 1.0 - 4.0	1.59 (.78) 1.0 - 4.0
Organize feedings/ diaper bag/ outings	1.67 (.89) 1.0 - 4.0	1.53 (.71) 1.0 - 3.0	1.48 (.82) 1.0 - 4.0	2.17 (.54) 1.0 - 3.0
Buys clothes or toys	--	2.14 (1.12) 1.0 - 5.0	2.02 (.99) 1.0 - 5.0	2.26 (.70) 1.0 - 4.0
Plans Activities	--	--	--	2.32 (.60) 1.0 - 3.5
Total Childcare Duties	2.15 (.31) 1.2 - 2.8	1.94 (.38) 1.1 - 2.8	2.20 (.38) 1.25 - 3.25	2.52 (.31) 1.79 - 3.35

Note: 1 = "always mom"; 2 = "mostly mom"; 3 = "about equal"; 4 = "mostly dad"; and 5 = "always dad"
[a]Study 1; [b]Study 2

Do childcare duties become more shared as the infant gets older?

To examine whether childcare duties become more shared as infants get older, data from Time 3 in Study 1 (when infants were twelve-month olds) was compared to the data from Study 2 (toddlers ages 18-35 months). Using an independent sample t-test, comparing the Time 3 means from Study 1 with the means from Study 2, a statistically significant difference was found (t (116) = -4.91, p <.001). These results demonstrate a trend toward a more equally shared distribution of child care duties during the toddler years. However, as noted above, the overall mean is below 3.0, indicating that childcare duties are still primarily the responsibility of the mother.

DISCUSSION

This research adds to our understanding of the division of childcare duties of Canadian parents of young children through an exploration of mothers' and fathers' prenatal intentions regarding the division of childcare duties in their own families, and the actual division of childcare duties during the first few years of parenting. In terms of prenatal intentions regarding the division of childcare duties, our findings indicate that Canadian parents expect mothers of infants to be disproportionately responsible for childcare duties. In fact, only one of ten surveyed duties, "bathing the baby," was viewed by expectant parents as a task that would be equally shared between mothers and fathers. Thus, despite the dominant cultural rhetoric regarding shared parenting duties (Daly; LaRossa), the families in this study did not intend infant care giving to be a shared responsibility within their own families. This finding highlights the importance of focusing research questions regarding support for egalitarian parenting models on parents' intentions for their own families, as opposed to families in general. More importantly, it raises the question of why contemporary Canadian families intend for mothers to shoulder the majority of childcare duties for infants.

One explanation for these intentions may be found, ironically, in Canadian policies regarding parental leave. The federal government's Parental Benefits Program (PBP) currently provides up to 35 weeks of parental leave for employed parents that may be shared by either mothers or fathers. This is in addition to 15 weeks of maternity benefits, which can be claimed by birth mothers. One of the objectives of this program is to increase the proportion of fathers who take parental leave and thus increase the sharing of benefits between spouses (HRSDC). However, the most recent available data indicate that for families outside of Quebec (which has unique guidelines for parental leave), the percentage of fathers participating in this program has remained virtually unchanged from 2003 to 2006, at approximately ten percent (Marshall). Those theorists who have focused on societal and economic explanations of gender inequality in parenting might explain this fact by claiming that men tend to have greater earning power and thus families seeking to maximize income while actively parenting are encouraged to have mothers take the leave. Other explanations are available, however. In particular, this decision may reflect the intention of couples to have mothers do the majority of child care. This, in turn, may reflect parents' views about mothers' unique role in terms of breastfeeding, or a sense of which parent is more inclined toward the types of tasks involved in parenting an infant. Thus, it may be that, as it is currently structured, the federal PBP continues to be more conducive to mothers shouldering the majority of childcare duties. While parents may intend for there to be a shift in childcare duties once the mother returns to the workforce, prior research, as well as the findings from our toddler study, suggest that this happens in a very limited way. Thus, although Evans may be right that "parental leave programmes ... shape, as well as reflect, gendered responsibilities for paid and unpaid work" (120), the federal PBP may be falling far short of its stated aim of promoting equal sharing of parenting responsibilities, and, in fact, may be entrenching a division of labour along gender lines.

Another explanation for the intentions of Canadian parents to have mothers primarily responsible for the childcare of infants reflects the nature of the childcare duties during infancy. Caring for infants primarily involves physical care tasks, such as feeding and dressing. Given the biological fact that only mothers can breastfeed, and the fact that many Canadian agencies promote breastfeeding as the best food source for infants, it makes sense that many mothers are responsible for infant feedings. Previous research has shown that mothers tend to spend their childcare time doing physical care tasks, while fathers spend the majority of their childcare time doing physically active tasks such as playing and engaging in recreational activities (Craig). Since children require less physical care as they get older, there may be a subsequent shift in the allocation of childcare duties. In support of this explanation, in this research, we found that the task of "playing with children" was reported to be a shared parenting task by the time children reached toddlerhood.

Our findings indicate that by the time infants were one year of age, the division of childcare duties became significantly more shared than at the three-month time period. This trend toward equally shared parenting then continued during the toddler years with fathers significantly more involved in the care of their children during this time then at the one-year period. These findings are consistent with research demonstrating that fathers tend to be more involved with their children as they get older (Pleck and Masciadrelli). It is possible, though, that the families in this study intended mothers to be the primary caregivers during infancy but also intended to share parenting duties more equally if the mothers returned to the paid work force. In that context, it is interesting that our findings indicate that mothers continued to perform the majority of childcare duties when their children were of toddler age, despite the fact that the majority of them were engaged in paid work outside of the home (Daly; Pleck and Masciadrelli).

Francine Deutsch notes that equally shared parenting does not occur accidentally, but rather is characterized by several discrete choices that parents make while their children are young. Choices, such as which parent will take parental leave, may influence future decisions regarding which parent will be primarily responsible for the care of children. And as long as couples choose for mothers to take PBP leave, the program may actually reinforce an unequal distribution of parenting responsibilities that may carry over into later years as well.

In sum, given that the roles mothers and fathers play within the family have changed considerably in the last 60 years (Haddock, Zimmerman, and Lyness), the lack of intent for and actual shared parenting found in this study was surprising. This serves to underline that while the cultural discourse surrounding family life has evolved (Daly), the actual behaviours of parents in general, and fathers in particular, has not kept pace with this shift in ideology. Ralph LaRossa was among the first to identify this disconnect between the culture and the conduct of fathering. He suggests that the culture versus conduct split will be minimized among well-educated, upper middle class families. However, as the sample of parents surveyed in this study could be described in those same terms, the fact that the mothers continue to perform the majority of childcare duties is thus all the more remarkable. Both cultural and individual beliefs about gender remain powerful organizers of our daily lives and influence how families organize their lives (Haddock *et al.*). Having a better understanding of how cultural messages influence individual gender ideologies in new parents may shed more light on the process by which couples divide childcare and other domestic work. Also, future investigations could examine a broader array of work done in the private sphere thus incorporating and moving beyond care giving duties. Perhaps such an exploration would provide evidence of a more equal allocation of domestic duties overall.

WORKS CITED

Ajzen, Icek. "The Theory of Planned Behavior." *Organizational Behavior and Human Decision Processes* 50.2 (1991): 179-211.

Bryant, Alyssa N. "Changes in Attitudes toward Women's Roles: Predicting Gender-Role Traditionalism among College Students." *Sex Roles* 48.3-4 (2003): 131-42.

Cabrera, Natasha J., Catherine S. Tamis-Lemonda, Robert H. Bradley, Sandra Hofferth, and Michael E. Lamb. "Fatherhood in the Twenty-first Century." *Child Development* 71.1 (2000): 127-36.

Cowan, Carolyn P., and Philip A. Cowan. *When Partners become Parents: The Big Life Change for Couples*. New York: Basic, 1992. Republished by Lawrence Erlbaum Associates, Fall, 1999.

Craig, Lyn. "Does Father Care Mean Fathers Share? A Comparison of How Mothers and Fathers in Intact Families Spend Time with Children." *Gender and Society* 20.2 (2006): 259-81.

Daly, Kerry. *The Changing Culture of Parenting: Contemporary Family Trends*. Ottawa: The Vanier Institute of the Family, 2004.

Deutsch, Francine M. "Equally Shared Parenting." *Current Directions in Psychological Science* 10.1 (2001): 25-28.

Evans, Patricia. M. "Comparative Perspectives on Changes to Canada's Paid Parental Leave: Implications for Class and Gender." *International Journal of Social Welfare* 16.2 (2007): 119-28.

Fish, Linda S., Rebecca. S. New, and Nancy J. Van Cleave. "Shared Parenting in Dual-income Families." *American Journal of Orthopsychiatry* 62.1 (1992): 83-92.

Fishbein, Martin and Icek Ajzen. *Belief, Attitude, Intention and Behaviour: An Introduction to Theory and Research*. Reading, M.A.: Addison-Welsey, 1975.

Flouri, Eirini. *Fathering and Child Outcomes*. West Sussex: Wiley, 2005.

Gaetner, Bridget M., Tracy L. Spinrad, Nancy Eisenberg, and Karissa A. Greving. "Parental Childrearing Attitudes as Correlates of Father Involvement During Infancy." *Journal of Marriage and Family* 69.4 (2007): 962-76.

Gaunt, Ruth. "Biological Essentialism, Gender Ideologies, and Role Attitudes: What Determines Parents' Involvement in Child Care?" *Sex Roles* 55.7-8 (2006): 523-33.

Haddock, Shelley A., Toni S. Zimmerman, and Kevin P. Lyness. "Changing Gender Norms: Transitional Dilemmas." *Normal Family Processes* (3rd ed.). Ed. Froma Walsh. New York: Guilford, 2003. 301-36.

Human Resources and Social Development Canada. *Summative Evaluation of EI Parental Benefits*. (HRSDC Catalogue No. HS28-25/2005E.) 2005. 4 Aug 2008. <http://www1.servicecanada.gc.ga>.

Ishii-Kuntz, Masako and Scott Coltrane. "Predicting the Sharing of Household Labor: Are Parenting and Housework Distinct?" *Sociological Perspectives* 35.4 (1992): 629-47.

Julian, R. *Fathering in the New Millennium*. Wellington, NZ: Office of the Commissioner for Children, 1999.

LaRossa, Ralph. "Fatherhood and Social Change." *Family Relations* 37.4 (1988): 451– 57.

Marshall, Katherine "Fathers' Use of Paid Parental Leave." Perspectives on Labour and Income 9.6 (2008). (Statistics Canada Catalogue No. 75-001-XIE.) 25 Jul 2008.<http://www.statcan.ca/emg;osj/freepub>.

Milkie, Melissa, Suzanne Bianchi, Marybeth Mattingly, and John P. Robinson. "Gendered Division of Childrearing: Ideals, Realities, and the Relationship to Parental Well-Being." *Sex Roles* 47.1-2 (2002): 21-38.

Pleck, Joseph. H. "Paternal Involvement: Levels, Sources and Consequences." *The Role of the Father in Child Development* (3rd ed.). Ed. M. Lamb. New York: Wiley, 1997. 66-102.

Pleck, Joeseph. H., and Brian P. Masciadrelli "Paternal Involvement by U.S. Residential Fathers: Levels, Sources and Consequences." *The Role of the Father in Child Development* (4th ed.). Ed. M. Lamb. New York: Wiley, 2004. 222-71.

Renk, Kimberly, Rex Roberts, Angela Roddenberry, Mary Luick, Sarah Hillhouse, Cricket Meehan, Arazais Oliveros, and Vicky Phares. "Mothers, Fathers, Gender Role and Time Parents Spend with Their Children." *Sex Roles* 48.7-8 (2003): 305–15.

Sanchez, Laura and Elizabeth Thomson "Becoming Mothers and Fathers: Parenthood, Gender and the Division of Labor." *Gender and Society* 11.6 (1997): 747-72.

Birth, Bureaucracy, and Life Thereafter

Recognizing Queer Mothers and Families in British Columbia

MICHELLE WALKS

> Nevertheless, it appears that part of what it means to *be* a mother is to be recognized as a mother.
>
> —Fiona Nelson, *Lesbian Motherhood* (100)

FOR MANY YEARS, governments in the western world have understood kinship in very strict terms, posing a problem for families with only one parent or more than two parents, families with multi-racial parents and/or children, foster families, and queer-parented families (Cannell; Luce; Modell; Moraga; Owen; Toevs and Brill; Wozniak). In recent years, policies have started to change, showing an increasing acceptance and recognition of diverse family formations. In British Columbia, groundbreaking legal changes have increasingly demonstrated the government's acceptance of and respect for queer folks and their families. The unique political and social climate of British Columbia, in regards to queer-parented families, lays the foundation of my study of queer couples' birthing experiences. This presents an opportunity to explore some of the diverse choices and experiences that queer couples have in British Columbia, a place not only with a variety of legal options surrounding birth (including midwifery) available, but also home to some of the most queer - (family) -friendly laws and policies in the world. This paper explores the various experiences of interviewed queer-identified couples regarding birth certificates (with the B.C. Vital Statistics Agency) and/or parental leave (with Human Resources and Skills Development Canada [HRSD]; formerly HRDC), the federal agency responsible for parental leave).

Queer parents in British Columbia are relatively fortunate because the province is at the forefront of queer-family-friendly policy changes. (In other provinces and in the territories, for example, two women still cannot be named on a birth certificate as birth parents, and government bureaucracies have a hard time dealing with non-traditional families.) Three particular changes have been monumental for queer families in

B.C. First, in 1996, the provincial government amended its Adoption Act to include "any person or any two persons [to] adopt" children in B.C., regardless of their sexuality (Luce 34; also findlay; Owen). Second, in 1997, the same government altered its definition of "spouse" in order to recognize legally same-sex partners, and, in 2000, the federal government followed suit (Kranz and Daniluk; Luce; Owen). The legal recognition of same-sex marriage then occurred in the province of British Columbia and within Canada, in July 2003 and June 2005, respectively. Third, in August 2001, the British Columbia Human Rights Tribunal ruled that disallowing the naming of two women on the birth certificates of children conceived via anonymous sperm donation and born to lesbian parents is discriminatory[1] (findlay; Kranz and Daniluk; Luce). Recently, in January 2007, a judge in Ontario ruled that, legally, a child can have three parents (Gandhi; Wente). This case involved a family comprising a child, his biological mother and father, as well as his biological mother's lesbian partner who had planned the boy's conception with the other two parents.

THE STUDY

Between July 2005 and March 2006, I interviewed ten couples, in a total of 16 interviews. Participants were recruited via word of mouth or by email listserv. The participants in this study were all female-identified at the time of the study and had some post-secondary education, and the majority of participants were Caucasian (with one of South Asian descent, and one of First Nations' heritage). The participants ranged in age from 31 to 51, and the couples had been in their current relationships between 2.5 and 24 years. The ten couples were either between 31 and 38 weeks pregnant, at the time of our first interview, or they had birthed within the last three years. With the six couples that were pregnant during our first interview, I conducted follow-up interviews between four and 13 weeks post-partum. All of the interviews occurred in the homes of the participants, and were conducted with both parents simultaneously, allowing both partners to narrate their own experiences, as well as add information and anecdotes while listening to their partner's experience.

The interviews covered a wide range of topics and experiences. However, the most emotional topic to emerge was the legal recognition of both partners as mothers to their child or children. Despite the Human Rights Tribunal ruling five years earlier, the couples revealed that many wrinkles had yet to be ironed out in terms of familial and parent recognition.

BIRTH CERTIFICATES AND "LEGAL" PARENTS

Birth certificates play a fundamental role in how births, and those involved in them, are legally and socially recognized, and accounted for. In addition, they are used by vital statistics agencies to acknowledge new citizens and their families. The struggle for lesbian parental recognition on birth certificates has centred on the fact that by not being able to name both lesbian parents on birth certificates, they "[suffer] discrimination and [have been] made to feel that their relationships and families could not measure up to those of heterosexual families" (Makin). When the B.C. Human Rights Tribunal acknowledged the discrimination that was occurring by not allowing all couples who use anonymous donor sperm to conceive to be fully acknowledged on the birth certificate, they also acknowledged the importance it played for families and parents, whether queer or heterosexual, to be recognized.

Not long after the 2001 Tribunal ruling, a "Parent 1/Parent 2" birth certificate was created for families with more than one "mother." When I spoke to couples about filling out their birth certificate applications, not all of them were aware of the existence of this form, as they all had been given a "Mother/Father" application by the hospital or midwife. All of the couples knew (or felt) that they were both legally entitled to be named on the birth certificate, but were not sure how to proceed with the "Mother/Father" form. It is not surprising, therefore, that they had different responses to and experiences with their "Mother/Father" applications.

> **Leah[2]:** *We just filled it in with Andy as the father, cause we figured, they haven't changed their forms yet. It's the same when we got married. One of us had to be the bride, and one of us had to be the groom. And we just figured, oh whatever!*
>
> **Beverly**: *With Arianna, there wasn't a parent-parent option like there was the second time around. We talked about it, and decided to put my name on as father and it went through. My first name, obviously, can be a male or female name. It isn't so common for men, but it is also a male name. We half expected to be rejected. We know a number of other lesbian-headed families, who have children roughly the same age as Arianna, and, in most of those cases, a female "father" was rejected. But in my case, it wasn't. So, we were initially given a birth certificate with both of our names on it. We decided to hold back my initial adoption—the fact that my name is listed under father means nothing. It doesn't recognize my relationship with Arianna, because I'm female.*
>
> **Jenn:** *What's funny is when the birth certificate came in the mail, cause I had crossed things out on the form. So, instead of "name of the father," I put "name of second mother," and instead of*

> *"name of mother," I put "name of birth mother." But, they didn't change the form, so when the form came back it said Trish is the father. So Trish's gotten a lot out of that one.*
>
> **Alexis:** *And when the birth certificate actually came, the first one said, "mother/father," even though you'd crossed it off and put "parent/parent." And then I remember barbara findlay, our lawyer, saying she had won a case, which then made the B.C. government people, staff people, have to change the form. So she was surprised it said, "mother/father."*

Three couples had their initial application returned to them when they attempted registration as "mother" and "father" on the standard form. With their rejection came the co-parent form for them to re-start the application process. Two of the other couples phoned the B.C. Vital Statistics Agency before sending in the paperwork. As a result of their phone calls, they had the co-parent application sent to them. The inconsistency that the couples dealt with, and the fact that the co-parent forms were not available at hospitals, through midwives, or through the Vital Statistics website, was confusing for and disrespectful of these and similar couples. However, the problems with the birth certificates, and having the non-biological parent recognized, did not end here.

Three of the couples I spoke with used a known donor to get pregnant. Legally, in situations of known donors, non-biological mothers were not to be listed on the birth certificate. While two of the couples ignored this legality, Lisa and Patti did not. The frustration of trying to have both Lisa and Patti legally recognized as mothers is clear in their narrative.

> **Patti:** *We went to fill out the paper work, and we ended up phoning and saying, "Ok, how should we fill this out?" "Oh, okay, you need a special form" [Lisa: A co-parent form], a co-parent form. So, then they sent us the co-parent form, and we read the fine print at the bottom, and the fine print said, "Do you—" How did, how was the wording?*
> **Lisa:** *The donor has to be anonymous.*
> **Patti:** *Yeah, and so we didn't fit into the category. So again, I could not be recognized. So, I'm totally off the paperwork, and, we're back to the same procedure as adopting Seamus.*

Moreover, Lisa and Patti pointed out that while the B.C. Human Rights Tribunal decision permitted two women to be listed as parents on the birth certificate, legal rights for the non-biological parent did not accompany this decision. Adoption is necessary to obtain these rights. While lesbian parents in Québec were granted full legal rights with the change of the birth certificate legislation there ("Québec Adopts"; Greenbaum *et al.*; Séguin), the same cannot be said for parents same-sex parents in British Columbia or Ontario (every province is a little different with information changing on a monthly basis currently), who are legally advised to go through adoption in order for the non-biological parent to gain full legal status as a legitimate parent to her child.

Three couples informed me that they went through the process of adoption. Cheryl and Alexis explained why they went through the process.

> **Michelle:** *So, was it barbara findlay that said you should go through the adoption process?*
> **Cheryl:** *Yeah. She advised us. Because there was this whole issue of getting married, and does that afford us the same legal rights in terms of parenting, that it affords a straight couple? But it's so new, so there's no precedent. So, she advised us that we should go through the whole adoption—the traditional approach for same-sex parents used for adoption—to have those rights guaranteed.*
> **Alexis:** *My big concern was that if something happened to Cheryl—Cheryl being the birth mom—that I would run into problems for custody issues. And it's really hard to say. I mean, how that would turn out? But I wasn't willing to risk that, I mean, I just, there's just, I couldn't live with that.*

Unfortunately, bureaucratic red-tape affecting recognition of two birth mothers expands beyond birth certificates and adoption. It also affected the couples' applications for parental leave, through the federally-administered Employment Insurance (EI).

PARENTAL LEAVE

Three couples spoke of their intent to apply for Employment Insurance (EI) Parental Leave. Two of these couples spoke at length about their experiences, yet all three of them raised it as an issue in our interview because the non-biological parent would be applying for the leave. It is important to recognize that Human Resources and Skills Development Canada's (HRSD) understanding of who is eligible for parental leave did not recognize the non-biological parent within a queer parented family. As each family pointed out in their interviews, HRSD explicitly states that in terms of parental leave, one must be either a biological or adoptive parent. At the time of birth, the non-biological parent is officially neither since no adoptions in British Columbia can be finalized until the child is six months old. Cheryl and Alexis managed their way around this. Alexis was named as "father" on the birth certificate, and due to her androgynous name, this was upheld and accepted by HRSD in her application for parental leave. However, this was not the case for Lisa and Patti, or for Sheila and Beverly.

> **Patti:** *For EI you are either the adopted or the biological parent. So, if you read that on their website or on the form...*
> **Lisa:** *If you are a heterosexual couple, you just say you are the parents.*
> **Patti:** *Yeah, but technically, you'd be lying. That's what I'm just saying is that the fine print...*
> **Michelle:** ... *to be all legal* ...
> **Patti:** ... *yeah, so the situation is that I'm still, I haven't adopted Finn until, I guess, until he's six months or a year.*

> **Beverly:** *We delayed my actual adoption of Arianna until Sheila went back to work, with the plan that I would then take adoption leave from work, so I would be home for the second year. We knew other lesbian-parented families that have made that choice. It was kind of a little dream we had, and we didn't know if it would backfire on us or not, but we thought, you know, if we were adopting Arianna from China, I'd be eligible for adoption leave from my employer, so I thought I'd apply. So I applied, and they gave me leave. And I said, "Okay, let's see if I can get EI." And I went to the EI office, and I was very truthful, because I didn't want to get bit in the bum in a year when they say, "You owe us several thousand dollars of, you know, incorrectly claimed EI cheques."*
>
> *So anyways, when I went there, I talked with a staff person, and I was really, really clear and I explained my situation, and they looked at me like, "I had never heard this scenario before," and he said, "Your argument is perfectly valid. You have no legal relationship with this child. And therefore, why should you not be able to get EI like you would if you had adopted this child from another country or from the ministry or whatever." And I said, "Exactly." So he went away and talked with his supervisor, and he came back and he said, "We've never seen this scenario before, but why shouldn't you, so we approve it." So, I was home with Arianna for almost nine months, and I say the down part of having to pay to adopt my own child was that I got to have another year home with her, and that was a huge goal of ours. We simply repeated the same situation with Rose—and I got EI again.*

Lisa and Patti were not aware of the EI understanding of "parent" until it was time for Patti to apply for parental leave, just before her son was born. When I spoke with them, their frustration about not being properly recognized or legally able to take parental leave until Patti adopted her son was evident. While this was detrimental to Lisa and Patti's situation and plan, Beverly and Sheila found a loophole and used this policy to their advantage—doubling the usual amount of parental leave given to parents.[3] Beverly and Sheila felt proud that their family could be recognized, maybe not just as a heterosexual-parented birth family, but for the unique qualities and situations that queer-parented families possess and experience. All the same, it did not seem right to those I interviewed that non-biological parents need to wait for their adoption to go through to be able to have parental leave through EI. Although the wording on the HRSD website now states "partner of the biological mother," applicants only have the option of identifying themselves as adoptive or biological parents when filing their application. This lack of comprehensive and equal recognition of parents demonstrates an overall lack of understanding and preparedness of government policies to accept and respect queer-parented families.

CONCLUSION

Before my research, I had no idea that "lesbian" birth certificates were not easily accessible and that non-birthing/non-biological parents are not legally eligible for parental leave upon the birth of their child. What I was aware of was that when Québec's legislation passed in 2002, allowing two-women to be recognized on birth certificates and giving full parental rights to both women (Greenbaum *et al.*; Séguin), it also included a clause that allowed past births to be re-registered, listing both mothers. Moreover, Québec's new forms were easily accessible within weeks of the legislation being passed.[4] While neither a clause for re-registering past births, nor for granting parental rights ever passed in B.C. (or Ontario), the parents I spoke with were grateful for the rights they did have. At the end of her interview, one participant, Rachel, noted, "We've come a long way, baby. Right? I mean the same questions a couple of years ago would have had a very different … ramification and outcome, so we're in a pretty nice time that way as lesbians in our own country."

While what Rachel said is true, the couples' satisfaction or complacency regarding government bureaucracies' treatment towards them shocked me. The extra steps that these couples had to go through to gain access to the correct birth certificate application, to gain full legal rights as parents to their children, and to take parental leave, reflects a second-class treatment by government bureaucracies. This sense is strengthened by my knowledge that it this is due to the B.C. provincial government's laziness—at least in comparison to that of Québec—as opposed to simply an "adjustment time" or "transition phase," as Alexis described it. While queer parents may be lucky in comparison to queer folks living in other places, they are still treated like second-class citizens by our bureaucracies, which is not acceptable.

Having one accessible, standardized queer-friendly birth certificate application makes things much easier for registering and acknowledging the full family involved in the birth of a child to queer mothers. As Nicole pointed out in her interview, "I don't know why they don't just have a standard [Parent 1/Parent 2 birth certificate] form anyway." This form would work for all parents, equally. In fact, Ontario's new birth certificate application works for same-sex and differently-sexed parents alike. I believe having different forms continues to reflect the marked difference in the government's perception of queer- and straight-parent-led families, as does the federal government's formal lack of acknowledgement of the parental status (via the parental leave application) of the non-biological mother. While the British Columbian and federal governments have shown progressive steps in changing legislation regarding same-sex partners, many more steps need to be made to show that they fully respect and understand the needs of alternative families. Until this changes, Farah Shroff's argument that "[H]eterosexism permeates virtually every aspect of Canadian culture: language, guiding practices of all institutions, and social interactions" (287) will continue to hold true.

EPILOGUE

In August 2007, British Columbia Vital Statistics created and made available a new birth certificate application. This new application (available both online and through midwives and hospitals) merged the Mother/Father and Co-parent forms into one. While this new, unified form addresses many of the issues—in terms of treating two-mother families as second class—confusion and ambiguity still exist. Since the creation of this form and its availability, seemingly no effort has been made to make new parents, midwives, or doctors aware of the changes it entails.[5] Moreover, while it equally allows for the naming of a "father" or "co-parent," no definition of "father" is given. It might be presumed by Vital Statistics that everyone *knows* what they mean, but a "father" may be defined in more than a purely *biological* context—which I expect is the definition to which they are inferring. While this ambiguity allows for trans-dads or lesbian-partners to be labeled as "father," I do not believe this is the intent of Vital Statistics who defines "a co-parent as a person who is in a spousal relationship with the mother of the child, is not the father of the child and the mother and co-parent have agreed to be the parents of the child." Moreover, it also makes ambiguous an issue that has been raised repeatedly since the Human Rights Tribunal ruling: the naming of a second mother in families who has used a known donor to get pregnant, as no statement regarding the known/anonymous status of donors is mentioned on this form, contrary to the previous co-parent form and Tribunal ruling. Although updates to the birth certificate has been a step in the right direction, it is obvious that further steps still need to occur in order for both mothers (and any other adults involved in the planning and raising of children in queer-parented families) to be fully recognized as legal parents to their children.

[1]As of December 2007, Québec, Manitoba, New Brunswick, Nova Scotia, and Ontario are the only other places in Canada where two women can be legally recognized as parents on a birth certificate; each province has different measures regarding how and when this can occur ("Mom and Mom Now Allowed"; Wente; Epstein; Canadian Press; Greenbaum *et al.*; Makin; Séguin).
[2]All participants' names have been changed to pseudonyms.
[3]Federally-organized parental leave is legally one year shared between parents. Beverly and Sheila managed to acquire double the leave, as one parent took leave as a birth parent, and the other for adoption—two separate types of Parental Leave.
[4]This information was obtained through personal communication with Mona Greenbaum, co-coordinator of L'Association des mères lesbiennes in Montréal.
[5] This information was obtained through personal correspondence with midwives and new parents, in the months following the release of the new birth certificate application.

WORKS CITED

B.C. Vital Statistics Agency. "How To Register A Birth." *British Columbia Vital Statistics Agency*. 16 August 2007. <http://www.vs.gov.bc.ca/births/breg.html>.

Cannell, Fenella. "Concepts of Parenthood: The Warnock Report, the Gillick Debate, and Modern Myths." *American Ethnologist* 17.4 (1990): 667-86.

Epstein, Rachel. "Queer Parenting in the New Millennium: Resisting Normal." *Canadian Woman Studies/les cahiers de la femme* 24. 2/3 (2005): 7-14.

findlay, barbara. *The Law Office of barbara findlay, Q.C.* 28 June 2005. <http://www.barbarafindlay.com>.

Gandhi, Unnati. "The Ontario Court of Appeal Ruled Tuesday That a Boy Has Three Legally Recognized Parents." *Globe and Mail* 6 Jan. 2007: A5.

Greenbaum, Mona, Michael Hendricks, and Eminé Piyalé-Sheard.

Civil Union—Good News for Lesbian Mamas. 2002. 7 March 2007. <http://uwo.ca/pridelib/family/articles/a-civil-union.html>

Kranz, Karen C. and Judith C. Daniluk. "We've Come A Long Way Baby ... Or Have We? Contextualizing Lesbian Motherhood in North America." *Journal for the Association for Research on Mothering* 4.1 (2002): 58-69.

Luce, Jacquelyne Marie. *Queer Conceptions: Lesbian/Bi/Queer Women, Assisted Reproduction and the Politics of Kinship*. Unpublished Diss. York University, 2002.

Makin, Kirk. "Two Mothers Should Be Allowed on Birth Documentation, Judge Says." *Globe and Mail* 7 June 2006.

Modell, Judith. "Rights to the Children: Foster Care and Social Reproduction in Hawai'i." *Reproducing Reproduction*. Ed. Sarah Franklin and Hélène Ragoné. Philadelphia: University of Pennsylvania Press, 1998. 156-72.

"Mom and Mom Now Allowed on N. S. Birth Registration." *CBC NEWS*. 20 Sep 2007. 3 Dec 2007. <http://www.cbc.ca/canada/nova-scotia/story/2007/09/20/birth-ns.html>

Moraga, Cherrie. *Waiting in the Wings*. Ithaca: Firebrand, 1997.

Owen, Michelle. "'Family' as a Site of Contestation: Queering the Normal or Normalizing the Queer?" *In a Queer Country: Gay and Lesbian Studies in the Canadian Context*. Ed. Terry Goldie. Vancouver: Arsenal Pulp, 2001. 86-102.

Nelson, Fiona. *Lesbian Motherhood: An Exploration of Canadian Lesbian Families*. Toronto: University of Toronto Press, 1996.

"Québec Adopts Same-Sex Union and Parental Rights." *Globe and Mail* 7 Mar. 2002.

Séguin, Rhéal. "Gay Couples in Quebec Get Full Parental Rights." *Globe and Mail* 8 Jun. 2002: A1.

Shroff, Farah. "All Petals of the Flower: Celebrating the Diversity of Ontario's Birthing Women within First-Year Midwifery Curriculum." *The New Midwifery*. Ed. Farah Shroff. Toronto: Women's Press, 1997. 261-310.

Toevs, Kim and Stephanie Brill. *The Essential Guide to Lesbian Conception, Pregnancy, and Birth*. Los Angeles: Alyson, 2000.

Walks, Michelle. *Queer Couples' Narratives of Birthing: A B.C. Focus on the Intersections of Identity, Choice, Resources, Family, Policy, Medicalization, and Health in the Experiences of Queers Birthing*. Unpublished Diss. Simon Fraser University, 2007.

Wente, Margaret. "Two Mommies and a Daddy." *Globe and Mail* 4 Jan. 2007: A15.

Wozniak, Danielle F. *They're All My Children: Foster Mothering in America*. New York: New York University Press, 2002.

Contributor Notes

Dianne Hancherow Anderson lives and works in North East Saskatchewan while pursuing her life long interest in the study of medicinal plant culture. Her current photographic research explores the themes of ancestral myths and legends and the role that photography has played in the transmission of familial history.

Judy Anderson is a Cree artist who works in multi-media including painting, installation, and video. She is an Assistant Professor in the Indian Fine Arts Department at the First Nations University where she teaches both studio classes and Indian Art History. She is the mother of daughter, Riel, born in 2002, and son, Cruz, born in 1995.

Jane Arsenault is an Acadian writer from Summerside, Prince Edward Island. Her writing interests include creative non-fictional expressions of personal survival and success, and interpretations of well-known lyrics of contemporary songwriters. She plans to write an English-language novel set in turn-of-the-century Acadia. She has three teenaged sons.

Sylvat Aziz teaches at Queen's University. She studied Visual Arts at the Pratt Institute and Concordia University. Aziz's research includes issues ranging from traditional representations and adaptations of industrial methods and materials to contemporary studio practices. Her work has been exhibited in major Canadian and international galleries including the Venice Biennale.

Angelina Baydala, Ph.D., is a registered Clinical Psychologist and Associate Professor in the Department of Psychology at the University of Regina. Her research focuses on histories, cultures, and theories of psychological healing. She regularly teaches courses on the history, theories, practices, and systems of psychology and psychotherapy, theories of personality, and yoga psychology.

Corrina Beesley-Hammond is primarily a painter and is currently working on a collaborative painting project with painter Michael Dowad. She is also available to perform Domestic Interventions for the occupants of cluttered and unorganized households. Corrina and her husband have one son.

Linda Bell holds a doctorate in Clinical Sciences (Nursing) from the University of Sherbrooke and a postdoctoral fellowship in the Child Development Unit of the Children's Hospital in Boston. Her clinical and research work focuses on maternal and infant health and, more specifically, bonding between parents and infants.

Margaret Bessai, B.A., is interested in the humour of everyday life, and finding the personal in history. Based in Regina, she has exhibited and published her drawings in the local community. Family, community, and collaboration are important to her work and her life.

Shannon Wall Bixby is a "Mompreneur" who runs a social enterprise called Eggplant Inspiration. She lives by the sea in Vancouver with her husband and three young sons.

Elizabeth Blanchard is a fiction writer from Dieppe, New Brunswick. Her short stories have appeared in a number of literary journals and will be appearing in an upcoming anthology published by Killick Press. She is a recipient of a New Brunswick Arts Board Creation Grant.

Glenda Tibe Bonifacio, Ph.D., is an Assistant Professor in Women's Studies at the University of Lethbridge. Her works on Filipino women have been published in *Asian Women*, *Asian and Pacific Migration Journal*, *Review of Women's Studies*, and *Frontiers*. Glenda is the co-editor of *Gender, Religion and Migration: Pathways of Integration* (Lexington 2009).

Carrie Bourassa, Ph.D., is an Associate Professor of Indigenous Health Studies at First Nations University of Canada. Carrie's research interests include the effects of colonization on the health of First Nations and Métis people and Aboriginal women's health. Carrie belongs to the Riel Métis Council of Regina and resides in Regina with her husband, Chad, and her daughter, Victoria.

Sheree Bradford-Lea is a cartoonist. Her cartoons have appeared in many magazines, ezines, books, journals, and the Herstory calendars. She also teaches cartooning courses and workshops. She lives in Ottawa with her husband Jim, and their children, Zoë and Monica.

Yael Brotman is a visual artist from Toronto. She teaches Visual Arts at the University of Toronto, Scarborough. She has exhibited in public, artist-run, and commercial galleries across Canada and beyond, most recently in museums and galleries in Jingdezhen, Sanbao and Taiyuan, China. She has a daughter and two sons.

Rosa Hong Chen is a poet and dancer, and a Ph.D. candidate, Educational Philosophy, at Simon Fraser University. Her publications include *Choosing the Ferry of Life* (forthcoming); *A Journey of Writing the Self; Pedagogical Approaches: A Discussion of Poetic Forms & Cultural Awareness; Analyzing Discourse to Uncover Power Relations in Verse, Still Remember the Moments;* and *I Want to Go Beyond.*

Sorel Cohen lives and works in Montreal. Her art practice, which is largely autobiographical, weaves original links between photography, painting, and film. In 1988, she was awarded the Canada Council's prestigious Duke and Duchess of York Photography Prize. She was recently inducted into the Royal Canadian Academy of Arts.

Nicole Côté, Ph.D., Associate Professor of French at the University of Regina, has published several articles on French- and English-Canadian literature. She has translated numerous Canadian authors and has co-edited *Varieties of Exile* (2002) and *Expressions culturelles des francophonies* (2008). Her research focuses on questions related to identity, gender, and minorities, as well as on cultural transfers.

Pamela J. Downe, Ph.D., is an Associate Professor in the Department of Archaeology and Anthropology at the University of Saskatchewan. As a medical anthropologist, the majority of her research is ethnographic and community-based with a focus on infectious disease, violence, gender, and maternal health.

Isla Dowling studies at McGill University, in the Faculty of Law. In addition to her focus on childcare issues in Canada, her research interests include gender parity in French politics and minority language rights. She pursued undergraduate studies in French and Political Science at the University of Regina.

Cara Driscoll earned her B.A. in Visual Arts from the University of Regina. She set up her ceramic studio in Regina in 1993 and continues to work from there. Cara is currently enrolled in the Prairie Jubilee Program for Spiritual Direction.

Joy Eidse has mothered three boys: the first was stillborn; the second and third are healthy, rambunctious toddlers, ages two and four. She and her partner currently reside in Winnipeg, where they provide a supportive living environment for people at risk of homelessness. Joy is studying Social Work at the University of Manitoba, and has written several plays.

Michelle Glennie is an artist and writer from Saint-Bruno, Quebec. She studied art at Central Tech in Toronto and English Literature at Western and Carleton, graduating with an MA. Michelle's drawings have been exhibited in Canada and her poetry has appeared in many Canadian journals. She has two young children.

Jewell Goodwyn is an artist/arts advocate from London, Ontario. She has explored identity and gender in her work. She is the founding director of Artist-Run Centres and Collectives of Ontario (ARCCO) and leading member of other art service organizations, provincially and nationally. Jewell is the proud mother of Hannah.

Troni Y. Grande, Ph.D., is an Associate Professor of English at the University of Regina. She teaches early-modern drama, genre theory, and feminism. She has published *Marlovian Tragedy: The Play of Dilation*, and poetry in *CV2*; and co-edited *Northrop Frye's Writings on Shakespeare and the Renaissance* (forthcoming) for the *Collected Works of Northrop Frye*.

Libby Hague, Toronto, is a visual artist who works primarily in print installation. Her recent exhibitions include "One step at a time" and "Everything needs everything." She is featured in the British book, *Installations & Experimental Printmaking* by Alexia Tala, and won the 2009 Open Studio National Printmaking Award.

Mary Hampton, Ed.D., is a Professor of Psychology at Luther College. She is also a researcher with the Saskatchewan Population Health and Evaluation Research Unit and is Saskatchewan Academic Co-ordinator for RESOLVE. Her research areas are intimate partner violence, end of life care, and sexual health of Aboriginal Youth. She is married with two children and four stepchildren.

Kathryn Hatashita-Lee is a stock photographer and office assistant. Her publications include "Remember, Chrysanthemum" in *Winds Through Time: An Anthology of Canadian Historical Young Adult Fiction*. Her images are marketed by *iStockphoto LP*. She lives in Vancouver with her husband Roger and their teen-aged son Edward.

Marie Hatem, who has trained as a midwife and nurse, holds an M.A. in

Health Administration and a doctorate in Public Health. She is an Associate Professor and the graduate director in the Department of Social and Preventative Medicine at the Université de Montréal. Her research lies in maternal mortality and midwives in developing countries of the Francophonie.

Alison Hayford, Ph.D., is the Head of the Department of Visual Arts and the Associate Dean, Undergraduate, of the Faculty of Fine Arts at the University of Regina. She is also a Professor in the Department of Sociology and Social Studies. When she has time, she does research on gender, place, and space.

Reinie Heydemann is a retired professional chaplain who worked in hospitals and nursing homes. She has told many stories based on her profound experiences with people who faced critical times in their lives. She now lives on Vancouver Island and enjoys her friendship with her four granddaughters.

Elizabeth F. Hill is a stay-at-home mother, currently residing in Edmonton. The holder of a Ph.D. in Intercultural Education, she has been a sessional instructor at the University of Alberta and a research assistant at Charles Sturt University (Australia) and at Aichi Gakusen University (Japan). She enjoys her family, music, literature, travel, sports, and creative writing.

Grace Rose Holyer lives and works in Weyburn, Saskatchewan. She always wanted to be an artist; it is her passion in life and has been since she was a young child. As she married young and had three children, she did not receive formal art training until she attended university as a mature student. Grace holds a B.F.A., a B.ED (Arts Ed.) and an M.F.A. degree.

Claudine Houle completed her M.A. in Nursing at the Université de Montréal in 2006. Her article in this anthology is a summary of her M.A. thesis. She works as a clinical councillor at the Institut en Santé Mentale Douglas. Her clinical practice is informed by her focus on clients' needs, systemic familial intervention, and increasing accessibility to services.

Helen Hoy, Ph.D., has taught at the Universities of Toronto, Manitoba, Lethbridge, and Minnesota, and is a Professor of English at the University of Guelph. Her most recent book is *How Should I Read These? Native Women Writers in Canada* (2001). She has mothered a stepson, a birth son, an adopted daughter, and, briefly, a grandson.

Patrice Keats, Ph.D., is an Assistant Professor in the Counseling Psychology program at Simon Fraser University, where she engages in teaching, research, and practice. Her research interests involve qualitative explorations of secondary trauma, post-traumatic stress, expressive trauma treatments, and visuality. Art is her hidden passion.

Marsha Kennedy lives in Regina, Saskatchewan and teaches painting and drawing at the University of Regina. Her art practice probes the compelling interactions between culture and nature. Her solo exhibition *Mapping the Land and Body* was at the Vernon Art Gallery, B.C., in 2007 and the Prairie Art Gallery, Alberta, in 2006.

Lois Klassen is an interdisciplinary artist based in Vancouver. Besides small-run publications, she has produced collective-action projects, performance, video, and installation works in Canada and abroad. She is the mother of two sons.

Belinda Kriek's research and studio practice explores themes of the corporeal body and its psychological and metaphysical manifestations in the social world. A South African born artist, Kriek resides in Regina, where she is currently completing her Bachelor of Visual Arts at the University of Regina. Belinda and her husband, Giel, have two sons, Uysie and Johann.

Aurélie Lacassagne received her doctorate from Sciences Po Bordeaux (France) in 2008. Since she immigrated to Canada eight years ago, she has been teaching in the Political Science Department of Laurentian University. Her work focuses on international relations and, in particular, immigration and identity questions. She has two daughters.

Marie Lacombe holds a Ph.D. in Nursing from the Université de Montréal. Her research interests lie in perinatality and family. Her work deals with breastfeeding, postpartum depression, children's temperament, interactions between parents and children, and perinatal mourning.

Donna Lester-Smith is a Ph.D. student at University of British Columbia. She is of Métis/Algonquin, English, Irish, and Scottish descent. Her work and study interests focus on Indigenous knowledge(s) and methodologies, and ethically sound community-based research. Her academic, creative writing, and editing contributions have been published in numerous journals and books.

Maria Lezon was born and raised in the Basque Country of Spain. A B.F.A. graduate from the University of Saskatchewan, she works and lives in Ottawa as a full-time artist. Her latest series of works "The Dangers of Motherhood" have been on exhibit in Canada, Spain, China, and the U.S.

Jennifer Linton is a visual artist working in drawing and printmaking. She holds a B.A. in Art and Art History from the University of Toronto and an M.F.A. from York University (2010). Linton lives in Toronto with her partner, Richard, and their children, Ridley and Nigel.

Lisa Loewen is a mother and artist living and working in Regina, Saskatchewan. She is a graduate of the B.F.A. program at University of Regina.

Elizabeth MacKenzie is a Vancouver-based artist whose work explores maternal ambivalence and the complexity of familial relations and their representation. Her drawings, installations, and videos have been presented in numerous exhibitions and screenings across Canada and elsewhere. She maintains an ongoing commitment to collaboration, writing, and teaching.

Kim McKay-McNabb is an Assistant Professor of Psychology at the First Nations University of Canada, and is completing her Ph.D. in Clinical Psychology. Her research interests include assisting in creating culturally competent care in health, specifically in mental health. Kim is a member of the George Gordon First Nation. She resides with her husband, Patrick, and children, Raymond, Rowan, Shay, and Isaiah.

Elder Betty McKenna is from the Aninishnabae Nation, Shoal River Band. She is very knowledgeable on many traditional teachings and she was appointed by former Premier Roy Romanow to the College of Physicians and Surgeons Council of Saskatchewan. She serves on a number of committees, including the National Elders Advisory and Correctional Services Canada.

Patricia Miller-Schroeder teaches Women's Studies at the University of Regina, where she has developed several courses including Women the Environment and Change; Reproductive Technologies; Feminism, Gender, and Science; and Motherhood and Mothering. Her current research includes women's life writing, story telling, and empowerment. She is the mother of three adult children.

Elena Neiterman is a Ph.D. student at the Department of Sociology, McMaster University. Her research interests include sociology of the body, health, and gender. Her dissertation analyzes the transformation of self during pregnancy. Elena has four young sons who were all born during her graduate studies.

Pam Patterson, Ph.D., focuses her research, art, and teaching on the body and/in culture. She is Associate Researcher, Centre for Women's Studies in Education, Ontario Institute for the Studies of Education of the University of Toronto (OISE/UT), Director, WIA projects, which presents exhibitions, screenings, performances, and interdisciplinary arts-based workshops, and educator for the Art Gallery of Ontario. As a performance and visual artist, Patterson exhibits and performs internationally.

Wendy Peart is a Regina-based artist whose work considers familial relationships, ecological territories, and interspecies societies. She works as an instructor in Visual Arts at the University of Regina and as a mentor artist with Learning through the Arts. She is the mother of two children.

Susan Picard is the youngest child of a northern Alberta farm family. She has been singing and songwriting for most of her life and has taught grades six to ten for more than ten years. She holds an MA from the University of Calgary. Her poetry has appeared in *Writing the Land: Alberta through its Poets.*

Rochelle Rubinstein is a Toronto-based printmaker, painter, and fabric and book artist. She facilitates art projects with battered women, people with eating disorders, and health workers. Her work can be found in the collections of the Museum of Modern Art, New York, and the Irish Museum of Modern Art, Dublin.

Phillip R. Sevigny is a Ph.D. candidate in Clinical Psychology. His research interests focus on the evolving roles of fathers in families and on understanding the similarities and differences in parenting beliefs between mothers and fathers. He lives in Regina with his wife Jennifer and daughters Ayla and Alise.

Jody Salerno is a queer, femme feminist mother of three inter-racial (Sri Lankan, Métis, and Italian) adult children, grandmother of one, and other mother to several. She studied Women's Studies at York University, and is an advocate for intersectional feminist perspectives. She is the Director of Women's Services with the BC Yukon Society of Transition Houses.

Susan Shantz lives, with her son Lief, in Saskatoon, where she is Professor of Art at the University of Saskatchewan. She works in sculpture and installation, and exhibits her work across Canada and internationally.

She has received grants from national and provincial arts councils and her art is in numerous public and private collections.

The Skeleton Crew is a Regina group of subterranean subliminalists, dedicated to making art that is gritty, giddy, and inside-out. Robin Poitras is the co-founder and artistic director of New Dance Horizons, Seema Goel is a sculptor and writer with engineering leanings and a penchant for collecting degrees, and Steve Kirkland is a matrix theorist at the Hamilton Institute, National University of Ireland, Maynooth.

Paula Stromberg's writing, photography and art designs have won 50 national and international communications awards. She has a B.A. Honours in English Literature from Concordia University and a Certificate in Creative Writing from The Writer's Studio 2006 at Simon Fraser University. Currently, she works with gay and lesbian (GLBT) refugees and immigrants in Canada, and is involved in the field of women's micro-finance.

Gaëtanne Sylvester graduated with a B.F.A. from University of Waterloo in 1990. Since moving to Winnipeg, she has pursued research into the beginning of life, fertility, femininity, and genetics in her chosen media: clay, printmaking, and installation, exhibiting locally, nationally, and abroad. She is a member of MAWA (Mentoring Artists for Women`s Art), Winnipeg.

Dominique Tanguay holds a Baccalauréat in International Studies, an M.A. in International Relations, and a Diplôme d'études doctorate supérieures spécialisées in Feminist Studies. She mothers three children while pursuing a doctorate in Orientation Sciences at Université Laval. Her thesis deals with mothers' and fathers' abilities to persevere in their doctoral studies.

Maureen J. Thompson is a Master's candidate in Clinical Psychology. Her research interests are reflected in the experiences of first-time parents, and include balancing work and family responsibilities, knowledge of infant development, and infant-parent relationships. In her spare time, Maureen likes to read and write.

Edward Z. Tronick, Ph.D. and Professor in the Department of Society, Human Development, and Health in Boston, heads the Child Development Unit of the Children's Hospital in Boston. The studies conducted at the Child Development Unit mainly focus on the factors that influence the socio-emotional development of young children, as well as the role of parents.

Valérie Vézina is a journalist living in Montreal. She contributes articles to *Sélection du Reader's Digest*, *La Presse*, and other Quebec publications. This mother of twins holds degrees in Communication and Information Technologies, and is keenly interested in culture, home, urbanism, gastronomy, and twinship.

Michelle Walks is a Ph.D. student at the University of British Columbia, Okanagan campus. While her MA (Anthropology) research concentrated on queer couples' birthing experiences in British Columbia, her Ph.D. research focuses on "butch lesbians' and trans-men's experiences of infertility." Michelle lives in Kelowna with her partner and their toddler son.

Natalie Ward is a Senior Research Associate at the C.T. Lamont Primary Health Care Research Institute and is a Ph.D. candidate in the University of Ottawa's Department of Anthropology and Sociology. Beside her interest in academics, Natalie is an avid photographer and writer.

Lori Weidenhammer, aka Madame Beespeaker, is a Vancouver-based performance-based interdisciplinary artist originally from Saskatchewan. Her collaborative media works with Peter Courtemanche have been shown in Canada and abroad. She is passionate about art that transforms the relationship between the artist and the viewer and creates community bonds.

Carol Wylie is a figurative/symbolist artist. She received a B.F.A. degree in Studio Art in 1996. She lives and works in Saskatoon. Her work has been exhibited across Western Canada and the U.S., and is part of public and private collections. She has three daughters.

Sylvia Ziemann's homey miniature installations explore our growing fear of the domestic other and our neighbours, and the creeping anxiety that our cocoons might be breached from without or within. She lives in Regina, Saskatchewan with her husband and two daughters.

About the Editors

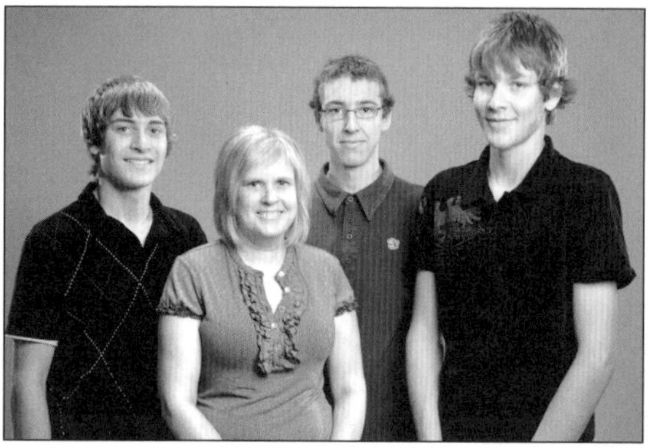

Photo: Trevor Hopkin

Shawna Geissler holds an M.Sc. in Biology from the University of Regina. After seven years as a full-time mother, she earned her M.A. in English. In 2007, she chaired the University of Regina's Graduate Students' Research Conference. She has published and presented papers on a variety of topics including children's fiction, holocaust narratives, and apocalyptic literatures, as well as on the evolutionary relationships among grasshoppers. She teaches critical reading and writing at Campion and Luther Colleges, and, in 2007 and 2009, won the Inspiring Sessional Award. She mothers three teen-aged sons: Justin, Adam, and Evan.

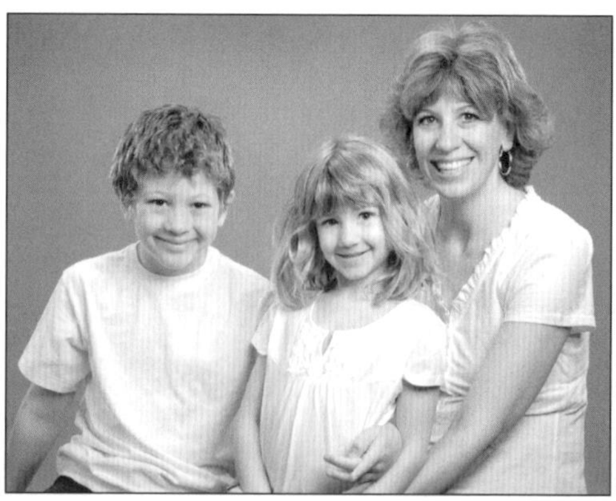

Photo: Trevor Hopkin

Lynn Loutzenhiser, Ph.D., is an Associate Professor of Clinical Psychology at the University of Regina. Before joining the faculty in 2003, she worked as a child clinical psychologist with children experiencing developmental and/or mental health difficulties and their families. Her research has been funded by the Saskatchewan Health Research Foundation, the Saskatchewan Interprofessional Education for Collaborative Patient-Centred Practice, and through the University of Regina's SSHRC/President's Fund and the Dean's Research Fund. Her current research interests lie in the areas of mothering and fathering, with a particular focus on the experience of new and first-time parents. She and her partner have two children, Maya and Joshua.

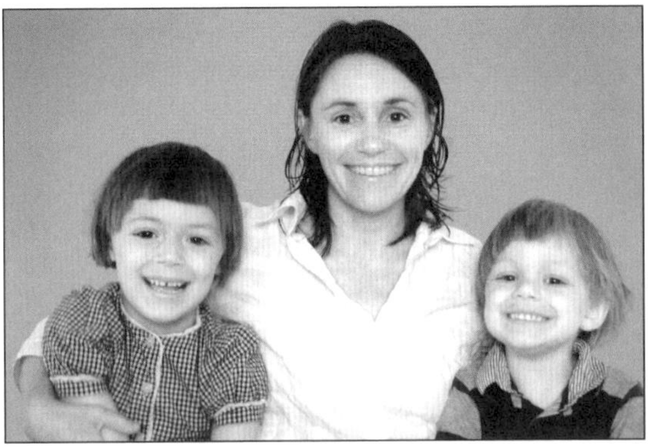

Photo: Stéphane Kostiuk

Jocelyne Praud, born and raised in France, holds a doctorate from the University of Toronto. She is an Associate Professor of Political Science at the University of Regina. Her research and writings have primarily dealt with the political representation of women in France, English Canada, and Quebec. Ever since she worked in a daycare center in France, she has been keenly interested in comparing different child care systems. Together with Sandrine Dauphin, she is presently revising their book entitled *Towards Parity Democracy: Women's Political Representation in Fifth Republic France* to be published by University of British Columbia Press. She and her husband have a daughter, Justine and a son, Franz.

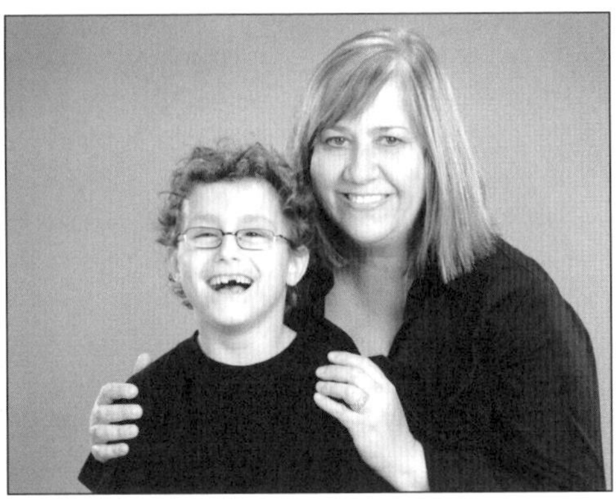

Photo: Trevor Hopkin

Leesa Streifler is Professor of Visual Art at the University of Regina. She holds an M.F.A. from Hunter College, New York and a B.F.A. (honours) from the University of Manitoba. She has exhibited widely and her work is in public collections including the National Gallery of Canada and the Canada Council Art Bank. She is the recipient of grants from the Canada Council for the Arts, the Saskatchewan Arts Board, the University of Regina's SSHRC/President's Fund, and the University of Regina Dean of Fine Arts

Research Fund. In 2005, she founded a Mothering Research Group at the University of Regina. Her feminist, multidisciplinary studio practice focuses on the female body through the lens of mothering, aging, and familial relationships. Leesa and her husband are parents to Daniel.